Praise for
Portraits of France

"Some books just read themselves. This is one of them. *Portraits of France* is not mere travel writing nor is it popular history, and yet it is somehow both, written in the winning style of a personal essay."
— *Pittsburgh Press*

"A beautifully evocative collection that holds up to wonderment many of France's multifarious aspects. . . . Daley goes to rich lengths."
— *Booklist*

"A treat for Francophiles and Daley fans alike. An engaging story of a man's love affair with a country, and a congenial portrait of one writer's life."
— *Kirkus Reviews*

"You can read it as a guidebook, as a kind of conversational history, as a memoir, or as a journey with a bestselling writer. There are lines in this book I've copied out to keep and I only can say that I'm taking it with me to France next time."
— James Salter

"*Portraits of France* is a touching and captivating account of one man's Gallic odyssey whose memory, like one of those marvelous restaurants worth a detour, lingers on long after the last page."
— Larry Collins

"A superb song of love for my country."
— Dominique Lapierre

"*Portraits of France* is like one of those pleasantly surprising *buffets de gare* that offer a number of *spécialités du pays,* all of them tempting, well prepared, and guaranteed not to give you a *crise de foie.*"
— Ted Morgan

"A delightful blend of history and anecdotes mixed with a little travelogue to provide an intimate, refreshing look at France."
— *Library Journal*

"*Portraits of France* is a wonderful personal memoir of France, good sides and bad, by one who knows it well. . . . An absolute winner!"
— *Greenwich Times*

"A wonderful book — informative, entertaining, sometimes stirring, always fascinating."
— *Los Angeles Daily News*

"Robert Daley's book is a veritable fount of information. In wonderfully literate yet simple prose he writes of people, places, and things in a country he knows so well."
— *San Gabriel Valley Tribune*

"An eclectic and wide-ranging tour through past and present, emphasizing some of France's most unusual places and personalities."
— *Newport News* (Virginia) *Daily Press*

Portraits of France

By Robert Daley

Portraits of France

ROBERT DALEY

LITTLE, BROWN AND COMPANY

BOSTON   NEW YORK   TORONTO   LONDON

Pour P. Avec Tout

First Back Bay Edition

Library of Congress Cataloging-in-Publication Data
Daley, Robert.
    Portraits of France / Robert Daley. — 1st ed.
        p.   cm.
    ISBN 0-316-17185-9 (hc) 0-316-17181-6 (pb)
    1. France — Civilization.   2. Daley, Robert — Journeys — France.
3. France — Description and travel.   4. National characteristics,
French.   I. Title.
DC33.D27   1991
944 — dc20   90-25071

10 9 8 7 6 5 4

MV-NY

*Published simultaneously in Canada
by Little, Brown & Company (Canada) Limited*

Printed in the United States of America

Contents

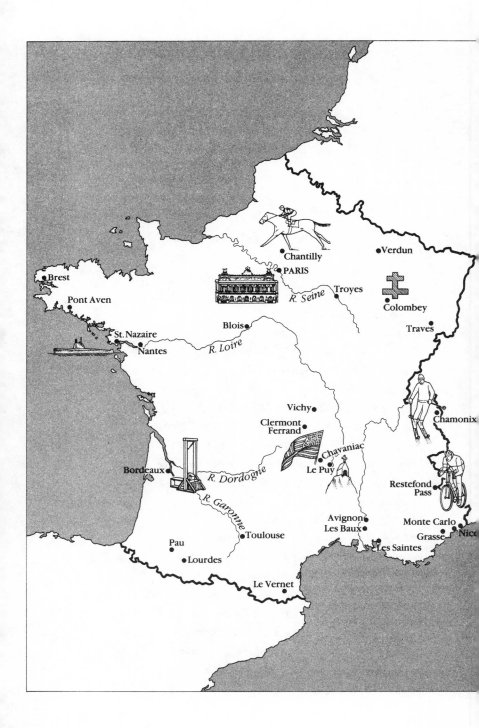

Brest

Pont Aven

St. Nazaire
Nantes

Chantilly

•Verdun

PARIS

Troyes

R. Seine

Colombey

Traves

Blois

R. Loire

Vichy

Chamonix

Clermont
Ferrand

Chavaniac

Le Puy

Restefond
Pass

Bordeaux

R. Dordogne

R. Garonne

Avignon
Les Baux

Monte Carlo

Toulouse

Grasse

Nice

Pau

Les Saintes

Lourdes

Le Vernet

Portraits of France

Portraits of France
PROLOGUE

There are a thousand years of French history in this book, but it is not a historical treatise; there is much about France's wars, but only the one battle that changed her forever is described in detail; there is much about religion, but it is not a catechism; much about food and wine, but it is not a cookbook; much about places of interest (*), some of which may be worth a detour (**) or even a journey (***). However, it is not a travel guide. There is (inevitably) much about the author, but it is not an autobiography and you can skip those parts if you wish. Each chapter as I wrote it was meant to stand as a portrait or aspect of a country that I know in some respects better than my own. It was my hope that these separate portraits taken together would result in the reader's mind in a single canvas representing all of France.

A thousand years. The writing took on rules of its own. Each portrait had to bear on France as a whole. Apart from that I would write about places, things, and people I had stumbled on or gone looking for that had seemed notable to me, that had impressed or in some cases shocked me. Conques, a village of curious legends, impressed me; it huddles under ancient slate roofs around a church that seems to be dragging it backwards into the Middle Ages, and in its museum abound strange artifacts done 1,000 years ago, mostly in gold. Rocamadour in its canyon above the river impressed me; it is perched not so much atop the cliffs as in them. In a country full of perched villages, it may be the most stunning.

The first two interviews I ever did in France were with priests. I would take any assignment I could get in those days; I was not a religious specialist. The first was with Bonaventure Fabron, 90 years old the last I saw of him. In his dusty cassock and clodhopper boots, a sack over his shoulder, he was plodding through the Maritime Alps collecting the herbs which, when he had mixed them, would give up a healing broth he called Fabronine. I was struggling to learn French at the time, and my trade as well, I had no vocabulary in herbs, and it was hard. The old priest took orders from all over the world, sent out packets by mail, and with the proceeds supported his parish. Finally he commissioned a futuristic, reinforced-concrete church on a shoulder of mountain where no one lived; it is there now, though he of course is not.

The second was a Jesuit named Aime Duval, who moved along the roads on a motorcycle with a guitar strapped to his back, singing songs of his own composition in bars. This was his mission duly approved by his superiors; when a crowd of drinkers had gathered around him he would talk about God. His lyrics were intricate and poetic and beyond my then French. So was much else of what he told me. Father Duval became famous and even sang from the stage of theaters in Paris, same as Maurice Chevalier or Edith Piaf. He died recently, an alcoholic.

La Roche Canillac, a village in the Corrèze, impressed me. The cows there are red, the slate roofs are heavy and bowed, we once owned the remnants of the village castle, and in the cemetery I have peered down on the tombs of ancestors of my children. It seemed to me very strange that they should have roots in rural France, where I did not.

The Eiffel Tower is not in this book, nor Versailles, nor much of what tourists see first and quickly. The cathedrals of the north are well enough known; I have preferred to describe the one at Le Puy. I never heard of it until I saw it. It is just as beautiful, older, more curious. And besides, it charmed me. As for museums, the Petit Palais at Avignon is stranger than the Louvre, with a bizarre story behind it, satisfying to write about certainly, and with luck to read about as well.

The personalities in this book are often those whose lives, however tenuously, touched me, touched mine: Lafayette, because he too discovered another country as a young man and afterwards could not forget it; and de Gaulle, under whom I lived; and Tobias Smollett, who invented what became the "fabulous" Riviera, in whose glow the world basked for 200 years; and Grace Kelly, who was my age, who arrived in the south of France the same year I did, and who saved Monte Carlo — not her original intention, surely.

I have written about families: the Pontacs, who dominated Bordeaux for 300 years; and the Sansons, who operated the guillotine through six generations. I have set down much that touched great events but that is otherwise little known: the concentration camps in the Pyrenees during World War II; the French-run Gestapo led by a renegade Paris cop; even Vichy's attempts forty and more years after the fact to rehabilitate its reputation.

There are other portraits too: of French opera, sports, schools, perfumes, chefs; of the police, of the penal colony in French Guiana. In those places where geography is dominant, the portraits become landscapes — stony vineyards, tidal beaches, the volcanoes of the Auvergne — for geography shapes a people more than any single factor. As much as possible I have based my descriptions on scars that can still be seen today — the battlefields, castles, works of art, manuscripts, tombs, ruins — scars in the flesh of the country, each one dating from some accident in its past. It was my hope that all this would evoke the rest — some of the rest, anyway, the best I could do, and that even the personal parts, insofar as they too represent France, might have some interest.

Nice
THE PROMENADE OF THE ENGLISH

He stood against the rail in the dark, pressed as far forward as passengers were permitted, leaning into the wind. He had been up for hours and out on deck, though it was cold and he could see nothing, not the shore towards which the liner was gliding, not even the black water hissing by three or four stories below. With first light would come his first glimpse of France, and he was waiting for it, but it was February and the dawn was slow. He was tall and skinny and wore the short haircut of the time. He wore his old air force raincoat buttoned to his throat. His face was cold. His coat, the only one he had with him, was thin and even the hands in his pockets were cold — winter was evidently going to be colder on the Riviera than he had imagined. But he did not go below. No lookout working for Columbus ever peered forward more intently.

High above the night there suddenly appeared the dawn-struck summits of the Maritime Alps. They had simply popped into view, floodlit, a whole range of them close behind where the coast must be, miles and miles of rock and snow, pink peaks floating unsupported in the black sky. Mountains he had not even known were there.

So that was the first he ever saw of France, not so much a view as a vision, like an apparition of the Virgin. It stirred his soul as well as his eyes. Up forward, chains began to rattle. The anchor went down. The engines stopped. The steamship had approached as near to the still-invisible coast as the captain intended.

Having seen France, the young man soon could smell it, or thought he could. The harsh wind had disappeared, and now in his face he felt a mild breeze. It brought him odors more subtle by far than those of the past two weeks. He had crossed in a cabin for eight on D deck in a once-luxurious ship that was old before he was born. Only one of his cabinmates spoke English. With the door closed the cabin air was stupefying. Outside in the corridors the ship smelled of rust and vomit. Now on the breeze came the fragrance of a continent about which he knew little and whose edge he still could not see.

Next he heard France. That is, a tender had come out and was bumping alongside, and from below near the water line came French voices, the French language. A door in the rusty hull opened, emitting a square of light, and men began handing cargo up and down. The young man had studied freshman French. The teacher's name was O'Sullivan — you can imagine. He listened to the stevedores below, listened to muttered commands, warnings, and probably curses, and found the sounds romantic.

As the sun rose up out of the Mediterranean, a second tender took the passengers off. The young man stood up all the way to the pier. The sun ignited the villas on the hills, the roofs of the town itself, the masts of many yachts, the tousled palm trees that lined the streets. Palm trees. Wow.

The hotel in Nice was at the top of a shabby flight of stairs. There was a counter with a head behind it. This was the owner. The young man was shown a room on the fourth floor. The owner was out of breath when they got up there. The young man was not. The room was big. The walls bore huge water stains, and the ceiling seemed to sag. The bed looked lumpy. In the corner was a sink, and on the floor beside it a bidet. The young man had never seen a bidet before and stared at it curiously. It must be a douche bowl, he thought. The owner threw open the shutters. Sunlight flooded in through floor-length windows, and the young man looked out. The rooftops around him were orange. The view was down through hanging laundry into a courtyard.

"You like?"

"How much a night?"

"Two dollar."

The young man grinned.

He had with him three pieces of luggage. One was his type-writer in its wooden case. Once the owner had departed he took the machine out, set the case upon the bidet and the machine on top of the case. The height was about right. It would make an adequate typing table. In later years, he imagined, once he had become famous, journalists in their articles about him were going to note that he had started his career on top of this douche bowl on the French Riviera.

He went out. The first job was to change money. Not in a bank, but on the black market, for he had a dealer's address from someone on the ship. At the end of a dim hallway he knocked on an apartment door. The dealer took his traveler's checks and closed the door on him. As he waited he was pleased. In France only a few hours and already in contact with the underworld. Then he became nervous. Perhaps the man had absconded with his money. Finally the door opened a crack and a sheaf of francs was handed out. He tried to engage the dealer in conversation with some French phrases he had memorized, but the door closed on him.

In the street the young man studied his money. In exchange for a number of $10 traveler's checks, he had in his hands these thousands and thousands of francs. The notes were beautifully printed in pastel inks. Each denomination was of a different size and color from the others. The two biggest were the size almost of washcloths and had to be folded in four to fit into his billfold.

He strolled through the town. The war had been over eight years, but France was a defeated country and a depressed one, and the young man saw this. There were bicycles and motor scooters in the streets, most of them not new, but no traffic signals at any of the corners. Cars moved across intersections as they willed. But there were few of them. They seemed to him exceptionally tiny, the type he had seen midgets pile out of at the circus.

No one he knew had ever been to this part of the world. He was seeking to match what he saw to a vocabulary he was familiar with.

The pastel walls of the buildings were so faded there was almost no color left. The storefronts were shabby, too, and seemed to hold little stock. A dress shop had a single dress in the window staked out by pins; another had only two. Through a shop window he watched a woman manipulate an instrument he had never seen before; it repaired runs in nylons. American girls threw ruined nylons away and bought new ones.

But there were beds of flowers blooming, even now, in winter, in the public gardens and along the Promenade des Anglais as well, and the Mediterranean seemed to him bluer than blue. It needed no paint job, nor did the bright orange rooftops of the town. But the rest seemed forlorn, as if waiting without much hope for its legendary past to return. He was being observant, not critical. It was legend that had brought him to this particular place rather than another. The fabulous Riviera. A place featured in songs, in movies, in novels that had moved him. Kingdoms won and lost at the tables. "The Man Who Broke the Bank at Monte Carlo." Yachts, jewel robberies. A place frequented by the titled, by the famous — by great writers too.

The legend was so strong in him that it could survive any number of disappointments — the shabbiness of the town, for instance, or the stony beach at his feet that was not even sand. He had come here in search of life with a capital L, and legend with a capital L also, and he did not realize that as goals they were incompatible, for one was behind him, the other ahead. Sooner or later he would have to choose between them. In the meantime he was enchanted with Nice, and with himself for being here. This was where he would stay until his money ran out. All he needed now was a girl. It was essential that he find one. He would fall in love with her. He would start looking right away.

The legend.

The cemetery gates are wrought iron and taller than a man. There is a notice encased in plastic attached to the bars, and when I have read it I wonder if one of its purposes is not to end the legend once and for all. No telling who signed it. It bears an illegible signature and the official stamp of the Mairie de Nice. This is the French way. City hall signed it. Blame city hall.

The hinges are rusty. The gate creaks. I go through and find the same notice inside tacked to a tree.

Ocean liners no longer ply the Mediterranean ports. I have reached Nice by plane and driven up here through the heavy afternoon traffic. At the beginning this cemetery was well outside the city limits. Now it is well within, surrounded by villas and apartment buildings, overhung by the city's smog. It lies to the west on a man-made terrace partway up one of the steep hills that loom over the town on three of its four sides. Before it was a cemetery it must have been an olive grove or a vineyard — part of a farm, in any case, part of a different time and world. It is not a big cemetery, only five or six tree-shaded gravel alleys with plots to either side, perhaps 300 or 400 in all. Many are not really graves but tombs in the French style. They are rather deep, their walls lined with brick or cinder block depending on their age, and sometimes they contain whole families, the flat wooden coffins stacked one on top of the other and the tomb covered over with a marble slab to allow ease of access the next time. There is much about the French way of death which, as I learned it, seemed strange to me.

Of course most of the people entombed here were not French.

There is a small stone cottage just inside the wall under the trees. Now the concierge appears in the doorway. Her name is Mme Gagnes. We shake hands and discuss what has begun to happen here. She is a small, gray-haired woman with a local accent. You don't hear that accent much anymore. Having filled up with people from other parts of France and French émigrés from North Africa, Nice is cosmopolitan now. Its accent has become almost neutral, and Niçois, the local patois, which was common in the streets even twenty years ago, seems to have disappeared almost completely.

Mme Gagnes was born in this small cottage inside the cemetery. Her father was concierge then, as his father had been before him — they were all in a sense caretakers of the Riviera legend. Perhaps the job was in the family for generations further back than that. This too would be the French way.

In any case, the dynasty is finished now. She is the last of her line. The notice on the gate, and on the tree inside, was quite clear about that. From where we stand I can see that many of the tombs are in a state of disrepair. There are statues with heads or hands broken off, and stone crosses that have fallen forward or back, and tombs that have heaved or caved in. There are marble slabs so overgrown with nettles that the inscriptions can no longer be read. The town doesn't want the tombs cared for anymore, Mme Gagnes remarks bitterly, it wants them back so as to empty them out and sell them again. Nice has become an extremely crowded place with hardly room enough even to die. The town has changed the cemetery's name. It's now the Cimetière Ste. Marguerite. An era is passing, she adds. Worried as she must be about her home and her livelihood, I am surprised she is aware of any eras passing, though why should I be? This special cemetery, one of the most remarkable in France, was both her inheritance and her life.

It means something to me, too, principally because it is also almost the only place left — for a little time longer — where it is possible with a certain accuracy to reconstruct the "fabulous Riviera" that once so dominated the imagination of the world. Legends are living things. They are born, they flourish for a certain time, they grow old, die, and are interred. There are cemeteries for them. I am not being facetious. This is one of them. The Riviera legend, most of it, is interred here.

In origin that legend was English, not French. It was the English who took a few fishing villages fronting on a few miserable strips of beach and gave it all a name and termed it fabulous. Afterwards, for 200 years, they only tried to make it live up to the image they had created.

Of course the English were never the majority here, though they behaved like they were. They imposed their own culture on top of what they found, ignored nearly everything that was local except the weather and the gorgeous jagged coastline, and they ruled as absolutely as if in Singapore or Lahore. There were British consulates and Anglican churches and chapters of the British Legion and of the Freemasons in all the major Riviera towns. In Nice in the 1820s the English built a path beside the sea on which to stroll away the hours of incredible winter sunshine — incredible certainly when compared to London — and the locals, or someone, called it the Promenade des Anglais, and that's what it has remained to this day: the Promenade of the English. In every town they had their Cook's tourist agency, plus outposts of Barclay's Bank — at a time when international banking was rare. They had their own real estate agents. They had their own bookstores, their own lending libraries, and even their own hospital staffed by English nurses. It stood above the lower Corniche between Nice and Villefranche facing out to sea, and on a clear day convalescing patients could sit out on their balconies and they could see Corsica. The hospital's name changed from time to time, and that's all. When Victoria died it became the Queen Victoria Memorial; much later it became the British-American Hospital. Recently it was demolished and replaced by luxury flats.

How many English could there have been here on any given day? They stopped at hotels named the Westminster, the West End, and such — hotels that still exist. They bought their Jaguars and Rolls-Royces at car dealerships run by men as English as themselves, and these dealerships are still there, though French-owned now. They patronized their own pubs and restaurants, which are all gone. They had their own burial ground, and I am standing in it: the English Cemetery. For 200 years, until that notice went up on the gate, it had no other name.

The legend started small. It became a vogue first, a legend only after. It began with a single man, Tobias Smollett (1721–71), a Scottish-born London physician and surgeon who suffered from asthma. In 1748, at a time when he was still cutting people open with the crude instruments of the day, he published a novel called *The Adventures of Roderick Random*. This was a success. Three years later he published *The Adventures of Peregrine Pickle,* an even bigger one. It is difficult to understand what literary success amounted to in 1751. There was no competition from television; on the other hand, not many people could read.

Smollett abandoned medicine for the literary game and shortly thereafter set out with his wife for the Mediterranean coast, where it was said that a man with asthma would find it easier to breathe. Having crossed the channel to Boulogne, the Smolletts started south. They reached Nice in December 1763 after two weeks in a stagecoach.

Nice today is the fifth biggest city in France (after Paris,

Marseilles, Lyon, and Toulouse), about 350,000 people; count in all the satellite towns from the Italian border to Cannes and the Riviera population adds up to about a million and a half. There is scarcely an unused space left anywhere except for the vertical ones. The Nice of December 1763 was a town of 12,000. According to Smollett it was "wedged in between a steep rock and the little river Paillon, which descends from the mountains, and, washing the town walls on the west side, falls into the sea, after having filled some canals for the use of the inhabitants." Smollett found no hotels, no yachts, and the beaches were useful only as a place for the fishermen to spread and dry their nets. The narrow streets of the old town were already there, same as today, as was the ruined chateau on its rock high above. The port was new, only twelve years old.

Smollett found the Niçois lazy, probably because they were Catholics, and he thought the shopkeepers inclined to cheat him. He lived in a rented ground-floor apartment whose rooms were "large, lofty and commodious." Describing the view from the ramparts he wrote, "The small extent of country which I see is all cultivated like a garden. Indeed the plain presents nothing but gardens, full of green trees loaded with oranges, lemons, citrons and bergamots, which make a delightful appearance. If you examine them more nearly, you will find plantations of green peas ready to gather, all sorts of salading, and pot-herbs in perfection; and plats of roses, carnations, renunculuses, anemonies and daffodils, blowing in full glory, with such beauty, vigor, and perfume, as no flower in England ever exhibited." Nice was a place, he added, where "robbery and murder are altogether unknown" and the weather was perfect. "You see nothing above your head for several months together but a charming blue expanse without cloud or speck."

When spring came he had himself carried out onto the beach in a sedan chair. It is unclear exactly which beach this was. The Promenade des Anglais at the time was a sweep of stones that ended in bushes. "The people here were much surprised when I began to bathe in the beginning of May. They thought it very strange that a man, seeming consumptive, should plunge into the sea, especially when the weather was so cold; and some of the

doctors prognosticated immediate death. But when it was perceived that I grew better in consequence of the bath, some of the
Swiss officers tried the same experiment, and in a few days our
example was followed by several inhabitants of Nice."

These days you often see heads bobbing in the sea in spring,
and there are sunbathers even on warm winter days, mostly shopgirls at lunch hour who strip to the waist and lie there with their
breasts flattened out, exposed both to the sun and to middle-aged
tourists in overcoats who stand at the railing peering down at
them. Such scenes as this would have greatly scandalized Smollett,
who wrote that "the fair sex must be entirely excluded, unless
they lay aside all regard to decorum; for the shore is always lined
with fishing boats and crowded with people. If a lady should be
at the expense of having a tent pitched on the beach, where she
might put on and off her bathing dress, she could not pretend to
go into the sea without proper attendants; nor could she possibly
plunge headlong into the water, which is the most effectual and
least dangerous way of bathing. All that she can do is have the
seawater brought into her house, and make use of a bathing tub,
which may be made according to her own or physician's direction."

Smollett stayed a year and a half, then went home to London
and wrote *Travels in France and Italy,* which was published in 1766.
It became a bestseller, whatever that term may have meant, and
the vogue that would become a legend was launched. Four years
later, when King George III was on the throne and the American
Revolution was five years off, the Duke of Gloucester, one of the
King's brothers, wintered in Nice. The Duchess of Cumberland
followed, and the Duke of Bedford, together with many wealthy
and titled Englishmen, and a colony sprang up that resulted soon
enough in the creation of this cemetery in which I stand.

Nice also had a Russian colony for a time. About 1856 the
Czarina arrived for the winter with her entourage, and a number
of grand dukes followed, one of whom founded the golf club near
Cannes; photographs of him still hang on the wall there, or at
least they did the last time I went by.

For generation after generation the Riviera remained the

world's most fashionable playground. Edward VII, when Prince of Wales, frolicked here every winter; his mother, Queen Victoria, lived quietly in Cimiez, a new residential quarter on one of the hills above Nice. The sumptuous Hotel Regina was built up there; the English aristocracy kept it full season after season. A statue of Victoria in her later years was erected nearby, and it still sits on its pedestal brooding over the city.

All these people contributed to the legend, then died or went away. The legend went on without them, as today we go on without it. A few years ago the Hotel Regina was broken up into flats. The palatial hotel became a cooperative apartment house. Even the promenade along the sea that the English built has fallen on hard times. The Michelin guide has downgraded it from three stars to two; a miasma of automobile exhaust hangs over it most of each day, and eight lanes of bumper-to-bumper traffic, four in each direction, pass ceaselessly by.

The young man strolled through the old town. In here was the original Nice, unchanged since Smollett's time. Narrow alleys. Rooftops so close together that only a thin strip of sky showed overhead. The young man had never seen an old town before, nor heard of Smollett. There were no sidewalks. Women with string bags shopped for dinner. He inhaled the pungent odors that rushed out of doors at him and made him hungry: bread hot from the ovens, coffee, spilled wine.

When he had come out of the old town he saw things that to him were stranger still, one of them a nightclub, closed at this hour, that seemed to promise topless dancers. He studied the photos outside. He had heard about this, but was not sure he believed it. In America strippers stopped when still wearing net bras or pasties. Anything less would land them in jail.

And on certain streets prostitutes cocked their heads at him and murmured:

"*Tu viens, cheri?*"

They seemed to patrol several meters of sidewalk each. Some walked along swinging handbags. Some stood beside or were led along by lapdogs on the leash. All looked to him expensively dressed. Some were young and pretty. It was broad daylight and he didn't even realize they were whores at first. He had never seen whores on sidewalks before. He was curious and tried to question them, but they quickly lost interest. Perhaps they did not understand his French. Perhaps they thought he was mocking them.

He came to a restaurant and stopped to read the menu posted outside. This place served roast beef with Yorkshire pudding and other English dishes, and even English beers. He had become acutely conscious of his inability to converse with anyone, and he needed a place around which he could orient himself. He went in and sat on an oak stool at an oak bar and ordered Coca-Cola. There were two waiters in white coats, one behind the bar, the other in the dining room preparing for the dinner service. There was a charwoman washing dishes in the kitchen and a gray-haired woman behind the cash desk reading *France-Soir* and smoking. These people spoke French to each other, and none spoke English to the young man.

A girl came in through the door. He must have stared. She seemed startled to see him sitting there.

The trouble was, her language seemed to be French too. The woman behind the cash desk was evidently her mother. The waiters addressed her respectfully as "miss." When she asked for a coffee, the barman said:

"*Oui, mademoiselle.*"

She stood quite near the stool on which he spun from time to time, wanting to get a look at her but trying not to stare. The girls he was used to wore penny loafers, bobby socks, and barrettes in their hair. This one stood on thin high heels, a fashion he did not know because it had not yet reached America. She wore nylons and a gray-green tailored suit. Nor were her looks American looks. She was young and fresh faced, of course. She had high cheekbones, large blue eyes, and big white teeth. She was tall for a French girl, about five foot six. Her hair was dark brown, as thick and lustrous as a horse's tail, and parted on one side.

He decided to speak to her, expecting a cute French accent in reply. But her accent was British. She spoke like the Queen of England. He hid his disappointment. In response to his questions she told him she had learned English at 9. A war refugee child, she had landed in England and was sent to a boarding school in Sussex. For months, understanding nothing, she had spoken not a word to anyone. She smiled at the young man. They must have thought they had a 9-year-old deaf mute on their hands, she said.

Language as a topic had now been exhausted, and the young man could not think of another.

"Would you like to live in America?"

"No."

"You wouldn't?" But he had been led to believe there were only two kinds of people in the world, those who were Americans and those who wished they were Americans. "Why not?" he asked incredulously.

She said, "I'm French, you see."

He decided he better leave before he said something equally stupid. Her smile seemed definitely cooler. If he asked for a date tonight she would probably refuse. He was not a fool, he wanted to tell her. He just needed time to digest all this strangeness. He would come back and he would do better.

Mme Gagnes has gone back into her concierge's lodge. It is her habit to greet any mourners who come and then to withdraw. Hers is a profession that demands discretion. I move forward into the cemetery, and the changes are shocking. Cemeteries above all things ought to be timeless, and therefore changeless, or so it would seem, but in France this is not the case. Normally they belong to the state, which sells *concessions.* Families — referred to in legal documents as *concessionaires* — can buy a cemetery plot for a specific period of time, such as ten years, or they can buy one *à perpétuité,* which means forever. But in France, as far as graves are concerned, forever doesn't mean very long. The state will move to reclaim the grave site just as soon as there appear to be no relatives left to protest. There are very few old tombs in France. Once a headstone has collapsed into the hole and no one comes by anymore to put flowers down, that to the authorities is an abandoned grave, and they empty it out and resell the space. In French cemeteries the dead, like the living, come and go. Which is what the notice outside on the gate is all about. An attempt is being made to contact the *concessionaires* of those tombs that seem to be abandoned. They had best make themselves known. Otherwise . . .

Originally the English Cemetery was private and the state couldn't touch it. It belonged to the Anglican church down on the Rue de la Buffa. But today's parishioners are few and mostly they are transient. They provide not nearly enough money to support the cemetery. The vicar of a few years ago found a solution: he donated it to the town. What else could he do?

I walk along reading the tombstones.

To the memory of Frederick John Fargus "Hugh Conway"
British writer of great repute and greater promise
who died at Monte Carlo in his 39th year May 15, 1888

Sir Edward Beauchamp Bart. 17 years a member
of Parliament twice chairman of Lloyds

ALEXANDER ADAIR BRICE OF THE 23RD
ROYAL WELSH FUSILIERS
IN WHICH HE SERVED IN THE PENINSULA AND WAS PRESENT
ON THE STAFF OF HIS UNCLE GENERAL O'LOGHLIN
AT THE BATTLE OF WATERLOO

Ellen widow of J. B. Angelle
who died January 25, 1874,
at the age of 27 leaving an only son
who was all her earthly joy and care

SACRED TO THE MEMORY OF ANDREW MOSSMANN WHO DIED
FEBRUARY 1, 1868, IN THE 28TH YEAR OF HIS LIFE
THIS CROSS IS ERECTED BY THE EARL OF FIFE
TO WHOM HE WAS A FAITHFUL SERVANT

The English colony in microcosm: the writer, the tycoon, the soldier, the wife, the servant. Many of the deceased were retired military men who had served in India or Sumatra or some other warm place and who could not bear in retirement to return to the rain and gloom of the English winters. They stopped off here and stayed on. You can read their rank and regiment in the stone. Their women were buried under prayers instead:

And mother finds her home and heavenly rest
O call back yesterday, bid time return
She is not dead but sleepeth
Taken away suddenly by a terrible fall from a window

All these messages were chiseled out letter by letter by a succession of French stonecutters who did not know what they were writing. Many young people lie here too, some only teenagers, who perhaps were not true members of the colony at all. Tuberculosis killed most of them. That was the scourge of the young during the time that the English held sway. There was no known cure, but it was said to be easier to breathe in the sunny south of France than in dark English houses, and many young people were bundled off to Nice, often alone, and they sat in the sun for a while, and then they died.

The alley of cypresses comes to an end. In the sudden sunshine the view is quite magnificent: much of the city, much of the coastline, much of the Mediterranean Sea. But to the right, in what was once one of the oldest parts of the cemetery, the bulldozers have already been at work. The machines have skinned back that entire area. Neither trees nor tombstones are left. The dirt is almost orange. Soon there will be new graves there, French ones. Previously the English were all in here together, separated by generations perhaps but sharing, well, England. Now it is as if strangers will lie down beside them. Of course this is only a temporary condition. In time there won't be any English in here at all. Cemeteries are museums too; this is the only one the English left behind them, and perhaps an exception should have been made.

I turn into the newest section and pass among the graves of the final remnants of the English colony in Nice, and some of these people I knew. Here lies Jimmy Green, who was the cashier at Cook's on the Promenade; during the years I worked out of Nice he used to cash my checks for me; nearby lies Daisy Turner, and for a moment I am surprised to find no sign of Walter's name on that tombstone or an adjoining one. Then I remember that the family took Walter back to England. They left Daisy here. They didn't like Daisy.

And finally I stand over the grave of the man around whom the English colony was focused during the last forty years of its existence, the soul of the colony, so to speak — not something he ever claimed for himself. Nor, for reasons I will go into in a moment, would the others ever have conceded it to him.

After supper, wearing a beret he had bought, the young man went out of his hotel. He thought the beret might permit him to pass for a native. He went back to the nightclub he had noted earlier and waited at the bar to see if the show would fulfill what the photos outside had promised.

He sipped Coca-Cola. The show started. "Le Spectacle," the French called it. A girl came out wearing a long skirt and a shawl. As soon as the music started and she threw off the shawl, he saw that she was naked to the waist. She had castanets above her head and she began to dance. Her breasts moved with her rhythm. No tiny bra or pasties. Nothing. Wow!

The next night, his second in Nice, the young man returned to the restaurant. But he had made another mistake. He was too early. It was the American dinner hour, not the French one, and the dining room was empty. At a table near the cash desk the family was being served by one of the waiters: mother, father, brother, and the girl.

The waiter showed the young man to a table and took his order: steak, french fries, and an apple tart — he was not an ad-venturous eater. The waiter offered wine or beer, but he asked for milk. This was brought without protest; he was not the first American they had seen here. The french fries were succulent. The steak was pink inside and came with a wine sauce that he mopped up with the crusty bread. The apple tart was served with the delicacy the French call crème fraîche. To the young man it tasted sour.

The bill caused him some concern. He would not be able to eat here very often.

He moved to the bar. This place seemed to have filled up with exotic people. He stood listening to a Turkish prince and a member of the enormously rich British Sassoon clan. But he kept stealing glances at the girl. She had finished her dinner now too.

He had been thinking about her all day. He kept hoping she would come over and talk to him, and presently she did. They shook hands. They touched each other for the first time. The famous Nice carnival was to begin that night, and they talked about it. Why was he so shy with this girl? Finally he got up his nerve — would she come with him to the carnival? After a moment — a long moment for him — a smile came on and she nodded her head.

Then as now carnival was focused in the Place Masséna, whose walls were festooned with colored lights and with gigantic wooden cutouts in the shape of toys — the carnival motif was toys that year. They walked into an explosion of color and light. The walls, the lampposts, the entire square seemed ablaze. Bleachers were filled to overflowing. Streamers arched out from buildings, and confetti floated down like pink and blue snow. Music blared from loudspeakers. The Mediterranean fleets of all the allied nations were anchored offshore, British, American, French. Such a concentration of warships had not been seen off the coast since the invasion of southern France in 1944, almost ten years before, and the square was swarming with sailors.

The carnival parade came up the Avenue de la Victoire and into the square, pink clowns first, and mummers wearing grotesque heads that swayed awkwardly as they danced. Then came the great floats, a long line from far down the street. Horns caterwauled. The floats were in the form of toys that were larger than life: a sprawled blue train, an upturned toy box, a leering jack-in-the-box. They floated around the square and out again. The King of Toys came last, a merry papier-mâché giant with gilded crown, a fuchsia vest, indigo sleeves, rouged cheeks, and grinning red lips. When he had been ensconced on a throne in the center of the Place, the crowd spilled down out of the bleachers, and the first of the nightly battles of confetti began.

The confetti was sold from booths in swollen bags in two sizes, *gros,* which means fat, and *formidable.* Handfuls of confetti were flung into the grinning faces of total strangers. Impromptu dances began, for the music continued to blare. Halos of dust rose up to soften the multicolored lights, to dim the stars and blur the contours of the moon.

Escaping at last from the tumultuous square, the young man and the girl plunged into the public gardens, into darkness, into quiet. There was confetti stuck in their hair, on their clothes, on their faces. They were excited by the carnival, they were excited by each other. They held each other tight, hearts beating inside overcoats. They were laughing and half out of breath.

He walked her home. She had to be in by eleven, she said. When he had left her he did not know where to go, what to do. There was still noise from the Place Masséna, but for him the city was empty. He went to stand in the dark on the Promenade facing out over the Mediterranean. The sea was black. He listened to its short rush over the stones. He could hear glass tinkling brokenly in the shallows.

The opulence of the carnival, which continued day after day, was still another strangeness. In the afternoon there were Battles of Flowers. Horse-drawn carriages paraded by, each one so heavily decorated with flowers that it could scarcely be seen. In each carriage rode one or several pretty girls. They threw flowers at the crowds who lined the streets, and the crowds threw the flowers back. There were nightly fireworks as well, and the young man was confused. In a country as poor and desperate as France, how could so much care and craftsmanship and so much money be lavished on a carnival?

He did not realize that during this time the hotels stayed full, the shops as well. He did not realize that the Riviera was still trying to live off this and a few other events that had become traditional during its lurid past, was still trying to attract the very rich, who, apart from the Americans, no longer existed, for Russia was closed, Spain was closed, Germany and large parts of Italy were still devastated. England was bankrupt. The only English left in Nice were bank clerks, airline personnel, and such, still a small permanent colony but definitely not the same one as in the past.

The local economy had become dependent on American tourists, who were too few to take up the slack, and who did not stay for the season; and on the American navy. Nearly all tourists still came over by boat, usually debarking at ports in the north. Many brought their fat American cars along in the hold. But most of them only passed through Nice on their way somewhere else. They accorded it only two or three days. The U.S. Mediterranean fleet was not reliable either. Although its home port was Villefranche, three miles to the east, it was often at sea, or showing the flag in other ports. It was keeping other towns afloat besides Nice: Genoa, Barcelona, Athens. It ranged as far as Turkey.

The young man and the girl were together every day. The car rental business did not yet exist in France, and he could not have afforded a car anyway. But public buses were cheap and, in the absence of other traffic, swift. He and the girl rode buses to Eze, where he saw his first perched village, and to La Turbie, his first Roman ruins, and to Cagnes, his first feudal castle. He gawked at Eze, which clung like an eagle's nest to a rock crag 1,500 feet high. From its ramparts the view was straight down into the sea. The ruins at La Turbie, he decided, must once have been a temple of some kind. He had studied Latin in school. Showing off for the girl, he tried to decipher the engravings in the stone. The castle at Cagnes, which today can barely be seen for all the tall buildings around it, at that time dominated not only the hill on which it stood, but much of the surrounding countryside. Inside, it had been turned into a museum. Renoir's wheelchair was there and a palette and some brushes, for he had lived in Cagnes the last twelve years of his life.

The girl had seen all this before. The young man had not. He was dazzled by it, and by her. They drank innumerable cups of tea in tearooms, usually before boarding the bus back to Nice, and told each other who they were, and this subject to them was entrancing.

She had been evacuated from Nice in 1940 when France fell, she told him. In London she went every night with her mother to a shelter, and bombs fell, and dust and plaster came down from the ceiling, people screamed, and once her mother fainted — the only person in that shelter who spoke the child's language lay on the floor unconscious. In the shelters, before she'd even learned to speak English, she learned certain English card games and how to play chess.

After seven years she came back to Nice and entered art

school. Although she now spoke English like a duchess's daughter, she found to her horror that an English accent had crept into her French. Her schoolmates called her "L'Anglaise." It took her months to lose the cursed accent. Art school was the first time she had ever attended class with boys, and she did not know how to handle them. At first they twitted her about her accent and then about her haughtiness. They passed her love notes in class, they formed archways of brushes or books for her to pass through as she entered or left the building. At the end of the term they voted her both most beautiful and most bitchy — *la plus belle,* but also *la plus pimbêche.*

On her way to and from school policemen would stop traffic so she could cross; from their pedestals in the center of intersections they would give her elaborate bows. Men sometimes followed her in the street. One followed her all the way home and in past the bar. She fled into the kitchen. Her father knocked him cold with a wrench and had to go down to the police station. After that when men followed her she would go round and round the block trying to lose them. She couldn't go home — she would seem to be leading them into a bar.

At the end of her second year in art school she won first prize, which was an art scholarship to Paris. She was thrilled — all she had ever wanted in life was to be an artist. She was also apprehensive, and she asked the professor to come around and speak to her father. "No daughter of mine is going to Paris alone," her father told the professor, and her art career ended then and there.

The movement for equal rights for women would not begin for another fifteen or twenty years — even later in France.

Lately she had worked in a shop that sold expensive leather goods to tourists. The "English Spoken" sign in the window was her. She was 22 years old. The shop was on the Avenue de Verdun, Nice's swankiest street. She had earned the equivalent of $54 a month, the going wage for French girls, even bilingual ones, that year. But not enough tourists came in, and a few weeks ago the shop had closed. Since then she had been trying to get a job as a model for one of the local couture houses, but without luck so far. Perhaps she wasn't tall enough or skinny enough.

She had been invited aboard warships by officers who came

into her father's place. The French navy served wine and champagne at these receptions, the English navy gin, and the American navy an insipid, nonalcoholic fruit punch. She was not allowed to date sailors. She had dated officers, though, particularly Americans. Most had been somewhat older men, up to the rank of lieutenant commander. They took her to nightclubs and attempted to ply her with champagne.

"Oh," said the young man. He had imagined himself probably the only American she had ever known.

It was his turn to speak, but what could he tell her that was even half as interesting as what she had told him? He was from New York, the son of a newspaper columnist. He had started his first novel when he was twelve. In college he had majored in English literature. He had written for the college newspaper and won some swimming races. When the Korean War started he went into the air force, rose to the rank of corporal, and was bitterly unhappy not to be an officer — his natural station, it seemed to him. Anyway, that's why he was wearing this air force raincoat. He had turned down pilot training in order to get discharged sooner and begin his life's work. His life's work was to become the greatest writer who ever lived. He had completed another novel and many short stories. He hadn't sold anything yet. Everything he sent out came back rejected. But they would have to start publishing him soon, wouldn't they? It had been his ambition to be published even younger than F. Scott Fitzgerald, his idol, who had been 23, but his 24th birthday was coming up in a few months. He was working on new stories in his hotel room every day. He did not tell her that Fitzgerald had come to the Riviera thirty years previously, which was partly why he had come himself — in such ways do men unknowingly distort the lives of the generation that is to follow.

He did not brag that his desk was the bidet, nor that it was getting harder and harder to concentrate on working when the only place he wanted to be was with her.

At home he had an old car. Actually he and his brother owned it jointly. It was parked in his father's garage. He had a job to go back to. It was with a pro football team. It began next July 1 and would pay $85 a week. He had enough money to last until then, he hoped. If he sold a story to one of the magazines, he wouldn't have to go back at all. He could stay in Nice. He glanced at her hopefully.

They rode more buses up into the hills. She showed him St. Paul, a perfect jewel of a walled village, another first. They walked the cobblestone alleys, passed under stone archways. People were still living there at that time; it wasn't all shops as it is today. There were small galleries in which local artists showed their wares and working ateliers; they watched salad bowls being carved out of olive wood. From the ramparts they could see a series of hills dropping down towards the sea, with here and there a villa or a carnation farm.

They went on to Vence, where they gazed at a fifteenth-century square tower and at a great urn of a fountain with water slopping over its rim and down its mossy sides. They walked down a street to the chapel that Matisse had both underwritten and designed, and the young man bought tickets and they went in. The white porcelain walls were decorated with simple but extremely eloquent black designs, here the figure of St. Dominic, there the stations of the cross outlined in bold black strokes. The floor-to-ceiling stained glass was in green, yellow, and blue, but the sun coming through managed to cast a faint reddish shadow upon the floor. There was a drawing of the Virgin Mary with one breast exposed to symbolize maternity.

The young man had read about this chapel in *Life* magazine, and here it was in real life, a place of extreme sobriety and incredible luminosity. Over 80 and an invalid confined at times to a wheelchair, Matisse had said of it: "This chapel for me is the culmination of an entire life's work and the flowering of an enormous, sincere and difficult labor. It is not a labor I chose but for which destiny chose me at the end of my road. I consider it, despite all its imperfections, my masterpiece, an effort resulting from an entire life dedicated to the search for truth."

Behind the chapel was a small gallery where Matisse's preliminary sketches and designs were on display. The young man knew little enough about art, but he knew about first drafts, and these were the first drafts of Matisse, and as he moved from one to the other he was able to study Matisse's struggle to find the apparently simple drawings inside.

A few days after this they went to a Raoul Dufy retrospective in Nice. Like Matisse, Dufy was a longtime resident of Nice; he had died at 76 the year before. Nowadays the Riviera is dotted with small museums devoted exclusively, or almost exclusively, to single painters. There are Picasso museums in Antibes and Vallauris, a Fernand Léger museum in Biot, a Renoir museum in Cagnes, and Matisse, Chagall, and Dufy museums in Nice. But at that time none of these places existed, and the young man had never heard of Raoul Dufy.

He and the girl studied the canvases. She pointed out how the painter's style had changed over the years. His earliest paintings were in the style of impressionism, she said. Then he switched to fauvism, then to cubism. Finally he adopted the flat planes and the pure colors of these later canvases here, most of which depicted Nice during its most fashionable years: yacht regattas, beautiful people, the seafront, casinos. The structure of each painting was almost calligraphic. The brilliant colors somehow came out subtle. In these paintings, it seemed to the young man, was all of the Riviera legend, all of the gaiety and glamour that he had always imagined, and had come here to find firsthand. Dufy had captured it exactly.

When they came out he was in awe not only of Dufy, but of her. He had never met a girl who knew more about art than he did. The girls in his past had majored in home economics. They applied Toni home permanents to their hair, wore yellow chrysanthemums to football games. They hoped to marry advertising executives and have many children. Art was not considered important in America, and even his friends had scoffed at the young man's yearning to become a great writer; his parents had warned him that he was being unrealistic.

There were Dufy prints on sale. The girl stood close by him and helped him choose. He bought two, scenes of Nice, for the day when he would have to pack up his bags and go home.

He had cleaned out his bank account for this trip. Every childhood birthday present had been turned into traveler's checks, the profits from every summer job. He had been clutching it all when he landed, his life's savings, his entire earthly fortune, $500. On this he had hoped to stay until his job started, five months, even longer if his novel sold, or one of the new short stories he was writing and posting to America. Every day he stood on line at the mail counter at American Express hoping to receive an acceptance. But there had been only more rejections so far, while his money dwindled. He had begun to worry constantly about money, about how little was left, about how to cut back on what he was spending. He didn't want to leave Nice, didn't want to leave this girl.

Cheap as it was, his hotel was costing too much. Then he learned of an apartment that might be available. It sounded good. He would save on hotel bills, on restaurants, and he would have a real table to work on, not a bidet. The romance of crouching over a bidet with his typewriter between his knees had by now palled. Unfortunately there was a hitch.

One of the other inhabitants of his hotel was a man named Pierre, a Lebanese in his early thirties. Pierre was the hitch. It was Pierre who had suggested the apartment, Pierre who had found it, and Pierre with whom he would have to share it. Pierre and his girlfriend.

Pierre had been a sergeant in the British army during the war, so he said. He spoke five languages in all, so he said. He had much charm and told fantastic stories about himself, some of which were perhaps true. He did have a problem, though, and it was the same as the young man's: money. He was expecting some any day. Perhaps in the next mail. He wanted the young man to put up the front money for this terrific apartment.

"How much?" the young man asked.

Well, the landlady was asking two months' rent in advance and a month's deposit. But Pierre would pay him back as soon as his own money arrived.

The young man nodded. They were seated in a restaurant waiting for Pierre's girlfriend to join them. Pierre had found the restaurant too, and the young man was grateful to him, for it was cheaper than any he had found on his own. As for the girlfriend, he had met her and thought her fascinating, principally because of her occupation, which was nude dancer. Her name was Odette, and she was 21 years old.

Now he saw her cross through the tables — a blond girl, heavily made up and all curves, wearing a dress two sizes too small for her. She sat down beside him and she was giggling. As she had approached the restaurant, she reported, several of the prostitutes had misidentified her. They had told her angrily to get off their street. Wasn't that funny?

"What did she say?"

Pierre translated, then added, "We had best act fast on this apartment, or we'll lose it."

The young man could certainly see how the prostitutes might have made such a mistake. Odette so far was something of a disappointment to him. He had tried several times to converse with her about what it was like to dance nude but had been frustrated. The subject was simply too complicated for his French.

Pierre began to enumerate the arguments in favor of taking the apartment. He did not advance what was to the young man the most appealing argument of all, which was Odette — the prospect on his first trip abroad of actually living with an actual nude dancer. Sort of living with her, anyway.

The next day he signed over two-thirds of his remaining traveler's checks. He also signed the lease. His misgivings were momentary and he smothered them. Pierre would certainly pay back his share. Pierre was an older man. If the worldly and sophisticated Pierre couldn't be trusted, who could?

The odd threesome moved into the third-floor apartment. There were two bedrooms cluttered with derelict furniture and a kitchen containing a broken stove and no refrigerator. The bathroom, especially the tub and the toilet, had not been scoured in some years. The windows, however, looked down onto a garden that contained palm trees, various types of Mediterranean pines, and bougainvillea and wisteria that climbed the walls and clung to the balconies of their own building and all the surrounding ones. On hot spring days a perfume wafted up that was intoxicating.

In addition to trying to write stories, the young man was also studying French hard, memorizing new words every day, and he practiced, or tried to practice, on Odette. From their conversations he learned that she came from a village in eastern France. Her chilly trade was poorly paid, the equivalent of only about $3 per night. She was expected to drink afterwards with the customers, but this was difficult since they always took her to be a whore, which she was not. One day she invited all the girls from the nightclub home to tea. The young man sat with them and attempted to make conversation. They giggled and told him he was very droll.

The rest of what he came to know about Odette he learned from observation. She kept a hand douche syringe on the shelf in the bathroom, with her money rolled up and hidden in the nozzle. She had excruciating periods. She worked seven nights a week and slept till noon. Perhaps he had expected her to comport herself as nakedly around the house as she did in public, but she was an extraordinarily modest girl who moved about either fully clothed or in a dressing gown buttoned up to her neck.

Consequently he became increasingly curious. Hundreds of people had seen her naked but not him, and so one night he went to the nightclub and stood at the bar and watched her come onstage wearing the usual long skirt and shawl. She gave a terrific start to see him grinning at her a few feet away and as a result came in behind her music, threw off the shawl, and had to hurry to catch up. Her stage movements were constricted and stiff. Only her breasts moved rhythmically, and she never once glanced in his direction again.

Back in the apartment his visit to the nightclub was never alluded to by either of them in any way.

All this time Pierre was waiting, he said, for his money to come in. The young man waited also. Pierre appeared to have no job, no means of support. When asked, he said he was a businessman, but offered no details. He certainly did no business by telephone, for there was none in the apartment, and he did not seem to receive any mail either. The young man was beginning to be a little worried. He was in a number of businesses, Pierre murmured when pressed. Investments, sales — that sort of thing. He was a big man with a big, bold laugh. He wore thick tinted glasses and it was difficult to read his eyes. In the past his business interests had extended to Lebanon, Italy, Greece, he said impressively, but lately he had cut back.

The young man had begun to save money on food. He had very few traveler's checks left. Lunch was bread smeared with jam, and milk. For supper there might be meat. There were still many horse butcher shops in Nice, and throughout France as well; he had discovered that ground horsemeat was cheaper than beef, and horsemeat hamburgers tasted okay, if a little metallic.

Pierre brought home a man he introduced as an Egyptian. They conversed over supper in what was presumably Arabic. A few days later the Egyptian's picture appeared in the *Nice Matin;* he had been arrested as part of some international swindle. The young man's French was not good enough to decipher the details. But it made him worry a bit more about Pierre.

One night he and the girl took the train to Monte Carlo. They sat in a third-class compartment with eight places. Outside the window was the Mediterranean with the moonlight on it. The train ran along a ledge. Sometimes it plunged into tunnels reeking of coal smoke. When it came out the air was clear and there were lighted villas on the promontories and opalescent waves that washed onto the rocks below. The intervening stations were lighted, and flowers bloomed in boxes under the station windows.

The young man and the girl were sitting almost on top of each other. They were in a state of high excitement that had nothing to do with Monte Carlo. Directly opposite sat a frowning, middle-aged French woman. She had a red face, reddened knuckles and wore a thick cardigan over her dress. She watched them as if she were their conscience, or their mother, as if she disapproved of what they were doing. But they weren't doing anything. They weren't even holding hands.

Disembarking at Monte Carlo, they started up the stone staircase that climbed the cliff to the casino. There were handsome balustrades and landings decorated with urns of flowers, and they turned and looked out at the Mediterranean. It was as if golden dollars had been flung onto the sea. They were alone at last, and he kissed her. He had been wanting to kiss her since Nice. The thirty-minute train ride had seemed endless. He had thought he would die if he didn't kiss her soon, and at last he was doing it — a moment of absolute enchantment, the supreme moment of his life so far.

So that was Monte Carlo to him and would always be — a single chaste kiss, and never mind any of the other Monte Carlo legends, past or future. Perhaps he even imagined he would come back here many years later — he might be a middle-aged man by then — take the train to Monte Carlo, climb the same staircase, with this girl or another. But trains do not stop at Monte Carlo anymore. The station is gone altogether, replaced by a convention center and hotel built on pilings above the tracks.

The young man cashed a traveler's check, they sat down at a roulette table, and he looked around him.

The fluted columns, the decorated ceilings, were baroque and grandiose, but on the walls here and there were patches of peeling paint. The carpeting may have been opulent once, but now threads showed through. The draperies looked brittle with age. Most of the other chairs were empty. The gamblers were not only few but old; they looked like they had hung over these tables since World War I or before. Collars grown too loose for stringy necks. Knobby fingers heavy with rings. And notebooks beside each place. Hands that trembled slightly as they jotted down the numbers that came up, as if the last turn in some way regulated the next.

Certain men, the young man knew, had broken the bank at Monte Carlo. Others had flung themselves onto the rocks. He had come with some notion of winning money himself so that he could stay on here with this marvelous girl and not have to go home. But if he lost he would have to leave Nice even sooner.

Together they risked $10 and stopped. They made the $10 last a long time. When their chips were gone they went into the bar and had tea. There was no one else in there but the barman. They went back to Nice on the bus, and during the ride they laughed a lot.

They came into the streets of Nice and got off. By then the young man had ideas. He was in love and it seemed to him possible that she was too. He began walking her in the direction of his apartment. But when she realized where they were heading, her steps got slower.

They stood in front of his building, and he took both her hands. "Come up with me."

She shook her head.

"Why not?"

She stroked his cheek.

"Please."

But she shook her head again.

Those were more romantic times than now, and he was almost glad that she had refused. "I love you," he told her, and took her home.

One evening, his eyes glazed, giggling, Pierre came home waving wads of 10,000-franc notes. He had a cab waiting out in front, and he swept the young man out of the house.

He had won a fortune that day at the Casino Municipal, Pierre explained in the cab. He happened to be passing by, and went in, and in a few minutes won all this money. The casino was so pleased for him they had laid on a champagne dinner tonight for him and a guest. Too bad Odette was working. There was no sense wasting the casino's champagne, was there? He burst out laughing.

But inside the casino everyone knew who Pierre was. They bowed to him and addressed him by name.

So at last the young man realized what line of work Pierre was in. He did not "happen by" only this afternoon. He was not a businessman. His only business took place right here.

As they moved into the gaming rooms, Pierre dropped big chips on tables, calling out "*Banco!*" as they passed by. His voice was overloud and on the edge of hysteria the whole time. The young man followed a step or two behind, his mouth slightly agape, making notes in his head. Someday he would write a short story about a gambler like Pierre, he promised himself. "The Man Who Broke the Bank at Monte Carlo" was old hat. He didn't need it, he had Pierre, same thing, don't you see? Nothing had changed in sixty years except for time and place — mere incidentals.

He was at an age when he imagined that a few surface

impressions gathered in the course of a few hours were all the raw material any real writer would ever need.

Over the next several days he observed Pierre carefully. The winning streak continued, apparently. He paid off all his debts, including back rent to the young man, he had some suits made, and he bought Odette a coat with a fur collar. She was very pleased. She whirled around the apartment in it.

Then the rent came due again, Odette's coat disappeared, and Pierre's tailor came to the door, all in the same day.

Pierre asked the young man to pay the entire rent; he'd pay back his share as soon as his money came. The young man had no choice but to comply. He did not immediately realize that Odette's coat was gone, but he knew about the tailor because Pierre, hiding in the kitchen, sent him to the door with instructions to say he was out of town for a few days. He did this. It made the tailor plead for his money; he waved his unpaid bills. But the young man could only repeat his original message. His French, in such a situation, was not equal to more. The tailor was begging. There were tears in his eyes. Finally he stumbled towards the elevator, and the young man stepped back into the apartment.

The run of luck had stopped, and behind the bedroom door Pierre and Odette had a terrific fight.

"I wish I had my car," the young man said.

"What do you want a car for?"

"To take you for a ride."

"You don't need a car to do that."

This was in the street in the afternoon, and when they had gazed gravely at each other, both burst out laughing. But the laughter stopped, for each felt a moment of intense vulnerability.

"Why do you like me?" he asked.

An older man would have been embarrassed to pose such a question. An older woman would have answered with a laugh or a joke. Because, she told him, he wanted to be the best at something. He had big dreams and was willing to work to make them come true.

"Everybody my age is like that."

Not the Frenchmen she had known, she said. The only ambition of the young architect she had dated was to take over his father's practice. The young *notaire,* the same. The ambition of most other young Frenchmen was to become government functionaries.

"Well," he said, "I'm American."

But she had known plenty of Americans who were mostly quite arrogant, she said. They didn't even realize it. They thought everything American was better just because it was American. They belittled France and most of what was French. Some of them wouldn't eat the food, and not one even tried to learn the language.

"You're trying to learn it," she told him.

"It's not easy."

"You love everything you see here."

"Well, yes." Of course he did. How could anyone not?

"And most of them were liars. One might even have been married. He said he wasn't, but I was never sure."

The young man was astonished that anyone could lie about something like that.

One night the girl intercepted him in the street and told him he could no longer wait for her at the bar. Her father had been muttering all day that he was sick of people hanging around his daughter. The next time the American came in he would throw him out.

He knew he was unpopular with her father, to whom he had spoken only a few times. This had happened to him with other fathers and he accepted it as a fact of life: sometimes the fathers did not like you. That fathers might have special feelings for their daughters never occurred to him and would not, perhaps, until he had daughters of his own.

The young man was perplexed. "But why?"

The girl did not know about fathers and daughters either. "Once he said you were like all these Americans, thought America had won the bloody war."

The young man laughed.

"This is serious," she said.

"I know it's serious."

The places where they could be together had just been diminished by one, which was perhaps why, when he invited her to his flat for tea to meet Pierre and Odette, she accepted. This tea party took place a day or two later and was a failure. The nightclub artiste and the proper bourgeoise disliked each other immediately. Pierre saw this too and bustled about trying to be charming. The conversation took place partly in English, partly in French. The young man felt a strange kinship with Odette, for like himself she understood only half of what was said.

Pierre and Odette had gone out. The cups and saucers were drying beside the sink.

"Would you like to see my room?"

She followed him. His typewriter was open on the table in front of the window, and she touched it. He flipped through the latest of his short stories. "Maybe *Collier's* will buy it," he said hopefully. "Or the *Saturday Evening Post.*"

They looked at each other.

His money was almost gone.

They formed the habit of meeting every afternoon. She would come into the garden and call up to him.

Waiting for her, he found he could not work. Every morning he made his bed — formerly he had not bothered. He made sure his few clothes were put away. There was a carpet sweeper and a broom in the closet, and he used them. He became aware of how ugly the apartment was, that there were no curtains or drapes. It had always seemed a quite fine place to him, highly romantic, though not a garret, perfect for a literary man starting out. But now it did not. During the last hour that he waited for her each day he could not even sit at his typewriter. He kept going to the window looking for her, until at last she was there below in the garden. He always claimed he wasn't quite ready yet.

"I have to finish this paragraph, why don't you come on up?"

She always had to be coaxed to come up.

Afterwards they would walk hand in hand along the streets staring into the shop windows, or rather she would stare into the shop windows while he only stared at her.

Luminous days. He wanted them never to end.

But they did. Taking her by the hand, he led her through the streets and in past the bar and up to the cash desk where her mother sat reading the *France-Soir*. It was late afternoon. There was a barman behind the bar polishing glasses; they ignored him. They were holding hands and looked as concentrated and grave as if they had come to announce a death in the family.

"Could we sit down and talk, Madame?"

The woman behind the cash desk looked from one face to the other, and her chin began to quiver. She sent the barman to fetch her husband, then led them not to the family table, but to one already set for dinner in the farthest corner of the dining room. All three sat down.

"So you want to marry my daughter," her mother said. The young man's nod was followed by a silence during which the woman seemed to be searching for words she could not find. Turning to her daughter, she blurted out in French, "Oh, I wish I could speak English!" Then she burst into tears.

This was going to be hard, and the young man knew it. The mother, who perhaps saw what had been happening and even perhaps approved, had almost no English. He would not be able to explain anything to her or enlist her help. The father, who did speak English, would understand explanations, he just wasn't going to listen to them.

All three waited for the father — the middle-aged woman weeping and the two young people holding hands beneath the table. They waited for whatever his explosive reaction would be.

The English Cemetery. Standing over the grave I read his name and dates in the stone. The dates are 1891–1964. That is straightforward enough, and his incised name may seem so too, though it is not the one he was born with, nor even the one he was known by during the forty or so years he stood at the center of the English colony in Nice. Following his name are the letters D.C.M., M.M. Many of the names engraved in tombstones in this cemetery have letters following, usually the ones that indicate knighthood or some other honor conferred by the King, but these letters here refer to something else entirely, and no other stone has them.

During all the forty years he seemed to most of those with whom he came in contact the very epitome of an Englishman. And English was the way he wanted to think of himself. Few men had suffered as much as he to earn the right. But those who lived here knew the truth about him, or thought they did. To them he was not English at all — British perhaps, though only barely, and only on paper, less British certainly than themselves.

In truth his first language was German, not English. His parents were Swiss and he was born in Bern. He was raised in an orphanage there but ran away to England at 12 and found work as a busboy and dishwasher in a hotel staffed largely by other Swiss. The Swiss then as now were the world champions of the hotel business and could be found everywhere. Obviously someone helped him get to England. A 12-year-old boy could not have got there alone in 1903, but no one ever knew much about his background. If he was reticent about it, even embarrassed, this was because he had chosen to live his life mostly among a class of men to whom the accident of birth was all-important.

When he was a bit older and had learned English, he shipped as a cabin boy on a luxury liner and began to see the world. He grew into an extremely handsome young man, was promoted to chief steward, and came to know a number of rich female passengers.

World War I broke out. He was 23. There is no patriot fiercer than the convert, and he enlisted at once in the Rifle Brigade in the army of his adopted country, and except for the times he lay shot in hospitals, he served for the next four years in the mud in the trenches around Ypres in Flanders. The Rifle Brigade was a London regiment and in it the homeless youth perhaps imagined he had found a home, for afterwards, whenever anyone would ask where he was from, even forty or more years later, he would always reply: London. At the start he served as an officer's servant — being a foreigner, he could not hope to be commissioned himself. The officer died in his arms, victim of a sniper. "Get down, you silly bastard," he had said a moment before.

He became a sniper himself. He was a deadly shot and sent bullets into the heads of a number of German soldiers who had the effrontery to peek over their parapets when he was on duty.

He volunteered repeatedly for hazardous jobs. He single-handedly wiped out a German machine-gun nest that was holding up an advance. He put on a German uniform and crawled across no-man's-land to listen and gather intelligence; on the way back he lost his way among the shell holes and tumbled into trenches held by another regiment. Since he still spoke English with a German accent, the troops would not believe he was who he said he was. They bayonetted him in the buttocks. Some of them wanted to shoot him. He was fast on his feet and made an excellent battalion runner. He came to be considered unkillable. During attacks, with the telephone lines destroyed and the radios not working, he ran messages from the front to the rear and back again under the heaviest bombardments mankind had ever known up to that time.

He was decorated for gallantry in action twice, was wounded three times. A bullet took away part of a finger; he tied a string around it and stayed at his post. Another bullet, or perhaps shrapnel, removed part of his skull; it was replaced with a plate and he went back into the line. A machine-gun bullet went through his ankle, destroying the bone. He would suffer from this wound all his life. Fortunately the war was almost over, meaning that the doctors had time for experimental operations. After a number of experiments that failed, the missing bone was replaced with metal and pins. He lay on his back more than a year and then had to learn to walk again.

He was offered British nationality. It was almost like a reward for so much heroism, so much suffering, and of course he took it. He was offered a new name too, if he should so wish, as was normal in most countries on such occasions. It was thought of as starting with a clean slate. He selected his own first two names, Karl Ernst, and anglicized them. His first passport so read: Charles Ernest, British subject, naturalized 1920.

When he was released from the hospital, the grateful nation had offered him, along with his demobilization papers, money too, either a pension or a lump-sum payment. He took the lump sum and went south to Nice, where the sun was reputed to shine every day and his leg would not hurt so much, and he invested it in a hotel. His partner was his mother, who had somehow made contact with him during the war. He limped badly and needed a cane to get about, but the hotel prospered. Then he met a young woman, but it wasn't a simple boy-meets-girl story. Her name is there on the stone. Her casket lies above his in the tomb over which I stand. Towards the end of what was then called The World War — for there had been only one, and it was unimaginable that there could ever be another — she had run away from her village in the center of France to Nice because her parents had promised her in marriage to an older man she barely knew and did not love. Arranged marriages were still quite common in rural France at that time. She had always been an excellent student. She was so bright that the schoolmaster in the one-room schoolhouse in her village had recommended that she be sent to the nearest metropolis, which was Tulle, population about 10,000, to continue her studies, and this had been done.

Now, still not out of her teens and faced with an arranged marriage, confident that she was smart enough to make a living in a world for which there was still no room for unattached girls, she had run away and had managed to get to Nice. She sought refuge in a hostel for girls run by nuns and found work in a bank. She lost this job by catching typhoid. She was sick a long time, and when she returned to the bank to ask for her job back, a war veteran was sitting at her desk. She took in sewing. When she was stronger she began to look for work in a hotel because at one time her parents had run a small hotel near the village in which she had been born. She walked into the hotel run by the young British war hero with the funny accent and the game leg, and she asked him for a job.

But when they decided to get married his mother flew into a rage and threw them both out and sold the hotel. Virtually penniless, the ex–war hero limped about the city trying to borrow money with which to open something of his own. His French was still poor, and he refused both then and afterwards ever again to speak German; if a German tourist even asked him directions, he would answer in English or in French, and if the fellow didn't get it, too bad.

He did find money, not very much, and he bought a narrow storefront on the Rue Masséna and put in a solid oak bar, solid oak stools, and, in the dining room in back, solid oak tables and chairs. He decorated it with World War I cartoons and framed portraits of the victorious generals, and he named the place after himself: Charley's. He was the host and his new wife was the chef. The place was so small that unless it caught on in a big way, unless it was full every night, they were not going to be able to survive.

But it did catch on, and often was so full that customers ate standing up, packed between the bar and the tables. These were the so-called Roaring Twenties, when people had money and looked for ways to spend it, when Europeans tried to forget the late war by drowning themselves in revelry, when America was in the grip of Prohibition and people flocked to Europe simply to be able to buy a legal drink. Charley's became not only famous, but something of a literary hangout. Celebrities like the Aga Khan and Mistinguett came, but the Spanish novelist Blasco Ibáñez was a regular too, and Somerset Maugham and a number of American authors later to become famous whose names no one bothered to remember at the time. There were only a few of these celebrated European watering holes: Harry's New York Bar in Paris, and the other Harry's Bar in Venice, and Charley's in Nice, and one or two others, all of which stayed famous for forty years and more.

All day and sometimes far into the night the ex–war hero stood on his game leg and greeted those who came. He listened to their stories and sometimes loaned them money. They called him Charley as if they had known him all his life, until finally that became the name he was known by far and wide, the only name he had — to his employees, to his neighbors, he was Monsieur Charley. His wife became Madame Charley, his daughter Mademoiselle Charley.

With his profits he bought a car. Every day he would get it out of the garage and drive it around and park it in front of his place. Hardly anyone in France owned a car at that time. He sent his son to boarding school in England, and as World War II approached, ever the patriot, he gathered up all his money and backed the governments that were about to fight the hated Germans again:

he bought French and British government bonds. In the course of the war to come the French bonds would become totally worthless and the British bonds nearly so.

He also stocked up on enough wine and liquor to last for the duration. His cellar was full to the top. He and his wife and family would be safe in Nice. But then an astonishing thing happened. Almost without warning, almost without a fight, France capitulated.

There were few telephones in the south of France. The British consul sent emissaries through the streets. Within twenty-four hours the entire British colony was to be evacuated from every town on the coast. One suitcase each. Anyone who wanted to stay could of course stay, in which case His Majesty's government disclaimed all responsibility. There were two ships lying off Cannes. They were the last. There would be no others.

Twenty-four hours to decide. He could perhaps stay on in Nice and be quite safe. His wife and children were French. He himself could claim Swiss nationality if he chose — he dismissed the idea at once. He was an Englishman. To stay would split the family in two, for his son was at school in England. The war might be a long one. But to board one of those ships meant abandoning his business, his apartment, his car, his well-stocked cellar, even his small daughter's toys. One suitcase each.

The next day almost the entire English colony was at Cannes waiting to be ferried out to the ships, the sight of which was in no way comforting. They were old and filthy and normally were used to haul coal. The consul and his men moved up and down the quay shouting. The English are nothing if not orderly. In perfect order they were divided evenly, were assigned to one coal boat or the other, and were ferried out by tender. Presently the ships weighed anchor and started for Gibraltar.

One of them reached there on schedule. The other, Charley's ship, was torpedoed by a submarine that was presumed to be Italian because it did not stay to finish the job. For four days the ruined coal boat wallowed in the Mediterranean troughs while repairs were attempted and supplies ran out. There was no food or water except for the children. Everyone waited for another attack. Charley watched his daughter, covered with soot, clutch-

ing her doll and talking to everyone. She thought this was a pleasure cruise. His wife meanwhile was frantic, and he tried to
comfort her. But they made it to Gibraltar, and then to Liverpool.

Upon reaching London, where he had not lived since he was
a boy, he ran Hachett's, a well-known Piccadilly bar. He also
served as an air-raid warden and volunteer firefighter, and he
joined the Home Guard and reported regularly for drills. The
Home Guard was mostly old men with hunting rifles and pitch-
forks. It was meant to repulse the German invaders, if they came.

He had left power of attorney in Nice with a trusted barman.
When he came back within days of the liberation of France, everything had been sold or looted; his cellar of course was empty, his
place a shambles. The trusted barman was about to conclude the
sale of the restaurant/bar itself and disappear with the profits. In
another day or two it would have been too late. His apartment
had been used by the Germans, apparently as a brothel. Almost
nothing in it could be salvaged.

His life savings were gone, he was 54 years old, and now he
would have to start again. After borrowing money at ruinous
interest rates, he had his place repaired and redecorated, keeping
the World War I cartoons on the walls˙but changing the faces of
the victorious Allied leaders over the bar.

At first business was quite good. The American troops were
there, and much of the English colony had rushed back to Nice
to find out what was left of their villas, their businesses — whatever they had owned. They had to eat somewhere, and as a host
Charley was as congenial and sympathetic as ever. He listened to
their troubles, and he loaned a good many of them money when
he had it, or let them run up astounding tabs. His wife remonstrated with him. At times she got furious, but it did no good.
He would answer that these people were in trouble, and it was
his job to help where he could.

His son, known inevitably as Young Charley, had been in
the British navy during the latter stages of the war. Now he came
back to Nice and went to work for his father. Young Charley had
all sorts of ideas for bringing in business. It was clear to him that
the English colony could no longer support the place. Some effort
had to be made to attract a local clientele and to attract the new

tourists, who were Americans. Young Charley brought forth his ideas, but his father refused to listen.

He walked now with a more pronounced limp than ever and was in almost constant pain. Circulation in his foot was so bad that sores formed that did not heal. It was agony to put a shoe on, but his profession obliged him to stand near the bar smiling, greeting patrons literally night and day. He had a car. Cars apparently were important to him. He was one of the few people in Nice after the war to have one. He still parked it in front of his door every day.

Year by year business fell off.

Aggravated by diabetes, blood circulation past the plate in his leg worsened, and for long periods his foot was so bad that he could not leave his room. He began to lose his toes to amputation. Finally, with gangrene threatening, the entire foot was amputated. He had a special shoe made and resumed his post near the bar, smiling, greeting whoever came in.

He had been one of the founders of the Nice-Monaco branch of the British Legion in the early twenties. He was never the chairman but usually served on the committee, and most years it was he who carried the Union Jack in the Armistice Day parades.

The job of the British Legion abroad as at home had been to give help to the World War I veterans, for little or no social legislation had as yet been enacted. The Riviera had its share of indigent ex-soldiers, and some of them left destitute widows, and between the wars the Nice-Monaco branch raised money for them through its dinner dance and from the sale of poppies around Armistice Day. Poppies were on sale at Barclay's Bank, at Cook's Travel Agency, at Charley's, and elsewhere, with Charley himself the only man in Nice actively pushing them.

The legion chairman most of these years was a man named George Chadwick, and its official address was care of the British consul in Nice. Unofficially the chairman was Charley; the tables opposite his bar, or even the bar itself, served as headquarters.

Chadwick had been a captain during World War I. He was always referred to as Captain Chadwick. He was related to a duke, did not work, and was driven around in his Bentley by his chauffeur. Formal meetings might be held elsewhere, with Chadwick presiding, but whenever anything had to be discussed of an impromptu nature, the men met at Charley's and it was he who was the moving force behind the British Legion in Nice, and behind the Freemasons as well. Chadwick and others of the well-born English resented this. They were the leaders of the colony on the coast, not Charley. They did not mind letting him carry the flag or do most of the work, but saw no need to be nice to him. He was, after all, not one of them. Charley appeared not to notice. His children did. To Charley, if one of these people failed to greet him in passing, it was probably because he didn't have time. They did come to him if they needed help, for he knew everyone who mattered in Nice, or if they needed money. He loaned a man named Harrison enough one day to buy a farm, and although the money was paid back, Harrison was never very friendly to him after that.

It became possible after World War II for Chadwick and his successors to solicit honors from King George VI, and after him from his daughter Queen Elizabeth II. Nearly every member of the hierarchy of the Nice-Monaco branch of the British Legion sooner or later acquired at least an O.B.E. (Order of the British Empire). Harrison, now a pig farmer, got one. Jimmy Green got one, and he was only a bank clerk. Peter Wright, who owned the Rolls-Royce–Jaguar agency in Monte Carlo, got one. But to Charley no such honor ever came. The others continued to meet in his place, invariably they toasted their new awards there, and sometimes they did not ask for the check.

In time he got as old and feeble as the English colony itself. People died off and were buried in this cemetery on the hill. Their tombs are all around me. As membership diminished, the British Legion and the Masonic lodge met less and less often. Gradually the British-owned businesses fell into the hands of the French. Gradually, in the minds of tourists planning their vacations, the French Riviera no longer seemed such a glamorous destination. As business continued to fall off, Charley's wife and children begged him to sell his place while there was still something to sell; finally he did so. He was 73 years old. Three weeks later he died.

There is a curious French burial custom known as the *mise en bière*. The putting into the coffin. The undertaker's men were waiting in the morgue at the Hospital St. Roch when the family arrived. The coffin was already resting on the floor. The body lay on a slab. As the family watched, the undertaker's men carried it over to the coffin and thrust it into place. Two other men stood with the lid, ready to screw it down on top.

"One moment, please," said Young Charley. Bending over the coffin, he pinned his father's World War I medals to his chest. Medals for heroism awarded posthumously. Then he nodded, and the lid was screwed down on the box.

The London national newspapers carried news of Charley's passing, one of them on the front page under the headline "Charley Is Dead." He lay in state in the center aisle of the English church for two days, with the British flag covering the coffin. The church was packed for the funeral. Nobody had realized there were that many English left in Nice. His neighbors had come. Shops were closed or understaffed all along the Rue Masséna. A good many civic dignitaries were present as well. The mayor either came or sent a representative, for his card was found in the box in the vestibule, along with scores of others after the ceremony.

The pallbearers were from the British Legion, two of them rickety old men from the 1914–18 war, the only two left on the coast. The honor guard, also from the British Legion, carried black-veiled flags. The funeral service was that of a simple British soldier. The vicar in his eulogy described Charley as being sometimes overgenerous, but the ideal type of innkeeper. "With our thoughts at this Christmas season still focused upon Bethlehem, we can say with certainty that Charley would never have turned away any needy family from his door."

He was put into the ground in the English Cemetery among people he had known. I am standing over that tomb now. As ordered by his son, the letters D.C.M. and M.M. are incised in the marble after his name — Distinguished Conduct Medal, Military Medal, the second- and third-highest British decorations for gallantry in action. When he ordered those letters carved, Young Charley once told me, he was thinking not so much of his father as of Captain Chadwick and all the other snobs. "Let's see any of them match that," he said.

With Charley died an era. There are a few tombs more recent

than his, and of course Mme Charley survived him by twelve years. I look along the row. Eight or ten more tombs and the row peters out. I have been carrying flowers. I put them down on Charley's tomb, and walk back down the path, and the gates of the Cimetière Ste. Marguerite, formerly the English Cemetery, close behind me.

This was the man for whom a middle-aged Frenchwoman and a young couple holding hands beneath the table waited with such apprehension. An explosion of rage was what they expected, and no one had worked out what was to be said or done afterwards.

During the time that his daughter was in art school, Charley had taken her to Italy in his car, just the two of them, because he thought that, as an art student, she should see the art treasures there. He took her to Milan, to Florence, to Siena, to Rome. Most of the bridges were still out this soon after the war, and they crossed the rivers on barges. To him the trip was not a success. He was appalled to note that in the famous Italian museums many of the statues of Roman and Greek gods were without fig leaves over their private parts. To him this was not art but pornography, and not fit for the eyes of a young girl. He had been appalled to note also that his daughter had literally stopped traffic every time they crossed an Italian square to sit down in a café. Young men had collected around her, had begun to talk to her. He had glared and tried to look menacing; it did no good. Young men followed them into restaurants, into stores. It was as if the Italians had never seen a foreign girl before. Several times he had caused scenes.

He was a loving father but a strict one, and his wife, his daughter, and his prospective son-in-law waited for him. He was then 63 years old, short and stocky, bald, wearing spectacles, and he limped in the door behind his cane, passed in front of the bar, entered the dining room, and stood over the table at which the other three sat. Of course he had known his daughter must some-day marry — in the early fifties there were few other possibilities for a girl. But it had been his hope that she would marry a man some years older than herself, preferably an Englishman, one with money and a name, with — perhaps — a title. Several likely can-didates among his customers and acquaintances had seemed to him

suitable. He had introduced them to her, had watched their eyes
brighten; but his daughter had shown no interest whatever. Now
he listened to the halting explanation of this tall American boy
who did not look old enough to be out of school and who seemed
to own only one pair of shoes, only one or two changes of clothing,
and his expression did not change, and he did not sit down.

To everyone's surprise there was no explosion. The old man
was above all things a pragmatist, and he was perhaps too sick to
fight. "If that's what you both want," he said, "I won't stand in
your way." Then he turned on his heel, limped out past the bar
out the door, and was gone.

Which caused a new outburst of tears from his wife. She too
had married a foreigner. She too had gone to live out her life in
a place far from home. This was a situation she could identify
with and was perhaps seeing in a romantic haze.

"Tell the boy to take his meals with us from now on," she
sobbed to her daughter. "We can't send him back to America as
skinny as that."

The American Congress in its wisdom deplored marriages such
as the young man was proposing, and so did the vice consul
whom he went to see next. After the war, the vice consul explained
smugly, too many American soldiers had married the wrong kind
of women. Foreign women lied about their pasts, about their ages.
They all wanted to get to America, the greatest country on earth.

"How old is your . . . fiancée?" The vice consul managed to
make the word sound like a slur.

"Twenty-two."

"Are you sure?"

"I'm sure."

"Maybe she's 30, did you ever think of that?"

"No."

"Does she have a police record?"

"No."

"Maybe she's a shoplifter or prostitute?"

In his hands the vice consul held a list of the documents that
would be needed before any marriage could be performed.

"Can I have that list, please?"

"Some of these women have gone through marriage ceremonies with one of our boys when already married here in
France."

"Please give me that list."

"Some of them have been infected with communicable diseases, even venereal diseases."

"Are you going to give me that list?"

Even if he fulfilled all the requirements, the vice consul continued, there was no guarantee that his "wife" would be admitted
to the United States. At best, visas were never issued in less than
three months.

"Three months?"

"Minimum."

"May I have the list, please?" the young man said. "Give me
the goddamn list."

Seated on a bench in the public gardens, he studied it. How
much time would it take to acquire all these documents, and what
would it cost? And the bride's visa, three months — my God! He
did not have enough money to wait with her here for three or
more months, and he would lose the job on which he hoped to
support her. Even if they reached New York together, the im-
migration authorities on the quay might be dissatisfied by something. If so, she could be sent back.

He wrote a letter to his father requesting the required American documents and then, riding a borrowed motor scooter, started
through the streets after the French ones. The girl sat pillion behind
him, her arms around his waist, her chin on his shoulder, and this
felt very good indeed, and gave him hope.

The American consulate had been modern: plenty of IBM
machines. At the French agencies papers were written out by hand
and then attached to other papers by straight pins through the
corners. There was form after form to be filled out, they waited
on queues, and some days they obtained one of the needed certificates, other days none. They paid filing fees and for photos.
Money kept vanishing.

At one agency an essential document was refused.

They were standing at the counter. The girl turned to the
young man. "He says I can't have it because I'm not French."

The clerk nodded. Since her father held a British passport, making her mother British too, according to British law, then how could she herself be French?

Close to tears, the girl kept pushing her French birth certificate, French identity card, French passport, across the counter. The clerk pushed them back. He was desolated, he said, but there was nothing he could do.

Stepping in front of her, the young man pushed the same three documents at the clerk. He wanted to shout at this man. He wanted to shout: She was born in France, and that makes her French. But he didn't have the words.

The clerk had waved the girl aside. His decision had been made. He was asking the next person on the queue to step forward.

"*Elle est née en France,*" the young man heard himself shouting. "*Elle est française.*" And ever afterwards he wondered where the words had come from. Over and over he shouted them, while other officials crowded around.

Five minutes later the young couple was out on the sidewalk, document in hand, jubilant.

Among the documents required by French law was a *certificat de coutume,* proof that he was legally free to marry. At the American consulate he found a French clerk who seemed more sympathetic than the vice consul. Such certificates were not easy to come by, the clerk said, for there were forty-eight states, forty-eight different sets of laws.

"But I'm over 21 and I've never been married before."

Unless an American lawyer agreed to take his case, the clerk told him, he was lost. Only an American lawyer would know the laws of his state and could undo all the legal tangles and provide the certificate. Fortunately there was such a lawyer just across the street, the only American lawyer in Nice, who might be willing to help, and the clerk steered him there. As he steered all Americans in distress, the young man would realize when he was older, receiving finder's fees in return.

The only American lawyer in Nice was a middle-aged man who wore a silk foulard and a velvet smoking jacket.

"Age?"

"Twenty-three."

"Married before?"

"No."

He signed the form. "Take this back to the consulate and they'll stamp it for you, and you'll be all set. Legal fees come to $20."

"Twenty dollars?"

It was four or five times the highest filing fee so far. It was money on which the prospective bridegroom could survive for a week, perhaps longer. He stormed out without the form, returned to the consulate and argued, but the clerk answered blandly that there was nothing he could do. No certificate, no marriage.

The young man began leafing through phone books. There was an American lawyer in Cannes also, and he phoned him.

"But you have an American lawyer right there in Nice."

"He wants $20."

"Hmm, yes. He's the one you want to see. He'll fix you up in a jiffy."

Several days later the young man rang the bell, handed over the $20, and took the certificate.

The experience nearly broke him financially, and emotionally as well. Getting married had turned out to be a legal experience, and a financial experience. Love had nothing to do with it. Love had got lost somewhere. There was no romance involved at all.

"You want to get out of it, don't you?" the girl said to him on the street.

Pedestrians stepped around them.

"If you don't want to marry me, just say so. You don't, do you?"

It was all too much for him, and at that moment the answer was no. He looked into the upturned face of this stranger with whom he proposed to spend the rest of his life. He was too young to have to cope with this, and too alone. For other people the hard part came later; for him it came right now. He did not even have a friend he could talk to. Then he thought: Yes I do, one, and he put his arms around her.

"We're getting married," he said, "and no one is going to stop us."

*   *   *

In America his mother had taken to her bed, it seemed. His father was not happy either. Some French adventuress had got her hooks into their son. It had not been possible to telephone them. Transatlantic calls at that time were prohibitively expensive and took hours to go through.

Money. Her steamship ticket to America, third class, same as his, would cost about $200, which of course he didn't have. He needed additional money on which to live until the banns were published and the marriage could take place. He wanted also to give her a ring if he could, and it would be nice if they could have a honeymoon, even if only for a couple of days.

He needed over $400. None of his ex–college friends had that kind of money, and his father, if asked, would probably refuse as a way to stop the marriage.

He began to write travel articles. He wrote them as fast as he could and mailed them to the Sunday travel sections of various New York papers. The *Times* paid him $40 for one, the *Herald Tribune* $20, and the *Paris Herald* $10.

It was not enough. Where else could he get money?

The French tobacco industry then as now was a government monopoly. French factories produced the popular Gauloise cigarettes, among other brands, all made of harsh black tobacco, and these could be bought only at licensed tobacco counters. They were heavily taxed, making them, relatively speaking, very expensive. Imported American cigarettes, spoken of in France as "blonds," were even more expensive.

Gangs of smugglers operated out of Tangier, a duty-free port where blonds could be bought for the equivalent of seven cents a package; the legal price in France was almost ten times that. Fleets of speedboats, even war surplus PT boats, raced across the Mediterranean and offloaded cargoes of blonds off the Riviera towns in the dead of night. Judges, cops, prosecutors, all smoked Chesterfields, or Lucky Strikes, or Philip Morris, or Camels — the four most popular brands — and passed on to each other the names of reliable dealers.

But recently the mood had changed. The happy-go-lucky operators of the past had been forced out. The trade was now in the grip of the *milieu,* the Corsican mafia, and there had been some killings. As a result the embarrassed authorities had begun to crack down. Special units had been deployed. The Riviera harbors were being closely watched. Informants were everywhere.

The young man did not know this. All he needed to enter the cigarette trade, he believed, was a source of supply, and he thought he had one.

Duty-free blonds were also sold aboard U.S. warships. Any sailor or officer could walk up to the commissary and buy them. Having gone aboard a cruiser to visit a young officer he knew, he saw that he was taken for an officer himself. He was the right age, his college ring was as big as anybody's, and he wore civilian clothes — enlisted men were not allowed civilian clothes on board. The next day he went back out to the ship, stepped up to the commissary window with a satchel, and bought as many cartons as he could cram in.

This was at anchor at Villefranche. The only problem was to get his contraband ashore. With a dozen or so young officers he rode the launch in to the quay. Customs guards came out of their shed to watch the officers disembark. The young man strode past them with his loaded satchel and was not stopped.

He sold that load in Nice, and went back and got another, and another after that. He walked each satchel past the customs guards on the quay. He became very impressed with himself: international traveler, international lover, international smuggler.

By the time the cruiser put to sea, he had earned most of what he needed, provided he could count on the money owed him by Pierre. But Odette's engagement at the nightclub was ending. Perhaps they would vanish. Sometimes the young man would mention money to Pierre, who always gave his big, bold laugh and promised to pay the day some commissions arrived. But the magic day had not yet come, and perhaps wouldn't. Every time he entered the flat the young man looked to see if Odette's trunk was still in the hall. Or he would detour in the street so as to walk past her nightclub. There were gold stars pasted over her nipples in the photos in the window. He would stare in at the photos, not for prurient reasons but because the naked Odette meant they were still in town.

By the day of the wedding Pierre still hadn't paid. There were to be in fact two ceremonies, civil and religious. The first would be legally binding and the second, legally speaking, was froth. Only after the civil wedding could they apply for the girl's visa to America, which might or might not be accorded, and which might take three months.

The wedding party — the young couple and the two witnesses — entered the courtroom. A deputy mayor wearing a tricolored sash entered by another door, together with a clerk. The clerk demanded that the foreigner's translator step forward.

The young man had been warned that, as a foreigner, he must be represented at the ceremony by an official translator. Being unable to afford one, he had decided to try to bluff it through.

"What do I need an interpreter for?" he said in French with pretended nonchalance. He had been practicing his lines for days and declaimed them like an actor. "I speak the language perfectly."

After studying him a moment, the deputy mayor nodded and decided to begin the ceremony. It was extremely short. When it ended he kissed them both on both cheeks and went out the door.

But that night the bride's mother sent the bridegroom back to his apartment alone. The church wedding was what counted with her, and it was two days off. The bride was staying with her parents until then.

So the young man went home, and Pierre was there.

"I'm married," he told him.

Pierre was delighted. He opened some bottles of beer, and he paid back all the money he owed. To the young man it meant that friends could always be trusted and would never let you down.

It meant they could have a honeymoon.

Later he lay in the dark and imagined his bride several streets away, also lying in bed alone, and he thought: Is this what it's like to be married?

For the church ceremony the bride wore a kind of two-piece white cocktail dress made from a heavy brocaded material she had found and brought to her dressmaker, who was also the wife of one of her father's barmen. She had designed this dress herself: tight waist, flaring skirt to just below the knees, short sleeves, and a cloth belt cinched with a bow. She had bought a wide-brimmed white hat and white open-toed, high-heeled shoes. She looked very nice, but the bridegroom, though he said nothing, would have preferred something more traditional, perhaps satin with a long white train. He was really, despite everything, a conventional young man. He himself was wearing the only suit he had with him, which luckily was dark blue. Most of the now much reduced Nice English colony was in attendance, but on the young man's side of the aisle sat three young officers off the cruiser, his only guests. Although he had wanted to invite Pierre and Odette as well, the bride had convinced him that they were perhaps too raffish to feel comfortable in such company.

The newlyweds went to Milan on their honeymoon. They traveled third class by train and checked into a third-class hotel, where the clerk demanded both their passports. Since the bride's was of a different nationality and in another name, they didn't dare hand it over lest the clerk think they weren't married. Every time they went in or out past his desk, he addressed the girl as mademoiselle, or miss, or fräulein, or signorina, and each time they were mortified.

They went to see Leonardo's *Last Supper*. They walked through the streets eating cherries out of a paper bag. They were awed by the great cathedral. Crossing into Switzerland, they sat on wooden benches on a cog railway taking them up to Zermatt, where they walked in the mountains and gawked at the Matterhorn. Their *pension* was very clean. The floor of their room was so shiny the twin beds kept sliding apart. The young man bought string and tied the legs together each evening, untying them each morning before they went out. On the train coming down from Zermatt he realized that he had forgotten to untie the beds before leaving. He worried about it most of the way back to Nice, not so much for himself but for the girl. What would they think of her in that hotel?

Her requested American visa had been on his mind all during the honeymoon. It was on his mind still. If it took three months to be accorded, what then? His money was now definitively gone. Suppose it were not accorded at all? What would he do? What could he possibly do?

He had written his father about this. He was totally dependent on his father now. He had reminded him that one of his old friends was presently serving as an assistant secretary of state. Could he ask his old friend for help? In emergency cases visas could be authorized by cable. They could be accorded in a few days. The assistant secretary could do it if he wanted to. If his father asked him. Could his father ask the assistant secretary to send the cable? Would his father do this on his behalf? Please, Dad.

But no answer had come back.

From Nice they rode the train third class to Marseilles, where the visa would — or would not — be accorded. They took a room in a third-class hotel near the consulate. It was noon. The hotel clerk asked if they wanted the room for an hour or all night. They were both embarrassed. Why wouldn't people believe they were married?

As they went into the consulate their hearts were thumping with fear. But the visa was there. Authorization had been cabled by the assistant secretary that very day. A vice consul stamped it into the girl's passport. He was very annoyed to have to do it. What about the three-month waiting period? Proper procedure had not been followed, he said.

Aboard ship, their arms about each other, they stood on the third-class deck and watched the coastline of Europe recede. Both of them wondered if they would ever see it again. They disembarked in New York with under $3 in their pockets, and that was the end of one young man's first trip to France.

Monte Carlo
A SERIES OF GAMBLES

That same year a Hollywood company was at work on the Riviera filming a movie called *To Catch a Thief,* starring Grace Kelly, 24, and Cary Grant, 50. On an off day some of the actors, including Miss Kelly, visited Monaco and had lunch at the castle with Prince Rainier. This marked the start of an entirely new Riviera legend that in no way matched the ones already in place.

Rainier Grimaldi, Prince of Monaco, had been educated in Switzerland, England, and Paris, and had served as a captain in the French army during the war. The French army had quickly capitulated, and he had sat out the rest of it. He was now 31, somewhat portly, with a somewhat receding hairline, and he did not have much to do. He had a royal title, sort of, and a reputation as a playboy. In addition to his castle he had a villa down the coast in France, which he sometimes shared with a French actress named Giselle Pascal, to whom he was not married. Illicit romances were considered scandalous in 1954, and this one had greatly titillated France and Europe.

The Grimaldi family, which had bought Monaco from Genoa in 1308, was no stranger to scandal. The Grimaldi princes — their title had been conferred by Spain, which had occupied the principality between 1524 and 1641 — had not always behaved with princely restraint. Prince Jean II was killed by his brother Lucien, who in turn was assassinated by his nephew. Prince Honoré I was thrown into the sea by his subjects. There had been a number of more personal, more recent scandals, and the family had been trying without much success to live them all down.

Rainier himself was a man with a singular problem.

Since the war Monaco had known bad times to exactly the same degree as the rest of the Riviera. It had no industry except tourism, not enough tourists came, and there was no money for upkeep or promotion. The casino had grown shabby and no longer attracted the rich gamblers of the past. Even the celebrated Grand Prix race through the streets of the town had been allowed to lapse, and for the second year in a row.

None of this touched Rainier personally, however. His own hefty yearly stipend was still being paid by his subjects. His problem was not tourism and it was not money.

Monaco was one of the tiniest independent countries in the world, about 20,000 people. Its fame rested on the legends spawned by its casino, and on the appealing notion that its citizens paid no personal or corporate income taxes. But it would revert to France, according to a 1918 treaty, if ever its ruling prince died without issue. Its independence and privilege would end and taxes would begin.

So Rainier needed an heir. He was a man who had to get married.

Miss Kelly was the daughter of a Philadelphia bricklayer who had grown into a wealthy contractor. She attended a convent school, got rejected by the college of her choice because of too few academic credits, and applied to the American Academy of Dramatic Art in New York. Upon being accepted she left Philadelphia forever, took a room in Manhattan's Barbizon Hotel for Women, and forthwith began to change the way she talked. Later her sisters made fun of her, called her snooty, but when she reached the screen it was precisely this new voice and diction, this personal, patrician, and, yes, snooty way of speech that made her seem so refined, so repressed, and so very, very sexy. If her speech was unique, so was her face. She was beautiful, of course, but it was a regal, almost icy beauty that only love could melt. The word most often applied to her was *class*. The bricklayer's daughter had more class than anyone.

She began as a model, then acted on television. At 21 she went to Hollywood. She made only eleven films, nearly all of them before she met Rainier, and she won an Academy Award for *The Country Girl*. As amazing as everything else about her brief career was the identity of the actors with whom she starred — some of the biggest names not only of her day, but of all time: Gary Cooper, Clark Gable, James Stewart, Frank Sinatra, William Holden twice, Bing Crosby twice, and the aforementioned Cary Grant.

Interviewers found her dull copy. She would tell little about herself then or ever; in any case there was not yet much to tell.

Her engagement to the Prince of Monaco was announced in Philadelphia, with Rainier present. They had seen each other only five or six times before that moment. No one had been aware she even knew him. Love at first sight, Rainier said, which in French comes out as *coup de foudre*, lightning bolt. The story made headlines, of course, and at first they were nice ones. Hollywood's princess would become a real princess. It would be a fairy tale come true.

The outside world now took a close look at Monaco for the first time. Why had no one ever heard of Monaco, whereas everyone had heard of Monte Carlo? Inasmuch as part of the castle in which Grace would live dated from the thirteenth century, whereas Monte Carlo 100 years previously didn't even exist, there was something peculiar here. How had Monte Carlo come to cast such a powerful shadow, and Monaco none at all?

What was Grace Kelly getting herself into?

Considering the identity of the scoundrel who had both founded Monte Carlo and named it, its notoriety was perhaps not surprising. His name was François Blanc, and he was born near Bordeaux about 1805, making him one of the few Frenchmen ever to be responsible for any of these Riviera legends. In his youth there were no casinos as we know them today, but all the big cities boasted gaming houses in which men bet principally on two-handed card games like piquet, *écarté,* and baccarat. Blanc went into some of these houses. He was a fast man with a deck of cards. He had fast hands. With his winnings he opened a stock brokerage in Bordeaux. He saw stocks as just another card game: find an edge and you could make killing after killing. Was there some way he could learn of price fluctuations in Paris before his customers did? If so he could fleece them all. In the 1830s a state telegraph service already existed. Messages were signaled from hilltop to hilltop by semaphore. Men with telescopes took the arriving messages down, and men with flags sent them forward. After studying this system, Blanc decided he wanted code letters attached to messages to show whether certain stocks rose or fell in Paris, and he set out to subvert the officials in charge.

For two years he bribed whomever it was necessary to bribe, and profits from his advance information were enormous. Then he was arrested, tried, and convicted. On the stand he admitted guilt. He was quite charming about it. He made his scheme sound merely clever and, after all, whom did he hurt? Only rich, greedy people, who could afford it. He charmed the jury. He charmed the court. Or else more bribery was involved. His sentence was only to pay the costs of the case. His profits were untouched even by a fine.

Of course, afterwards he couldn't go back to Bordeaux. He went instead to Paris, intending to set up a gaming house. Before he could get established, however, legal gambling in Paris was abolished.

Germany at that time was a collection of independent city-states where almost anything was possible if you paid money. Blanc went to the Landgrave of Hesse-Homburg, bought a gambling concession, and built a casino. Its walls were covered with silver-gray silk, there were paintings and tapestries, gilt furniture, and crystal chandeliers. On opening night 200 invited celebrities sat down to a banquet. Blanc bribed French railway officials to extend their tracks towards the Rhine as speedily as possible, meanwhile advertising in the major French newspapers. The salubrious qualities of the waters at Homburg would cure almost any ailment, he claimed. The spa was restful and its casino, at which fortunes were being won every day, was filled with "young, lovely and exquisitely dressed women perfumed with the fragrance of flowers and animated by music and dancing."

Blanc's casino began to attract all the nearby German princelings, then the Russian aristocracy, and finally from Paris Prince Charles Bonaparte himself. Soon it was the number-one casino in the world.

But public opinion began to turn against casino gambling. One by one the German casinos closed. Blanc's eye fell on Monaco. A gambling concession could probably be had there for almost nothing because the reigning prince, Charles III, was nearly bankrupt.

It was 1863 when Blanc reached Monaco. Or perhaps it was two years later — the dates here are a bit vague. Contemporary accounts describe him as 57 years old, small, wearing glasses and a mustache, with "darting eyes and nervous gesticulations." Monaco, he found, was three churches, five parallel streets, and six alleyways. There was no Monte Carlo at all. The site of his possible casino was an arid plateau called Les Spelugues, completely barren except for a few withered bushes, some grazing goats.

The principality today, and also when Grace Kelly first saw it, is half the size of Central Park, so small that its golf club, tennis club, beach club, and even its cemetery are all outside the border, in France. This was the size when Blanc arrived also, but it should have been much bigger. Charles III was so impoverished that he had been forced two years previously to sell Roquebrune and Menton, more than half his territory, to France to raise funds.

The idea of a casino on the Spelugues plateau had been in the air for some time, and the Prince had attempted both to start a casino and to sell the land around it for development at the equivalent of two British pence per square yard. No one would buy.

Blanc bought. He knew just how to turn the Spelugues into a gold mine, and his first job was to rename it. He toyed with several possibilities, one of them Charlesville, for to flatter Charles III would be a good idea. Finally he did flatter him, though somewhat obliquely. Henceforth the arid plateau would be known as Monte Carlo.

Within twenty years the "worthless" land up there was virtually priceless.

Nice at the time was 40,000 people. It already had its substantial English colony and during the season was filled with aristocrats of all nationalities. This was a considerable pool to draw
from, except that Monte Carlo, though only twelve miles away,
was almost inaccessible. It took four hours to get there by carriage
over the high corniche. The road up to the corniche was so steep
the horses had to be frequently rested, and the descent to Monte
Carlo was a series of writhing dirt lanes. By steam launch — there
were no speedboats in the 1860s — Blanc's casino was scarcely
much closer.

So his first priority was to bribe railroad officials to bring the
tracks in from Nice fast, at whatever cost.

At the same time he began a publicity barrage. Although his
first Monte Carlo casino was a kind of atrium — very small, a
place of marble pillars and echoing walls — he brought journalists
in from everywhere and paid them to extol the place. He also
provided them with the names of fictitious gamblers, winners of
stupendous fictitious amounts, and these stories too appeared all
over Europe and made exciting reading. One of the most influential journalists was an editor of *Le Figaro,* whom Blanc brought
down from Paris and installed in his own luxurious villa, alone
except for all the servants. The man lived there for the season on
the arm and wrote all the laudatory copy Blanc could have wished
for. But soon after he got back to Paris this editor changed his
tune and began attacking Blanc and Monte Carlo in print. Instead
of getting angry, Blanc invited him down again, turned his house
and servants over to him again, and the laudatory tone of the
man's articles quickly reappeared.

The railroad came to Monte Carlo in 1868. The next year
taxes were abolished. In 1871 some 140,000 visitors were recorded.
In 1872 the Prince of Wales (later Edward VII) came. He was
followed by the Emperor of Austria, four Russian grand dukes,
the King of the Belgians, Archduke Ferdinand, and King Oscar
of Sweden. Blanc publicized it all. He popularized the practice of
throwing a black shroud over the roulette tables if any lucky
gambler should break the bank. Breaking the bank meant only
that the table had been cleaned out of whatever funds it had been
supplied with that day, but the sight of the black shroud had an

incredibly dramatic effect — it excited the imaginations of would-be winners far and wide.

A great many people lost entire fortunes in Monte Carlo. Casino gambling was still so new, rare, and dazzling that some men lost all reason and were wiped out. Some also lost all hope, and rushed out the back door and plunged off the terrace onto the rocks. One year there were at least eight suicides, four in one week. Inevitably this too was publicized, whether by Blanc himself is difficult to tell, but it certainly spread the "fame" of his casino.

Blanc himself said, or was supposed to have said: "Sometimes red wins, and sometimes black wins, but Blanc always wins." It sounds even better in French: "*Rouge gagne parfois, et noir gagne parfois, mais Blanc gagne toujours.*"

At his death the convicted swindler left a personal fortune of about $20 million, colossal for the time. He was succeeded by his son Camille, who carried on the good work, adding only a bit more class. In 1878 the new casino, designed by Charles Garnier, architect of the Paris Opera, was completed: it contained sumptuous restaurants and bars, sumptuous gaming rooms, even an entire opera house, and it offered dazzling views of the sea. The greatest composers of the day, particularly Massenet and Saint-Saëns (and later Puccini), were commissioned to write operas that were premiered there. The famed Ballet Russe de Monte Carlo came into existence as well. That is, a sustained and extremely expensive effort was made to present Monte Carlo as a bastion of culture, rather than what it was.

Probably the most celebrated gambler Monte Carlo ever saw, and never mind all the princes, dukes, moguls, and tycoons, was Charles Deville Wells. Three movies and a very pretty song were inspired by his exploits. The movies are forgotten now, but the song was so catchy that it has kept his story alive to the present day. For Charles Wells was "The Man Who Broke the Bank at Monte Carlo."

The casino never begrudged a man his winnings; a big winner only served to lure more losers to the tables. But it was better if he was an aristocrat, or at least rich. Charles Wells was instead a thief and swindler gambling with stolen money — a man after François Blanc's own heart, so to speak. Wells arrived in Monte

Carlo in July 1892. He wore a loud checkered suit, spoke loud Cockney English, and he bellied up to the roulette table. His capital amounted to 400 pounds sterling — some accounts say 4,000 — which he had conned out of society matrons, offering worthless patents in exchange. In London warrants were out for his arrest, and the desperate Wells was hoping to win enough money to stall his creditors and avoid jail. As his first bet he plunked down the maximum permitted sum, approximately $200, on number 5 — and it came up. Stacks of chips appeared in front of him, and his fantastic two-year career in Monte Carlo was launched. He left his original bet on 5 twice more; it won both times.

He became somewhat cautious, playing mostly on *manque, rouge,* or *impair,* where the payoff was only even money as opposed to 35 to 1. If he lost, he doubled his bets, the so-called Martingale system, until finally he won again.

By evening Wells's winnings had passed the 100,000-franc mark, and crowds had collected to watch him play. He was drunk with excitement. Towards midnight, after eleven straight hours, having won more than 250,000 francs, he at last stood up. He would be back when the casino opened in the morning, he announced to the crowd. He intended to break the bank before noon.

No one knew who Wells was or where he came from, but by the following morning Monte Carlo could talk of little else. A crowd followed him from his hotel to Barclay's Bank, where he had a sizable deposit credited to his account in London. From the telegraph office he dispatched wires to his more aggressive creditors, suggesting they examine his bank statement. Then, having gained financial breathing room, and with his disciples gathered breathlessly around him, he strode into the casino to fulfill his boast of the night before. The maximum bet again went down on number 5. The white ball spun around and tumbled into the slot. It took him just thirty minutes to break the bank. The black shroud went down over the table.

Every day a crowd of gamblers waited in the street to escort him to the casino, some pushing close enough to touch his coat for luck. His third day saw him break the bank a dozen times. The fourth day, after losing 60,000 francs at roulette in half an hour, he switched to *trente et quarante* and won it all back. Few gamblers could have resisted the impulse to stay with *trente et quarante,* but Wells, springing to his feet, darted back to the same roulette wheel that had betrayed him only moments before. This time he won, then won again. And again, and again. Suspecting collusion, the casino began to change croupiers and dealers every few minutes. Wells kept winning.

The crowds around his table became unmanageable. Those close enough staked on whichever number Wells favored. Those in the rear began to arch chips over heads onto the table, begging the croupiers to place their bets with his. Near riots ensued, for it was impossible to tell who had bet what, and finally the casino decreed that only seated gamblers could play. The disappointed remainder attempted to play Wells's numbers at other tables, a practice that ruined most of them.

Soon it was impossible for Wells to stroll the streets of Monte Carlo. He became loud and boastful. He was an inventor and already rich in England, he declared. Among his patents was a perpetual-motion machine. A Bavarian count and a French marquis gave banquets in his honor. British peers and peeresses, taught from the cradle to snub Cockneys, nonetheless begged to meet him socially. It was believed that he had already won $500,000, that whatever system he employed guaranteed an income of $10,000 a day.

He returned the following November at the start of the main winter season and had another astonishing run of luck. In January he was back again, this time aboard a magnificent steam yacht called the *Royal Palace* that seemed, in Monaco's tiny harbor, almost a battleship. It boasted a ballroom in which more than sixty guests could be accommodated during Wells's lavish parties. According to the press, his guests one night included five British peers and their wives, a German millionaire, three American millionaires, a distinguished French diplomat, and several members of well-known English families. The song about him appeared. It swept two continents, and in the streets of London the barrel organs seemed able to play nothing else.

Having returned to the tables, Wells actually broke the bank six more times.

✳ ✳ ✳

Suddenly, as incomprehensibly as it had started, his luck turned. Day after day he lost, and since he continued to oblige his public with maximum bets, it did not take long to dissipate his entire fortune.

Aboard his yacht the lavish entertainments continued — for a while. Then the bills came due. Abandoning the yacht, Wells attempted to flee by train but was arrested by agents of the Sûreté as he was about to board a ship at Le Havre. Extradited to England, he was tried, convicted, and sentenced to eight years in jail.

Upon his release, he changed his now famous name to Davenport, went into partnership with a defrocked Church of England clergyman, and together they sold much stock in Wells's inventions. This earned them three years in jail each. Afterwards Wells crossed into France, swindled successfully for a time, was caught, and served five years in a French prison. By the time he came out this time he was an old man, and all the brash courage was gone.

He was penniless too, of course. Although by nature a reckless gambler, he had lived in fear of old age and had spent a lifetime buying annuities with a portion of the profits of each swindle. But these had been attached and seemed lost to him.

Charles Wells now worked his final swindle. Summoning his creditors, he threatened to kill himself unless paid a regular sum on which to live. Suicide would end his annuities, and his creditors would get nothing. He wanted 5 pounds a week — take it or leave it.

One by one Wells stared his creditors down. He had won his final bet.

From that day until his death in 1922 — some sources say 1926 — he lived on what he proudly referred to as his pension. He died alone in a furnished room on a cold, rainy day. He was about 85. No one mourned him, but all over the world people were still singing the song that had made him famous:

> *You can hear the girls declare*
> *He must be a millionaire*
> *You can hear them sigh*

And hope to die
You can see them wink the other eye
At the man who broke the bank at Monte Carlo.

Grace Kelly was married in April 1956 in a long white dress that even then seemed somewhat out of date. She looked as pure as the dress. She carried a bouquet of flowers. She looked demure, yet somehow regal, very young and very beautiful. Rainier, now 33, wore a uniform so brightly draped with epaulets, with gold braid, with elaborate piping, that it could only be described as splendid. The entire left side of his chest was hung with medals, some of them enormous. He looked every inch what a prince was supposed to look like 200 years ago. The couple pronounced their vows, then waited through the long nuptial mass — masses were still being said in Latin at that time. Grace scarcely raised her eyes, she was so demure, and she sat with her bouquet clasped in two hands on her lap. She was now a European princess, which was perhaps the fulfillment of her every adolescent dream. Or perhaps it was not. She never told anyone, and the world never knew.

The site of the ceremony was a neo-Romanesque edifice of no architectural distinction built post François Blanc. In Monaco it was called a cathedral. The streets outside were jammed. So was the church. The bride and groom had had almost to fight their way in. The entire Kelly clan was there from Philadelphia, and so was every Monegasque dignitary, such as they were. But of major European royalty there was no sign, and this to Grace Kelly of Philadelphia was perhaps a major disappointment. So few international celebrities attended that the presence of Somerset Maugham, whose villa on the Cap-Ferrat stood not far from Rainier's former love nest there, was much remarked upon in the press. The author, 82, seemed to doze through most of the ceremony. Invitations had been sent to, among others, the Queen of England, RSVP. The Queen of England declined. Before Grace was born, her father, then a champion oarsman, had been refused entry into the Diamond Sculls at Henley on the grounds that he was a laborer. So being snubbed by English gentry was no new thing to the Kellys.

The bridal couple and tiny Monaco were much mocked in

the accounts of the day, and the usual adjective applied to them was "pretentious." Grace thought she was now royalty, it was written unkindly, but she was not; and her new domain was treated as a kind of international joke. This was perhaps inevitable, under the circumstances. About half of those in attendance inside the church seemed to be journalists and photographers, for this was a media event of the first magnitude. In the streets outside, and also outside the castle where the reception took place, the density of pseudo-journalists and paparazzi seemed even higher. All of the journalists, whether real or pseudo, were confined to certain spaces and treated with royal aloofness.

What celebrities the world over never seem to realize is that the press always gets the last word, and the last word on this royal wedding could not have made pleasant reading the next day on the royal yacht, as the royal honeymoon began. Rainier's yacht, by the way, visible all this time and for years afterwards in the horseshoe-shaped harbor, was dwarfed by the truly princely vessel parked alongside, a converted warship with gold faucets in its bathrooms that belonged to Aristotle Onassis, the enormously rich Greek shipping tycoon. Onassis was already famous in Europe, though not world famous as he would become when he married President Kennedy's widow many years later. It was Onassis who owned the Monte Carlo gambling concession, making him and not Rainier the principal personage of the principality. On the day of her wedding it seemed to the world that it was Onassis, not Grace, who owned whatever future Monaco might have.

In retrospect her entire reign seems to have been devoted to a quest for respectability, not so much in the eyes of the world as in those royal circles she wished to penetrate. Respectability cannot be earned quickly, like money. It requires patience and sacrifice. Although she sometimes invited Cary Grant, Frank Sinatra, and such people to the castle when they were passing through, she never made another movie. She received many offers too good to refuse; she refused them all. The world did not see, could not understand how or why she had made such a choice, and did not believe it would last, but it did. She had traded Philadelphia, Los

Angeles, New York, once and for all for Monaco, population 20,000. There the Academy Award–winning actress served as patron of the Monaco branch of the Red Cross. She kept her American passport but learned to speak French. She gave birth to three children. She became a matron. Her life must have satisfied her. She lived it twenty-six years without a peep.

She and Rainier became more and more famous, not because they did anything, for they didn't, but simply because they were. Grace was seen in public often enough. She was always present at the Grand Prix de Monaco, which was again one of the premier car races in the world, handing over the winner's trophy at the end. Once I saw her at a gymnastics exhibition in Antibes. One of her daughters must have been interested in gymnastics, as was one of mine. Afterwards she got into the back of a Rolls-Royce with Monaco license plates to be driven home.

She was much in demand not only by Hollywood, whose blandishments she refused, but also by the magazines of the world, particularly the American ones whose audience was women. A Princess Grace cover, it was said in the business, sold out. Very few subjects would do this: Sophia Loren, Jackie Kennedy, maybe Audrey Hepburn, but best of all Princess Grace — in America she was never Grace Kelly anymore, always Princess Grace, the only royalty America had. We were proud of her.

At some point she decided to put these requests for interviews to her own use. Instead of just refusing, she hired a public relations firm in New York to screen them and to pose conditions: the palace reserved the right to approve, or disapprove, the magazine's writer; and the resulting article must be submitted for censorship before publication.

Since I was living in Nice at the time, a magazine asked me to write such a cover story. But when I learned about the censorship, I refused to agree to it. Although I was as curious about Grace as anybody, and needed the money, I was not going to submit to censorship by some actress my own age. This was as much pique as principle; I'm not particularly proud of it. Between the magazine, the PR firm, and presumably the palace a good deal of negotiation ensued. Meantime I drove to Monaco and tried to begin preliminary interviews. But no one would talk to me. How had Grace managed to silence the entire town? On the subject of censorship the palace remained adamant. So did I.

In this way and certain others Grace — for Rainier in the past had never seemed to care — controlled the face that Monaco presented to the world. Always the first consideration seemed to be respectability. Grace and Rainier were respectable, and increasingly the casino's image was cleaned up too, and its importance downgraded, until it seemed that all those lurid legends must have belonged to some other place.

One of the casino's oldest and most traditional games of chance took place not in the gambling rooms but on a terrace behind the casino overlooking the sea: live pigeon shooting. For six weeks each winter rich men shot pigeons for purses and side bets. They used up a total of 25,000 pigeons per season.

But pigeon shooting was contrary to the image of Monaco that the new princess wished to present. She wanted it stopped. However, she did not control the casino, Onassis did. The tycoon had poured a great deal of money into refurbishments. The gaming rooms were again as sumptuous as in François Blanc's day. But Onassis faced competition that was intense. Casino gambling had been legal in France since 1933, and there were other casinos all around him — two in Nice, two in Cannes, others in Menton, Beausoleil, Beaulieu, and Juan les Pins. Gamblers could play the same games in all those places, but could shoot live pigeons only at Monte Carlo. Onassis had a lot of money invested. From his point of view, what Monte Carlo had that was special it needed to keep.

Grace's opposition remained. Monaco was not a gambling den where 25,000 pigeons a year were reduced to feathers. There followed a long behind-the-scenes struggle. It took a number of years, but she finally won. Live pigeon-shooting tournaments, first held in 1872, were abolished. Not long afterwards Onassis, who had seen his influence and access diminish year by year and who certainly did not need Monte Carlo, shrugged, sold out, and moved on.

By then other new money had poured into the principality. It was rumored on the coast that this money was American and that Grace had attracted most of it, some through rich builder friends of her father's. What was clear was that Monaco now underwent a building boom unprecedented on the Riviera and even in France. Many of the most luxurious villas of the past were demolished, and skyscrapers ten, twenty, thirty stories high went up in their stead. These were the first skyscrapers on the Riviera or indeed anywhere in France. Even in Paris the only high structure was still the Eiffel Tower. Into these luxurious towers moved tennis stars, racing drivers, and rich people of all nationalities, most of them attempting to avoid the high taxes at home. The population of Monaco rose by over 5,000 — more than 25 percent. Eventually all of France was to recover from the ravages of World War II, but Monte Carlo did it first and did it bigger, and it is difficult not to credit this to Grace Kelly of Philadelphia.

Meanwhile, she lived quietly with her husband and raised her children, and the scandalmongers had been silenced forever, or so it seemed, until the older of her daughters, Caroline, reached puberty and began to show a great deal of well-rounded flesh on beaches. Caroline, who came to be as indiscreet as some of her Grimaldi forebears, later married someone unsuitable and later still even got divorced — all of which proved only that Grace Kelly was no more able to control her children than any other parent in these times. The family linen was again being hung out to dry, but it was not her doing, and she made no public comment of whatever kind.

During these years Grace and Rainier moved about the world as rich people do, wintering sometimes in Gstaad, attending their son's graduation from Amherst. The bland articles about them continued to appear. They achieved such a level of respectability that they were no longer ostracized by the rest of European royalty, and when Prince Charles of England was married to Lady Diana Spencer in 1981, Grace and Rainier were invited to the wedding. Rainier skipped it, but Grace was there on the arm of her son, Prince Albert. It was a signal triumph and one of her last.

Among their several residences was a villa in France high up on the mountain above Monaco and connected to the principality by steep, narrow roads. Grace was descending towards the palace in September 1982 when her car went off the edge and plunged forty feet down into a ravine. Her daughter Stephanie, then 17, was with her, and was perhaps driving, though that would have been illegal in France; it was never clear who was driving. Mother and daughter were both badly injured. Stephanie lived. Her mother did not. Grace Kelly's funeral was carried live on television all over the world, an orgy of international grief. The only notable figure out of her past who attended was white-haired old Cary Grant, 78, with whom she had starred in *To Catch a Thief* on the Riviera twenty-eight years before.

Verdun

FEB. 21, 1916

We are five or six kilometers out of Verdun and lost. The night is dark, the temperature below freezing. We are on a long, straight road through a seemingly endless woods. The headlights show trees laden with fresh snow. There is smooth snow on the road, and no other tracks but the ones we are making. I am driving with extreme care. If we slide off here, they would not find us for a while. I picture the wait, shivering beside the derelict car. The hardship. The anxiety. How inconsequential compared to what once happened in these woods beginning fifteen minutes from now on this same day of the year at the end of a night identical to this one.

A road sign glares at us: Louvemont. Louvemont is one of the nine obliterated villages. There's nothing there except an indentation in the underbrush and a snow-covered monument. Then we are past it. The road continues as straight and empty as before.

Finally the forest ends. There is a fork, but no signposts. I guess, and turn right. Fields to both sides of the road. Another village: Ormes. I know the name. Ormes is an obliterated village also, I believe. I see no houses. Nor does the road widen.

Carefully I turn the car around, go back to the fork, and take the other turning. The night is no longer pitch-black. I drive as fast as I dare, making fresh tracks, hurrying. According to the dashboard clock the bombardment is to start three minutes from now, at 7:15 precisely, and it seems important to get there on time, as if to warn the soldiers to stay in their holes. On the other side of the lines everyone knows what is about to happen; men stand with their fingers in their ears. On this side no one knows, men are just beginning to stir, to urinate against trees, perhaps to heat coffee on spirit stoves. There are 3,000 or more massed guns about to go off. The shells will explode among them before they ever hear the noise of the firing.

The road has reentered the woods. I stay as far as possible from verges I cannot see under the snow. Finally there is a clearing, signposts. It is still too dark to read them from the car, so I get out, crunch across through the snow, and put my face up close: Bois des Caures.

All right, I have found it, but it is 7:25, getting light fast, and the shells are already falling. I am too late to warn anybody by seventy-one years plus ten minutes. Around me is absolute silence. I call back that this is indeed the Bois des Caures, and P. nods through the glass but declines to get out of the car. I am in snow up to my ankles. Women are said to be more practical than men, and this one is plainly unwilling to join my search for old ghosts. But for me the most murderous battle in the history of the world to that time, perhaps of all time, is now under way.

Old ghosts. The front that day stretched from the Swiss border to the Belgian coast, a distance of over 300 miles, only 800 meters of it being the Bois des Caures. The 1,200 young Frenchmen deployed in three lines in these woods had the bad luck to be standing in the wrong place at the wrong time. The weight of the German army has just landed on top of them. Many are dead already. All but 100 will be dead by tomorrow night.

In the clearing stands a panel showing the positions of both sides on this exact morning seventy-one years ago. There was no continuous trench line, as was usually possible in the flat plains to the north. Instead there were short lengths of unconnected trenches laid out according to the contours of the ground and the possible fields of fire. That is, once the bombardment started, no one could know what was happening two trenches away, or even one trench away, and once it had stopped after ten solid pounding hours, those who were left alive crawled groggy and stupefied to the tops of their holes, laid their rifles on the dirt, and fired bullets into the advancing horde, each man so far as he knew alone, each man firing until his bullets were gone or he was overrun. Overrun is a euphemism for being blown up by a hand grenade, or shot to death (the nicest way), or nailed to the mud by a bayonet, or done to a crisp by one of the new German flamethrowers, which this day made their maiden appearance in the world. The flame-throwers did not melt any snow. There would have been no snow left by then, the terrific heat of the bombardment would have turned it all back into water long before. There would have been few trees still standing either.

But the Germans had let their bombardment go on too long. Within two hours it was dark again, and the offensive stalled. The attackers settled down for the night in their new holes, while the defenders organized a hysterical counterattack, for one of the immutable dictums of that war was that each lost foot of ground, each blasted blockhouse, each half-caved-in section of trench had to be got back at once at whatever cost. The French rushed forward in the dark, and you had what the press of the time, and the history books to this day, have called savage hand-to-hand fighting. This phrase sounds rather brilliant. What is described was two groups of men spearing each other, clubbing each other to death with rifle butts. They — we human beings — were back to the level of the cavemen, an idea which, if it occurred to anyone seventy-one years ago, could never be mentioned in public.

In this way most of the lost ground was retaken, and by ten o'clock at night a calm had fallen over the battlefield. But in the morning the bombardment would start up again, and the gray hordes would come forward again. Were there enough Frenchmen left alive to stop them?

Leaving the clearing, following signposts, the only sound my boots on the snow, I come to the command post of Lt. Col. Emile Driant, whose sector this was. Driant was the first of the heroes produced by the battle of Verdun and almost the only one whose fame has lasted to our time.

His command post was a concrete blockhouse that looks to

be about twenty-five yards long. Most of it is below ground level.
I descend a little staircase and peer inside. It's about eight feet
across, just a long, concrete tunnel-type thing, and absolutely
empty, no furniture of any kind, no partitions, no rusting guns.
There isn't even any picnic garbage. Nor has anyone used it for
a latrine lately. That's a surprise. It would have contained desks
and tables with typewriters on them, probably, for armies generate
paper even during battles, and maps on the walls, bunks to rest
in, a kitchen of sorts; and it would have been crowded with people.
In here, in addition to Driant, were his staff officers, a doctor, a
priest, a multitude of clerks, and a group of soldiers whom Driant
would use one by one as runners. That was a war of poor com-
munications. Forward posts like this one were connected to the
rear by buried telephone lines. It was of course impossible to bury
them deeper than a shell could penetrate, so all lines would always
be cut almost at once. The radio transmitters of the time were
enormously bulky and needed enormously long and elaborate aer-
ials as well; these never survived a bombardment either. The result
was that messages had to be carried back and forth through bursting shrapnel by frightened young men whose only armor was
woolen overcoats. A battle such as this one used up a good many
runners quickly.

At the far end of the blockhouse the roof is half caved in. A
direct hit. Eight of the men in here were wounded, and Driant's
secretary, a lieutenant, was killed. The shell did not actually penetrate the roof, I see. The lieutenant must have been sitting directly
under it, was perhaps killed by a falling chunk of concrete. Or
perhaps he was standing up and the roof sagged down and crushed
his skull.

High up in the walls are rifle embrasures. The walls themselves are more than two feet thick, and the roof appears to be
about four feet thick. Driant commanded two battalions of *chasseurs à pied* — light infantry. When I first read about this battle, I
wondered how he could have survived for two days when everyone around him got wiped out. I never imagined a blockhouse as
tough as this one. I also never imagined that it would still be here,
though if the German bombardment couldn't dent it, how could
civilian demolition experts do better?

The trees outside are mostly low beeches, all of them of course new since the battle, and the forest floor is pocked by shell holes still four or five feet deep. It is amazing this long afterwards that so many craters as deep as this still exist. The entire woods, I see as I walk on, is pocked and cratered, but it is particularly bad close to the command post. The Germans must have known where it was. They must have lobbed a few thousand shells at Driant personally. They never got him.

In summer this woods is a picnic ground. I pass picnic tables and benches here and there. I also pass stretches of blasted trench lines, though one of them zigzags through the trees like the teeth of a saw, which is the way trenches were supposed to be dug. It is still four or five feet deep. Trees grow up out of it every which way. Some have planted themselves in the floor of the trench, others halfway up the walls — all at different levels. The new trees have stabilized the ground, have preserved the trenches and shell holes this long, and possibly will preserve them forever. The original trees, the ones they replaced, must have flown through the air like trapeze artists. I wonder how many soldiers got killed by flying tree trunks, by chunks of boughs, not to mention chunks of each other, rather than by bullets or shrapnel.

The light has risen a good deal by now. Off in the woods is a row of tiny concrete pillboxes half hidden in the underbrush. Finally I come to another blockhouse, much smaller than Driant's, which must have suffered a direct hit, perhaps several — certainly something demolished it. Great slabs of concrete lie tilted at strange angles and out of them grow trees, bushes.

About 200 yards from Driant's command post is the first of the monuments that are to be found in these woods, unless the pillboxes and blockhouses are to be counted as monuments. This one is surrounded by a semicircle of graves, thirteen in all, each cross labeled *chasseur inconnu*. When applied to infantrymen, *unknown* becomes one of the saddest words in the language. There is a fourteenth tomb in front which ought to be Driant's, but isn't. It's a mock tomb among real ones, which seems odd. A path leads off into the woods, and at the end of it is another monument, and this is where Driant's body lies.

He should not have been in this woods at all. He was 61 years old and a deputy to the National Assembly as well, so on two counts should have been excluded. He was born at Neufchâteau, a town of under 10,000 about sixty miles southwest of Verdun, on Sept. 11, 1855. He entered St. Cyr at twenty and came out fourth in his class. He was promoted to lieutenant in 1883, to captain in 1886, to battalion chief in 1896. He was an idea man, which perhaps explains why promotions were so slow and would continue to be; at his death, eighteen months into the most murderous war in history, he was still only a lieutenant colonel. But the French army of those days seems to have been hostile to any new idea of any kind, and Driant not only proposed ideas, he also wrote books. The best known was called *The War of Tomorrow*. Another was called *Toward a New Sedan,* Sedan being the site of the French surrender in the war of 1870. Driant wrote under the pen name of Captain Denrit — junior officers, like small boys, were to be seen but not heard. His pen name failed to fool the generals. They knew who he was. In 1906 he resigned his commission and became a novelist and journalist. Four years later he ran for the National Assembly from Nancy and was elected. All this time he kept crying out that France was unprepared for the war that was coming. Hardly anybody listened. In August of 1914, with the German invaders at the gates of Paris, he resigned from the assembly, rejoined the army, and demanded a command.

He was one of those officers, the French army was full of them at the time, who believed in leading charges personally — and charges then were conducted at a walk. During the battle of the Marne he walked calmly at the head of his men into a storm of machine-gun bullets and was not touched; and when one of his soldiers asked him about it he remarked: "I don't want it said that Driant died showing his back to the Boches." This style of leadership remained popular even into the last year of the war, so it is impossible to say with any accuracy how good an officer by today's standards Driant was. Of course, by the standards of his own day he was magnificent, and would remain so. Cited for heroism on the Marne, he was awarded the Rosette of the Legion of Honor, which was then and is today basically a civilian decoration, meaning reserved for what might be called gentlemen only.

So Driant conceived the idea that there ought to be a purely military decoration that even common soldiers could win, and its only criterion would be gallantry in action, and he wrote and sent forward a report to this effect. Originally he had intended to call his proposed decoration the Cross of Military Merit, but now in the writing he changed his mind. The new decoration, he wrote, should be called the Croix de Guerre.

Most of the last year of his life he spent in the Bois des Caures reinforcing defenses that he knew would be inadequate, given the weight of the German preparations opposite him, and he wrote letter after letter to Paris imploring former colleagues in the government to bring his concerns to the notice of the general staff. This was done, and the general staff, in the person of Marshal Joffre, supreme commander of France's armies in the field, flew into a rage. How dare any subordinate officer criticize superiors, Joffre cried. He demanded to know who had criticized him, and though at first the politicians concealed Driant's name, Joffre promised to move heaven and earth to find out who he was, and then to court-martial him.

So Driant at his death was about to be disgraced, perhaps even imprisoned. Instead, thanks to whatever German implement killed him, and to these monuments here, he is today a far more revered figure than Joffre himself. Not many Frenchmen can say where Joffre's tomb may lie, but the "grateful nation" (as the saying goes) seems to have dedicated this entire woods to the memory of Driant.

Near midnight in the lull between the first day's battle and the second, Driant made his way from post to post to comfort and encourage his troops. Picture a 61-year-old man slithering down the sides of holes on his back in the dark, then having to scrabble his way out again. There must have been wounded men whimpering or screaming in the darkness, but these noises have not come down to us. The night was freezing cold, and once more it was snowing. Driant's men knew that the bombardment would resume in the morning, followed by another attack, and that this attack would be more violent than the first one. Driant himself did not pretend otherwise. A Lt. Robin said to him: "But what am I to do? I've only eighty men left."

To which Driant replied: "My poor Robin, our orders are to hold here."

The shelling that began at daybreak was more intense, if possible, than the day before. It lasted until noon, stopped abruptly, and was followed by a sudden momentary silence. Then came the flood of enemy troops in long gray overcoats skirting the shell holes, rushing across the new open ground. Not for Driant the safety of his blockhouse. He was outside it, one knee on the ground, a rifle at his shoulder, firing as fast as he could reload.

By three o'clock in the afternoon the Bois des Caures was surrounded. The enemy had got a field piece behind Driant's command post and had begun shelling him from the rear. He turned his machine gunners around and told them to take out the field piece if they could, but a shell came down and blew them all up. Even Driant could see that it was time to retreat before they were cut off. They were cut off already. He sent his men out in three groups, leaving a rear guard. The third group included Driant himself. He walked without haste, swinging his cane with superb nonchalance. Behind him the rear guard was annihilated.

The photographs of him show a small man still trim for his age, wearing a fierce black mustache. Now at this moment he seemed to his men, and to the whole country later, the epitome of French panache, the epitome of heroism. Or else he was the epitome of some other quality much more difficult to name. He was like an actor onstage concentrating so hard on his role that he didn't realize that the theater was on fire. Bullets whizzed all around him. Bursts of shrapnel filled the air. He came to a wounded soldier and stopped to bandage him up, and continued on with no more haste than before until he reached a shell hole in which two sergeants cowered, and for a moment he stood over them. Suddenly he spun around, muttered "Oh, my God," and was dead.

So fell the Bois des Caures, a mere incident in that war, an incident even in the battle of Verdun itself, which was to last with unimaginable savagery for another ten months and was to result in the slaughter of nearly 400,000 young men on each side.

Almost instantly German troops converged on the shell hole,

took the two sergeants prisoner, and dug a grave for Col. Driant. Dug a grave in the midst of a battle? It sounds unlikely. Nonetheless, that is the story, and a grave remained there until 1922, when the existing monument was posed on top of it. A German Countess sent Driant's belongings via Switzerland back to his wife — apparently her husband had commanded the troops who killed him.

The account of his death comes from the two sergeants, who, of course, were not heard until many months later. According to them Driant was hit in the head, a neat little wound, and killed instantly.

Funny the way certified heroes always die such neat deaths. None of them ever lingers in agony with his legs blown off or disemboweled or minus his face. None of them ever screams with fear and pain.

Anyway, Driant was lost, and more than 1,000 men with him, all in this little woods, all in the space of about thirty-six hours. The little woods was lost too, of course. France gained nothing except a hero, which was badly needed if the country was going to be able to live with what had happened here, what was still happening all along the 300-mile front, what would continue to happen for almost three more years.

I trek through the snow back to the car. It is full daylight now, and we drive down the road and out of the woods into open farm country. We are looking for a village with a café where we can get breakfast, and so come upon Flabas, a huddle of gray stone buildings containing a school, a *mairie,* a post office, and no shops that I can see. Certainly there is no café. There are a few parked cars with snow on them and some snow-covered farm machinery. Flabas is not much of a village. The nine obliterated villages must have been much like it. It was behind the German lines, and the artillery pieces stood in the fields nearly wheel to wheel, firing over the village most likely, using the village houses as protection from the inevitable counterbattery fire. Flabas was only destroyed, rather than obliterated, and was rebuilt after the war.

We find a café in another village, Bras, and sit down against the wall opposite the bar. The coffee comes in enormous cups, half coffee, half hot milk. The bread is half of a crusty French loaf sliced down the middle, the two halves thick with butter. The room is unheated, or nearly so, and we eat breakfast in our overcoats. From time to time truck drivers or farm laborers come in through the door singly or in pairs and step up to the bar and down glasses of red wine, and go out again. Some things about old France never change.

As I warm my fingers around my cup, I am still brooding about Col. Driant. In those days, and into my lifetime as well, men believed absolutely in duty and honor, which were considered not vague obligations but articles of faith, as holy as belief in God. As near as I can tell, duty and honor are not considered holy anymore. Today one does them from nine to five, five days a week. Maybe. One does them if convenient. It is as if the world saw in which direction duty and honor could take nations, never mind individuals, and gave them up at last.

For it is not weapons that make wars possible, but ideas, and it is duty and honor that lead men straight to the most insidious idea of all, which is heroism. Were Driant's men heroes? The trouble with heroism is that no one has ever defined what it is. When you subject men to the conditions of the Bois des Caures, the conditions that generally obtained throughout that war, when you leave them eating, sleeping, shitting, freezing, day after day in the same two feet of muddy trench and then subject them to a ten-hour bombardment — when you do this you remove from them all dignity. You reduce them to the level of slavering animals. They exist on the level of animals. Their psyches are overpowered by the most basic and also the basest (we have mostly been taught to think) of emotions, namely fear and rage. They become crazed. Are crazed men responsible for their actions? Some become catatonic and are killed where they cower, sometimes by their own men. Others in their hysteria fight like demons, a more accurate word than most people commonly realize. They literally no longer know what they are doing. The difference between coward and hero may even be chemical, the presence or absence of a single hormone, perhaps, something that could be added or subtracted from their soup. The hero may have no more control of himself than the coward. To me, especially in that snowy woods this morning, it seems as unreal to call one man coward as to call another hero. As for Driant himself, was his conduct not preconditioned to such an extent that it became, therefore, preordained? Is it possible in an age that has at last become skeptical about heroes and heroism to decide that he was the victim of such an incredible mind-set that he literally had no choice but to behave as he did?

An hour later I stand on top of Fort Douaumont, the number-two tourist attraction hereabouts — the Bois des Caures is far down the list, and we will get to the number one in a moment. Douaumont must be seen next partly because it is the most spectacular relic of that war, mostly because it must be understood if the battle of Verdun is to be understood, if the war itself is to be understood.

Douaumont is possibly the most enormous single chunk of concrete in the world. It is half a mile long, a quarter of a mile wide, a concrete carapace whose walls and roof are said to be more than eight feet thick. It was the strongest fort in existence at that time.

It is so vast that, standing in the snow on its roof, I can't even see all of it. The snow all around is studded with rusty turrets. There are paths and even in places handrails that draw me forward from one turret to the next. The turrets are low and round like studs on the soles of boots and were retractable in their day. They will never retract again. Rust and disuse have accomplished what no shell ever did. Here and there lie fragments of barbed-wire entanglements that perhaps guarded observation posts, and certain profound indentations in the snow are identified by signs. In this one landed a 420 mm shell on a specific day — the date is given. Over there landed another months later, and that date is given too. A 420 mm shell weighs over 2,000 pounds. The business end of it (minus the cartridge) is taller than a man, and these were direct hits, but they only dented the carapace, they did not seriously damage the fort.

The rest of the roof, and also the ground all about, are incredibly pockmarked still. There are supposed to be parts of the Verdun battlefield that were hit by so many shells, were blown up over and over again so many times, that after the war nothing would grow. Perhaps it was just a case of all of the topsoil becoming buried many feet deep; or perhaps the repeated shelling destroyed all the life that existed in the earth itself, pulverized even the microorganisms that give rise to life. There are obviously fewer such areas now, so many years later, but it is said that some still exist, and perhaps it is that way around this fort. Because of the snow I cannot tell for sure.

The view to all sides is stupendous, which of course was why the fort was built here in the first place. Although clearly impregnable, Fort Douaumont fell to the Germans without a shot being fired. It was retaken eight months later almost to the day, also virtually without a shot being fired. In between it cost the French 100,000 lives. All it ever was, was a symbol. How they did believe in symbols in those days. In that war men died for symbols by the millions. Verdun itself was a symbol — the German generals had mounted their offensive against the one spot in the 300-mile-long front that French honor would feel obliged to defend to the last man. And of course the very war was a symbol. It was supposed to be "the war to make the world safe for democracy." And if that slogan didn't convince you, it was also supposed to be "the war to end all wars."

Fort Douaumont dated from 1885. By 1915 the French general staff considered it obsolete, and it was stripped of its guns, which were needed elsewhere. Only three days after the fall of the Bois des Caures, which is about six kilometers to the north, a small German detachment wandered in here. It is amazing they didn't get lost in the subterranean levels, the labyrinthian corridors under my feet. They found an elderly artillery guard and a handful of men, who were immediately taken prisoner. Col. Driant was hardly yet cold in his tomb, if there was a tomb. And if he was lying out on the floor of the ravaged woods along with 1,000 or more of his men, he — they — had not yet started to rot.

So for the next eight months the French shelled their own fort, and they mounted assault after assault, all of which were beaten back. The Germans in the fort never had an easy time of it. There was never enough water. Ventilation was nonexistent. The noise and concussion of the ceaseless bombardment destroyed their nerves and their hearing. They could not use the fort to advance. It became a munitions dump and a rest home for troops.

One day a store of hand grenades accidently exploded. It killed 679 German soldiers, splattered them all over the walls, I imagine. That particular gallery was immediately sealed. It is still sealed, and there is a chapel where tourists sometimes kneel to pray. Finally in October, as another massive French counteroffensive got under way, fire broke out in one of the casemates. The German garrison fled and the French strolled in.

Douaumont was never really good for anything except publicity. Its loss had plunged France into despair. Its recapture caused national rejoicing. Though militarily of little value, it was and remains one of the mightiest symbols of World War I, and of course one of the most costly. Nor did the symbol die there. When the fort was found to be essentially undamaged after eight months of shelling, a new idea began to take root in the French soul, and its most prominent expression was a man named Maginot, once a soldier at Verdun, now a deputy to the National Assembly, who argued that France needed only a line of such forts extending from Switzerland to the Belgian frontier to be ever afterwards safe from invasion by any power to the east, especially the one most feared. The Maginot Line would do the trick; no other preparation would be necessary. And in the event, no other was ever made, and the Germans in 1940 conquered France in a matter of days.

Alone in the snow on the roof of Fort Douaumont, I look at the ravaged shell of the fort and at the ravaged countryside all around it. I cannot comprehend the vastness of the numbers of men who died here, or perhaps don't want to try. Instead I concentrate on all the work and money that went into the months and months of shelling. The constant rearrangement of the terrain around the fort, and the earth and concrete on top of it. For me that's easier. Never mind the grand strategy. Never mind the dead.

I'm cold. My hands are cold. The soldiers must have been cold too. It's one thing to be frightened, to be running, to be diving for cover and so on. A man's body gets warm, but not his fingers. And if they're freezing, how do you reload your rifle? How, after a time, do you even pull the trigger? How do you get the pin out of a grenade and then throw it? There must have been guys whose hands were so cold that they dropped the thing and blew themselves up. Many of them.

At the foot of the snow-covered ramp is the narrow steel door through which the paying customers enter and leave the fort during the season — from Palm Sunday to Dec. 1 there are busloads of tourists here, and upon payment of a fee they file inside. The French have managed to commercialize these battlefields and to extract profit from them in the same way that the Italians have managed to profit from their Renaissance art — national treasures in both cases. I went into Fort Douaumont some years ago. There is a small war museum, and you are shown some galleries, some casemates. I also visited Fort Vaux, which is not far away and whose story is distressingly similar. But both forts are closed now in winter, for it is impossible to heat them. They weren't heated during those years when soldiers lived in them under bombardments, either.

It's snowing again. From behind the steel door a telephone begins to ring. It is the only sound anywhere about. It rings and rings. Nobody home.

Beside the site of what once was Fleury, another of the nine obliterated villages, there has stood since 1967 a two-story square building in white stone that identifies itself in letters over the entrance doors as "The Memorial of Verdun 1914–18." What it is of course is a museum, but in the French mind the word *museum* has to do with the fine arts. A memorial is something else.

The Verdun battlefields abound in memorials of one kind or another, but this one is the biggest, the most complete, and the most moving. Fleury is a fitting site for it, for the village, which still has a mayor and an official existence but no houses or people, changed hands sixteen times — some reports say twenty-six — until not one stone was left upon another. Inside, there's enough space for two of the flimsy pursuit planes of the time, a Nieuport and a Fokker III, to dangle from the ceiling over a simulated battlefield, a patch of real earth that is as pockmarked and pounded as photos show the actual battlefields to have been; a battlefield littered with real iron junk from the period, with ruined weapons, caved-in dugouts, blasted cannons, and so forth.

This is the central exhibit, but there are many others. In display cases are the uniforms, the equipment, the weaponry, of the competing armies — one can note how all this changed over the years, for no one wore steel helmets at first, and the French private soldier, who later found himself not only khaki-clad but also almost permanently encrusted with mud, started out wearing bright red pantaloons.

And there are photo blowups on the walls. One shows a French soldier lying faceup on the ground. He still wears his helmet, his greatcoat. He is a young man with a mustache. He does not appear to be suffering. Both legs have been blown off at mid-thigh. Another photo shows an intact hand, its fingers spread, lying on top of the mud — intact except that it is not attached to anything. Whether a French hand or a German one the caption does not say, not that it matters anymore. Press censorship being absolute on both sides of the lines, such photos did not appear until years after the war — they might have hurt the war effort, don't you know. It was all right to show German corpses in French publications and French corpses in German ones, but not the reverse. I have at home two leather-bound tomes of *L'Illustration,* the number-one French picture weekly then. They show captured German trenches that are always full of corpses, but in hundreds of pages, thousands of photos, there are no corpses of French soldiers anywhere, not one. On the contrary, in text and photos week after week life in the trenches was made to seem not half bad.

The memorial's segment of battlefield is accurate up to a point. The earth did look like that, not the moist black soil that the plow turns over, but earth that had come from much deeper down, that had never before been exposed to the light of day, that was orange in color, that had never known life of any kind, desiccated earth that looked somehow obscene. And its surface would have been littered with iron junk as here, too. But it also would have been littered with corpses, and pieces of corpses, and bloody shreds of uniforms and bones.

So this scene is not real life. In real life the remains of most of Verdun's 800,000 murdered young men, though buried and reburied dozens of times, were never formally buried even once. When the war ended they were still there. And so was all manner of other garbage which, if touched, was lethal. To find out how these battlefields were cleaned up, I sought out the director of the memorial, Léon Rodier.

Rodier is a retired army colonel. He was born in the last year of that war. His father fought at Verdun, which is not even curious, for so did 70 percent of the French army, but he also survived Verdun, which, once you have seen the state of the still-devastated terrain outside these walls, seems remarkable. Col. Rodier is also a delegate to the Comité National du Souvenir de Verdun, the private organization that both built and runs the Fleury Memorial, and he begins by telling me about the various monuments, museums, and memorials that now stand on the battlefields, rather than about the battlefields themselves. All were paid for not by Paris, but by private groups or even by single individuals. French grief, once the war had ended, evidently ran so deep that collecting the necessary contributions posed no problem whatever.

At first the battlefields drew what Col. Rodier calls "pilgrims," the remnants of families who had lost sons, husbands, brothers, fathers, in the war. Today of course few such people are left, and the visitors who come are tourists of all nationalities, most of whom have little idea of what the war was about, or how the various battle sites fitted together. There seem to be fewer of them each year now; admissions to his memorial are down 20 percent from peak years. Meanwhile, groups like his see to it that the monuments are cared for, that the paths, approaches, and parking lots are kept cleared, and that visitors are reminded from time to time that they are in a holy place and that certain kinds of dress and certain boisterous conduct are not appropriate. For instance, as you approach Fort Douaumont there is a sign that reads: "From here on no picnicking, camping, or loud talk."

It is Rodier's opinion that it will be 150 years before the scars in the terrain completely disappear. It is my opinion, if the terrain can recover no better than it has done in the more than 70 years so far, that he is being optimistic.

At first France was so utterly exhausted both emotionally and financially, says Rodier, that little effort was made to repair the immense empty landscape that had been the battlefield. It took more than ten years just to collect all the bodies and pieces of bodies. Much of the work was done not by the government or the French army but by charitable organizations, many of them composed of idealistic young people, including the Boy Scouts.

In 1919 a provisional ossuary was built as a place where the unidentifiable bones could be stored till a more permanent memorial could be built — the Bishop of Verdun had already started to collect funds by means of subscriptions and lecture tours in France and abroad. Tons of iron junk were carried away as well, and there were the inevitable accidents. Not far from Col. Rodier's museum is a monument to a group of Boy Scouts who happened to pitch their camp and build their cooking fire over an unexploded shell, whether French or German no one will ever know.

In all, the bones of 130,000 unidentifiable people were collected, and included in this total no doubt were the remains of the ancestors of the inhabitants of the obliterated villages, for in the indiscriminate shelling their coffins went up into the air over and over again as well. In a sense the collecting of bones from the Verdun battlefields has never stopped. They are still being found. So are the unexploded shells, which seem to work their way up to the surface a few inches every winter, until finally one spring they erupt into view. There are still posters being freshly printed and freshly hung — I saw one in a café yesterday — that show such a shell nosing out of the dirt. The caption reads: "*Touche pas, ça tue.*"

The area containing the nine villages was called the *zone rouge*. The inhabitants were not allowed back, and partly this was because of danger from unexploded ordnance. More than that, the earth surrounding those villages was no longer capable of supporting life, or so it seemed. French peasants used to live together in their hamlets and walk out into their fields each day. Or they rode out behind farm animals. But in 1919, even if they were allowed to rebuild their villages, there were no fields close by that they could till, and therefore no way they could support themselves. Nor was it possible to commute to other work some distance away, for they had no transportation. So they were compensated for their houses and land, and eventually they stopped begging for permission to return and established themselves elsewhere.

Meanwhile, everyone waited for the raw earth to give birth to green growing things, but this did not happen, and ultimately the government came in and planted trees. In the Bois des Caures, for instance, rows of spruce trees were planted in 1920, Austrian pines and beeches in 1922, and still more beeches of a different type in 1925. Ultimately there as elsewhere these seedlings took root and began to grow, though there were always plots where nothing happened, seedlings simply died, and the government nurserymen were obliged to come back ten or twenty or thirty years later and try again.

At the end of the war there was of course no game left alive anywhere in the battle zone, and the only creatures that thrived were the rats and the crows that fed off corpses. Over the years many attempts were made to restock the new woods with deer, wild boar, rabbits, and other game. But even animals seemed to find the area inhospitable. Within a year or two all had migrated elsewhere, and a new attempt to restock would have to be made. According to Col. Rodier, deer and other animals now live comfortably in the Bois des Caures and in other once-ravaged areas, and in the last five or six years even the songbirds have come back at last and sometimes you can hear them singing — songs not heard in these parts since 1914.

Adjacent to the museum are the woods where Fleury used to stand — the usual multiplicity of shell holes and trenches. The thing about ground such as this that's so hard to describe is that it isn't normal, isn't natural. The eye looks at it and somehow is shocked every time. Amid the shell holes here are snow-covered monuments, not only a major monument for the vanished village itself, but also many smaller ones marking former village streets, former village buildings. Once about 400 people lived in Fleury.

The signal attraction of the entire Verdun battlefield has all this time been visible on the near horizon, or rather its colossal spire, if you can call it a spire, has been visible. Rising 150 feet into the air above the highest plateau around, it draws all tourists forward ultimately, even those like me who know what it signifies and might have hoped to avoid getting any closer. This is the Ossuary, the supreme monument to the war, the monument that ought to have ended all other monuments, though of course it didn't. It was built on the Thiaumont crest close beside another of the battlefield's ruined forts between 1920 and 1932 out of white stone in a style of architecture that might best be described as twentieth-century blockhouse. In front stretches a vast lawn out of which in even rows sprout 15,000 crosses. These represent those soldiers who, when harvested, were still recognizable. They were, one might say, only slightly killed.

Inside the Ossuary itself have been collected the remains of the men who were more thoroughly destroyed, separated into individual crypts according to the sectors in which their bones were found. One can criticize the Ossuary as grisly, though that is not my intention here — what else was the nation supposed to do with all these human remains except pile them together and then try to devise a suitable tombstone? The Ossuary is really a church, a kind of militaristic cathedral. There is a chapel whose stained-glass windows glow not with biblical symbols but with images of war, with soldiers instead of saints. Nearly every foot of every pillar, every wall, has been engraved with dead soldiers' names, units, and dates, and vigil candles burn. It is all very beautiful in its way, and of course, unless you have a heart and mind of stone, incredibly moving.

The Ossuary is unheated. It is icy cold in here.

We go outside where it is not much warmer but where at least there seems air to breathe. On the road between the cemetery and the Ossuary five or six cross-country skiers pole their way along. They're wearing bright parkas, one red, another yellow, and they are laughing.

Around behind the Ossuary on the parking lot side there are windows in the exterior wall of each of the crypts. They are small windows, and so low down that you have to crouch to peer through. I don't know why they were put here. Perhaps they shouldn't have been, for what do they satisfy except the prurient curiosity of people like me? Behind those windows are the piles of bones that each crypt contains: tibias, vertebrae, thousands upon thousands of ribs — I had not realized until now how much ribs dominate the human skeleton — and of course skulls. There is a hole the size of a silver dollar in one skull. It is above and slightly behind where the right ear would have been. Was some young man wearing that skull at the time, or did the hole happen afterwards?

Does it matter?

Turning to P., I remark that of course the Holocaust, the murder of 6 million European Jews, must never be forgotten, but the so-called Great War must never be forgotten either. Then I add hopefully, "And it won't be. This place will keep it alive." "Won't be forgotten?" she snorts. "It was forgotten almost immediately. We had another war barely twenty years later, did we not?"

Above my head a bell starts to toll. The bell up there weighs over 5,000 pounds. You can climb the 204 steps and look at it, if you choose to. There's a small museum and a projection room as well. At night there is a beacon whose beam sweeps out over the different battlefields.

The spire itself is not like other church spires. It was built in the form of a bullet, or in the form of one of the shells that so devastated all those men, all this terrain. And it does resemble a bullet or shell, if that is the way your mind is fixed. It also resembles an upthrust phallus, and I wonder if no one ever thought so at the time that it was conceived, designed, built. To me it seems to celebrate the virility of France, its ability to procreate, as well as to fight and die, to celebrate and deplore war at one and the same time.

The bell above is still tolling. Anyplace else I would stop and listen, not here. We get back into the car. I can't get away from this place fast enough.

We return to the café in Bras and sit in our overcoats and order lunch. We have taken the same table as this morning. There are farmers drinking red wine at the bar, and the woman comes out from behind it and hands over the bill of fare. This is not the sort of place you find listed in the Michelin guide. There is a sink in the corner. Above it, attached to a rod, is a bar of soap shaped like a small football. A towel hangs down off a hook. The toilet, we are told, is outside in the shed; we decide to forgo that.

Our first course is a plate of raw country ham and a basket of crusty bread. It is good ham and there is more of it than either of us can eat. The second course is steak with fried potatoes. French dinner plates are bigger than American ones, and the steak on this one hangs over the edges. It is splendid. The other half of the plate overflows with equally delicious fried potatoes. The woman comes out and stands over us and asks how we like the steaks. They were grilled over an open fire and there are herbs stuck to them. She is proud of them. After our plates are removed she brings wedges of Camembert, then dessert. The coffee is very good. The bill comes to 153,70 francs — about $22.

The river Meuse slices through the center of Verdun, running from south to north, and all the battlefields we have visited so far are on the right or east bank of the river, where the German push started, and even though they took the Bois des Caures and Fort Douaumont and much else, French resistance was so stubborn, French counterattacks so relentless and so spendthrift, that the Germans decided the left bank might be easier after all, and they tried it, starting about thirteen kilometers northwest of the city where there runs a series of gentle, low hills — *mamelles,* the French troops called them. The female breast is a *mamelle,* and in contour these resemble the breasts of a young girl lying down. They are wooded now but were cultivated over most of their surface at the time, and the French trench lines were at the top. The hill closest to Verdun was known as Le Mort Homme, which means the dead man — this was its name long before the war. The adjacent hill to the west had no name so the generals gave it one: Hill 304.

The gently sloping Le Mort Homme was by military standards a commanding elevation, but on it there were no ravines, trees, or natural defenses of any kind, just belts of barbed wire many feet thick lying out on the dirt in front of trenches open to the sky. The Germans brought forward seventeen trainloads of artillery ammunition and expended them all. French guns fired back just as fast. On March 6, 1916, in a blinding snowstorm the German troops in their long gray overcoats finally attacked, running up the tortured north slopes of Le Mort Homme towards whatever Frenchmen were left alive at the summit. French guns emplaced on Hill 304 cut them to pieces.

Day after day the German troops attacked and were mowed down. Day after day the French troops crouched under ferocious bombardments. Neither side attempted to improvise any new scenario. Before March ended — that is, in three and a half weeks — the Germans had lost 81,607 men on Le Mort Homme, the French 89,000. The Germans then decided to attack Hill 304 instead. The same thing happened there, although the numbers were smaller. The French lost only 10,000 men, hardly worth talking about.

We have driven north out of Verdun on Route D38 passing through Thierville, Marre, and Chattancourt, from where a dirt road leads up towards the summit of Le Mort Homme. To either side are cultivated fields that are smoothly white under the snow. All these fields were fought over — which means they were cleared after the war, what a job. Even farmers who didn't manage to blow themselves up must have had a hard time of it. Either their plows were ruined on chunks of steel just under the surface or else they kept disinterring corpses or pieces of corpses which, once partially revealed, had to be dug up completely and carried to the side of the road.

Soon the cultivated fields fall away and we are in a pine forest. The road is smooth and white as it climbs, but in the forest is rumpled ground that is worse even than over on the other bank. There are trench lines, and blasted trench lines. There are shell holes that are partially filled in, and there are some still enormous craters, and out of all of this ground grow trees, all growing at different levels. The government forestry men planted them right on top of the mess. Why should these pounded forests have such an effect on me? Perhaps it's because a forest is a living thing and it can't recover from that war. These are like still-open wounds. Broken bones that never healed properly. The forest is crippled. Whatever Col. Rodier says, it is difficult to believe these holes will ever close now.

At the summit we come out into a clearing, and there is a monument. It's a standing skeleton carrying a furled flag in one hand, its other fist upthrust. Very heroic. But to me it looks like a soldier who has just been hit and throws up both arms before he falls. In the course of the battle Gen. Pétain, the French commander, exhorted his troops with the message, "Courage. They shall not pass."

The inscription at the base of the monument reads: "They did not pass."

Well, actually they did. At the end of three months the Germans had the whole hill, though they paid a terrible price for it. After that the French counterattacked and got it back. The same battle was fought a second time in the opposite direction, which of course more than doubled the total bill.

Le Mort Homme rises only a few hundred feet higher than Verdun itself. But since its slopes are for the most part so gentle, it is enormously broad. Its summit must measure a mile and a half in diameter. It is difficult, when reading about the battle of Verdun, to imagine how so many men could have been killed on this single hill. But stand on its summit, drive up and down several of the alleys that loggers have cut, and such carnage becomes easier to comprehend. The distances become, relatively speaking, vast. The summit of the hill is vast. Because of smoke from the explosions, because of folds in the ground, each part of the hill was isolated from each of the others. By all accounts the trench lines on both sides were packed solid with men, there was no other cover, and the shells kept threshing the ground, threshing the men — who, of course, were not only replaceable but immediately replaced. The generals of that war thought nothing of moving platoons, companies, even whole battalions up into the line in the midst of a bombardment, knowing very well that only a few men would get through, but so what, a few was better than none. A Capt. Augustin Cochin wrote to his mother about crouching under a ninety-six-hour bombardment: "The last two days soaked in icy mud without any shelter other than the narrowness of the trench which even seemed to be too wide. Not a hole, not a dugout, nothing, nothing. The result: I arrived there with 175 men. I returned with 34, several half mad." His shattered trench, he said, was "inundated with the blood of the wounded, who came to take refuge close to me, as if I could do anything." An aviator — that's what they were called in those days — described looking down from his flimsy pursuit ship at villages that had become gray smears, at the wide swath of brown where nothing grew, where nothing seemingly could live, where man had "murdered nature." He described "monster projectiles" that hurtled past his plane, leaving it rocking violently in their wake — projectiles that then fell on the men below.

As we drive west towards Vauquois, another particularly ghastly place with a message and relics all its own, we pass many cemeteries, and signs where lanes lead to others. There are forty-three French military cemeteries in this area and twenty-nine German ones. (There are two American cemeteries too, and I shall speak about them presently.) In the French cemeteries lie 80,726 identified bodies, and in the German ones 54,845 bodies. Add the approximately 130,000 men whose bones lie in the Ossuary, and you arrive at a total equal to about one-third of the men killed in the battle of Verdun. So where are the other bodies?

You guessed it.

Wherever there are villages there are monuments — the design and building of monuments must have been the number-one industry in these parts after the war. Some are quite beautiful, one or two are shocking, and all are moving.

Here and there we pass statues of the Virgin that stand as war memorials as well: Our Lady of Resignation, Our Lady of Silence. At Malancourt the figure on the war memorial is a woman in a long stone dress. She wears a French soldier's helmet and stands with her hands crossed on the hilt of a stone sword whose point touches the ground.

Farther on is a monument honoring the French 69th Regiment, 1,800 men, 80 of whom survived the battle on this spot. An official communiqué is reprinted on the plaque. It says that the men had only shovels and pickaxes, their rifles, bayonets, and machine guns having been destroyed in the bombardment, but their "superb behavior limited the progress of the enemy." It mentions the name of the commander, a Maj. Navel, and cites him for having got his troops to do this. Well, their standards were different in those days. Navel was perhaps a hero, or perhaps he was a lunatic who should have pulled back but instead sent his disarmed men in to be slaughtered. I don't know, and perhaps too many years have gone by to speculate, but I have the impression that if Maj. Navel had commanded this same group in, say, Vietnam, they would not have obeyed his command to grab their shovels and pickaxes and attack. Instead they might have fragged him — that's a word that came into existence in Vietnam. They might have rolled a grenade into his tent. A good many unpopular officers in Vietnam got fragged for less. In some ways the world's perceptions and deportment have changed 180 degrees in the last seventy-one years, and of course in other ways they have not changed at all.

We drive on. There is no sun and the temperature outside is just below freezing. There's not a soul on all these gloomy roads — nothing coming the other way, and when we stop nothing passes us. It's as if nobody's alive around here. Even the villages we drive through seem empty.

At Montfaucon the monument is American — an enormously high column has been established amid the ruins of the village that once existed here. The Americans were late getting to this part of the world but paid heavily once they did. There is a new Montfaucon a few hundred yards away that is of little interest. The old one is a place of ruined walls, freestanding fireplaces and chimneys, a ruined church. The inevitable plaque gives the history of the village from A.D. 587, when it was founded, until the day, only six weeks into the war, when the Germans captured it, chased out its 900 inhabitants, and burned the place down. In the ruins they built seventeen blockhouses in all, one of which is now known as the blockhouse of the Crown Prince. A sign with an arrow shows the way there, but this tourist is not tempted. How could a blockhouse compare to these ruins in which generations of French families once lived?

For four years after the Germans captured Montfaucon the French shelled it, which resulted only in the complete destruction of the village. It is one thing for invaders to shell the enemy's houses. But what was it like for French soldiers to shell French houses? The Germans were still here when the Americans showed up on Sept. 26 and 27, 1918, and drove them out. "To commemorate the more than 100,000 U.S. soldiers who died or were wounded in the battlefields in this area," I read, "the United States has erected this column as a testimonial." You can go inside the monument, where there is a museum, but I have seen enough of these museums; and you can climb to the top of the tower and look out over the countryside if you wish, but by now I know very well what the country looks like. This monument celebrates the American push through the Argonne forest and there is another that is at least equally impressive and to my mind more beautiful not far away at Montlec in the St. Mihiel Salient, which commemorates the American push there. That one is round, a sort of white marble Greek temple on top of an imposing flight of stairs on top of a high steep hill. There is no roof. The temple is open to the stars and to the snows. As with most of these monuments, the American like the French, the numbers of the combat units are incised into the stone, together with the name of the architect, but not a single name of a single dead soldier. That is, the soldiers remain as nameless in death, as far as these monuments are concerned, as they were in life. Generals — all the generals, including the American ones — simply sent them forward by the numbers to be massacred. The American offensives were frontal assaults just like the French and British and German ones of the previous four years, and in not much more than eight weeks of fighting, the last eight weeks of the war, the Americans managed to get 126,000 boys killed. Chicken feed compared to the French, German, and British losses, of course, but not bad. The American frontal assaults succeeded where the others had failed because the troops were big and strong and new, they vastly outnumbered the depleted German divisions on their fronts, and they believed to the fullest extent imaginable all of the old notions of honor and heroism and glory that the older armies had learned by now to live without.

A bit further on from Montfaucon is the principal American cemetery of this region, 14,246 graves. The crosses are white marble, the rows perfectly aligned. I have read someplace that the crosses were embedded in concrete ties and the ties buried so that the rows would remain perfectly aligned forever.

Here is the grave of Pfc. George Harssel, 111th Machine-gun Battalion. He was from New Jersey and won the Distinguished Service Cross. He was killed Oct. 12, 1918. A bit further on lies Pvt. Jacob Walart, 319th Infantry, from Massachusetts, Nov. 2, 1918. He almost made it. Pvt. Adolph Simonsen, 128th Infantry, was from Pennsylvania: Nov. 10, 1918. The war ended the next day. If he had kept his head down just a few more hours . . . The date on a cross in the next row is Nov. 11. I find I don't have the boy's name in my notebook. Perhaps my eyes misted over and I was unable to read it. The war ended at the eleventh hour of the eleventh day of the eleventh month in the fifth year of the war. There would have been only four hours of daylight for the boy to be killed in. Why? How? Was he just unlucky? Was he perhaps determined, as the winds of war died away, to become a hero in the final seconds, even if it killed him? Perhaps he was shot much earlier, and dying on the final day of the war was a mere coincidence.

Do I feel something special here merely because these boys were American? But I have been feeling these same emotions more and more strongly each day even though, until now, all of the victims at every site were German or French. The cemeteries of the three nationalities are all so different. All the crosses are perfectly aligned everywhere, of course. The German crosses are black, the American crosses are white marble, and the French crosses, which are also white, are narrower in design and bear brass plates on which is incised the name and unit of the fallen hero. The British cemeteries in the north are different again; they're usually much smaller, and they exist in incredible profusion. Whatever the nationality of these cemeteries, in their perfect rows they are unbelievably orderly, unbelievably neat; they make order out of chaos after the chaos is over, peace out of war, a very human need, I guess, I don't know why.

On to Vauquois. This is really very strange country. Basically it is a flat plain, out of which here and there rise hills. Some of them are vast, smooth hills like Le Mort Homme, and others are buttes, steep, abrupt hills ending on top in a plateau. A snowy track leads up to the summit of the butte of Vauquois; but it is narrow and steep, and if the car starts to skid I see no possibility of even turning around. So I park and climb to the top via a succession of staircases put there for tourists. No staircases existed for French assault troops so long ago. According to a plaque on a tree the butte is 295 meters high — that's almost 1,000 feet. "Climbing these staircases will give visitors some idea of the difficulty French troops had when they stormed the summit," the plaque says. There are other plaques too. "*Messieurs les touristes*" are forbidden to pick up "vestiges or engines of war." "It is forbidden and dangerous to leave the delineated paths or to penetrate the underground galleries."

On the summit is a white stone monument: a French soldier standing in front of a ruined tree stump is about to heave a grenade. It is a pretty monument, and behind it is a pole from which the French flag blows in the breeze.

The view up here commands the countryside all around. This butte is totally isolated, a freak of nature sticking up out of the plain. Far off is a railroad line that could not be used for as long as German guns were planted here.

When they first took Vauquois they installed concrete dugouts in the walls overlooking the plain, they fortified the summit as well, and the French, trying to come to grips with the problem, at first merely shelled this summit, shelled the perched village which had stood here since medieval times or before. The shelling accomplished nothing except to destroy this village too, so it was decided to dig mine galleries straight into the base of the butte, and load them with explosives, and blow the top off it — blow everything on the summit to smithereens. This was done, and the resulting craters are still here, and I peer down into them. These are the biggest man-made craters I've ever seen. They are ferocious craters, at least four separate ones, one of which must be fifty yards in diameter and almost that deep. There's a sign on the shoulder between two of them: "Here stood the Church of Vauquois before 1914." The sign points out into empty space. The church is gone, and the fifty or sixty feet of earth underneath it as well. I find these craters astonishing. That must have been a hell of a noise at the time. And since then, seventy years of silence.

The first mine to go off was not dug deeply enough into the hill. Tons of earth and stone rose into the air, and much of it came down on the forward French trenches, killing and wounding thirty men. Two others failed to go off at all. The French attacked anyway while a military band in full view played the "Marseillaise." German guns decimated the attacking troops, and after that the band.

More mines were dug. The French kept attacking. Units or parts of units got all the way to the summit, where they could not be supplied and where German guns hidden in the ruins of the village destroyed them. The battle for the butte of Vauquois lasted five months. From time to time the Germans were forced off the summit or forced far back to the edge, at which time they dug their own mines under the French troops and blew up everybody. The fighting here and the grotesque losses that went with it continued off and on until late September 1918, when the Americans finally cleared the Germans out for good.

There are still barbed-wire entanglements all over the summit, except where there are craters. Some of them are wrapped around the steel sawhorses the French called *chevaux de frise* — the first I have seen since I owned tiny replicas of them, together with World War I lead soldiers, when I was a little boy.

Verdun's best hotel is the Coq Hardi. It was its best hotel before 1914 too, and high-ranking officers always stayed there whenever they came to inspect the "impregnable" Verdun fortifications. Then the war started and almost at once the German troops were less than ten miles away. There they stopped, and for the next seventeen months this was a quiet sector, and most of Verdun's prewar population of 14,000 remained in place.

But as their 1916 offensive started, the Germans moved up big guns and began to pound the town. The civilian population dropped quickly to 3,000, and soon after that to almost nothing at all. There were 2,736 houses in Verdun before the war, only one of which survived the shelling intact. Only about 100, supposedly, were sufficiently sound afterwards to be repaired.

The Coq Hardi today is essentially the same building it was then, four stories high, forty-three rooms. Its corridors are full of wonderful old paintings and polished antique furniture. In the lobby there is a great old fireplace in which a log fire has burned every night of our stay. Old brass cooking implements hang from the walls, one of them an enormous copper caldron full of flowers. There are flowers in our room every day as well, and a big firm bed, and each morning when I peer out the second-floor window the cars in the street below are covered with fresh snow.

The first night here we sat up in bed reading and were cold. My nose was cold. Even my fingers were cold, and I finally got

up and patted the radiators and only then realized that someone
had turned them off. In old France, even in rather elegant hotels
like this one, that is what happens. Chambermaids are sent up
behind you as soon as you go out each day to turn off the heat.
There are *minuteries* on all the hall corridors too. You push the
button for light, and you have about thirty seconds to get your
key in the door and get inside before the light automatically goes
off, throwing the corridor and you into absolute darkness.

Tonight, having returned from Vauquois, we dine in the hotel
restaurant, which rates one star in the Michelin guide, a quite high
rating for a provincial town such as this one. The restaurant is
handsome: beamed ceiling, thick linen tablecloths, heavy silverware, fine crystal glasses.

It is a leisurely, elegant, and at times exquisite dinner; but
part of the reason we enjoy it so much, or so I imagine, is because
we have been confronting horror, or rather the remnants of horror,
all day, and in fact for several days running.

Afterwards I sit in front of the fire with Patrick Leloup, who
is not only the proprietor of the hotel but also the director of the
Verdun tourist office. The town's population today is about
24,000, and according to Mr. Leloup it draws about 400,000 tourists per year. But this number, like the attendance at the memorial
in Fleury, has begun to diminish, and it is Leloup's opinion that
Verdun must change its image if it is to continue to attract visitors.
The young people of today, he says, are no longer interested in
that war. For them it is too long ago. They don't want to hear
about the suffering of the soldiers.

If this is true, he argues, then the battlefields must be sold to
them as history, and by this I understand him to mean ancient
history, an intellectual exercise rather than an emotional one. One
of the problems, as far as the young are concerned, is that the
battle of Verdun no longer offers any villains. To past generations
the battlefields were proof of the barbarism and hatefulness of
Germans and Germany. But the Germans are now France's closest
friends and allies, as every schoolchild knows. Therefore the emotional impact of the battlefields is much reduced, if not removed
entirely. The soldiers are no longer seen as hated aggressor and
heroic defender, but as victims one and all, and even in a deeper

sense as brothers in adversity. One of the latest and most popular of the posters/postcards on sale here shows a German soldier and a French soldier standing in a military cemetery embracing. In front of them is a cross with a loop of barbed wire hung over it, and the cross bears the legend "Verdun."

And in addition, Mr. Leloup goes on to say, Verdun has much more to offer the tourist than battlefields, and he presses into my hands the newest of the publicity folders and brochures that his office is putting out, urging me to take a look at them when I have time.

In our room I unfold them. First of all Leloup's office is sponsoring a "Verdun smile" campaign: "Traditional, rural, sporting, avant-garde, Verdun will weave the web for your most beautiful memories," I read. Verdun is young and sportive, the brochures tell me, Verdun offers the unexpected. How about a motorboat cruise on the Meuse? How about hiking in the forests? Or fishing in the streams?

In these brochures the city itself is made to seem special. It is "famous," for instance, for its sugared almonds and also for its circus school, the only one in France. And the town itself should wow any tourist, it is written, for there are a number of remnants of medieval walls and gates and a handsome cloister attached to the cathedral. And don't forget the Princerie Museum with its ceramics, its old paintings and furniture, its carved wooden statues dating from many centuries ago; or the bishop's palace, which was built in the middle of the eighteenth century; or the seventeenth-century town hall.

Well, okay. The town tourist officials can go in that direction if they like, but I don't know if they will have success, for even within the city itself the principal tourist attraction is none of the above. It is not the cathedral of Notre Dame either, although part of it dates from 1048. The cathedral has been so mauled over the centuries by incompetent bishops, and their untalented architects — and also for a time by German artillery — that it bears today no resemblance to any architectural style and seems to me without distinction.

No, the town's principal attraction is not dedicated to the god of saintliness or to the god of art at all, but rather almost inevitably to the god of war. I am speaking now of the Citadel, down the street from the hotel.

The Citadel is still another massive, mostly underground fort. Begun in 1567, its construction continued off and on until 1893, by which time there were four or seven or fifteen kilometers (I've seen all three figures printed) of underground galleries fifteen meters beneath it. In these galleries, once the bombardment began, lived up to 25,000 people per day. At first the remnants of the civilian population cowered there, sleeping on mats in the corridors the way the street people of Calcutta live on sidewalks; and when a girl baby was born underground in the midst of a bombardment they named her France. For a time the municipal government functioned down there, and shopkeepers set up their stands and sold what goods they had. But mostly the hordes who populated the galleries were troops, not only battalions or even regiments moving to and from the front, but also the headquarter's staff, the hospital personnel, and inevitably the burial squads, for the wounded were brought into the Citadel, where, given the rudimentary facilities available, many of them, even most of them, died.

You can take a guided tour — it comes with a Sound and Light show — of the Citadel today. A ticket costs 14 francs, and the "guide" turns out to be a series of loudspeakers high up in the corners of the successive rooms and corridors. As the description of each room is completed, its particular loudspeaker falls silent, and all the lights go out in the one room and come on in the next and we — by this time we are part of a small group of tourists — move forward behind it.

Some of the galleries are outfitted like barracks, with rows and rows of steel double-decker, double-width bunks. Troops slept side by side, four to a bunk, on board mattresses, apparently, and they slept not only in their clothes but wearing their greatcoats as well because there were no blankets. We pass small wooden cabins, almost like changing cabins on a public beach, where officers and important civilians lived, and then come the kitchens that fed all these people. Water was pumped up from the Meuse, which is only a few yards away and which also furnished the water power that generated the electricity. Giant fans twice a day tried to clear out the fetid air. There were no bathing facilities, the crude toilets were overwhelmed, and since there were always a great many corpses on hand that could not always be promptly removed, the stench in here, so the loudspeaker tells us, was often overpowering. I'll bet it was. The loudspeaker directs our attention to copper fixtures on the walls of the corridors in which incense burned night and day in an effort to improve the almost unbreathable air.

We move past cases displaying the usual uniforms and weapons, into other rooms which are virtual wax museums. Famous generals, famous politicians, stand around handing out medals to famous heroes while the loudspeakers above our heads give forth their speeches. In 1920 coffins of eight unknown soldiers were laid out down here in rows so that one among them could be selected for burial beneath the Arc de Triomphe in Paris. Life-size wax figures reenact this scene too, the coffins are there, and the loudspeaker harangues us. One thinks of the original coffins and wonders what was in them. The politicians and generals made a terrific ceremony out of choosing among the eight, and they made another in Paris when they planted the selectee. It was as if they were trying to invent ceremonies grandiose enough to match what had produced the coffins in the first place.

But presently we are out in the street again, walking back to the hotel along sidewalks that in places are only eighteen inches wide. The Citadel has put me in a bad mood. Compared to the terrain we have been looking at, this museum — any museum — is a joke. The terrain is the true monument to the battle of Verdun. The terrain is somehow alive, you can somehow still hear the men screaming. In a museum, because of the Sound and Light show and the other tourists, you can't hear anything. At least I can't. Verdun calls itself the "*Haut Lieu De L'humanité.*" I don't know why. What was done here or, worse, what was permitted to happen here did not have much to do with humanity, it seems to me, and the more I see the relics of such monstrous acts and the more brooding I do, the less possible it is to comprehend any of it.

There were always many qualities on display in that war, but dignity was never one of them. They marched the troops for hundreds of miles. They marched them from Reims to Verdun, for instance, and once there they marched them up under the guns. The men were treated like sheep and cattle, and several times they baa-ed like sheep while being marched to the front. But on the whole they allowed themselves to be so treated. Those who reached the trenches alive stood in mud and water up to their knees, without latrines, with rotting and disintegrating corpses all around them. The generals hardly seemed to feel that they owed it to these men to preserve their lives if possible; they certainly didn't owe them any comfort whatsoever — comfort is the wrong word here. What seems most clear today is that the generals, and behind them the politicians, did not recognize the dignity of the human beings under their command. They had no respect for human dignity in itself. They thought of troops as battalions, regiments, divisions, as numbers of troops only, not as some young man, living, breathing, laughing, hoping — who gets slaughtered. The men didn't believe in their own dignity, it wasn't just the generals. Of course afterwards all the cemeteries were very beautiful, and they have been kept impeccably to our day — the men are accorded far more dignity dead than they were ever accorded alive.

The next day we leave Verdun, driving south out of the city. It is bright and sunny and the road is clear and dry, though the fields to either side are still smooth with snow. Ahead is Hattonchâtel, where we hope to find a restaurant and have lunch and behave like ordinary tourists. Hattonchâtel is a medieval perched village. It's supposed to be beautiful. It had nothing to do with the war, or so we imagine. We have had enough of war. We don't even want to talk of it any longer. However, we are still within twenty kilometers of Verdun, it is still all around us and we cannot get away from it; when we come to a crossroads, one of the signs points in the direction of Les Eparges. Ineluctably we are drawn there.

Les Eparges is another of these buttes — like Vauquois, like Montfaucon where the Americans fought, like Hattonchâtel, which we have not yet seen. In this part of the country these steep-sided hillocks pop out of the plain every so often, like a soldier sticking his head up above the level of a trench. They are all similar in height, 300 or so meters above the valley floor more or less, and the invading German army grabbed most of them immediately in 1914.

Les Eparges is more extensive than most of the others, almost a ridge. It measures about a mile from one end to the other, and it represented then, and still does, not only a steep climb but a slippery one, for the many springs high up tend to overflow down its flanks. It was in some respects before any shelling ever started a mountain of mud. The Germans fortified it. In places they built five levels of fortifications, tiers of trenches, tiers of blockhouses, five levels of fire, and no way to get past any of them. Well, the assaulting troops would just have to ignore them then. Loaded down with gear and fear, they would just have to scrabble on up the steep, slippery slopes and throw the Germans off the top. The French generals evidently had no trouble deciding that this is what their troops would have to do.

The first thing one sees upon reaching the foot of the butte is the cemetery, which certainly sets the tone. It occupies part of the gentle lower slope and is very beautiful. It's open to the road in front and entirely surrounded by a pine forest on three sides. And it is small, only 1,653 graves. All of the other Frenchmen who died up there, a minimum of 10,000 of them, disappeared into the mud without a trace.

There is a plaque near the cemetery. It says that on Feb. 17, 1915, four heavy mines exploded under the west bastion of the Les Eparges ridge. The French 106th Infantry immediately climbed up and occupied the craters. Shells exploded around them. For most of two months the two enemy lines "measured their strengths in grim hand-to-hand fighting." The decisive French assault came from April 5 to 9 under torrential rain. "Rain, blood, flesh, and bone made a heaving mass indistinguishable from the mud where the combatants floundered. Hundreds of wounded soldiers fell and the dead were lost. At the price of enormous sacrifices the survivors withstood the counterattacks of the enemy."

It is amazing that anyone should try to describe one of these battles in a paragraph.

A postscript is attached: On March 13, 1985, in memory of

the Les Eparges combatants, 270 trees were planted by school-children from the nearby village of Fresnes, and by visiting children from Belgium.

From the cemetery the road winds on up to the crest. There is fresh snow here and I drive carefully. There are trees to either side of the road, the usual pine forests that were planted afterwards because nothing else would grow, and the forest floor is pocked and pounded, the same shell holes we've seen elsewhere, and trees grow in them and on the walls of them and on the rims of them. In many places I can discern real trenches, the deepest and most defined trenches yet.

At the top I get out of the car and am stunned by what I see. First there is the view. On a clear day I suppose you could see for fifty miles in all directions, perhaps further, which is why the Germans took the hill and fortified it, though it does not entirely explain why the French were willing to pay such an enormous price to get it back. Then there are the craters. Mine craters that are stupendous in size. Below is flat, peaceful farmland, and to gaze from such peace and beauty into the grotesque craters that litter the summit can give a man a sudden emptiness in the gut.

The craters here are bigger than at Vauquois, and there are more of them. Faced with those five levels of fire and the failure of their first assaults, the French dug mines into the side of the butte and blew the summit off it, as well as whatever German soldiers were standing there, and occupied part of it, and the Germans in their turn dug mines and blew up the French. How many bodies or pieces of bodies are at the bottom of that crater there? Or this one? Or this one? There exists an aerial photo taken during the worst of the fighting; it shows sixteen mine craters. I don't count that many now. I walk along. There must be others hidden out in the new forest. I pass trench lines that extend out into the trees, well-defined trench lines that, even though they have now been collecting falling pine needles for seventy years, were and remain deeper than a man is tall.

And the monuments. Here is one to the engineers who dug the mines. I pass monument after monument. There must be fifteen on this one small hill. One is dated 1957 — people were still putting them up more than forty years later. Monuments seem to make everybody feel better. They seem to pretend that something wonderful happened on this butte, that somehow a celebration is in order. Never mind the terrain, the still-visible trenches, the shell holes, the craters — the evidence of all that killing.

The soldiers wrote letters home. They are still being found, still being published. In one of them a young Frenchman describes the explosion of a mine here on Oct. 19, 1916. He was not even a lieutenant. He was an *aspirant,* an officer-cadet. He had spent the night moving from post to post visiting his men. At dawn he got back into his dugout which was well built, revetted with timbers. He was fifteen feet into and under the earth, safe from shelling, and for a time he lay listening for any sounds that might be coming from deep underneath him. The Germans had been working on a mine. Everyone had heard them until two days ago. Since then, nothing. The Germans had given up on their mine, the boy decided, and he went to sleep. In the afternoon some muffled explosions woke him up. It sounded like firecrackers. An instant later the earth shook under him. His dugout seemed to turn upside down. The light outside disappeared. The doorway disappeared. There were several men in there with him, and they were tossed on top of each other in total darkness.

Candles were lit. In the feeble light the young officer saw — everyone saw — that they could not get out. They were buried alive, and when they tried to shove a rifle through the mud where the door had been, they realized it was obstructed by at least ten feet of earth. Furthermore, one wall of the dugout had split open, and a nearby spring had begun running in on them. The dugout was filling up with water. They began trying to dig their way out, but the former entrance had been so narrow that now only one man could dig at a time, and he had to dig lying on his stomach in the rapidly rising water.

An hour passed. Two hours. The water rose. The air got more and more rare. "I can't describe," the young man wrote, "the anguish of a man who feels his end coming, who sees it coming and realizes there is nothing he can do." Three hours passed. The candles had all gone out. The water was up over their knees. They could breathe only with great difficulty, and they had begun to get dizzy. Suddenly the man digging gave a cry. He had been able to push his rifle barrel all the way out. Some air came in. They were able to light a candle again. Thirty minutes' more digging and they crawled one by one out of their hole. They were the only survivors of their section. All their comrades had simply disappeared.

Off in the woods some iron pickets jut up that once anchored rolls of barbed wire. God knows what else is in there lying on the ground under the snow. Maybe in summer you can still find helmets amid the pine needles, broken rifles. This is a battlefield you don't hear much about, though Verdun is only twenty kilometers away. Not many tourists know about it.

I get into the car and we start back down. We didn't think there was anything left to see today, but there was this. Our education continues. On the slippery narrow road I worry about sliding into one of the craters, which would then claim one or two more victims, not to mention Hertz's car. Why did the French feel obliged to make those repeated frontal assaults at such cost? Why not besiege the place, starve it out? Why not anything, rather than what was done? We pass a young couple and a little boy walking in the road. The man is wearing red pants. The girl wears a red sweater, and the little boy walks between them holding their hands, kicking up snow. But the French saw Les Eparges and Vauquois and so much else as blots on the national honor. Honor demanded sacrifices, so the French — the generals and the troops both — consented to them. However frivolous such reasoning might sound today, it was sufficient at the time.

A mile past Les Eparges there is a scarecrow hanging in a snow-covered field. It wears a German helmet from the earliest days of the war, the kind with a spike on top.

Presently we are in Hattonchâtel, walking past the lovely old buildings, looking for a restaurant. We pass the fifteenth-century cloister, with its series of handsome Gothic arches. The church attached to it looks at least that old, and inside there is supposed to be a magnificent retable dating from 1523 and attributed to Ligier Richier. But the church door is locked tight, though it is one o'clock on a Sunday afternoon. At the end of the one street a café is open.

Afterwards we walk towards the château, but it too is locked and shuttered. The air of the village smells of wood smoke. Part of this château dates from the fifteenth century. It is as gracious and well proportioned as any we have seen. Why is it not better known? In addition it stands on the highest part of the crest, making for a commanding view of all the country below. According to a plaque outside, it was restored by Miss Belle Skinner of Holyoke, Mass., who died in Paris in 1928. The Germans held this butte too, it seems. Though it was strategically every bit as important as Vauquois or Les Eparges, the French made no frontal assaults, expended no 10,000 lives here. Why not, since that was evidently what they liked to do?

Instead the Germans stayed until the American offensive of 1918 drove them out. As they left they burned the château down behind them. Enter Miss Belle Skinner.

We drive on to Nancy and are out of the battle zone at last. We turn in the rented car, walk through the streets for a while, and have dinner. About nine o'clock we walk to the railroad station. The train, a sleeper, is just coming in. We have a compartment. That night I wake frequently, usually because the train is in a station and there are people moving by on the platform below my window. Each time I lie in the dark and brood about Verdun, about World War I in general. It was perhaps the saddest war in history. It killed 1.5 million French troops, 900,000 British, 1.7 million German, 126,000 American, and God knows how many of all the other nationalities, more than 10 million young men altogether. Not to mention the three or four times that many gassed or maimed who would suffer all their lives. And the 10 million women who would never marry. It caused the communist revolution in Russia, the rise of Lenin and Stalin, and after that it led to Hitler's Germany, to the massacre of 6 million Jews and World War II. It also destroyed the French army, which could not face any more Verduns and in 1940 gave up without a fight.

When I wake up in the morning the train is moving through the towns and villages along the Mediterranean coast. The houses all have orange tile rooftops, and there are green growing things in the fields because here it is already spring.

Lourdes
SANCTITY IN THE OFF-SEASON

Lourdes under the November rain is a city of wet, empty streets. For minutes at a time no car passes, nor any pedestrians either. I am on foot on the Boulevard de la Grotte, which leads from the business center to the basilicas, to the sacred grotto, to the place of the miracles; it is a row of iron shutters pulled down to sidewalk level and padlocked. Every souvenir shop, every hotel is closed. The Hotel Jésus-Marie, the Hotel Annonciation, the Pension St. Joseph, the Hotel Notre Dame Auxiliatrice, the Hotel St. François Xavier, the Pension Ste. Eva — all closed. One walks past corrugated shutters for block after block. The walls above are sightless too, wooden shutters shut smoothly tight all the way up, no windows showing. It is like walking through the streets of a ghost town. The rain continues to fall.

At the river are more hotels packed shoulder to shoulder, all closed: Hotel Madona, Hotel Notre Dame de France, Pension St. Paul, Hotel Notre Dame des Champs, Hotel Good Shepherd. Lourdes in November is a city of 18,000 people, many of them absent, and 17,000 hotel rooms, nearly all of them empty. In total hotel capacity it is the second city in France, behind only Paris. As a shrine to attract pilgrims it is most likely the second city in Christendom, behind only Rome, and in religious fervor it may be first in the world. The entire city is a shrine, or pretends to be.

During the season, that is, not now. The season is reckoned to run from Easter to October, which adds up to as much as 190 days in the years when Easter comes early. Sanctity would not seem to be, on the face of it, seasonal, but it is here.

The river is the Gave de Pau, thirty yards wide, a mountain torrent tumbling under the bridge at the end of the Boulevard de la Grotte. Lots of noise and foam. The mountains all around have come into view. Up there it is snowing, not raining. The snow line is quite low, only about 300 feet above the town.

Just across the bridge standing open are the great iron gates that give onto the holy places. Past the gates begins a vast esplanade and then, rising at the end of it, a neo-Gothic mass that is not one church but three different ones more or less piled one upon the other. There are three separate steeples sticking out on top, the middle one taller than the others. The whole is embraced by semicircular ramps leading up to the topmost level. The overall effect is not Gothic at all, but Byzantine, almost Moorish — Middle Eastern anyway, not French.

The esplanade can hold 100,000 or more people, and has. Today there are six or seven of us standing in the drizzle or plodding along under umbrellas. Ahead is the door to the lower basilica and it is open, but the natural impulse of most visitors, pilgrims or not, believers or not, is to ignore it, moving with a certain impatience around to the side. What one wants to see first is the grotto.

Nothing else matters very much compared to it, or so it seems. The grotto is where in 1858 all of this started, all of modern Lourdes, every bit of it, from the astonishing religious fervor the place can evoke to the astonishing commerce it can also evoke and that goes on side by side, commerce in candles and religious medals and plastic bottles in every size and form in which to take samples of water from the supposedly miraculous spring, including a popular model shaped like the statue of the Virgin herself — the halo, which unscrews, serves as a cork. From the hordes and hordes of pilgrims (in season), whether crippled or dying and hoping against hope for a miracle or healthy enough but burning with piety anyway and constantly glancing around so as not to miss any miracle if by God one happens, to the vast parking lots filled with

tour buses (about 1,200 per year) and the railroad yard, which is
twenty-two tracks wide so as to receive the approximately 700
special trains; from the hundreds of bars and souvenir stands named
after saints but closed six months of the year, to the policemen
sighted earlier today, traffic policemen in summer but patrolling
now in pairs as if the empty town were not only crime-ridden but
also as unsafe for cops as Harlem or Watts — but in November
what else is there to do with them apart from sending them out
in pairs or even in small bands?

On Feb. 11, 1858, Bernadette Soubirous, together with a
younger sister and another girl, was sent out along the Gave to
gather whatever firewood might have been washed ashore. Firewood was not something the Soubirous could afford to buy. Nor,
sometimes, was food. Bernadette was sickly. All eight of the Soubirous children were sickly, and four of the eight died young.
Bernadette's father was an out-of-work miller. The family lived
in one ground-floor room on the Rue des Petits Fosses. It wasn't
a room but a former jail cell called the *cachot*. There were bars on
the windows. Inside were six straw pallets on the stone floor, a
fireplace, a sink with two shelves over it, a discarded table, and
some three-legged stools.

Today this *cachot* constitutes one of the prime tourist attractions of the city. Admission is free. Tens of thousands of people
troop in and out every year. There is a second somewhat similar
attraction on the Rue Bernadette Soubirous called with some hyperbole "the family home," meaning the apartment above the mill
in which Bernadette was born. There is in this apartment a kitchen
with an open fireplace, three beds, and very little space left over.
In the past, tourists moving through were in the habit of whipping
out penknives and whittling off pieces of bed to keep as holy relics
or else just souvenirs. The effects are still visible. The beds these
days are caged by grillwork. Admission to the family home is free
too, but access is via a substantial souvenir shop owned by one
B. J. Soubirous, who bills himself in the window and on his
wrapping paper as "grandnephew of the saint." He will sell you
any imaginable pious memento on the way in or out, and he is
open year-round, unlike nearly all his competitors, who must close
for six months for lack of customers.

Bernadette and the other two girls walked along the riverbank collecting twigs. About half a mile below the town there rose beside the river a mammoth cliff that was wooded on top, for it constituted the start of a ridge that climbed southwest up into the Pyrenees. The face of the cliff was smoothly eroded gray rock, and it was higher and steeper than a house. In places it overhung the river and it shut out the light. Into it over the millennia the river had carved out a number of grottos. Although today the world speaks only of one, there were and are several, certain of them deep enough almost to be called caves.

Afterwards the river was moved some distance away and made to run between concrete banks. This created room for tens of thousands of pilgrims to crowd up close to the cliff face to pray or to gawk. But at that time the river lapped at the base of the cliff, and the three girls stepped carefully from stone to stone.

Then Bernadette Soubirous looked up, and in one of the grottos about fifteen feet up the wall she saw "a lady." The other two girls saw nothing.

This was the first of eighteen apparitions, most of them in the days immediately following, but the last not until July 16, more than four months later. Word spread quickly and crowds began to follow her out to the grotto every day. No one ever saw a thing there except her.

Some days the lady was silent, Bernadette said. But other days she begged the girl for favors — for instance, she wanted a chapel built on that spot — or else she begged her to pass on messages so theologically complex that they baffled the local priest Bernadette took them to. "I am the Immaculate Conception," for instance. What did that mean? Bernadette certainly didn't know. She was 14 years old, could neither read nor write, and did not even speak French, her native tongue being the local Pyrenees dialect. Luckily this appeared to be the lady's native tongue also, and in it they conversed. The lady addressed Bernadette as *vous*, like an equal, and at first this was what impressed the girl above all else. It was marvelous. No one in the world had ever called her *vous* before.

By Feb. 25 there had been nine apparitions. The ninth was the big one. The lady told Bernadette to kneel down and scratch at the soil. The girl did so, and before the stupefied crowd that by now dogged her every step a spring welled up that had never existed there before.

The prefect of the department was in the habit of sending monthly reports to his superiors in Paris. His report for February, dated March 4, 1858, stated that nothing significant had occurred last month. "I must nonetheless inform you of something that has caused a quite lively agitation in Lourdes and its environs. A girl of 12 [sic] who seems subject to hallucinations and catalepsy pretends to be visited by the Holy Virgin at the entrance to a grotto she goes to every day." According to the prefect's report, the authorities were worried about public order, for in addition to the supposedly miraculous spring, people were throwing crutches away and stepping out of wheelchairs and claiming miraculous cures. Tumors shrank or disappeared, paralytics walked again, cancers appeared to go into remission. The grotto now attracted great numbers of people, all of them stepping from stone to stone as Bernadette had done. "Monsieur le commissaire de police de Lourdes has estimated the crowds these last few days at 4,000 at least."

The population of Lourdes in 1858 was 4,155.

The local bishop, believing none of it, sent in a team of experts. After an investigation lasting four years he was forced to conclude, he wrote, that there was no explanation for the phenomena that had occurred and were still occurring other than a supernatural one.

The lady had wanted a chapel built on that spot, according to Bernadette — on top of the cliff, apparently, which is where the nave of what is now the middle church was hewn out of solid rock in three months by twenty-five men, including Bernadette's father, working night and day. Called The Crypt, it was finished almost immediately (as these things go) and was consecrated in 1866 in the presence of 50,000 people, including Bernadette herself.

The upper basilica was ready five years later. On one wall engraved in marble is the text of the bishop's administrative decree authorizing the cult of Our Lady of Lourdes. The bishop's prose is measured, his reasoning impeccable, if a bit tentative, as if he didn't quite know what to do. Few men in history have been faced with a decision such as his. He knew very well he was creating a traffic jam, though he could not have dreamed of the ones that exist these days. About 35,000 cars enter Lourdes every day in summer, then go round and round looking for a place to park. On the sidewalks the crowds are so dense that people walk along elbow to elbow, chest to back.

Neither crypt nor upper basilica can be called a chapel. The bottom basilica, which is bigger still — it can hold 4,000 persons — was finished in 1889. A huge mosaic of the Virgin surrounded by angels fills almost the entire apse. At Easter, concerts of sacred music are held in this lower basilica to get the season off to a good start, so to speak. The area under the mosaic serves as the stage. The musicians, who are of international stature, draw big crowds, and the acoustics of the church are said to be splendid.

Even the lower basilica was far from the end of it, and new construction has rarely slowed down since: outbuildings, chapels, conference rooms and press rooms, three hospitals, the fourteen baths fed by the miraculous spring into which hundreds of hopeful or desperate people are plunged every day (in season), life-size bronze stations of the cross climbing the hillside for almost a mile, parking lots. The river was confined to its concrete trench and the bridges rearranged. In 1958 still another "basilica" was ready — the meaning of words was being rearranged too, for this basilica was entirely underground. It was 200 yards long and could hold almost 30,000 people during concelebrations, liturgical processions, and the like. Oval-shaped, it lies buried under the turf beside the esplanade. Imagine a gigantic buried almond. It is served by ramps, six of them, not doors. How else do you move 30,000 people in and out? It is a church that contains toilets. The altar is in the center. Imagine a boxing arena. There are no pillars. The ceiling, thirty-six feet above the floor, is held up by soaring rafters of reinforced concrete that meet a central spine. Imagine the veins of a gigantic concrete leaf. An engineering marvel and thrilling to behold. There are of course no windows underground, but inset in the walls of the circumference of the basilica are *gemmaux* representing the mysteries of the rosary: designs in shards of colored glass that are backlit, thus giving the illusion of windows.

The exit ramps now in November are stacked with hundreds upon hundreds of wheelchairs and gurneys, by means of which during the other part of the year the sick and the dying are moved from ceremony to ceremony. Most are hung with signs bearing the names of whoever donated them.

The underground basilica was not the end of it either, and we pass now a kiosk that houses a wooden model of a new 5,000-place church that, according to a sign there, is "desperately needed." The message on the sign is printed in several languages. The faithful are urged to contribute: "All gifts, even the smallest, will be gratefully received." Forty francs will buy one stone, it seems, 800 francs a choir seat, 2,000 francs a priestly vestment. The New Church — that's all it's called at the moment — is already partially constructed and is in plain sight on the opposite bank of the river.

Having passed the various basilicas, we have come at last to the grottos. There is an altar in the biggest one, which is at pavement level, and a life-size statue of the Virgin occupies the one up in the cliff face where Bernadette once saw the lady. In front of it about a dozen people are standing or kneeling, some apparently praying, others only peering up at the statue. In a third grotto old crutches, some of them very old, hang from a cable. Presumably they were discarded by people who no longer needed them, or thought they didn't. In any case they left them behind.

To one side stand a number of small, roofed iron trolleys that are ablaze with candles. Masses are said here every day — in season for an audience of thousands. The priests at their altar and the Virgin in her niche and the candles in their trolleys are protected from the elements by the overhanging cliff, but the faithful are not, and many of them will be lying out on gurneys and stretchers unable to move. It rains a lot here, about 150 days a year, and when it does such people can do little except lick the rain off their lips and hope that something marvelous might happen. About 4.5 million people come to Lourdes to this grotto each year — and although we are living it seems in an irreligious age, the figure keeps rising. Of course the vast majority are ambulatory, but about 70,000 each year are wheeled in by family or attendants.

The spring that Bernadette scratched from the soil is not visible. Instead its water has been funneled to the left of the grottos into a row of brass fountains and faucets in the wall, at which people drink or fill their plastic bottles or both, and also to the bathhouses on the right. The bathhouses contain a number of tubs, and there are attendants on duty to help people in and out who are too ill or crippled to manage by themselves.

The fountains and the baths are free. All else must be paid for. A short distance away stands a kiosk for masses. To have a mass said one pushes across money or, if there is no one on duty, through a slot. The price, 65 francs or the equivalent, is announced by signs in sixteen languages, as is information to the effect that there is no need to leave one's name or the name of the loved one for whom the mass is to be said, just the money. God will know the names without being told. "Masses are said for the intention you have in mind," reads the sign. The candles on sale in racks next to the grottos are all at least two feet long and the smallest in diameter is the size of a quarter. It costs 10 francs. The really big ones are on sale in the shop near the drinking fountains, along with other mementos: 600 francs for a candle weighing twenty-four kilos, 1,650 francs (about $300 at this year's rate of exchange) for the seventy-kilo monster. One goes up to one of the iron trolleys, fits the candle in among the others, and lights it.

Today, although many candles are burning, there is nonetheless plenty of room for new ones. In season this is often not the case, but more signs in many languages advise the faithful to leave their offerings anyway. An attendant will light their candle for them as soon as there is space for it, and their prayer, of which the candle is the symbol, will mount to heaven. This may of course take weeks, and some of the candles burning now were no doubt paid for last summer, for attendants are carrying them out in armloads and lighting them in bunches of about fifty.

P. lights a candle and we leave the grotto.

Only two of Lourdes's 420 hotels are rated by the government in the four-star category, and there are no first-class restaurants at all. The people who come here do not come for that and do not seem to care. Besides which, since most of the hotels and many of the restaurants are closed for six months at a time, owners find it almost impossible to keep first-class personnel from year to year. There is a terrible unemployment problem here in the off-season. Workers and even shopkeepers must go miles away to find jobs. In season they cater to persons who are often poor, and although almost all nationalities are represented, pilgrims from Italy and Spain account for about 60 percent of the foreign visitors. Of course, there are many French too, a proportion of whom are merely driving through, merely curious. Whereas the foreigners have all come a long way. It has cost them sometimes their life savings. They are not looking for elegance and could not pay for it if they were. They are here because they believe.

Bernadette's tomb is not at Lourdes. After the apparitions she was taken in by an order of nuns and after eight years of schooling entered their convent at Nevers in the center of France, where she took the veil. She was 22. She suffered from asthma and tuberculosis for most of the rest of her short life, while behind her Lourdes grew and grew as a site of pilgrimages, and she died sitting up in a chair at 35. Dead, the nuns kept her. They did not send her back.

For thirty years she lay sealed in a lead coffin that was venerated in their chapel. Then as her canonization loomed she was exhumed in the presence of sworn witnesses for the ceremony known as the Identification of the Body. The mayor and deputy mayor were there, together with assorted doctors, ecclesiastics, and nuns, plus the necessary carpenters and stonemasons, two of each.

When the coffin was cut open there was not the slightest odor of putrefaction, the witnesses swore, and Bernadette's body was perfectly preserved even though her habit was damp and the rosary was rusting in her fingers. The doctors' report stopped short of calling this a miracle. It contained many details such as: "The stomach had caved in and was taut like the rest of the body. It sounded like cardboard when struck."

The nuns washed the body, re-dressed it, and it was resealed in its coffin. In the few hours exposed to air it had begun to turn black.

Ten more years passed. In 1919 Bernadette was exhumed again for the second Identification of the Body. Similar audience, same sworn oaths. Again there was no odor. The body was practically mummified, according to the doctors' report, though covered with patches of mildew: "The skin has disappeared in some places . . . some of the veins are still visible." Again the coffin was resealed and reburied. Six years after that, in 1925, came the third Identification of the Body. Bernadette had been dead forty-six years and two days.

The audience this time was more numerous than ever: the nuns from the community, the bishop, the vicar general, the police commissioner, and many others. There was still no odor of putrefaction. The surgeons cut out pieces of Bernadette's ribs, part of her diaphragm and liver, fragments of muscles from the outer thighs, and both kneecaps, as instructed, to serve as relics. One of the surgeons wrote that he was amazed at the condition of the liver, an organ basically soft and inclined to crumble. When he cut into it, it was almost normal in consistency, which did not seem to him a natural phenomenon. The face was now tinged with black and the sunken eyes and nose were no longer pleasant to look at.

Wax impressions were taken of the face and hands and given to a sculptor together with photos of Bernadette alive, and he was asked to make masks of what she had once looked like and of her clasped hands. Some weeks later the masks were ready, as was a glass coffin ordered from a firm in Lyon. The nuns dressed Bernadette in a new habit, the light wax masks were placed over her face and hands, she was sealed into her new glass shrine, and she went on permanent public display.

In Nevers, not Lourdes. Some visitors to Lourdes are disappointed to learn this, but if the glass-encased mummy of an authentic Catholic saint is what they have come here to see, there is another one close by. It is not advertised, or poorly advertised. Hardly anyone realizes it is there. This is at Betharram, ten miles west. The corpse is that of St. Michel Garicoits (1797–1863), a Basque priest who was known far and wide during his lifetime, as was Betharram. He was the holiest man around, meaning that church authorities liked to consult him whenever saintly matters seemed complicated or tricky — the case of Bernadette, for instance, for his life overlapped hers slightly. When she began having

these apparitions, the bishop and his men went straight to him.
The church and sanctuary at Betharram had been receiving
pilgrims since the Middle Ages. For a time Betharram was perhaps
the most famous pilgrimage site in France. It was known as the
place of miracles. The archbishop of Paris attested to twenty-two
of them between 1620 and 1642. The blind, the paralyzed, the
cancerous, all were delivered from their ailments by celestial intervention. Over the centuries the church and sanctuary had been
dedicated to Notre Dame of the Star, or Notre Dame of Calvary,
or finally Notre Dame of Betharram, but the Huguenots burned
the place down in 1569. It was built up once more only to be
destroyed a second time in 1793 during the Revolution.

Enter St. Michel Garicoits, who rebuilt it still again beginning
about 1840, hiring the best artists and artisans he could find. He
also established a seminary, an orphanage, a hospital, a school.
He fed 300 persons a day. He begged what he could and borrowed
the rest. He founded the missionary congregation of the Priests
of the Sacred Heart, who today work in fourteen countries, and
he bore the cost of feeding them, training them, and sending them
out. The pilgrims kept coming to Betharram in ever-greater numbers, and because of their generosity he was able to support these
enormous expenditures.

Then Lourdes happened.

The bishop of the diocese that included Lourdes sent Bernadette to see Father Garicoits. He turned out to be the only person
who believed in her apparitions absolutely from the very beginning. He made several pilgrimages to Lourdes himself, and he
began to accept donations for Lourdes and to send the money on.
There were people around him who objected strenuously to all
this. They said that Lourdes would be the death of Betharram,
and of course they were right. But the saint replied: "What does
that matter as long as the Blessed Virgin is honored."

He was canonized in 1947, Bernadette in 1933.

Colombey les Deux Eglises
A MAN'S HOUSE

Many times the President of the Republic drove out this same road to his house. He used to leave Paris by the Porte de Bercy, as we have just done, planning to follow the N19 through Provins, through Nogent sur Seine, through Troyes. The N19 was a two-lane road — it still is — and his house was 135 miles away. The drive took him between three and four hours, depending on the traffic. Of course in those days, which were not that long ago, there was rarely much traffic on the roads of France. Certainly the N19 was usually largely empty.

Today the traffic jam starts on the Périphérique, the eight-lane superhighway that is like a tourniquet around the city's throat, and it continues. The *agglomération* of Paris seems unending. The working-class suburbs on the other side of the Périphérique constitute what is often called the Red Belt — red meaning communist. They are cities in their own right, some abutting Paris, the rest abutting each other, all singularly unattractive. They are jammed with blue-collar workers and blue-collar architecture: railroad yards, housing projects, factories, office buildings, warehouses, storage tanks, gas stations. The office buildings and the blocks of low-rent flats are, by Parisian standards, skyscrapers: shoeboxes standing on end. The warehouses are the same boxes lying flat, and the storage tanks are great domed cylinders that expand and contract as if the ground under them were breathing. The forms are quite geometric and also quite unlovely. The Paris that is behind us is a nineteenth-century city: stately, calm, permanent. Then comes this: new, crowded, still in flux. These towns are like an active earthquake. The plates underneath keep moving. Most of this sprawl the President of the Republic never saw. It wasn't here yet, and the Paris he knew had not changed since Baron Haussmann designed and cut through the *grands boulevards* between 1852 and 1870.

But once these ugly suburbs have dropped behind, the whole country opens up under the wide sky. Ripening fields of grain undulate gently toward the distant horizon, and it is possible, particularly on a bright spring day such as this one, to imagine that France has not changed at all, and will never change. The villages are widely separated, each one resembling all the others: gray stone buildings, a small square dominated by a church whose belfry until quite recently was the tallest structure that anyone living could possibly imagine. These villages were there centuries before this particular president passed through, and now that he is gone they will stand there for centuries more.

All this country he crossed many times. He used to drive out to his house every Saturday afternoon and come back Sunday night, and sometimes he must have stopped in one or another of these village cafés and sat outside with his wife under an umbrella and ordered tea or an aperitif. Of course, this would have been before so many people dedicated themselves to trying to kill him. Once the "Revolutionary Tribunal" had condemned him to death he would not have been permitted to stop at all; very soon he was no longer permitted even to make the trip by car. Airplanes and helicopters were put at his disposal. This did not stop the attempts on his life. His weekends merely became much less pleasant. But he kept going out to his house. The various groups of plotters could count on it. They had only to rearrange their plans, and they did. Any plotter seeks a focus, and the great man offered very few. His life was oriented around three people, two places, and one concept — not much to get a handle on. The three people were his wife and his two surviving children — and his grandchildren, of course: he had no friends, no other intimates. The two places were the presidential palace in Paris, which was well guarded and presumably impregnable, and his house at the end of this very road. The one concept he cared about was France. In her name he had already been shot at many times and been hit, and he had been condemned to death once previously in absentia. He was not afraid.

His house then. But how to do it?

Riding the N19, we slice across the bottom edge of Champagne. For mile after mile the country is treeless, smooth, flat, as undramatic as Kansas, which it resembles, even to the folds in the ground. There is no way to perceive these folds from a distance or to know what the next one might contain. In Kansas in the past they sometimes hid Indian war parties or entire buffalo herds. Here in Champagne such a fold contains something much more surprising, for now we suddenly come upon a medieval walled city complete with castle, cathedral, narrow streets, and a population of 12,000 people. This is Provins, and it rears up suddenly. There is no warning. It is invisible until we are almost on top of it, the steep-roofed, octagonal keep of a superb twelfth-century castle beginning to show above the wheat fields.

Beyond it, like one of those retractable turrets that once defended Fort Douaumont, a cupola slowly rises; presently the cupola is seen to sit atop a gigantic dome, and this too keeps rising, a turret to surpass all turrets, but attached to nothing, it seems. In this agricultural landscape there is no reasonable explanation for its existence. The keep keeps growing higher. Under the octagon the castle itself is square, though with conical towers attached to each corner, and the great stone base that it sits upon is round, and the wall around it is round. It is geometrically pleasing and of splendid proportions. Meanwhile the dome has risen higher still, until at last the roof of the cathedral to which it is attached begins to appear, followed by other rooftops, and then by the ocher walls of the city.

Provins surprises me every time I see it. Did it sometimes surprise the president as well? In France you get used to walled cities on hilltops; they were put there for purposes of defense. Was Provins hidden in a fold in the ground for the same reason?

We did not plan to stop here this afternoon, but it seems

absurd not to. I drive through a gate in the ramparts. It is Sunday, and the town is full of tourists, most of them out from Paris. Provins has not been restored like new, it does not attract many foreigners, and the only language we hear in the streets is French.

All this country was ruled in feudal times by the counts of Champagne. The word *champagne* in those days signified not a drink but a world power: certain counts were capable of raising armies of up to 2,000 knights, and the province did not become French until Jeanne de Champagne married Philippe le Bel of France in 1284 and brought it to him in her dowry.

In modern times the major city is and has been Reims to the north, with its hotels and fine restaurants, its famous champagne houses open to busloads of tourists, and its cathedral, one of the half-dozen greatest in Christendom, where many of the kings of France were crowned. But in the Middle Ages the tourists, such as they were, congregated here to the south, and the money was here in the south. The court of the counts of Champagne was often here at Provins, which was one of the world's great cities, being the same size then as now, and full of wonders; and which was also, along with Troyes, one of Champagne's two principal market towns. There were two fairs a year here at Provins (as at Troyes), and at those times the city bulged with foreigners, with merchants and moneychangers, with weavers and dyers, and tavern keepers and entertainers, and with swindlers of all kinds. Flags flew from the tents that served the fair as warehouses, shops, lodgings. A police force, one of the first in Europe, had to be created to cope with the crowds.

At first the city was down at the bottom of the fold in the terrain. Gradually it grew up the western slope. The cathedral was built about halfway up beginning in 1160, and in it, according to a plaque on its wall, Joan of Arc, together with Charles VII, whom she had just crowned in Reims, heard mass on Aug. 3, 1429. There are churches all over Champagne, not to mention all over France, with similar plaques on their walls, and the cathedral at Le Puy even claims a visit from Joan of Arc's mother.

The Provins cathedral was begun before Gothic architecture had really taken hold and was continued for over 500 years by a variety of architects. This is obvious, for each of them seems to have added some feature especially pleasing to himself. There are some Romanesque features, some Gothic, some baroque, and the present massive dome with its overriding cupola was added last, after a fire in 1662 burned down whatever preceded it. It doesn't just sit atop the roof. It sits atop a stone cylinder as massive in girth as itself, like a weightlifter's smallish head atop a massive neck. The effect is, to say the least, peculiar.

We sit down in a gravel courtyard overhung with linden trees and breathe the fragrance that goes with them, and a waitress serves us tea together with a *tarte tatin,* which she says is the specialty of the house; later she stands smiling beside the table to ask how we like it. Delicious, we assure her. A *tarte tatin* is not simply an apple tart. It is a layer of pastry overlaid with plump chunks of apple, the whole somehow carmelized in the baking. It is almost impossible to get a bad one in France, and this one is very fine.

As we sip our tea we talk of the President of the Republic, because there was a time when he dominated to some extent our lives. We lived in Paris then. Certainly he moved me around Europe and North Africa a good deal: to Marseilles and later to Montpellier to write about the refugees from French Algeria who streamed across the Mediterranean and who disturbed in profound ways the cities in which they collected; and to Tunisia to describe the brief brutal war he instigated there, its ruined city, its hundreds of dead upon a hillside. In addition, because of him, bombs exploded all over Paris for months, one of them on our street.

At Nogent, the next town of size, there is a choice of roads. The D442 goes off to the right. It is thinner and less traveled than the high road but rejoins it further on. Surely the great man must have come this way from time to time, if only for a change of scenery, but we take it for a more particular reason. About two kilometers further on we come to the ruins of the abbey founded by Pierre Abélard (1079–1142). It was here that Héloïse and Abélard lived, here that they were buried side by side, the final act in one of the most celebrated and most touching real-life love stories of all time. It is a place I've always wanted to stop, but never have until now. I was given Abélard to study in college, making him in a sense part of my heritage — he was part of the President of the Republic's heritage too, of course, his more than mine. In that particular course we studied the philosopher, not the man. Abélard the man was not considered important, and Héloïse was mentioned only vaguely.

Abélard was a theologian, a dialectician, a poet, a writer. He is regarded as the founder of the University of Paris. As a philosopher he was one of the founders of Scholasticism, which seeks to understand God and the universe and the relationship of man to both through the use of pure reason; although Scholasticism did not reach its fullest fruition until Thomas Aquinas came to Paris to live and write 150 years later, it has dominated Catholicism, and the interpretation of Catholic doctrine, from Abélard's time until now.

But if Abélard's name has remained alive for more than 800 years, this is because of none of the achievements just noted. He is remembered almost exclusively as Héloïse's lover — not what he would have wished, surely.

On the surface their story was a banal one. Think of him as a popular college professor; he was 39. Think of her as a college freshman, age 16. He was eloquent, domineering, and, in the intellectual world in which he moved and to which she aspired, famous. She was dazzled by him. He seduced her. She got pregnant — this was not a new story even then. She was sent to the country to have the baby so that no one would know. It was Abélard's sister who took her in. A son was born. (The sister later raised him; he became a priest.) When Héloïse saw her teacher again she flew straight into his arms. In secret they got married.

Abélard had opened his own school at the age of 23. Wherever he taught, students flocked. They were all rich, and he was well paid. But he was a contentious man and evidently an arrogant one. He was constantly involved in bitter quarrels, usually with someone much more powerful than himself. As a result he was constantly on the run, and his students had to work hard just to find him, much less fathom his thought. He was obliged to move his school from Melun to Corbeil and then to Paris. He was known as a continent man. He did not chase skirts. He was perhaps a priest — neither his own writings nor those of any of his contemporaries make this clear.

Why he had set out now to conduct a clandestine love affair with a very young girl from a powerful family is not clear either. Héloïse attracted him both by her beauty and by her "knowledge of letters," and he decided coldbloodedly to seduce her, a thing that seemed to him "very easy to be done," as he wrote later, adding, "So distinguished was my name, and I possessed such advantages of youth and comeliness, that no matter what woman I might favor with my love, I dreaded rejection of none." Apparently she was supposed to be only prey, but to his surprise he fell in love with her.

If Héloïse had a last name, it has not come down to us. She was the niece of a man named Fulbert, Canon of Notre Dame, and lived in his house. He thought her a lovely girl also, and in addition saw her as a brilliant student. He was incredibly proud of her, wanted the best for her, and he had gone so far as to hire the best possible tutor, Abélard, to give her private lessons on the side.

To Abélard this was almost too good to be true. The tutoring would go better, he told Fulbert, if he actually lived in Fulbert's house; of course he would pay a small sum in rent.

Fulbert agreed. "The man's simplicity," Abélard wrote, "was nothing short of astounding to me; I should not have been more filled with wonder if he had entrusted a tender lamb to the care of a ravenous wolf."

The lessons took place night and day. "Our speech was more of love than of the books which lay open before us: our kisses far outnumbered our reasoned words. No degree in love's progress was left untried by our passion, and if love itself could imagine any wonder as yet unknown, we discovered it. And our inexperience of such delights made us all the more ardent in our pursuit of them, so that our thirst for one another was still unquenched."

Abélard was so smitten that he began neglecting his school. The passion of the lovers was obvious to everyone, except to Fulbert, who did not find out until Héloïse's belly began to swell.

After the birth of their son, after Héloïse's return to Paris and their marriage, the lovers lived apart. Héloïse stayed at a convent outside Paris. Abélard's lodgings were secret, for he feared the wrath of Fulbert. But they continued to meet furtively.

Abélard had the misfortune to be living in the wrong century, when churchmen were all-powerful and when God could not be allowed to seem to condone sin. To inflict righteous punishment on evildoers in God's name was a holy act. Fulbert hired a gang of ruffians. A bribed servant admitted them to Abélard's sleeping chamber in the middle of the night. Some of their number pinned him to his bed. Another produced a knife or sword, tore open the writhing scholar's nightclothes, and sawed off his genitals — certainly his testicles, and perhaps his penis as well. We know all this because like many another author before and after, Abélard sought to purge himself of personal trauma, insofar as was possible, by writing about it. The girl's relatives had "cut off those parts of the body with which I had committed the acts that had offended them." Written in Latin, the work was called *Historia Calamitarum Mearum,* The Story of My Calamities. The ruffians ran out leaving Abélard in ruins in his bed. No ambulance sirens were heard. There was no sterile emergency room to take him in. The miracle is that he did not die. It all happened so fast, he wrote later, that it scarcely hurt; it was not the loss of his manhood that drove him now into a monastery, but shame. The ultimate disgrace had been visited upon him, for God abhorred the eunuch, as was written in the Bible. In an instant his fame and renown had been taken from him, and he had become, he believed, an object of derision to all.

The traitorous servant and one of the assailants (though not Fulbert) were later brought to justice. They were emasculated in turn, and their eyes were put out.

Abélard entered the monastery at St. Denis and he caused Héloïse, apparently against her will, for he describes her as "sobbing and weeping," to take the veil in the nunnery at Argenteuil where she was staying.

Abélard had always had other enemies besides Fulbert, and they were legion, for he could be an egotistical and insulting man. For instance, he used to attend the lectures of certain of the other famous teachers of the day. He would sit listening to their pronouncements with contempt, and not hide it. In his own lectures, and also in his writings, he would disparage their thought. One of his books, *Theologia,* delved into the mystery of the Trinity.

His enemies had him summoned to the Church Council at Soissons in 1121. He was ordered to bring his book with him. His eloquent defense of this book, every word and letter of which he had drawn with his own hand, was rejected. *Theologia* was condemned as heresy, a fire was prepared, and he was ordered to throw his book into the flames while his enemies looked on. He did this. The book, which must have been written on parchment and which today would be worth tens of thousands of dollars at auction, disappeared in smoke. Fortunately he had previously loaned it out to other scholars, and one or several transcriptions had been made. He would revise *Theologia* from time to time in the future, and it would keep getting him into trouble with ecclesiastical authorities.

Now as a monk at St. Denis he applied his dialectic method to the subject of the community's patron saint, proving that the original St. Denis, and the one whose intercession the other monks sought every day in their prayers, had been two different men. Since St. Denis was a royal abbey, this amounted to the crime of insulting the crown — certainly a felony at the time. But Abélard, as he was about to be brought to trial before the King, fled to Provins, where he put himself under the protection of Count Thibaud II of Champagne.

Count Thibaud gave Abélard a piece of land, and I am standing on it now, this spot here near Nogent where these ruins are left today. It was deserted at the time, which was fine with the great teacher, who believed his public life was over and who was resolved to live out his remaining days as a hermit. Out of straw and mud he built himself a chapel, but such was his fame that the students began to come, first a handful, then many, congregating around him and demanding to be instructed. His popularity with students was truly amazing. To all those other teachers who considered themselves his betters, it must have represented a bitter dose, one they had to swallow again and again.

As the years began to pass Abélard was obliged to build a bigger chapel, this time in wood and stone, and other buildings too. An abbey came into existence. The students paid for it. They also gave him money, clothing, food. This was enough to bring on attempts to shut him down by again accusing him of heresy. The argument used was an interesting one. He had named his abbey the Paraclete, after the third person of the Blessed Trinity, "because," as he wrote, "I had come as a fugitive, and in the midst of my despair I had found repose there and the consolation of divine grace."

But how could he name his abbey after only one person of the Trinity, the argument went, when as everyone knew the three persons were inseparable?

Abélard brought Héloïse from her convent to the Paraclete, and he founded an order of nuns with his former lover as abbess. Thus for a time they were together again. It seemed to him that no one could complain of their proximity one to the other. He was a eunuch who could do nothing. But he was wrong. Insinuations of carnal misconduct, in addition to the charges of heresy, abounded as well. Forced to leave, he accepted election as abbot of a monastery near the sea in remote Brittany, a wild place whose language he did not even speak. There he attempted to impose a stricter rule, quarreling so intensely with the men around him that attempts were made to assassinate him. Once he was given poisoned food. Not being hungry, he passed it to the monk next to him, who ate it and died. Another time men waited with swords, but he took another road.

He remained in Brittany about ten years. It was during this period that he and Héloïse exchanged their famous letters.

There are seven of them, four by him, three by her, but some are very long, one running to twenty-two printed pages, another to forty-eight. They have often been called love letters; they are not that exactly. Abélard's are often cold, distant. He addresses Héloïse as his "sister in Christ," quotes scriptures, propounds piety. He lays out rules for her and her nuns to follow.

Only rarely does he let his feelings show, as if the strain of denying himself to her had become unbearable: "Thou knowest that after the pact of our marriage I a certain day did come to thee privily to visit thee, and what the intemperance of my desire then wrought with thee, even in a certain part of the refectory itself, since we had no place else where we might repair. Thou knowest, I say, how shamelessly we then acted in so hallowed a place, and one consecrated to the most holy Virgin."

"Beloved," he calls her on another page, "thou knowest to

what great infamies my immoderate lust had sacrificed our bodies . . . and thee also unwilling and to the utmost of thy power resisting and dissuading me, being weaker by nature, often with threats and blows I drew to consent. For with such ardor of concupiscence I was attached to thee that those wretched and most obscene pleasures which even to name confounds us, I preferred both to God and to myself."

The letters, written by both parties in Latin, have been translated into many languages. Those by Héloïse are much less formal, much less restrained: "The voluptuous pleasures of lovers that we have tasted together were to me so sweet that I cannot feel guilty about them, nor even suppress the memory without pain. Wherever I turn, always they bring themselves before my eyes with desire for them. Not even when I am asleep do they spare me their illusions. In the very solemnities of the mass, when prayer ought to be most pure, the obscure phantoms of those delights so thoroughly captivate my wretched soul to themselves that I pay heed to their vileness rather than to my prayers. And when I ought to lament for what I have done I sigh rather for what I have had to forgo. Not only the things that we did, but the places also and the times in which we did them are so fixed with thee in my mind that in the same times and places I reenact them all with thee, nor even when I am asleep have I any rest from them. At times by the very motions of my body the thoughts of my mind are disclosed, nor can I restrain the utterance of unguarded words. O truly miserable I."

Finally Abélard went back to Paris to teach and to write, and his fame and the hordes of students he attracted seemed greater than ever. In a revised edition of *Theologia* he praised Aristotle and other pagan philosophers for arriving by use of reason at many of the fundamental aspects of Christian revelation. He wrote a number of other philosophical treatises, including *Ethica,* in which he analyzed the notion of sin: sin was not something done, but was uniquely the consent of the human mind to what it knows to be evil.

Among his pupils were youths and men destined to be famous, including the English humanist John of Salisbury and the future pope Celestine II. Abélard was as idolized as a baseball player or film star, and in the hearts and minds of his colleagues and competitors resentment smoldered anew. They not only formulated new charges of heresy against him, but some among them went to enlist the support of the most important churchman in France, the man who has come down to us as St. Bernard of Clairvaux — not the other St. Bernard, after whom the dog and the Alpine passes are named, who was a contemporary. If they could bring in Bernard on their side, then this plague who was Abélard could be got rid of for good and all.

Bernard, who was eleven years younger, worked out of the Cistercian monastery at Clairvaux that he had founded. He was so eloquent and zealous a preacher that he is credited with having launched the second crusade. Meanwhile, he was a mediator for peace among various squabbling European rulers. He was also a popemaker: he led the successful fight to seat Innocent II; and Eugene III, who succeeded Innocent, was said to make no move without his advice. Bernard never held high church office, nor wanted to, and he refused to let himself be made a bishop. He was seen as a man of immense piety, immense brilliance of mind, and some said he was the most powerful man in Europe of his time.

Under the influence of this holy man a church council at Sens in 1140 condemned Abélard and his teachings and sentenced him to silence; he was forbidden ever to teach again. The scholar, although by now old and infirm, started immediately for Rome to plead his case personally before the pope; but news of his condemnation reached Rome first and was approved before he got there. There was nothing left to do but turn around and try to make peace with St. Bernard — on the saint's terms. Abélard was obliged to give up teaching and to retire to a life of contemplation in still another monastery where he died soon after. He was 63.

In one of his letters to Héloïse he had begged that after his death his body be brought back to the Paraclete. This was done. Héloïse was waiting there to receive it, and presently she watched the man who had been her teacher, her lover, and was still her husband laid in his tomb in the abbey church. She survived him by twenty-two years, and upon her death in 1164, according to her will, was laid in that same tomb beside him.

Two hundred years later English invaders destroyed the church. When it was rebuilt in the following century, the lovers were reentombed within it, although this time apart, the abbey's founder on one side of the choir, its first abbess on the other. But they were not to be left alone, it seems. In 1621 they were moved into a crypt behind the choir and in 1780 into one of the chapels. By this time troubadours and poets had been celebrating their story for more than 500 years, and tourists from many countries, particularly the English, came to the Paraclete to brood or pray over their tombs.

During the Revolution, as churches were being profaned throughout France, the abbey was dissolved and the various pieces of it sold, and the remains of the lovers were carried to the Church of St. Laurant at Nogent and interred again with great ceremony. But a few years later they were jerked out of there and brought to Paris — it was becoming comical. The remains, by now in a lead case divided by a partition down the middle, had been bought by a man named Alexandre Lenoir — how he got them is not clear. He was the owner of a private graveyard known as the Museum of French Monuments, and Héloïse and Abélard were to be his prize exhibition. After selling off bones and pieces of bones of the lovers as relics or perhaps souvenirs, he placed what was left in two containers, put the containers inside a sarcophagus, and built a little chapel over them in his museum garden. The museum lasted only until 1814, at which point Héloïse and Abélard began still another journey. They were carried in a hearse to the Church of St. Germain des Prés, where a high mass was sung over them. After that they were borne to the Père Lachaise cemetery and installed there in still another small chapel, and generations of tourists have been trooping solemnly by them there — whatever is left of them — ever since.

Today the site of Paraclete Abbey is a farm owned by a man named Walckenaer. The buildings fell into ruin long ago, and little is left: part of a cellar, a chapel, and an obelisk marking the spot — or one of the spots — where the lovers once lay.

I don't know if the President of the Republic ever was touched by the Héloïse/Abélard legend or whether he ever came by here to see what was left of the abbey. He was an austere man, enormously tall and gawky as an adolescent, and now as president still enormously tall but grown heavy, baldish, and myopic. He was an extremely adroit politician, as practical and as hard-edged as the stone cathedrals hereabouts, softened only in places by time and adversity, an entirely serious man. His sense of humor, at least in public, did not show. It is difficult to imagine him ever having had much success with girls, or much interest in sensuality. His wife was a staid woman who kept in the background and who, someone once wrote, always seemed to be suppressing a desire to knit.

So the story of Héloïse and Abélard might not have appealed to him. On the other hand, he too was a poet in his way, some of his ideas were romantic in the extreme, and at times he wrote of love as eloquently as Héloïse and Abélard ever had. But there was a difference. The mistress he loved was France: "All my life I have thought of France in a certain way. This is inspired by sentiment as much as by reason. The emotional side of me tends to imagine France, like the princess in the fairy stories or the Madonna in the frescoes, as dedicated to an exalted and exceptional destiny. Instinctively I have the feeling that Providence has created her either for complete successes or for exemplary misfortunes. If, in spite of this, mediocrity shows in her acts and deeds, it strikes me as an absurd anomaly, to be imputed to the faults of Frenchmen, not to the genius of the land. . . . France cannot be France without greatness."

As we drive on towards his house, there begin to be vineyards near the road. According to the popular notion, all Champagne vineyards are in the north within the triangle formed by Reims, Epernay, and Châlons sur Marne, but this is not accurate. There are plenty of growers down here who have equal right to the Champagne appellation, who make good champagne, not great, whose grapes are sometimes shipped up to the major houses to be vinted or else are vinted and bottled locally under lesser-known labels, in some cases by cooperatives. The soil here is chalk, same as up there, and therefore of extremely poor quality. Rainwater goes right straight through. Before fertilizers, irrigation, and modern machinery came into existence, much of Champagne, but especially the southern region, was considered barren and was so designated on maps. Nothing would grow except grapes, whose roots will search for the water table however deep it is, but there was not much market for them until champagne (the drink) was invented about 1720. As a result, except for the cities and the fairs, the region was sparsely settled. It was the place to graze immense herds of sheep. It was the place during the Middle Ages to set up monasteries, the more severe the better: Clairvaux, the Paraclete, and many others. After the monasteries died out, lower Champagne became a place to put military installations. As a boy Napoleon spent five years in one at Brienne le Château learning to become an artillery officer.

It was also a place where vast armies could maneuver, the better to fight what history books call decisive battles. Generals made and lost reputations in this part of Champagne for centuries, and their troops ravaged the land many times.

The major city hereabouts is Troyes, whose rooftops are now in view, and as we come into the streets we resolve to stop for the night; we will go on to the president's house in the morning. I pull up in front of the Grand Hotel.

It's big, 100 rooms, and well situated at the corner of a tree-lined boulevard and a vast, attractive square. Its appeal, we soon find, ends there. There is no one on duty at the entrance, and the reception hall appears to be one flight up. There is a bird-cage elevator, but its use, according to a sign, is restricted to hotel personnel only. Lugging bags, we troop up the steps into a reception area that is spacious and graceful according to the tastes of fifty years ago.

But there is no one on duty here either. When I have called out several times a young woman sullenly appears, allows me to sign in, and pushes across a key attached to a chunk of wood so large that no departing traveler would be likely to take it with him. The parking lot, she says, is out back; she gives a jerk of her shoulder in the approximate direction and disappears. Eventually I find the parking lot. Eventually I find our room too. It is painted a kind of faded orange. The bedspread is none too clean. We have stayed in worse hotels than this, but not recently.

Troyes has played important roles in French history. It was at Troyes that the treaty of 1420 was signed during the Hundred

Years War, delivering France to the English. Within hours Henry V of England was married to Catherine of France, the King's daughter, in one of Troyes's churches, and that sealed it; France was now English, presumably forever. William the Conqueror had just been reversed. But nine years later along came Joan of Arc, a 17-year-old girl driving the 26-year-old Crown Prince (Charles VII) like an ox towards his own future, and the future of France. Joan's army freed Troyes and kept going towards Reims and the coronation. Within six years the war was finally over, but the pillaging by soldiers who got left behind continued for many years more. The countryside was laid waste, entire villages were deserted by their terrified inhabitants, and there were said to be 3,000 beggars here in the streets of Troyes and 2,000 at Châlons, which was a much smaller place.

A century later came the wars of religion. Champagne was again pillaged. In the Napoleonic Wars, same thing. During the winter of 1814 Napoleon had his headquarters at Troyes, and he won what were to be his last victories nearby. There were battles nearly every day, and Napoleon won them all; but finally he had only 20,000 men left. The allied armies had lost heavily too, but still had more than four times that many. On March 20 there was one final battle, and the invincible Napoleon was obliged to break contact as he was about to be crushed. On April 6, 1814, he abdicated. Of course, he escaped from Elba the next year, raised another army, and was finally, definitively beaten at Waterloo. Meantime, more than 350,000 soldiers of both armies had passed through Troyes, and this part of Champagne had been devastated.

For all of that Troyes was lucky. It got its wars early before weapons were developed of sufficient power to eliminate 1,000 years of civilization in a matter of hours. The two world wars passed by to the north, and there can be few more delightful cities than Troyes anywhere today. We see this when we come down to breakfast in the morning. It is the second biggest city in Champagne, population 65,000, a third the size of Reims. It owes its charm and its beauty to its manageable size, to its incredible prosperity during the century of Abélard and the ones just after, and, curiously, to a fire in 1524 that burned for two days and destroyed most of the houses of the town.

The sun is still low as we stroll through the streets. The light strikes the buildings on their sides, making sharp, dramatic colors. Almost at once we come upon a church so old and of such imposing bulk that I imagine it must be the cathedral, but in this I am mistaken. It is dedicated to St. Madeleine, I find. Inside a notice reads that its first stones were laid in the middle of the twelfth century; Héloïse was still alive then, and perhaps Abélard as well; it is the oldest church in Troyes.

But it is not the cathedral, and we stroll on. In two and a half blocks we come to another church of approximately the same age and much greater in size. Its roof and its flying buttresses tower over the roofs of the houses. The adjective *soaring* has been used often enough to describe buttresses, but these seem to be soaring across whole streets, a truly impressive sight.

We sit down outside a café on the Grande Place and order breakfast — café au lait and croissants — and study it. In response to my questions the waiter tells us that, no, this isn't the cathedral either. It is the Church of St. Jean, where Henry V married "Kate," as Shakespeare calls her, in 1420. We sip our coffee and watch the sun resculpt the edges of the buttresses, paint vivid color onto the upper reaches of the church and the rooftops around it. The streets all around us are closed to traffic, and paving stones have been laid down to resemble those that were there in the Middle Ages, and all the buildings have been restored to their original aspect. Almost all of them date from the years just after the 1524 fire. They are timber-framed houses, with ocher-painted stucco between the timbers. They have steep, overhanging roofs and often gables. Almost all of them are richly ornamented, with handsome windows and chimneys, and at street level there are attractive shops. The houses are of varying heights and widths, all pressed tightly against one another; and either the ground has subsided underneath them or there was a shortage of plumb-bobs and carpenter's levels when they were built, for there is hardly a straight perpendicular line to be seen anywhere. They are buildings that tilt, now this way, now that. Most of the streets are narrow, some almost alleys, but here and there is one on which horse-drawn coaches might have passed abreast. In its day it must have been considered a boulevard.

The waiter has pointed out the direction of the true cathedral — it is down this street and across the canal. We pass handsome public buildings, certain of them built in the classic style of 200 years ago, and a pleasant square, and we are approaching a park when we come upon still another massive Gothic masterpiece from the thirteenth century. Surely this one must be the cathedral at last, and we stand admiring it. Its construction is as unusual as any in France, for there are two sets of flying buttresses, one high up to support the walls of the nave and the roof and the other at ground level supporting the outer walls. This bottom row of buttresses is anchored in the grass. The church looks like some gigantic stone spider standing motionless on its curving, outstretched legs.

However, this is not the cathedral either, but rather the St. Urban Basilica, which was built by and named after Pope Urban IV, who came from Troyes. From where we stand part of the true cathedral can be seen further along this same street. It had already been under construction for more than fifty years when Urban became pope in 1261. He ordered construction stopped immediately. The cathedral Troyes needed was not that one but the one he would build for it himself right here. He would build it on the site of his late father's former cobbler shop. He would pay for it himself. Troyes was in an uproar. He did not even own the terrain in question. It belonged to an order of nuns. This to him was of no consequence. He expropriated the terrain. Within a single year the architect's plans had been drawn up and approved and ground was broken. The nuns were furious. Blocks of stone began arriving on wagons from the quarry. The stonecutters were on hand, and Urban's cathedral, to be named modestly after himself, was going up.

The nuns protested in every way available but got nowhere, for in those days no one won disputes with popes. Finally, led by their abbess, they invaded the construction site, drove the workers away, and sacked as much of the place as they could. Urban was only pope three years, and the basilica was still unfinished when he died. A bishop arrived to consecrate his tomb on the site, but the nuns and their abbess, still without satisfaction of any kind, burst into the ceremony, and with their whistling and hooting drowned out the bishop's prayers. But the construction of Urban's basilica continued; by 1286 it was finished. It had taken only five years. Urban must have left plenty of money. Work on the true Troyes cathedral, on the other hand, continued until the seventeenth century.

Troyes is full of great old churches. There are at least seven that are noteworthy. As everyone knows, there existed in France during the thirteenth century a rage to build massive Gothic cathedrals. Most of them were so huge that the entire population of the town and sometimes of the province could fit inside at one time. What is less well known is that the rage to build was not confined to one church per town. Almost all of the cathedral towns, Reims, Rouen, Chartres, and others, have at least one other gigantic Gothic church from the same period. Nonetheless, and even considering the standards of the age, Troyes seems to have got more than its share.

We come at last to its cathedral, which turns out to be big enough to contain any two or three of the other churches at once. Its stained glass, much of it dating from the thirteenth century, is intact, which is more than many of the more famous cathedrals can claim. The Reims cathedral was bombarded by German artillery during World War I; the Amiens cathedral was within range of German guns during most of those same years. The Rouen cathedral was damaged by British bombs in 1944. Troyes escaped all that, and its windows are splendid and have been justly praised for centuries. The cathedral also contains various other works of art brought here from St. Bernard's Clairvaux monastery at about the time it got turned into a famous prison, including eighty-two carved choir stalls, an organ, and various statues and portraits of the sainted man conceived and executed long after his death.

But to me the most striking feature of the cathedral is something that receives only passing notice in the guidebooks, or else no notice at all. I'm speaking of a series of paintings on oblong wooden panels that are to be found in many of the chapels. They date from the sixteenth century. I have seen nothing like them anywhere else, for the panels are painted on both sides and mounted on hinges so that, as fragile as they must be, they swing out from the wall to be examined by anyone who happens by. In most cases one side has been painted with a biblical scene, the other with more recent saints. All this is unique enough, but in addition in each case one side has been painted in color, the other in black and white. Both sides appear to have been painted by the same artist, about whom only two things are known: that he was a man of consummate skill and that he did not sign his work. These panels are four to five feet wide, two and a half feet high. One of the best of them hangs in a chapel on the left side of the cathedral. Saints Augustin, Hierosm, Gregory, and Ambrose are seen in black and white in prayer, fine portraits all; on the reverse side in color is Christ, dressed like a sixteenth-century bishop with a stole on his left arm, teaching in the temple.

I am so curious to know who this artist might have been that I begin to leaf through all the brochures and guidebooks on sale in the vestibule of the cathedral, but few of them mention the paintings at all, and none gives the name of the artist. So we leave the cathedral and walk back to the tourist office on the Boulevard Carnot to ask about them. But no one here can answer my questions either. A good many additional brochures and guidebooks are dug out from under the counter, and even from the director's office, but in none of them is the artist identified. Before long the entire office staff is clustered around me until finally, simultaneously, everyone seems to give a hopeless shrug.

"*Je regrette, monsieur,*" says the director.

Well, life is not a place where all one's questions always get answered.

Continuing our journey to the house of the President of the Republic, we cross the rest of the plain of Champagne until, just past Bar le Duc, his country's principal monument to him comes into view. It shocks us. We round a turn in the road and there it is. We are simply not ready for it yet. We are still twenty miles away, but there in the distance on the crown of a low, wooded hill, the only hill anywhere around, stands a gigantic Cross of Lorraine. There is no other structure in sight in any direction, not a farm, not a house. It towers above the hill, above the trees, above the world. It is 150 feet high. It weighs, I learn later, 1,500 tons. It dominates all this landscape just as the man himself used to dominate the nation, not only its political life, but, more important, its image of itself.

As we get closer the cross, with its four arms sharply etched by the sun, seems only to increase in size. It is as if the president is standing there still alive, arms outstretched like a medieval saint, but magnified 10,000 times. During his tenure the satirical magazines, the sharp tongues, frequently mocked him. His great height was a target, and his prominent nose, even his strait-laced wife. This monument would have silenced such carping, but of course it did not yet exist. It is as if, before it was raised, no one ever truly recognized the stature of the man who once walked among us. "Your legend has only just taken flight," said his successor, Georges Pompidou, at the inauguration of the memorial in 1972, "and already the shadow of its wings covers all of France." We knew he was big, but perhaps it is only in the presence of this monster cross that we realize how big.

Having parked below, we climb towards the cross that for the last many miles has beckoned us forward with such insistence. The hill is steeper and higher than it looks. Halfway up there is a small gift shop/museum. One can buy postcards, ashtrays, and such with his face on them. As a museum its principal exhibit is the black Citroën Traction Avant parked in the small — and locked — garage alongside. A sign says that the president owned and drove the car himself during his years in exile here. When he became prime minister and then president in 1958 he ordered it sold. That buyer and his successors must have used it with great care. It was still running when the great man died, and there it is shined up and on display. That is, it is visible through the not-too-clean garage windows. The exhibits one sees in provincial museums, which is what this one is, are often exceedingly strange.

The path winds still higher through the trees, then comes out into a clearing, where rises the immense cross. It is as high as a fifteen-story building. To see all of it one has to peer almost straight up. Across its base are the words:

AU GENERAL DE GAULLE

That's all. The grandiose monument bears not one other word. The absence of flowery language is completely unexpected, but so is the word *general*. Why not Charles de Gaulle, or President de Gaulle? Why General de Gaulle?

He did not invent the Cross of Lorraine, which was Joan of Arc's cross 500 years before him. She did not invent it either, as it was used by armies of various local strongmen during the century that preceded hers. De Gaulle adopted it in the summer of 1940 as a banner free Frenchmen might rally to. He certainly had nothing else to offer. At the time he escaped to London he was an obscure brigadier general — he had been promoted to general officer only three weeks previously. He was an equally obscure minor cabinet minister, under secretary of state for national defense, a post he had held only twelve days. He was virtually penniless and worried principally about his wife and retarded daughter, for he did not know where they were nor whether they might be able to make their way from France to London to join him, though eventually they did. He was 49 years old. The Cross of Lorraine was only a symbol, and the thought of using it was not even his own. In his memoirs he credits the idea to Maj. Thierry d'Argenlieu, a young army officer who had rallied to his side. As a symbol it would do, and he would hold it aloft until someone of higher rank, either a more experienced cabinet minister or some general or admiral senior to him in rank, came across the channel to supersede him. He expected this to happen. It did not.

From under the monument, de Gaulle's village, Colombey les Deux Eglises, though it lies just beyond the flank of the hill, cannot be seen because of the trees; and of course Joan's village, Domremy, lying about fifty kilometers further to the east, cannot be seen either, which does not change the fact that twice in history marching from this direction under the same banner have come forth saviors of France. Joan was listening to celestial voices; de Gaulle, though an ardent Catholic, made no such claim. He was listening only to the call of the greatness that was France. As a symbol the Cross of Lorraine is of course overtly religious. It was the only political symbol of modern times that was also a religious one. This is part of what gave it, and gives to this monument, such immense power. At times in history religion and politics are the same. If in 1940 God and France were one, then de Gaulle was some kind of commanding, secular saint. No other recent political giant has preached his creed from under a religious symbol, nor mentioned God less, nor adhered from beginning to end to such rigid principle, such lofty ideals, and the result is this monumental cross, the tallest and widest in the world.

We drive into the village of Colombey: gray stone houses, gray stone church. The population is about 350. It is indistinguishable from 10,000 other French villages except that the church graveyard on this Monday afternoon in late June is crowded with people, and there are policemen in the road controlling the cars. It is as if some village dignitary has just died and all his neighbors have turned out to watch him put into the ground. But no villager has died here for a while. These are not neighbors nor even mourners, but tourists, and the grave they have come to look at is of course de Gaulle's.

Many of them today as always have difficulty finding it, for it in no way stands out, and flowers and wreaths are not allowed to be placed upon it. The focal point of the cemetery is a monument surmounted by a rusty iron cross that may be 100 or more years old. The offerings are piled there, and today there is a profusion of them, not only wreaths and flowers that are often plastic, but also a great number of plaques bearing legends such as:

> From the 507th Regiment of Chasseurs
> to Its Chief
> the General de Gaulle.

Most tourists spot this monument and make straight for it, imagining that it is the great man's tomb, but it is not. The tomb is off to the side amid many others, a white marble stone covering the space of two graves. On one side lies the de Gaulles' retarded daughter, who died at 20, and on the other side her parents. The engraving reads:

> CHARLES DE GAULLE
> 1890–1970

And under that are his wife's name and dates, 1900–1979, for her coffin lies on top of his under the stone.

When de Gaulle died it came as a great surprise to France and the world that he wished to be buried here; according to malicious rumors that had swept Paris for years, he had already picked out a spot for himself under the dome of the Invalides next to or perhaps in place of the tomb of Napoleon.

Even more of a surprise was that he had managed to live as long as he did, for he was shot at, bombed, and bayonetted more frequently over a greater period of years than any world leader of modern times, certainly, and perhaps of all time. He must have come to believe he led a charmed life.

He graduated from St. Cyr in 1912, just in time for World War I. On his first day in action, Aug. 15, 1914, he was hit in the knee while running across a bridge at the head of his men. He was carried to the rear and operated on. He was out of action five months. When he returned to the front in January 1915 he carried out a series of dangerous reconnaissance missions, and was mentioned in dispatches. But a month later he was hit again — mortar fragments tore through his left hand. The doctors managed to sew it together again, but the damage was permanent; it would never function very well again. For four months he fretted before it had healed sufficiently for him to go back into the line.

His war ended near Fort Douaumont one week into the Germans' assault against Verdun in the winter of 1916. A frightful bombardment came down on Capt. de Gaulle and the company he commanded in trenches to either side of the Douaumont church. This was followed by a wave of German assault troops. As his position was overrun, de Gaulle was bayonetted in the thigh. Seconds later a grenade exploded, as he later wrote, "literally in front of my face." He lost consciousness and was believed dead, and dispatches describing this action mentioned him in the past tense: "He fell in the fighting. A peerless officer in all respects."

He was a prisoner of war thirty-two months, made five attempts to escape, and once was punished with 120 days of solitary confinement in a dark cell.

During the period between the wars he married a solid bourgeois girl, the aforementioned Yvonne Vendroux, fathered two daughters and a son, advanced slowly in rank, and published military tomes espousing new and radical ideas. In this he resembled Col. Driant, that other hero of Verdun, a generation and a half before him. The result was the same too. De Gaulle's ideas, and especially the effrontery of a junior officer daring to publish opinions in conflict with established policy, earned him the enmity of a great many powerful generals. But it also brought him to the notice of certain government ministers. He had no faith in the Maginot Line, he wrote: the next war would be fought with armored divisions, of which France had almost none.

In May of 1940 the German blitzkrieg broke through in a matter of hours and rolled almost unimpeded across the top of France. Only the 4th Armored Division commanded by Col. de Gaulle was able to slow them down, and even de Gaulle himself could fight little more than holding actions. On May 27 he got his first and only general's star. On June 5, with the French army in tatters and official military doctrine completely discredited, de Gaulle was invited into the government by Paul Reynaud, one of the politicians he had impressed years earlier, who was now prime minister. Even as he assumed cabinet rank, de Gaulle was advising his wife by letter to keep transport and passports available. Do it discreetly, but do it. Yvonne de Gaulle now made her way towards Brittany together with the retarded Anne. There she would be joined by the two older children and would wait to see what happened.

As a member of Reynaud's cabinet, de Gaulle saw indecision and defeatism all around him, plus a vacuum of power and will. Within four days he was on his way to London to meet Churchill at Reynaud's request. That was June 9; he flew back the next day. On June 11 Churchill flew to France to confer with Reynaud and his generals, including Charles de Gaulle, who sat beside him at dinner. De Gaulle had almost no English, but Churchill spoke a good deal of French. On June 13 Churchill flew to France again. More conferences. On the night of June 15 de Gaulle sailed to Plymouth by destroyer, drove to London, and lunched with Churchill and others, returning to France afterwards — the government by now had moved to Bordeaux — in a plane Churchill had loaned him. He discovered that the armistice with Germany was all but signed. As far as France was concerned, World War II was over. Churchill's plane was still at his disposal, and he himself had no intention of surrendering ever. Though fearful of being arrested, he decided to leave, at the same time trying to make arrangements for his wife and children to escape to England by ship from Brest. The next morning, June 17, he went out to the airport as if to see the plane off, but at the last second jumped into it and slammed the door. And so he escaped to London, a penniless refugee totally dependent on the goodwill of the British prime minister, whom he hardly knew and from whom he had no right to expect very much.

At the beginning he was virtually a creature of Churchill's. That is, he was always his own creature, but Churchill owned him. Churchill saw him as a political necessity. The idea of France as an ally of Britain had to be sponsored and maintained. Free French resistance to the victorious German army had to focus on someone, and there was no one else. It was Churchill who provided access to the radio transmitters with which de Gaulle began to make his nightly appeals to "free Frenchmen everywhere." It was Churchill who provided funds for the government in exile de Gaulle was trying to put together, and also the funds on which de Gaulle and his wife and children lived. It was Churchill who recognized de Gaulle — over the objections of his own cabinet — as chief of all free French forces. It was Churchill who championed him throughout the war to Roosevelt and others. Despite this total dependence on the British prime minister, or perhaps because of it, de Gaulle was most times totally intransigent in his demands for money, for materiel, for France's place at the table when those British war plans to which he was made privy concerned France. He and Churchill quarreled constantly. "The heaviest cross I have had to bear," Churchill is supposed to have said, "is the Cross of Lorraine."

The Allied leaders, especially Roosevelt, did not treat him very well during the war. He was kept in the dark about major decisions, was not informed until afterwards even of the Allied attack on the French fleet at anchor in ports in North Africa, which killed 1,300 French sailors. To all these other leaders de Gaulle seemed throughout the war to be arrogant, demanding, unaccommodating. All except Churchill sought an alternative figure but never found one, possibly because no one else cared as much for French honor, French grandeur — for France itself — as he did.

On Aug. 25, 1944, Paris was liberated. The next day de Gaulle walked from the Arc de Triomphe to the Notre Dame. Perhaps two million people crowded the streets. He walked through a storm of voices calling his name. "It is one of those miracles of the national feeling which mark our history down the centuries," he wrote. "We are one thought, one feeling, one voice together." He felt himself "not a person but an instrument of destiny."

The German forces were still nearby. Close to the cathedral sharpshooters began firing at him. Other men were firing back. Although he walked amid comrades-in-arms who had backed him in London, and generals, and Resistance leaders he had not met until this day, de Gaulle stood out among all of them by reason of his great height; and although others ran for cover, he did not deviate from his line of march by a single step.

Another fusillade occurred inside the Notre Dame during the mass. Again de Gaulle was not hit. A frantic search was made, while he remained imperturbably in his place and the mass continued.

He ruled in France for the next seventeen months. Bridges and railroad lines had been destroyed. Much of the country's rolling stock had been destroyed. Inflation was rampant and the franc dropped day by day. There was no capital available with which to start rebuilding the country. De Gaulle put a referendum before the people: Yes or no on a new constitution. The people voted yes. Simultaneously deputies were elected to a new National Assembly: the Communists, the strongest political party in France, won the most seats. The deputies unanimously elected de Gaulle president of the government, while at the same time constructing a constitution that gave virtually absolute power to themselves. That is, the deputies decided that France should have exactly the same type government as had functioned between the wars and had been responsible for the debacle of 1940 — government by political parties rather than by a strong executive.

It became impossible to govern.

On Jan. 20, 1946, de Gaulle summoned his ministers and read the following statement:

"The exclusive regime of the political parties has returned. I condemn it. But unless I use force to set up a dictatorship, which

I do not desire, and which would doubtless come to a bad end, I have no means of preventing this experiment. So I must retire."

And he came back here to Colombey to wait for his country to come to its senses and to call on him again. He never imagined he would have to wait so long — twelve years. During those years the franc continued to fall until it was at 500 to the dollar; the French army at one point was involved in three losing wars simultaneously: Indochina, Algeria, Morocco. In Paris the government floundered. Prime ministers changed every few months, sometimes twice within a single month, and sometimes the same man reappeared in the post years later and was just as ineffectual the second time as the first. As government after government fell, having accomplished nothing, the mood of Frenchmen and Frenchwomen was often one of embarrassment and shame.

For twelve years de Gaulle waited for the call. For him, though he loved Colombey, and though he used the time to write his memoirs, refusing to accept the pensions due him as a retired army officer, and retired President of the Republic, these were twelve years in the desert. Finally the third of France's losing military adventures, the insurrection in Algeria, boiled over, a military coup d'état was threatened, and the politicians turned at last to the most recent savior of France, asking him to save them again. De Gaulle imposed terms — he wanted still another new constitution and the end of rule by party. When this was granted, he accepted. But he did so with a heavy heart. He was 67. "It has come too late," he told someone. "I'm too old. There isn't enough time for me to do anything." But he left for Paris nonetheless.

The church beside the graveyard is cool and dark, and of course very old. The floor is made up of massive stone blocks worn smooth by the years and no longer completely level. The benches are hand-hewn and twenty feet long. One of them was de Gaulle's when he lived here. There is an enormous crucifix behind the main altar, a cathedral of a crucifix.

His house is on the other side of the road that runs in front of the church and about 200 yards further on. It cannot be seen from the road. The property is surrounded by a stone wall topped with a fence. Between the wall and the house is the equivalent of a small forest. Dense trees, dense bushes that create virtual darkness underneath. Admission tickets are on sale in a small gift shop opposite the gate. They cost 10 francs. In a country where politicians routinely become rich, where even Napoleon lavished pensions on all his relatives, de Gaulle left no money, and after his death it seemed that the estate would have to be sold. A group of former comrades-in-arms bought it and is seeking to keep it open as a memorial.

Inside the gate is a gravel path, and presently the house itself comes into view. The bulk of the grounds — the small forest — is to the left. There seem to be pathways in there under the trees. Of his property de Gaulle wrote during his exile: "I have walked around it 15,000 times." Apart from the occasional visit of a journalist keeping up the contact just in case, apart from the family at Christmas and in summer, he had no visitors. He had very little money but was too proud to make this known.

It is a long, low house with a hexagonal tower at one end. It is two stories high. Its walls are almost entirely covered with leafy vines. It is a house of good proportions, a noble-looking house without being in any way splendid. It contains a dozen to fifteen rooms, none of them enormous. De Gaulle bought it in 1934 when he was a lieutenant colonel stationed at Metz. He had been in the army by then twenty-two years. Retirement seemed not far off. "Where can a retired officer settle down except in the east, halfway between the Rhine and Paris?" he wrote. "Besides, I didn't have much money." The house was called La Brasserie at that time, apparently because the land that went with it had once been used for growing hops. De Gaulle changed the name to La Boisserie, a word he seems to have invented. The house was damp and unheated. De Gaulle gave the former owner, a widow, the equivalent of $1,800, plus a promise of $150 a year for the rest of her life. She died two years later.

We enter the house. It is clear at once that most of it is closed to tourists. One is allowed to peer into the dining room, the living room, the library, and de Gaulle's small study in the tower. The furnishings are plain, in no way remarkable. The upholstered furniture looks uncomfortable, as unyielding as the general's outward manner after he returned to power. There are no priceless antiques. The wooden pieces are not new, but do not appear valuable either.

There are a dozen or more fine paintings and pastels on the walls, some of them portraits of de Gaulle's ancestors. There is a TV set and on a sideboard a slide projector, as if the general, before he died, had forgotten to put it away. There are signed eight-by-ten glossies of world figures.

"To General Charles de Gaulle from his friend, Franklin D. Roosevelt."

"To General de Gaulle from Winston Churchill."

"To his excellency Charles de Gaulle, President of the French Republic, with the admiration and respect of his good friend Dwight D. Eisenhower."

Not much warmth in those inscriptions. Why did he want to hang them on his walls? To prove that he was an intimate of men of great stature? But the world had no doubts on the subject. Perhaps he himself had doubts — if so, it seems odd. No one ever came here to be impressed by such photos except, once, Konrad Adenauer, the chancellor of West Germany. To me the photos seem as odd as if I had hung my own walls with signed photos from fellow writers. The idea would never occur to me.

The study has tall windows and a splendid view, the same one today that de Gaulle stared out at during all those sad years. "Great, worn-down, sad horizons," he wrote during his exile. "Melancholy woods, meadows, planted fields and fallow land; an outline of eroded and ancient mountains, peaceful, rather poor villages, where nothing has changed, either in soul or in location, for thousands of years. Silence fills my house. From the corner room where I spend most of the hours of the day, I look out upon the land towards the setting sun. For fifteen kilometers no building appears. Above the plain and the woods, my eye follows the long slopes coming down into the valley of the Aube and then the heights of the opposite hills. . . . I watch as nightfall covers the countryside. Then, watching the stars, my being is penetrated by the insignificance of things."

He makes the view sound gloomy. On a summer June afternoon it's not gloomy at all, quite pleasant, in fact. Of course in winter in this part of France the sun rarely shines, and for de Gaulle during those years it was winter every day.

Now in May of 1958 he was suddenly back in power. The

army in Algeria was on the edge of mutiny. After four years of terror and tens of thousands of murders and battle casualties, a military junta was threatening civil war. De Gaulle flew to Algeria and calmed their passion with four words: "I have understood you." The army and the million white settlers, some of whose families had lived there for four generations, interpreted this to mean that the war would go on. There would be no independence for French Algeria. But de Gaulle had other plans.

He ruled by decree and by referendum, and he moved fast. He decreed into existence the "new" franc. He simply lopped two zeros off the old one. Overnight 100 old francs became worth 1 new franc. The people were used to buying groceries, to buying clothes, to counting out their money in the thousands, even the millions, and they would continue to do so for many years. Nonetheless, technically and legally, particularly on all formal documents such as bank statements, French currency was no longer debased by so many ridiculous zeros, as was still the case in Italy and such places. The franc began to take on weight. Confidence in it began to return. De Gaulle decreed that France would build its own atomic bomb. The *bombinette,* the people in the street called it derisively, even as French pride began to swell. De Gaulle withdrew from NATO, closed American bases on French soil, and forced American troops and their dependents into other countries. "France has chosen once and for all to be France," he said. "I invite everybody to adjust to this." He closed the Riviera ports to the U.S. Mediterranean fleet, and the villas on the precipitous hills around Villefranche and Nice began to empty out as American families departed. Business fell off for merchants and restaurateurs up and down the coast, some of them friends of mine, one of them my father-in-law. Even the whores drifted away.

De Gaulle invited Konrad Adenauer here to Colombey for two days of conferences. They ate off everyday china with everyday knives and forks. The German spent the night in the guest bedroom. De Gaulle never invited any other world leader into his house, neither before nor after. It was his way of showing France, and Germany as well, how far he was willing to go to heal the ancient breach between the two countries. Adenauer had tears in his eyes when he left: "You have treated me like one of the family."

Referendum succeeded referendum. The French voted on propositions de Gaulle put to them, yes or no. In this way time after time he bypassed the politicians, the National Assembly. Thus 80 percent of the electorate approved the new constitution; 62 percent approved the election of the president by universal suffrage. He did not invent referendums in France. Napoleon used them; how do you think he became Emperor?

De Gaulle announced that Algeria, where Arabs outnumbered whites ten to one, would decide its future itself; "autodetermination," he called it. In the ensuing referendum three-quarters of the voters voted yes, for mainland France was sick of the war, sick of the killing, sick of the cost. But in Algiers there was consternation, followed by a revolt by four generals, followed by the formation of a terrorist Secret Army there which put de Gaulle on trial, convicted him of treason, and sentenced him to death.

And commandos were sent to France to assassinate him.

There may have been as many as thirty attempts on his life. Certainly there were eight well-documented ones.

1. The plotters rented a house along the road to Colombey. They filled it with weapons and shooters like a duck blind. But the police, probably acting on a tip, raided the house and seized the stacked weapons.

2. Several unidentified light planes flew over La Boisserie. Air force fighter planes came and drove them off. Later the Secret Army announced that it had planned to bomb de Gaulle as he strolled in his garden.

3. De Gaulle was to be shot or stabbed as he watched a play in the Théâtre Français with a visiting chief of state. Again the police were forewarned and a search was made of the audience. In the confusion the assassin or assassins slipped safely out of the theater.

4. Explosives were planted along the road to Colombey near Pont sur Seine. As de Gaulle's cortege of cars sped by in the night, the charge was detonated. The whole road seemed to catch fire, the flames licking as high as the tops of the roadside trees. The cortege sped through the curtain of fire and no one was hurt. Most of the members of this particular assassination squad were caught almost at once and got long prison terms.

5. A five-man commando was sent out to kill de Gaulle during a political tour through the center of France. They were caught. The president was traveling by train. The police found and defused sabotage preparations along the track. They also found and confiscated bazookas and other heavy weapons, for if the sabotaged train failed, the commando had planned to blast rockets into the Elysée Palace. According to a second contingency plan, de Gaulle's car was to be rammed with a truckload of explosive gas.

6. During another provincial political tour, four men were arrested. They had planned to mine a railroad crossing as de Gaulle's car passed over it. The car would have been moving very slowly crossing the tracks.

By then the president had begun flying to Colombey, for the roads were too dangerous, and on political tours 6,000 gendarmes and security police were mobilized to protect him. But he had too much pride to hide behind such an impressive guard. On tours he would dart down into the mob to shake hands, and when moving about Paris he would simply jump into a car and go. I saw his car come out onto the Rue Royale several times myself, for the Elysée was not far from our office. Each time he was sitting bolt upright in the middle of the back seat as two motorcycle policemen tried to clear traffic so his car could proceed. He spoke disparagingly of his bodyguards as "gorillas" and refused to allow them to ride in the same car with him. If the police wanted him to fly to Colombey, then he would fly, but to drive out of the Elysée under police guard was not worth bothering about. Thus he approached his next rendezvous with an assassination commando one night in August 1962.

7. He sat in the back of a black Citroën with his wife. He was on his way to Colombey. In the front beside the driver rode his daughter's husband, Alain de Boissieu, an army officer. With a security car behind it and two motorcycle gendarmes as outriders, the car moved rapidly through the Paris suburbs towards Villacoublay military airport. No one in de Gaulle's car was armed.

Up ahead waited a commando of fifteen men armed with machine guns, grenades, and pistols in an ambush that had been planned with military precision.

It was getting dark rapidly. A lookout spotted de Gaulle's car coming and waved a newspaper as a signal. Three hundred yards down the road men sprang from a car and two panel trucks in which they had been hiding. They leveled their submachine guns and automatic rifles and opened fire on the presidential car as it came into range.

This plot, the most determined, most violent, and most nearly successful, was organized by Army Lt. Col. Jean-Marie Bastien-Thiry. A graduate of France's highest polytechnical institute, Bastien-Thiry was an engineer, not a line officer. To him, as to all the plotters, de Gaulle had shamed the army, shamed France, and lost Algeria. Bastien-Thiry collected nearly twenty men. One was Alain Bougrenet de La Tocnaye, who was from one of the oldest and proudest families in France and who was chosen for this reason. Another was Georges "The Limp" Watin. Bougrenet, a former army lieutenant and deserter, was second in command. Watin was to handle the submachine gun that would finish off de Gaulle. During all of the previous month this group had met to study the problems of the assassination and to assemble vehicles and arms.

It was summer as these plans were made, and de Gaulle was on vacation in Colombey. Although Paris is surrounded by official vacation retreats owned by the government and at the disposal of the president — former palaces built by kings for themselves and/ or their mistresses — de Gaulle continued to spurn them all. None of them was his house. La Boisserie was his house, and it was at Colombey.

The newspapers had announced his return to Paris on Aug. 8. He would board his plane at St. Dizier, which is about thirty kilometers from Colombey, and forty minutes later the plane would land at Villacoublay. From Villacoublay there were two possible routes into Paris, one through the suburb of Meudon, the other through Petit Clamart. Bastien-Thiry had men at both airports and a third man at the intersection of the two possible roads into Paris.

On the day of de Gaulle's return Bastien-Thiry and his men waited by a phone in a rented room about halfway between the two possible routes. Finally the phone rang. The lookout at St. Dizier reported that de Gaulle's plane had taken off.

For forty minutes hardly a word was spoken. Then the phone rang again. De Gaulle's plane had landed at Villacoublay.

In a few minutes came the third call. De Gaulle's car, with only two gendarmes trailing it, had turned left at the intersection. The choice of route was clear: through Meudon woods. The car would move into the heart of Paris along the Avenue de Versailles.

The assassins ran to their vehicles and sped to their prearranged rendezvous. They saw de Gaulle's car approaching, but then it unexpectedly veered off onto the Quai Blériot, a parallel street.

Of the plotters, only Bougrenet, sharing a Citroën with Watin and two other gunmen, realized what was happening. Since the Avenue de Versailles and the Quai Blériot rejoin each other a few blocks further on, Bougrenet sped on down the avenue and in a moment found himself on the Quai riding beside de Gaulle's car. Desperately he searched his rearview mirror for his colleagues' vehicles.

They were not there. The panel truck and the other car, seeing de Gaulle's car swing off onto the Quai, had not reacted in time. They were not following.

Bougrenet was enraged to find de Gaulle so close and himself so impotent. For nearly a mile his car ran within a few yards of de Gaulle's. At last he decided that to open fire would be too risky. He slowed down, and the president's car was soon out of sight.

The "study group" of the Secret Army sent Bastien-Thiry more men, including Jacques Prevost, a former paratrooper, and Pascal Bertin, 20, whose sister had an apartment near Petit Clamart. This gave the plotters a hideout close to Villacoublay airport.

De Gaulle, now back at Colombey, was scheduled to return to Paris for a cabinet meeting on Aug. 22. Again the plotters were nervously waiting, and at 8:50 A.M. came the first phone call from St. Dizier. De Gaulle had taken off. Forty minutes later his plane landed at Villacoublay, and the lookout there raced into a bar to phone Bastien-Thiry, but the phone was out of order. He dashed down the street looking for another phone. He lost ten precious minutes before he could find one.

When the call finally came, the plotters jumped into their

vehicles, three cars and two panel trucks, and drove rapidly to the point where they expected to intercept the presidential convoy.

It had already passed.

According to newspapers, de Gaulle would be engaged all day but would fly back to Colombey that same night, so Bastien-Thiry sent lookouts to the Elysée Palace. He and the others, fifteen in all, waited in the apartment of Pascal Bertin's sister at Petit Clamart. In the afternoon, Bastien-Thiry himself went out, entered a café, and began slowly sipping coffee and reading a paper, patiently waiting for the café phone to ring with news from the lookouts. At 7:45 P.M. the call came. De Gaulle's car had started for Villacoublay, and he was in it. Bastien-Thiry paid his bill, stepped out onto the sidewalk, and waved his newspaper. A lookout in the apartment window waved back. The plotters hurried downstairs to their vehicles. The two panel trucks had been parked outside all day, the back windows obscured by a coating of chalk so that passersby could not see in.

The street de Gaulle's car would come down, the Avenue de Libération, is wide and straight. The plotters were spread up and down this street for over 300 yards. Nearest Paris stood Bastien-Thiry, holding his newspaper and pretending to wait for a bus. When he spotted de Gaulle's cortege, he would wave the paper. The two panel trucks were about 230 yards down the street from him. A hundred yards further on was a Citroën containing Prevost, Watin, and Bougrenet. A second car was in reserve on a side street. On receiving Bastien-Thiry's signal, according to the plan, the men in the panel trucks would jump out and open fire head-on at the approaching cortege, using machine guns and automatic rifles. It was assumed that de Gaulle's car, hit hard and with the chauffeur dead, would come to a stop approximately opposite Bougrenet's car. Prevost and Watin were then supposed to march up to de Gaulle's car, yank open the door, inform the president that he was being executed, and do the job.

At 8:10 P.M. Bastien-Thiry finally saw de Gaulle's motorcade approaching fast. He waved his newspaper, but it was getting dark by then, and the lookout in the first panel truck did not see the signal at once. Six or seven seconds went by before the rear doors of the trucks erupted open. By this time de Gaulle's car, moving at about sixty miles an hour, was upon them. The machine guns and automatic rifles fired on it broadside as it went by. Two tires went flat, one bullet passed within five inches of de Gaulle's head, about ten bullets in all slammed into his car, and about five others hit the security car behind. Two bullets tore open the plastic helmet of one of the trailing gendarmes. A passing motorist was hit in the hand.

All this happened in a second or two. Then de Gaulle's car was past the trucks and abreast of Bougrenet's car. Watin and Prevost fired on it broadside too, but they had not expected to fire on a car moving so fast. They were not ready.

De Gaulle's chauffeur had floored the accelerator. The presidential car was now doing about eighty on two flat tires, but the chauffeur held it on the road, and in an instant the ambush was behind them.

That night the plotters dispersed, abandoning the vehicles. Bastien-Thiry went back to work at the air ministry the next day as if nothing had happened.

Even as de Gaulle's plane took off for Colombey, hundreds of security agents swarmed over the scene of the attack. Depositions were taken from dozens of witnesses. A few supplied partial descriptions. Others gave the make of Bougrenet's car and the color of the panel trucks. Someone had seen Bastien-Thiry waving his newspaper.

Nearly every policeman and gendarme in Paris spent the next few hours looking for the abandoned cars and trucks. They found them. Now the police asked themselves why Petit Clamart had been chosen for the ambush. There was only one possible answer: the plotters had a hideout in the neighborhood.

The police went through Petit Clamart on a door-to-door search. Other witnesses were found who had seen the trucks with their windows chalked over. One had been parked all day in front of a certain apartment house. Every tenant was questioned. Neighbors informed police that Monique Bertin was in sympathy with the anti–de Gaulle conspiracy, so for several days all four of her brothers were tailed. Pascal impressed the policemen shadowing him as nervous and worried, so suspicion fastened on him.

In the hope that he would lead the police to other members

of the band, he was arrested. This was done in a department store. He ran from the detectives trying to grab him and was chased between the counters among frightened women. But all the exits had been blocked and he was caught. In his pockets were found incriminating letters.

In France suspects may be held forty-eight hours for inter-rogation without charges being filed. This is known as the *garde-à-vue*. The suspects are supposed to be fed regularly and allowed to sleep, according to law, but in practice, especially in a case like this, such niceties are often ignored. Detectives have learned to deliver food to the suspect, then snatch it away immediately, not-ing down in the log: "suspect refused food." The food itself is then dumped in the toilet or the detectives eat it, but the receipt that came with it is stapled to the log. Similarly, notations can be made that the suspect chose not to sleep at night but preferred to answer questions. The interrogating detectives, meanwhile, come and go in relays. After forty-eight hours of *garde-à-vue* suspects often begin to babble.

Young Bertin was stronger than most. He denied his own membership in the conspiracy to the end, but did give up the names of other men whom he "thought" might be involved. The police checked every name. Some were false, but one was Prevost, who was living under an alias in Montmartre. Prevost was already under observation because he had paid his rent with a bad check. A dossier was now compiled of persons who had visited Prevost in his flat.

It was assumed that some of the plotters would head for Spain and Belgium by car, so roadblocks went up across France, each manned by a dozen gendarmes or security police armed with sub-machine guns. One night, near Tain l'Hermitage, a car carrying four men was stopped. One had no papers so the police took him into custody. He was a deserter from the French air force and had been a gunner in the reserve car.

More than a million people — on foot, in cars, on trains — had to identify themselves to the police. Many were brought in for questioning. Slowly the police ran down the other plotters. Two were pals of Bertin's at school, and Bougrenet was identified as a frequent visitor to Prevost's apartment. Soon so many of the plotters were in custody that it was easy to figure out who was missing. At first Bougrenet was assumed to be the leader, but he displayed such a wild temper under interrogation that the police decided he could never have arranged a cold-blooded ambush.

As the interrogations continued, the suspects began to be trapped by their lies and to make damaging slips of the tongue. Thus the police learned that the leader of the ambush was known as the "colonel." Also, the plotters had someone in the air ministry. Were there two men? Or were the "man in the air ministry" and the "colonel" one and the same?

Three weeks after the ambush Bastien-Thiry was brought in for questioning. Cheerfully he denied all knowledge of it, but the grilling continued so long and so fiercely that at last he could take no more. Out of hatred for de Gaulle and pride at being a major figure in the Secret Army, he began to brag that he, Lt. Col. Bastien-Thiry, was responsible for everything.

Ten of the fifteen plotters went on trial before a military court. Bastien-Thiry, Bougrenet, and Prevost were sentenced to death. Bastien-Thiry was executed by a firing squad, but de Gaulle commuted the sentences of the other two to life imprisonment. In fact, they were released less than six years later, and Bougrenet wrote a popular book called *How I Didn't Kill de Gaulle*.

Watin was still at large. A bull-necked man of 29 with a crew haircut and glasses, he now organized his own assassination plot.

8. Watin had once hidden out for a month in the apartment of Robert Poinard, 37, a captain attached to the Ecole Militaire, the French military staff college. With Poinard's help he moved several high-powered rifles into a room overlooking the courtyard in which de Gaulle, who was scheduled to visit the college, would review a detachment of troops. From so close the enormously tall de Gaulle would be an easy target.

But a sergeant stationed at the staff college saw something, or overheard something, and went to the police. The police found the room, found the high-powered rifles, and they connected Capt. Poinard to the plot. They began shadowing him night and day.

For the moment they had only Poinard, a minor figure. Given

time, he would lead them to someone, probably Watin himself, the most important and most dangerous plotter still at large in France.

When told of the plot and urged to cancel his visit, de Gaulle became furious. "France does not assassinate her chief of state," he cried, a line he had used in speeches. Such plots were alien to the dignity and grandeur of France. "Has France degenerated to the level of one of these South American republics which massacre their presidents every other week?"

He refused to let thugs and murderers alter his plan; his visit would take place as scheduled.

With this decision the police had no choice but to arrest Poinard, announce the plot to the press, and surround the staff college with security police. De Gaulle not only arrived on time, not only reviewed the troops in the courtyard, but even prolonged his visit by forty-five minutes to show his contempt for the men trying to kill him.

Eventually nearly all the Secret Army plotters were caught, and in still another of de Gaulle's referendums independence for Algeria was approved by the voters in the biggest landslide yet, 90 percent.

In all he reigned this second time for eleven years, not very long compared to the Sun King, Louis XIV, who sat on the throne for sixty-seven years, or to his dissolute great-grandson, Louis XV, fifty-nine years. Even Napoleon in one guise or another lasted longer, about fifteen years. But none of these men could have seemed more regal than Charles de Gaulle, even though they wore crowns and ermine and he did not. Command was in his bearing, in his eyes. He was, or at least became, a more austere, more unapproachable figure than any king. Note his press conferences, for instance. They represented at once an approach to the people and a godlike performance from on high. These press conferences were frequent; the reporters sat on straight-back chairs while members of the president's staff passed among them planting the questions the general wished asked. Press conferences in other countries were usually free-for-alls; not here. The general left nothing to chance. When he took his seat at the table in front of the television lights he sometimes wore his brigadier general's uniform; at other times he wore a business suit. He would recognize each questioner in turn, listen attentively to questions that were sometimes long and intricate but never frivolous. At the end of each question he would nod and say:

"*Bon.*"

Then he would recognize the next questioner, and the next and the next, each time nodding at the end of whatever the question might be.

"*Bon.*"

Finally he would begin a speech that answered them all one by one, and if an impromptu question had somehow got included, he would answer that too. His performance each time seemed to me remarkable. His answers were formal, complete, and delivered in beautiful classic French. There were no notes in front of him, no TelePrompTer. He could not have read from notes or TelePrompTer anyway, for his eyesight was failing fast and he was too vain to wear glasses on television. By the end of his reign faces had become such a blur that in a crowded room or on a political tour he sometimes shook hands with his bodyguards.

Eleven years. From time to time there were elections. He himself was elected to a second seven-year term as president. And there were more referendums, some of them vital to the health of France, or so he believed, some of lesser importance.

Eleven years. Time enough for the French to come to believe in a strong central government focused around a president who could not be dismissed at a moment's notice by squabbling political parties; it was the first strong central government the country had ever had under democracy.

Eleven years. Time enough to get the country functioning again and to give France and Frenchmen back their pride.

In April of 1969 de Gaulle called another referendum. It had to do with the reform of the senate, which had few enough powers in any event, and with changing the system of regional governments. He announced that if the referendum did not carry he would resign. The votes were counted and only 47 percent were in his favor, the rest against. He was here in Colombey where he had come to vote. He was still in his house when the results were announced. At once he issued a communiqué:

"I am ceasing to exercise my functions as President of the Republic. This decision takes effect at midday today."

This time he was in Colombey for good. He wasn't going back.

The referendum led to a good deal of speculation. There had been no need to tie his own prestige to its outcome. Why had he done so? Well, perhaps he had misjudged the electorate.

Or perhaps he thought he had done enough and could go home now.

He took no further part in the political life of the nation. He uttered not one further public word. During the next eighteen months private citizen de Gaulle and his wife traveled a bit. They went to Ireland, they went to Spain. They entertained their son, a navy captain, and their daughter and their seven grandchildren. But mostly they lived alone in this house in Colombey where one day was much like another. He would cross this library and go into his office in the tower at about 9:30 each morning and would work on his memoirs until noon. He would lunch with his wife, and then they would walk around the property for a while. In the afternoon he would go back to work on his memoirs. About 7:00 P.M. he would come out of his office and sit at the card table there almost in the doorway and play solitaire while waiting for the evening news on television. He had played solitaire for years, brooding on affairs of state as he watched the cards fall, solving whatever problem needed to be solved. Once someone dared ask him if he cheated at solitaire. "Of course," he answered. "I do not play solitaire to lose." On Nov. 9, 1970, he got up from his desk and opened his window so as to pull his shutters closed for the night. It was dark out. He could not see much. Then he sat down at the table with his cards. Suddenly he clutched his torso with both hands and cried out, "*Que ça fait mal*" and collapsed and died. In thirteen days he would have been 80 years old.

When he heard the news Georges Pompidou, de Gaulle's successor as president, said, "France is a widow."

The grandiose state funeral that all the world had expected, especially the cynical French, did not take place. The dead man lay in state in this house, to which no one but family and close friends were admitted, and when it was time for the funeral, his coffin was carried up the road and into the church on the shoulders of ten young men of the village: a carpenter, an electrician, a butcher, a pharmacist, a plumber, a cheese maker, a silversmith, a chef, a surveyor, a farmer; after which he was laid into the tomb in the village churchyard beside his daughter. There were no political figures present.

Although the politicians respected de Gaulle's wishes that they not come to Colombey, this did not prevent them from throwing a funeral ceremony of their own at the Notre Dame Cathedral in Paris. The world's major prime ministers, dictators, kings, and such were invited — and were obliged to attend under pain of giving insult to France. A command performance if ever there was one. The simple funeral mass here at Colombey and the lugubrious event in Paris took place simultaneously. The cathedral was packed with notables, but the guest of honor failed to appear.

Grasse
THE SCENT OF MONEY

The road north out of Nice runs straight and flat for twenty miles beside the Var. The Var is not only the major local river but also, as rivers go, an exceedingly strange one. Although half a mile across, its shallow bed is empty, or nearly so, during most of each year, a desert of sand and stones through which meander a few rills. But when it is in flood the water extends from bank to bank and ultimately it spreads its brown stain in a huge arc out into the Mediterranean. The variation in the Var's flow is prodigious — from 17 cubic meters per second during the dry months, to over 5,000 when the snows melt in the Maritime Alps in spring. It is not navigable at any season of the year, and never has been. You could never sail it, which is not to say you could never walk it or gallop a horse on it. For centuries it was the only highway around, and was so used.

On either bank the mountains rise abruptly — in some places almost like cliffs. On the cretes high above stand the perched villages. They are as isolated as sentry posts, and they frown down on the river. Many are totally depopulated today. They belonged to a time when errant crusaders or Moslem pirates or freelance knights tended to move up and down the Var requisitioning whatever food, animals, and women they required; a time when a village's only security was the impracticality of its location. The

people who built such villages also built ramparts around them,
and then they built concentric terraces that dropped below the
walls, and on these they cultivated enough crops to keep the village
alive. Every rainstorm washed the topsoil away, and the peasants
would descend with wicker baskets and carry it back up again and
level it and replant. Such terraces are still there, testimony to
decades of backbreaking labor by families long dead, a way of life
long dead. On them today nothing grows but weeds.

If still others of these perched villages have survived almost
intact into our time, this is principally because a road happens to
go through, and because they boast a restaurant. A restaurant does
more than merely attract visitors for a few hours a day. The
combination of the two — road and restaurant — makes the village itself seem attractive to people looking for places to build
weekend villas in which to escape the increasing pressure of the
cities. With the building of villas around it, the survival of the
perched village is assured.

Just past Plan du Var a truss bridge crosses the river to the
west bank, where, in a series of brutal switchbacks, the road begins
to climb. It climbs almost straight up, from sea level to about
1,800 feet, then enters Gilette, a huddle of gray stone houses on
the flank of the mountain, with the ruins of a medieval chateau-
fort sitting on top like a flower on top of a stalk. There are no
parking lots in villages like Gilette. The road as it goes through
is narrow and dark. Parking is at the exterior where the road
widens slightly in the sun. We pull the car snugly against the
retaining wall and get out. The air is amazingly cool and fresh.

Gilette's restaurant is called Bar des Chasseurs. It is not one
you have heard about, and I mention it chiefly to show that such
places in the last decade of the twentieth century still exist. Inside
the dining room are less than a dozen tables. The walls are hung
with the heads of the deer, chamois, and wild boar that are hunted
in these mountains during the season.

From seats at the window we look out over mountains that
shoulder away in all directions. Their flanks are covered with
forests, and the colors change constantly as clouds move across a
pure blue sky.

Service is by the proprietor, who serves also at his bar and at his *tabac* counter in the adjoining room — he is a busy man — and each time he comes through the beaded curtain with platters we can see men in rubber boots at the bar.

Lunch is copious. There are those among the French who eat daintily, but not in places like this, and *nouvelle cuisine,* which prides itself on its neat, small portions, is unknown here. The proprietor sets down a plate of raw country ham, enough to serve at least eight people, though we are four. Then comes a loaf of homemade terrine with a knife stuck in it, followed by homemade ravioli with a delicate, subtle sauce that any three-star chef would be proud of. Again there is enough to feed double our number, and when the proprietor returns with a fresh basket of bread, he tries to force seconds upon us. The only choice on the menu comes next — today it is roast duck or roast lamb. Some days there is rabbit or venison or boar or one of the game birds. After this come salad, cheese, homemade *tarte,* and coffee. The entire procedure takes close to three hours and requires numerous bottles of wine — usually a very pleasant Côtes de Provence — if one is to get it all down.

All this while gazing out at the amazing view. The bill when it comes is about a third of what such a feast would cost in one of the swanky restaurants down on the coast.

On this particular afternoon I have a rendezvous at a perfume factory in Grasse, and so we drive west out of Gilette, the mountains high and very steep, rising straight up out of deep valleys, the road still climbing. We pass through a number of other perched villages, and the air remains clear and pure, and the views keep changing. Sometimes we are high enough to see the sea. At other times we gaze over the tops of our own mountains at the much higher snow-capped peaks further inland. Sometimes the road runs along a precipice with a sheer drop to one side and no guardrail. Sometimes we run along the rims of spectacular gorges, at the bottom of which lie rivers that writhe like snakes.

These mountains are known as the pre-Alps of Grasse, and they reach almost 6,000 feet. But eventually the road starts to descend. The forests become thick — cork oaks, beeches, various types of pines — and a piney scent invades the air. We begin to pass fields of lavender growing carefully in rows, tiny mauve flowers peeping out of each clump. The lavender sends out the strongest odor yet.

The road drops down still further until it joins the direct traffic between Grasse and Nice. The traffic is suddenly heavy, and presently we enter the streets of the perfume capital of the world, where a miasma of exhaust fumes hangs in the air and both curbs are lined solid with parked cars.

Grasse, population 40,000, is the Riviera's only serious inland city, the Mediterranean being some twelve miles away, and perfume is responsible for its size and prosperity both.

As endowed by nature the Riviera figured to be poor indeed. The soil is poor, and the mountains come down so close to the sea that in most places there is not much of it. The centuries of peasants who scratched at the arid ground barely produced enough food to keep from starving. The stunted forests were no good for logging. Even the local sea is poor. The Mediterranean never had fish in the vast quantities of other seas. Nor was there much industry in the towns. There still isn't.

Except for Grasse, where perfume employs either directly or indirectly great numbers of people. There may be as many as thirty perfume factories here, only two of which are open to the public. One of the two, Fragonard, has a small museum whose exhibits amount to a short history of perfume. In one room are pieces out of Carthaginian, Greek, and Roman excavations: statuettes, scent bottles, toilet articles, all of which show how important perfume was 2,000 years ago and before.

It is not a recent invention. It began in ancient times with the use by priests of various strong scents, one of them myrrh, in the embalming of corpses, and with the burning of incense at funerals. The Egyptians anointed dead pharaohs with odorous oils, and the inner walls of certain pyramids contain fragments of formulas for perfumes. Herodotus wrote that the Babylonians perfumed their bodies with expensive odors. In Greece men scented different parts of their bodies with different oils. The Romans invented indoor fountains that sprayed perfumed water, and they loved to be massaged with scented oils. The Bible is full of references to perfumes. The Hebrews sacrificed perfumes to God, and two of the three gifts of the Magi were perfumes.

After Rome fell, perfume almost disappeared, except in the Arab countries, and when it drifted back to the West again it was once more religious. The church in which Clovis was baptized at Reims in 495 was illuminated by perfumed candles. Much later, Charlemagne received the Calif of Baghdad, who dropped a load of precious Middle Eastern perfumes on his desk. But it was not until the crusaders returned home from the Holy Land that interest in perfume started up again in Europe. By the fourteenth century, royalty in France sometimes wore perforated lockets containing mixtures of ambergris, musk, and other substances. Forks were invented in Italy in that same century but did not reach France and England until much later. In the meantime the French ate with their fingers, and it became the custom at court to wash the hands afterwards in bowls of rosewater.

The first charter for France's perfume industry was dated 1582, and the industry's foremost job was the perfuming of gloves, because as treated in those days, leather stank. When Catherine de'Medici came to France to marry Henri II, she brought along her personal glover, a Florentine named Réné Ruggieri. He became known as an alchemist who understood the dark mysteries of drugs. He was later accused of concocting and selling gloves impregnated with poison. Noblemen gave them to their rivals as gifts.

Grasse during most of its history has been a lucky city. The glove makers were already there, and now it was found that many of the world's most odorous flowers grew wild, or almost wild, nearby. The glove capital of France became the perfume capital as well. The city is built on a kind of escarpment at an elevation of 1,100 feet. Above are the mountains we have just come through. Below is terrain that drops sharply, extending virtually at sea level all the way to the Mediterranean, forming a plain that is ideal for growing jasmine, roses, and such. But the mountains are crucial too, for always perfumes have been blends, every ingredient vital, and the mountains provide the balsam, the sage, the moss, the lavender — plants that grow only at altitude. For instance, lavender suitable for perfume cannot be grown at all below an altitude of about 2,200 feet. In any case Grasse, needing to perfume its gloves, stood at the exact center of all the raw materials — or almost all — that its perfume factories would ever need.

The best years were to come. Beginning about 1750 the French nobility conceived a sudden, unprecedented, and almost all-consuming interest in their noses.

Preoccupation with odor was at first medical. It seems to have originated with doctors and chemists who propagated the notion that diseases could be diagnosed through a study of the odors that went with them. This led such men into what might be termed excruciating directions — they began to research and to try to catalogue odors, concentrating first on human excrement: they studied latrines, cesspools, and the like. They got their noses down close and afterwards conducted learned discussions.

Next they became fascinated with corpses in various stages of decay. The theory was that the careful sniffing of a corpse that had been hanging around for a while would permit a precise diagnosis of the disease that had killed it.

Like all fads, this one spread into new and unexpected areas. It made men and women conscious of their own odors, and those who could afford it, namely the aristocracy, began to want to disguise them. They had the money to indulge such whims, and so they built private toilets, or even private sewage systems, and also they began to slap perfume onto themselves — perfume made in Grasse. The idea became current that a man's body odor revealed his exact station in life — you could tell how high up the social scale he stood just by sniffing him. You could dress a poor man up in a rich man's clothing, but his putridity would give him away every time. Being poor, his very being stank.

A little soap and water might have ended such nonsense, but this was an idea whose time had not yet come.

Before long the profits from perfume surpassed those from gloves, and Grasse dropped out of the glove business. When the original Riviera tourist boom began early in the nineteenth century, Grasse's luck continued to hold. Despite being relatively far from the sea, it attracted its share of visitors. It was not beaches that drew the first tourists to the Riviera — beach worship is a recent phenomenon — but sun, smart shops, and parties, all of which Grasse could provide in as much abundance as Nice, Cannes, and the others, and once Queen Victoria chose to spend several winters here, Grasse's reputation was made.

The streets of the old town are too narrow for cars. The rooftops seem to close in over our heads. The people who built these narrow houses, who first walked these cobblestone alleys, did not work in perfume factories; they never dreamed of Chanel No. 5.

All the old towns of Europe have charm, this one more than most, perhaps because it is pitched on the side of the escarpment. One moves up and down steep little streets past lintels of carved stone — the usual decorated doorways. Often the thick doors have studs in them and heavy brass knockers in the shape of fists. There are a number of restaurants, one or two tearooms, and many smart shops, all with their lights on — for all their charm it is dark in these streets. It always was and it always will be.

We come out onto a little square and are facing the cathedral. It dates from the late twelfth century. Grasse was already a miniature republic by then. On its escarpment this far back from the sea it was apparently safe and prosperous at a time when other towns were not. It had strong trade links with Pisa. Out of the port of Cannes it sent soap, tanned skins, and olive oil to Pisa and got back raw hides and arms. It was administered by a town council whose members claimed to be "consuls by the grace of God," but in 1227 Raymond Bérenger, the Count de Provence, came in here with an army, slew a lot of consuls, and from then on Grasse belonged to him.

The cathedral is dark inside. It is also small. You could fit three or four buildings like this one inside the Notre Dame in Paris and still have room for a tennis court. It smells somewhat fetid, exactly like the narrow streets outside.

Also, it is full of rather spectacular paintings, including a major work by Fragonard, the famous court painter who was born in Grasse in 1732 and whose father, according to the present legend, was a perfumer. The painter was by far the most famous individual Grasse ever produced, though Adm. Count de Grasse (1723–88) was a close second. Neither spent much time here.

Fragonard lived in Paris from his teens until his death in 1806 at 74, except for a few of the most tumultuous years of the Revolution, when he hid out here in the villa of a friend — as a court painter he risked the guillotine. Apparently for want of something to do, he decorated the friend's staircase with revolutionary emblems and his doorway lintels with languorous love scenes. This villa is a museum today, and a number of drawings, engravings, and paintings by Fragonard are on display.

As for Adm. de Grasse, he lived most of his life at sea — he was a marine cadet from the age of 11. It was de Grasse who defeated the English fleet off Chesapeake Bay in 1781 and then blockaded Yorktown so that Cornwallis and his army could not escape. De Grasse was a legitimate hero of the American Revolution, even though his contribution and his name are largely forgotten today. Partly this is because he attacked a superior English fleet under Rodney in the Caribbean the very next year and was defeated. His ship was *The City of Paris,* 102 guns, supposedly the most powerful afloat. According to kindly local historians, de Grasse was "a victim of his own audacity." It was the custom to exchange high-ranking prisoners in those days. The English gave back the admiral but kept his great ship. When de Grasse got back to Paris he blamed his defeat on his captains, making unsubstantiated charges for which he was banished from court; he was still in disgrace when he died. In other words, Adm. de Grasse did not stay a hero long enough for his heroism on either side of the Atlantic to sink in — no pun intended.

The great paintings in these gloomy chapels I knew of in advance and am prepared for, but I am not prepared for certain of the cathedral's architectural features, especially the girth of the pillars that support the ceiling. They are like no others I have seen. There are four to either side of the nave, and though relatively short, they are incredibly stout. They must be five feet in diameter, yet they are striking, not graceless a bit. They make the vaults above seem to soar. Galleries at least fifteen feet off the floor run from front to back along both sides of the nave, further contributing to the surprising impression of delicacy that the cathedral achieves.

Above the door to the sacristy hangs one of Fragonard's rare religious canvases. Measuring about eight feet by twelve, it shows Mary Magdalene washing the feet of Jesus. I look at it for a moment, but this is not the painting I've come in here to see, and I move along the wall noting three paintings by Rubens, all done in Rome in 1601. The light in here is poor, and none of us have any coins to drop into the slot that would make the projectors come on to illuminate these paintings. In any case, I did not come here to admire Rubens either. At last, in the fifth bay of the south aisle I find what I am looking for, a fifteenth-century triptych on wood attributed to Louis Brea.

Fragonard has never pleased me very much, and I have seen better paintings by Rubens elsewhere, but with one or two exceptions paintings by Brea exist only in a few villages and cities close to Nice, where he was born about 1450: Luceram, Biot, Antibes, Fréjus, Gréolières, and here in Grasse. They hang almost exclusively in churches. Some of the best are in the monastery church at Cimiez, above Nice, whose graveyard, by the way, contains the tombs of both Matisse and Dufy.

Everyone knows about Fragonard and Rubens, but so far I have been unable to find anyone who can tell me very much about Louis Brea, or his brother Antoine, or his nephew François, both of whom worked for him. Apparently no one knows his exact dates. I do know that the Nice school — the appellation was invented by art historians 400 or more years later — flourished between 1470 and 1522, which seems to indicate that he lived to be 70 or 75. The Nice school was strongly influenced by the Italian Renaissance, and its own influence was limited to Nice and its environs, apparently. Apart from the Breas, the only other painter who was part of this school, whose name I have heard, was Durandi.

Most of Louis Brea's altarpieces and triptychs in this church and the others are unsigned. These are paintings that nobody really knew about or cared about until recently. No one protected them from vandals or mildew over the centuries; nonetheless, all the ones that I have seen are in beautiful condition. The colors have not flaked off or faded, the reds and greens are still vivid. The compositions, and especially the faces, are exceptionally striking, and there are dark contrasts and even a kind of early chiaroscuro.

In those churches that have them, no matter how full of other religious art or how good other individual paintings might be, the Breas stand out. One goes right to them. Louis Brea has been called the poor man's Fra Angelico, or else the "Provençal Fra Angelico." But to my mind he is as good as Angelico ever was, and perhaps better, and one of the places where you can admire his work is in this cathedral at Grasse. However, see that you have coins for the projector, or you won't see him very well.

At the Roure-Bertrand Fils et Justin Dupont factory there are no guided tours, no perfumery museum, and nothing is on sale. Roure's is not interested in tourists or retail sales or even in publicity, for it markets nothing under its own name. It is strictly a perfume factory. Its business is to manufacture for others some of the most famous perfumes of our day: Opium, Obsession, L'Air du Temps. Givenchy, Hèrmes, Halston, and Oscar de la Renta are all Roure clients. The company employs over 1,000 people worldwide and in addition to perfume also provides scents for antiperspirants and deodorants, detergents, floor waxes, and such. Although most people imagine that perfume is a mixture of self-indulgence and extravagance — pure vanity — Roure's seems proof of the contrary. Perfume and its offshoots are very big business indeed.

The Grasse factory includes a number of outbuildings that can only be described as sheds. Accompanied by a company executive, I walk through them. In one lies a layer of verbena measuring about twenty-five feet by fifteen and about a foot deep. Workers are forking this stuff into vats where it is to be, in effect, boiled until all its essential, highly scented oils are steamed loose, thirty to forty minutes on the boil for each batch usually. The oil will then be siphoned off the top like cream.

In another shed lie bales upon bales of hay or straw. The shed smells like a barn. And in still another are bales upon bales of moss, the entire shed smelling as fresh as a forest. If this were another time of the year, remarks the executive, there would be different products in these sheds, different odors. "Depends on what's being harvested," he says. It makes me wish I had come between August and mid-October, when the jasmine is brought in. Or during May, which is the time for tea roses. These are the principal aromatic flowers of the Grasse plain, though there are others.

In the next room are stacks of petal boxes. These are glass trays smeared with lard or some other fat on which flower petals are placed one by one, side by side, by hand. The frames are then stacked in a way that keeps the air out, and during the next thirty to sixty minutes the odor of the flowers goes into the grease in exactly the same way that butter, left open in a refrigerator, will pick up the odors of other foods. This is the most glamorous method of extracting perfume from flowers. Called *enfleurage,* it was invented when it was realized that cut flowers do not immediately die. They go on producing and exhaling perfume for some time. Much of this extra life can be captured via *enfleurage,* but not with the other two methods of obtaining flower essences — boiling off the vapors in a still and releasing them with solvents. But *enfleurage* is so labor-intensive that it is rarely used anymore, even though the quality it gives is superior.

The supreme personage in each perfume house is the "nose," the chief perfumer, the inventor of new scents, the guardian of the priceless formulas that determine the makeup of the classic old ones. Some major factories have two noses, but most have only one. Noses tend to be as temperamental as tenors, and as hard to get along with.

The major factories in Grasse train their own people, and this training begins at the age of 20 or younger. It lasts at least five years, during which the pay is poor. Apprentices start in the laboratory, learning and memorizing contrasting odors. They may first sniff lemon, then sandalwood, then cloves, anise, essence of rose, lavender, jasmine, civet, peppermint, in roughly that order, the next day memorizing ten other contrasting odors. After some weeks they progress to differentiating between ten related odors, such as the citrus family: lemon, orange, tangerine, lime, et cetera; or spice notes such as cloves, cinnamon, bay, nutmeg, pepper, juniper; or flower notes such as jasmine, tuberose, jonquil, narcissus, hyacinth, violet, mimosa — and so on. After that come the aldehydes and hundreds of other chemicals, then simple combinations of scents, then complicated ones. There are more than

2,000 different odors, and the serious perfumer must memorize each one before he ever starts work on a concoction of his own.

I am handed over to a perfumer who leads the way into the laboratory area, where other perfumers are making up existing perfumes according to elaborate formulas. I watch them measuring out quantities with eyedroppers. Formulas are extremely explicit, and some may be thirty pages long. A formula may call for, say, seven grams of oil of jasmine from field X from the 1982 vintage — the oil from field X in 1981 or 1983 would be a different odor. There are vintages in flower oils just like in wine. Eventually, of course, there will be no more 1982 jasmine from field X. At this point a nose must come in and find another jasmine from another field that is identical, or almost so, and thus the formula will be slightly rewritten. Chanel No. 5, for instance, was invented in 1920, and the provenance of its ingredients has had to be altered several times.

Once the perfume has been built up drop by drop in these laboratories, pure alcohol is added, about a pound and a half of the oil to each gallon of alcohol. This is the final mixture that goes into the half-ounce *flacon* that a woman receives as a gift at Christmas or on Mother's Day, which is when most perfume is bought — 70 percent of it by men, who get in and out of the shops as fast as they can.

Roure's research laboratory is crammed with futuristic and fantastically expensive devices. There are only two research centers as elaborate in France, only ten in the world. Most of the others, inevitably, are in America but staffed mostly by Frenchmen. The purpose of perfume research is to try to isolate the components of every scent existing in nature and then to reconstitute the original scent chemically. No one has yet developed, say, a synthetic jasmine as pungent as the natural flower. But suppose the components of jasmine could be found cheaply in other products. Eventually chemists could concoct a "pure" jasmine oil in the laboratory and, in addition to cutting costs, the industry would no longer be vulnerable to bad weather, bad harvests.

After components are isolated they go upstairs to the physics department to be identified. The physicist, Dr. Pierre Witz, stands in his laboratory surrounded by a nuclear magnetic resonater, an oscilloscope, and various other incredible instruments.

Dr. Witz is baldish, pale, wears glasses, and speaks in a monotonous voice. "To explain this in the most simplistic manner," he says, "the machine bombards the nucleus with hydrogen atoms. The azote is measured here, freeing the carbon molecules after passing through the magnetic fields and being fragmented into a proton minus two electrons — I'm oversimplifying, of course — then into the magnetic chamber to form a new separation. The result is on this graph here. You understand, of course?"

"Not entirely."

"What's your native language?" asks Witz. "English? Would you like me to explain in English?"

"I don't think it would help."

There is a natural antagonism between the pure research men and those who work with their noses, and as we leave the building my guide, the perfumer, says, "That man knows nothing about perfume, and doesn't even care about perfume."

After Witz and his team identify a chemical, it goes back downstairs to the chemists, who play with it a little longer before sending it on to perfumers, who experiment with it in scents; until finally the company directors come together to decide whether all that work is worth anything commercially.

Ninety percent of the research is wasted — it's that way with all research. But the expense is justified because perfume is far more than perfume. Modern man literally couldn't do without it. Most plastics stink and could not be used unless treated first with perfume. Insecticides are perfumed, of course, and paints and varnishes and many synthetic fabrics.

"We have isolated the odor of a new car," says my guide. "We sell it in aerosol cans to used-car dealers, particularly in America, who say their sales would drop without it."

He leads me into a kind of butcher's refrigerator where he takes a jar of jasmine oil down from a shelf. Why is perfume so expensive? he asks rhetorically. Well, about 350 roses weigh only one pound. It takes 3,500 pounds of roses to make one pound of the oil known as attar of roses. Jasmine is more expensive yet, for it is a night-blooming flower. It can be picked only from 4:00 A.M. till noon, while the petals are open. One trained woman in eight hours can pick only fifty-five pounds of flowers, but it took a ton of such flowers to fill this two-quart jar. He thrusts it at me. "That jar," he says calmly, as I receive it, "is worth over $10,000."

I thrust it back at him.

Most perfumes contain some flowering materials, some animal, and some chemical. The principal animal scents are ambergris, musk, and civet. Ambergris is a product of the intestinal tract of whales. Civet is an excretion of the civet cat of Asia, the East Indies, and Africa. Formerly the cats were wild and were hunted and killed for their scent pouches. Now in many cases they are raised commercially and kept in cages. Musk comes from the scent glands of the twenty-inch-high musk deer, which roams the Atlas and Himalaya mountains. The best of it comes from Tibet, where hunters are rapidly extinguishing the species for the sake of these golf-ball-size, hair-covered scent glands.

Animal products are used to bind and modify perfumes and to make the flowery scents cling. Also they are thought to impart an aphrodisiac quality to perfumes. They suggest the coming together of bodies, the contact of two skins.

Obviously the animal products are not produced in Grasse. More and more neither are the flowers. Formerly there were 2,000 nearby families growing jasmine alone. Now there are 200. Local jasmine production has dropped from 1,000 tons a year to 80. The growers — meaning ultimately the factories to which they sell — can no longer afford the hand labor. Some of the flowers must be picked petal by petal. Nor can Riviera farmers, it seems, long resist the pressure of the real estate boom. They sell out, make a killing, and fields that once sprouted flowers suddenly sprout villas and condominiums. The Grasse perfume factories must then buy their raw materials from Egypt, Madagascar, India, and such places, which is what is being done.

Here and throughout the perfume industry the noses are considered artists, for they combine scents the way a painter combines colors, and perfume making is considered an art, though perfumers sometimes sound defensive when they say so. A great perfume, they claim, can excite and give pleasure to the fifth of man's senses.

Is this not equivalent to the pleasure a beautiful painting gives to the eyes or a symphony orchestra to the ears?

Although revered in Grasse, noses to the world at large are anonymous. Few have seen their name in the papers. They do not give interviews on television. Anonymity is by no means the choice of most of them, but it is mandated by the chief customers of factories like Roure, who are usually the perfume branches of the Paris fashion houses. Perfume labels are small. There is room for the name of the house and for whatever exotic name has been awarded to the scent itself. Even Roure's name never appears on the label, much less the name of whichever nose concocted the scent in the first place. There is far more money in a successful perfume than in high fashion. The fashion houses do not mind paying a royalty to Roure, but they want the renown for themselves. The perfume sells the clothes, and vice versa. The house does not need Roure's name in the middle, and it especially does not need the name of some obscure chemist.

The most famous personalities associated with perfume therefore have never been noses. They have been instead people who knew how to market perfume, and usually they made sure that the only name associated with said perfume was their own. I will cite two examples.

François Coty was the first modern figure on the perfume scene. He was the man who first learned how to mass-produce it and also how to mass sell it. His big career began around 1900, and he died in 1934.

He was a Corsican working in Paris as a secretary. As a hobby, he haunted the backroom laboratory of a neighborhood druggist who made and sold his own eau de cologne. Fascinated, Coty took a job as a perfume salesman. What he learned dismayed him. Perfume ought to have romance, opulence, mystery, he felt. As the new century arrived, it had none of these things.

Even today perfume is an extremely secretive business. New formulas are still written in ancient books and locked up each one in its own safe. So there are more legends than facts about Coty. It is difficult to find out even what year he was born, much less what his exact talents were. That he was a marketing genius seems obvious. Whether he ever concocted any of his own fragrances seems unlikely.

But in 1900 he saw that packaging was poor, that no perfume house had managed to establish the brand-name concept, and that women scarcely knew what they were buying. So he "developed" a fragrance of his own, bottled it in an elegant crystal *flacon,* and made the rounds of the big Paris stores — which didn't want it. As he was leaving the great Louvre Department Store (where the finest and most expensive perfumes of the day were not sold, by the way), his sample *flacon* slipped from his hand and smashed on the floor, inundating the store with a delightful rose fragrance. Shoppers crowded around Coty demanding the name of his perfume. La Rose Jacqueminot — and Coty — was launched.

This is either the truth or pure invention.

In 1905 Coty invented the gold metal screw-on cap. The scent would be preserved weeks longer. Next he developed L'Aimant, which is still on the market today, and after that he dreamed up the idea of a *flacon* whose glass was so pure that its perfume would appear to be held by air. The glass was called *lalique* and was so fine a pinprick could puncture it. Rejects, the perfectionist Coty is supposed to have claimed proudly, ran to 83 percent. The man invented many other sales gimmicks: gold-leaf powder boxes, combination packages including perfume and powder, half-size *flacons* at a price even shopgirls could afford.

He amassed a fortune, bought a castle with walls six feet thick and a fantastic yacht. He decided to run for president of France, bought two newspapers to tout his fitness for the job and, when the syndicates of the day refused to display his newspapers on newsstands, bought his own chain of newsstands. He was never elected president of France. Apart from that, his mature life seems to have been one triumph after another. Were he alive today, however, he would be dismayed to learn that Parfums Coty now belongs lock, stock, and barrel to the Pfizer Drug Company of New York, N.Y.

The story of Coco Chanel, who might be considered the second principal figure in perfume in this century, is filled with hyperbole also. Coco Chanel of course was not a perfumer at all but a fashion designer. Most Paris fashion houses market multitudes of perfumes, most of them failures, most of them replaced the next year by something else. At any given time there must be 400 perfumes on the market. But for half a century Coco Chanel gave her name to only one. She changed her couture styles year by year — she was credited with some astounding innovations in women's clothes — but not her perfume. For fifty years she rejected all suggestions that she bring out another. She owned neither the perfume house nor the fashion house during most of those years, but she did own her name. She was the first person in either fashion or perfume ever to license her name, and her royalties from Chanel No. 5 in 1971, when she died at the age of 88, were said to total over $700,000.

As a child Gabrielle Chanel attended a convent school in Moulins, where the schoolboys wore black smocks and white collars with floppy black bows — an image that she would cause to reappear on grown women, rich women, in all the capitals of the world many years later. Upon leaving school she first worked as a seamstress, then went on the stage as a singer, but failed. She went to Paris, where she moved in with an Englishman to whom she was not married — certainly a daring adventure in the years before World War I — and began designing and marketing hats. Chanel never married, and the Englishman was the first of many public lovers. All her life she flouted conventions. She wore her hair almost as short as a man, lay bareheaded in the sun until she became deeply tanned, and in her couture sought to provide women with clothes that were as comfortable, as easy to wear as a man's, but which were still somehow feminine. She was credited with the invention of the little black cocktail dress, of simple, sometimes two-piece dresses in wool jersey, of the skirt with two pockets placed exactly where the hands would find them, of suits with cardigan jackets, of the pullover sweater and the clean white shirt. It was said of her that she freed women from yards and yards of petticoats, from dresses to the floor and great wide hats, and from veils. She pared down the clothes women wore and then added accessories, particularly chains, fake jewels, and ropes of fake pearls. She taught women to wear costume jewelry on casual clothes.

She closed her couture house in 1939 — during the war, fashion in Paris consisted mostly of bottles of makeup which women painted onto their legs to simulate silk stockings. When the war ended she was accused of collaborating with the Germans, for she was not one to hold men at arm's length, and this included officers of the occupying army. So it was not until 1950 that she reopened her couture house.

She had sold Chanel No. 5 in 1923, keeping only the royalties plus rights to her name. Presently she sold her couture house too, but stayed on. She had one of the longest careers in fashion history, during which she was responsible for but a single perfume. How much she had to do with the concoction of this perfume is not known. Coco Chanel was a genius at self-publicity. No one that the fashion world or the perfume world has ever seen before or since could match her in the ink she attracted. But Chanel No. 5 was certainly different at the time. There was no single dominant note in its scent, as had always been the case previously. Instead it was a blend of some eighty spices and flowers to which she suggested — or her nose Ernest Beaux suggested — the addition for the first time of something synthetic, namely aldehydes. There was already a rich blend of jasmine, May roses, neroli, ylang-ylang, sandalwood, and vetiver. The aldehydes blurred the floral outlines, resulting in a perfume that was both contemporary and uncopyable. It was the first floral abstract, a breakthrough, it is said, that has only happened three or four times in perfume history.

According to one legend Beaux created not one but ten perfumes at this time, and he presented them to Coco Chanel in sample bottles identified only by number. The first group was numbered 1 to 5, the second group 20 to 24. There was no other label. It was to be the equivalent of a blind tasting in the wine business — a blind sniffing. Coco chose bottle number 5, and when asked what exotic name should be given to her selection, answered: "Chanel No. 5. My collection is being presented on the fifth day of the fifth month and the number five has always been lucky for me." No one in the perfume business has ever been luckier.

For her new perfume she did design the packaging, or so she always claimed. The clear, square crystal bottle with the flat crystal top, the simple label, the rather stark white box with the thin black border — all this remains unchanged to this day.

She was capable of speaking eloquently on the subject of perfume, saying that its "voice" was both personal and secret; that it touched and confounded sensuality, hope, dreams, nostalgia, coquetry, love; that it was capable of evoking in both memory and heart the strongest of passions, the most fugitive of desires. And when a perfume was successful, she might have added, it became a source of legendary fortunes.

But most of the time, when Chanel spoke, it was difficult to tell where fact left off and fiction began. The origin of the name of her No. 5 was sometimes credited to the five fingers on her hand or to the five continents — she was charming and would say whatever might attract attention.

In 1983 a designer named Karl Lagerfeld took over the House of Chanel. He had never met Coco and is not sure he would have liked her, or that she would have liked him. Lagerfeld is often called the best designer in the fashion world today, but he does not own the House of Chanel. He is an employee. He finds himself obliged to preserve the "Chanel look," to adhere to a certain image, when what he would really like to do, apparently, is to hear the world speak of Karl Lagerfeld, not Coco Chanel. The Chanel dresses of the twenties, he told one interviewer, "looked a little like other designers' dresses. But now people think that she invented the look of the twenties. That is not exactly true, though her myth and her image survived better and she lived long enough in the public eye to tell people so." Lagerfeld names two other designers of the time, Vionnet and Patou, who died long before her and so could not claim their part in the evolution of the fashions of the twenties.

At one time Coco Chanel was called the queen of beige. Then she went off in a new direction entirely and began to design lace dresses and soft evening looks. "Schiaparelli invented another look for that period," Lagerfeld said, "with a stronger image than Chanel in those days, but she was not around long enough to tell the world what she did."

Under Lagerfeld there is again a new Chanel perfume — it is called Coco — but he is also marketing perfume under his own name, Parfums Lagerfeld, especially KL, which in one poll one recent year was voted perfume of the year.

"I like the idea of Chanel's life and everything she did," he said once. "I am not afraid of the old lady who hated knees and short skirts. She was perhaps right in her day, but today every woman can be proud of her legs and show them often and longer than any other part of her body. By fighting hopelessly against the short skirt for the last ten years of her life, she established perhaps the look — the famous little Chanel — better than any other look in the history of fashion except blue jeans, but the final effect was that it was considered a look for the middle-aged, the bourgeois, something you could still wear when fashion had passed you by. In fashion only the moment counts."

Artists and egos. The two are inseparable, I guess.

Bordeaux
THE FAMILY THAT OWNED THE CITY

Consider the map of France. Two-thirds of the way down the Atlantic coast comes a deep gash into the ribs of the country, extending downwards towards the navel. It is as if someone had swung an ax in there, then yanked it out again. The gash is the Gironde, one of the shortest but widest of the important rivers of the world. Where a ship enters from the sea it is nearly seven miles across; wooden sailing vessels had no trouble tacking back and forth during their up-river journey against the hard, heavy current. If it had been otherwise, the story to be told would have occurred elsewhere, or not at all.

After about sixty miles the river splits in two. The Gironde's name disappears, and it becomes two other rivers of quite ordinary girth and aspect. One is the Dordogne, which begins to meander eastward toward the Massif Central, becoming very quickly of not much consequence. The other, the Garonne, is the stream the major vessels always followed, and still do, for within ten miles, as it rises towards its source, it has sliced under the bridges of Bordeaux, the second most beautiful city in France, a city of parks, gardens, and lovely squares, of broad boulevards and handsome public buildings, a city built almost entirely on wine.

Bordeaux's beauty is an eighteenth-century beauty. It is elegant, harmonious, stately, much like Paris on a smaller scale. Perhaps as many as 5,000 private and public buildings remain from the years just before the Revolution, a period of great prosperity here. The most celebrated is the Grand Théâtre, finished in 1780, which stands at the head of the Cours de l'Intendance, the city's most celebrated street. Constructed in stone and marble by Victor Louis, one of the most famous architects of his day, it is probably the most classic in design of any opera house in the world, and certainly it is among the most handsome. Its facade is composed of twelve Grecian columns that support a high porch rimmed by a balustrade; atop the balustrade stand a row of marble statues, twelve partially undressed female figures representing the nine muses plus the goddesses of marriage, beauty, and wisdom. A Greek temple of an opera house.

Elsewhere in the old part of the city there are ancient churches and basilicas and, here and there, portions of former ramparts, and gateways that once were closed and guarded each night to protect the inhabitants while they slept. The great cathedral of St. André dates mostly from the eleventh and twelfth centuries. It is 400 feet long, longer and wider than a football field, only 20 feet shorter than the Notre Dame in Paris. Nearby, separated from it, is its steeple or belfry — I don't know what else to call it — growing up out of the grass like the trunk of some gigantic branchless tree. Adjacent to the Basilica St. Michel in another part of the city there is a similar tower, also Gothic in design, also isolated from the church to which it is conceptually attached. In this case it stands in the middle of the church square and it is surrounded most days by an outdoor flea market and milling bargain hunters. The steeple is 370 feet high, the height of a thirty-seven-story building, by far the tallest structure in the city, Bordeaux's Eiffel Tower.

Except for its beauty, Bordeaux is today a typical provincial capital — rather slow-moving, rather unsophisticated. The eighth largest city in France, its population is 211,000, with a metropolitan area of over 600,000, the whole of which is surrounded by vineyards — the epitome of the one-industry town. Of people of working age, one in six works in the wine trade. They and their families live off wine, and so in effect does everyone else. It may or may not be the best wine in the world. It is certainly the most distinguished, and most of the credit goes to the bizarre terrain in which it grows.

The Garonne, which rises in the Pyrenees to the south, is slow, muddy, and only about 1,500 feet wide as it moves through the city; not the Amazon by any means, but the fourth biggest river in France. As it makes its way northwest to become the Gironde, it delimits one side of a vast triangular peninsula — the other side being the Atlantic. The peninsula, which is the terrain of the great wine estates and, these days, of much else, is flattish, featureless, stony, sandy, mostly treeless, basically barren, an expanse of land inapt for the grazing of herds, incapable of sustaining most crops, and helpless in the face of natural disasters such as storms and floods; incapable during most of history of sustaining life itself. It is good for one thing only, wine.

It is land born in cataclysm. During the Pliocene epoch some twelve million years ago, when the horse had evolved almost to modern form and the manlike apes had appeared in Europe, and the last ice age was still in the future, the western Pyrenees had already risen up and had begun to be hammered by terrible storms. Clay and dirt were washed from the rock, and when that was gone gigantic flint cliffs broke off and, falling, mashed themselves to pieces. This debris collected at the base of the range and was transported north by the Garonne by the tremendous power of the rains. As they moved along, the chunks of cliff faces were reduced to chunks of flint, then were whittled down further into flat, smooth stones of the type the French call *galets,* beach stones, a shape able to withstand the 120-mile journey north for as many million years as it took to get there. From the mountains all the way north to the mouth of the Gironde this Pliocene garbage was spread out in layers, and it was a mixture of motley clay, yellow sand, and stones that, by the time they reached their destination, measured only a bit more than an inch in diameter. All of the rivers were running full at the time, emptying into a vast, low-lying marsh encompassing what is now Bordeaux and its outlying vineyards, creating a muddy, turbulent sea that was as thick as vegetable soup, in which the flat stones swam along like fish.

Millions of years passed, but the traumatic pressures on the land did not cease. The area between the Garonne and the sea, nearly flat to begin with and now buried under layers of clay, sand, and stones, was transformed again as the rivers canalized themselves and came with renewed force, carrying with them whatever got in their way. The Garonne, into which so many of these rivers fed, was churned up anew, overflowed its banks into the fields, spreading new and different stones. From the central Pyrenees far to the east came small- to medium-sized black Lydians and disparate stone matter pressed together and eroded and smoothed by so much travel. Presumably carried in by the original Dordogne came pale and agate quartz, and from the valleys of the Lot and Ayveron, which are tributaries feeding into the Garonne, came belts of a limestone called lias.

The various ice ages froze, melted, froze, melted — four or five times.

Still trying to carve out a bed for itself, the Gironde laid waste the entire valley, sucking away whatever clay and earth there was until only vast slopes of flat, round stones remained. Such clay and earth, which might have sustained life, was replaced by sand as huge gales were whipped up over the ocean and blown in across the land. The sand invaded all of the area now known as The Landes, completely submerging it, and much of the present wine-growing area as well. The beach in places extended thirty or forty miles inland and stretched in length from the mouth of the Gironde all the way south to where the Pyrenees dipped down to meet the sea. These sands raced towards the Garonne/Gironde and in some places reached it. They mounted the slopes of flat stones and seeped down through them.

Along the edge of the sea towering dunes began to pile up. They piled higher and higher upon themselves, miniature mountains, and behind them, because the rivers could not find their way to the sea, salt swamps of a particularly insalubrious nature came into existence. The rivers changed course constantly trying to get out, in the meantime covering over great tracts of land and rendering them useless.

The first men who happened by this wretched country had no idea what it could be used for, and some died and the rest moved on. But others came, for man is as persistent as the rivers or the sands themselves, and at last they learned about the land and how to exploit it and, in time, how to transform it in amazing ways.

First a wine economy came into existence, for vines could grow in sand and stones where grain and even feed for cattle would not; vines would go down thirty or forty feet looking for sustenance. It was not great wine then, only a product that could be sold, a way to live. As it awaited the birth of man the technician, the land remained in all other respects as desolate and inhospitable as ever.

It was the sixteenth century before the vagabond rivers were curbed. In some cases they had threatened existing towns or made the establishment of new towns impossible. Employing hand tools and oxen, men dug permanent new channels for them from far inland through the dunes all the way to the sea. Henceforth they would not interfere with whatever plans men might make.

With this job completed, the engineers found a way to stabilize once and for all the shifting dunes along the beach. They erected a wooden palisade 120 miles long, and as the sand piled against it they yanked it up higher and higher until the dunes were three to four stories high. On top they seeded a plant called gourbet, which grows in sand and has tightly interlaced roots. By the end of the seventeenth century it was done. The dunes would no longer move and towns could be, and were, built even on top of them.

The inland swamps remained, inhabited by a few herdsmen who stalked the marshes on stilts, tending their flocks. In the beginning of the nineteenth century drainage holes were driven into the hardpan deep beneath the surface, and as the water began to seep off, maritime pines and cork oak were planted to suck up what was left. More and more trees were planted until one of the greatest forests in Europe had come into existence, as did logging, paper factories, and the various industries based on pine tar. The dunes were the dividing line. On one side was the new forest, and on the other one of the world's longest and most magnificent beaches. Weekend villas began to be built atop the dunes, particularly at Arcachon, a miserable fishing village whose great shallow bay was about to be made useful by being seeded with oysters; the village became a town and then a resort city complete with casino. Later still a use was found even for the great inland lagoons, which remained despite everything: the outboard motor had been invented, together with water skis.

The first invaders to reach Bordeaux during what counts as recorded time had been the Romans. They either discovered a rude settlement already there and built upon it, or founded a new city. In any case, they named the place Burdigala. There may already have been vines growing. What is more probable, though difficult to prove, is that the Romans brought the grape with them. This was how they civilized any place they went. They planted grapes. One needed a product to export back to Rome; otherwise there was no point in starting a colony at all. The grape in question was called the Vitis Biturica, which is thought to be the same grape now called the cabernet sauvignon, the dominant red grape in Bordeaux and, some say, the noblest grape in the world.

By the fourth century Ausonius, whom the Burdigalians called Ausone, was cultivating vines and writing poetry on the banks of the Gironde. He described how the vines stretched back from the yellow-brown Gironde, and he was proud that the wines they gave were preferred by the Roman emperors over all others of the empire.

Then came the fall of the Romans and the onslaught of the barbarians, the Moors, the Normans. The wine that Ausone sang about virtually disappeared. The Normans came up the river in long straw boats covered with skin and, starting about a.d. 830, pillaged the region. The people huddled together in fear, the vineyards were abandoned, and there was famine.

It was widely believed that the world would end in the year 1000. During the final twelve-month countdown, work stopped and people began to do penance so as to gain eternal life.

To the general surprise the fatal hour rang and nothing happened, and the year of penance, in the Bordeaux area at least, was followed by disorder. The people gave themselves over to drunkenness — they had the means at hand — and to brutal passions. As the eleventh century progressed all laws were being ignored and there was no authority.

The English epoch began in 1153 and lasted 300 years. Eleanor of Aquitaine married King Henry II of England, brought him all of southwestern France in her dowry, and Bordeaux, which had once exported most of its wines to Rome, and after that to nowhere, now exported them principally to England.

In the Bordeaux archives receipts and bills exist which show how the vines were cultivated as early as 1332: planted in rows, kept low, and plowed four times a year, just like now. The men plowed and pruned; the women trained and tied the vines and picked up the vine cuttings, and for this traditional women's work they got the traditional women's wage, half.

Brittany, Normandy, and Flanders were also good customers during these centuries. However, England was often at war with Brittany, which put Bordeaux at war with Brittany too. During times of peace ships from Brittany would sail up the Gironde into the Garonne to Bordeaux bringing wheat and other grains, and they'd go back down carrying wine. But during wartime, trade ceased to exist, throwing numbers of Brittany sailors out of work. To keep eating, many became pirates. Ships out of Bordeaux bound for England, Flanders, or Normandy were obliged to sail within sight of the coast at all times because navigation was in its infancy, and the Brittany pirates, who kept lookouts on the cliffs to spot the sails, would simply go out and sack them. The Brittany pirates during the Middle Ages were the most dangerous enemies of Bordeaux's sea commerce — indeed, of nearly everybody's sea commerce. The ships took to sailing in convoys heavily armed or under the protection of warships. The dangers were compounded because the Brittany coast, as it protruded out into the shipping lanes, was both rocky and stormy. Many ships escaped the pirates only to pile up on the rocks anyway. His coastline, one of the Brittany princes of the age is supposed to have said, constituted the most beautiful pearl in his feudal crown. Finally the Duke of Brittany's right to exact a toll for ships passing in front of his cliffs was recognized by the commune of Bordeaux, and after that regular tribute was paid.

A document in the archives dated 1352 lists the ships that sailed that year. Not one was locally owned or built. They were English, Flemish, Breton, or Norman. The English ports of destination, about ten in all, were principally London, Sandwich, and Southampton. The ships weighed between thirty and forty tons each, big vessels for the day. One of the very strange things about Bordeaux all down through history is that it seems to have contributed to the sea trade nothing of its own except the wine — no navigators, shipwrights, or captains and few sailors.

At the mouth of the Gironde is a reef called the Rock of Corduoan. On the highest part of it there was a chapel dedicated to Notre Dame, and also a tower that served as a lighthouse to warn ships. The rock was inhabited by a hermit whose job it was to feed a fire all night. The hermit, with the waves lapping perpetually around his feet, earned two coins for each loaded ship that passed in front of the lighthouse, though he could not have had much to spend them on out there.

The convoys numbered sometimes thirty sails under the protection of two or more warships. The crossing to England and up the Thames took ten days. Pieces of the convoy would break off along the route to go to Ireland or a European port.

In the middle 1300s about 16,000 barrels of wine per year went from Bordeaux to England, Ireland, and Scotland. If the barrels were the same size as now, 225 liters, this adds up to about five million bottles per year. About 20,000 barrels went to Flanders, Holland, the north of France, and elsewhere. The records show that in 1372, 200 English ships arrived in Bordeaux to take on wine.

As soon as the ships had landed in England with the most recent harvest, last year's wine had to be tasted by experts and, if it had gone bad, spilled out on the ground according to law. The new wines were shipped immediately after the October harvest and were meant to be drunk as soon as possible, because by the following summer they had most often soured. In those days wine was seasonal; it did not keep, and wine lovers often had to wait months between glasses.

During all this period the wines from Bordeaux were distinguished one from the other as having come from the Graves or some other neighborhood, for vines were being grown for more than thirty miles above and below the city and on both banks of the river. It was already known that the stoniest, sandiest terrain, on the face of it the worst terrain, produced the best wines, and bills from the years 1490, 1491, and 1497 show that wines from

Graves were selling at up to three times the price of wines from the Médoc or Sauterne or any other place. Graves wines were always given to any dignitary who turned up in Bordeaux. No specific brand names or château names were yet known to anyone, but one was about to become famous.

Most of the foregoing geological information is readily available in Bordeaux, for over the years certain of the prosperous châteaux have commissioned scientific studies and borings. Partly their purpose was to understand what made their own wine so good, and partly it was an attempt to prove it better than their neighbors'.

As for the descriptions of how wine was sailed up past Brittany to the northern ports, these are based on documents in the Bordeaux archives that I came upon some years ago while nosing around in there looking for something else. Actually there are two archives; the Departmental at 13, Rue d'Aviau is the stronger of the two. The other is the Municipal at 71, Rue du Loup. It occurred to me at that time that the best way to tell the story of Bordeaux was to track a single important family over several generations, assuming such a family had existed, and before long I came upon the Pontacs.

They originated in a town called Pontac about 125 miles southeast of Bordeaux. Since the town bore their name, they evidently owned it, or most of it. For the earliest years there are only fragments of records. One Guillem de Pontac was one of the lords of Bigorre and in 1060 was credited with mediating a quarrel between two local armies. The Chevalier Albert de Pontac was appointed *maître d'hôtel* of the Duke de Guienne in 1120. Olmir de Pontac was a warrior for the Count of Foix in 1340. I found a letter of patent dated Feb. 20, 1375, and signed by King Charles V, in which Antoine de Pontac was one of five lords accorded royal permission to wear in the family coat of arms the order of the royal star. The document is signed "Le Roi."

The family evidently expanded in numbers and spilled over out of Pontac. Some of the sons came to Bordeaux. New lines of Pontacs began to accumulate there, one of them descended from Esteve de Pontac, a potter working in pewter at the end of the fifteenth century. His line led nowhere that I could see, but Arnaud de Pontac looked more promising. He was a merchant who imported cloth and exported wines and vine plants, honey, and pastel. Pastel is a plant whose leaves give up a blue dye. This was an extremely marketable commodity around 1480. Arnaud bought vineyards at Le Taillan, a few miles northwest of the city, and other land at Escassefort, several days' ride to the southwest. He appears to have been the first of the Pontacs to own land in or around Bordeaux. More important, he was the sire of the dynasty that was to dominate the city for the next 300 years.

The documents show that others among the important Bordeaux merchants also owned vineyards, either in the Graves or along the banks of the river close to the city walls. One or two had vineyards twenty or more miles north of the city in the Médoc, which is famous today but which was too far away and not safe. The roads out into the Médoc were bad, and they were unpoliced. The merchants were rich and could be robbed and killed, or robbed and held for ransom.

Not that these men were cowards. Most of them loaded their wine on board ships and then accompanied that wine north to wherever the market was, negotiating for the best prices in various ports speaking in Gascon, French, Latin, and English — sometimes in combinations of all of them. Once the wine was sold, the merchants would buy up goods to bring back to Bordeaux, sometimes redistributing these goods to points of sale along the Garonne in the upper country as far as Toulouse. They earned profits that were rarely less than 50 percent, and with their excess cash became moneylenders, charging 20 to 40 percent annual interest. Some were the equivalent of loan sharks. They furnished goods to peasant farmers in exchange for the peasant's mark at the bottom of a document. If the peasant failed to meet his interest payments, they took his property away from him. It was all quite legal.

Certain of these Bordeaux merchants financed voyages to the New World.

Their goal was the nobility. Always in the past a man had won noble rank with his sword only. But times were changing. The way into the nobility now was to buy land, and to buy political office. There are few enough specific references to Arnaud de

Pontac in these documents. Even his date of death is missing. As he acquired more and more land he won the attributions of Honnête Homme, then Honorable Homme, and finally in 1504 Noble Homme. This was as high as he got socially. In 1525 he bought the charge of king's controller for Bordeaux, the highest political rank he was to reach. He had two wives who gave him two daughters, who hardly counted in those days, but also six sons, one of them named Jean, a monumental figure from whom the dynasty would proceed.

Bordeaux at this time was a small, square, walled city. There were walls even along the riverbank. It contained an enormous number of churches and convents; it is possible on the early maps to count at least seven sprawling convents and fourteen churches. There were two brooding forces in the town: one was commerce, but the other was religion.

Outside the city walls to the north a new port came into existence called Les Chartrons. The merchants built their offices and warehouses there close to the river. Shops specializing in naval stores grew up, and after that inns, hostels, and a chapel. There were no quays. The ships dropped anchor out in the middle and were served by small boats. Casks of wine were rolled down the mud onto the small boats, which sometimes capsized. The ships sometimes dragged anchor and were blown up onto the bank. Presently a fort was erected between the new merchant quarter and the walls so that all those foreign ships could be kept under its guns.

The same ships came back year after year, and the men who sailed them became known around town. I found reference to a captain named Riou le Paing, master of the *Nonne* from Penmarch, who came to Bordeaux up to four times a year. The Englishman Richard Prow was seen along the waterfront for more than thirty years. Such people quickly found food, lodging, aid if they got in trouble, and especially long-term credit, without which commerce could not have gone on. Debts contracted in the autumn after the wine harvest would be paid when a ship came back the following spring. The documents seem to indicate that the merchants and sea captains were partners, whether officially or unofficially I could not tell, and even in times of war such partnerships continued.

For many of the captains and sailors Bordeaux was the last stop. They would disembark ill, be taken in by friends or companions who were members of the same trade guild, and they would make out their wills and die. These wills are still on file in the archives. They mention their home parishes, and their houses, and the steeples of their churches, and the odor of the sea that washed the shores of their distant homes.

Trade grew and the city grew. In 1509 a total of 587 ships went out of Bordeaux. They carried about 100,000 casks of wine, up from 36,000 a century and a half before. By 1563 this figure had more than quadrupled — the hermit out at the lighthouse was paid on the basis of having watched 2,556 ships go by. Salt, prunes, honey, and pastel were also being exported, but these products represented only about 20 percent of the volume and value of the wine.

Jean de Pontac, second in the line, was born in 1488. Like his father, he bought political office, he bought land, and he fathered children. He acquired immense power and wealth, and he held on to it for most of the next century.

Parliament had been established in Bordeaux in 1462, for the English era was over. The English had lost Aquitaine nine years previously at the conclusion of the Hundred Years War. By Jean de Pontac's time the Bordeaux parliament presided over most of southwestern France and supported nearly 10,000 clerks and officials. It is to be supposed that the peasants hated and feared their parliament, for the King did, and a later King, Henri IV, said: "You say that my people are being robbed? And who robs them but you and your company? All my parliaments are worth nothing, but you, Bordeaux, are the worst of all. Who wins his suit at Bordeaux but whoever has the fattest purse? Which peasant is there whose vines do not belong to a president or counselor of parliament? Which gentleman is so poor that he doesn't own land? It is sufficient to be a lowly counselor of parliament to be rich beyond words."

Jean de Pontac bought the office of *greffier civil et criminel* at the Bordeaux parliament in 1522. The *greffier* was a sworn notary or solicitor, and it was he who wrote down on vellum exactly what the law was, and what deeds were in force, and who owed what to whom. He took a piece of every transaction, not because he controlled the law but because he controlled what was written down. He controlled the word. Obviously *greffier* was a powerful office. It had become even more so now because in 1520, sixty-seven years after the fact, the official language of Bordeaux, which had been Gascon or Gascon mixed with English, had become French, a language few people spoke and fewer still could read or write.

The documents show that Jean de Pontac became the lord of at least ten different localities. He owned land as distant as Lacanau, out by the ocean about fifty miles to the north. He bought up a crossroads at Belin, thirty miles to the south, and there established a tollgate. Tollgates were a profitable business. The crossroads collected pilgrims from several directions enroute to Santiago de Compostela in Spain, and of course was used by other travelers too. From then on everyone who passed paid tribute to Jean de Pontac.

About half his properties were wine-growing domains. He owned the Château de Pez in St. Estephe, a well-known name in wine even today, though never classified as a *grand cru;* and in 1533, when he was 45 years old, he began amassing the pieces and parcels of land which came to constitute one of the greatest and most famous wine domains in the world, the Château Haut Brion. He bought the first piece of land from a Bordeaux merchant named Jean Duhalde for 2,650 livres — the bill of sale is on file. He bought at least two other pieces from local blacksmiths. It seems clear that he knew exactly what he was buying, for wine from these parcels had been the best and most expensive of Bordeaux wines for a long time. He bought parcels of land from whoever had it and in 1549 ordered the construction of the château itself. Documents dated Aug. 1, 1549, and April 27, 1550, give its original measurements: fifty feet by twenty-two. The English measure *pieds,* or feet, is the word used. The building was to be set off by four towers at its corners, of which three are left today, the fourth having been demolished to make way about 200 years later for what is now the "new" wing of the house.

The original château is, to modern eyes, almost feudal in aspect and rather austere. There is little decoration around windows and doors. Nonetheless, other great houses of the day had only one tower or two, and the enormously powerful Jean de Pontac had four. He was by then 62 years old.

He had married for the first time in 1525 at the age of 37. His bride was named Jeanne de Bellon; she bore him eight children who lived, at least four of them sons, and then she died. At 67 he married for the second time and fathered seven children in nine years, after which that wife died also. Jean de Pontac was what the French call a force of nature. At 75 he was still buying up more domains, for a document exists showing whom he bought them from and how much he paid. And his final child was born the year after that. He promptly married again for the third time, but fathered no more.

The documents indicate that he was either a religious man or a superstitious one. He kept a chaplain attached to his household; one of his sons was a bishop; he gave away part of the Haut Brion domain to the Carmelites — Château les Carmes Haut Brion still exists — and built them a church or chapel, stipulating that its central decoration was to be his tomb. And finally he became involved in a religious conspiracy that ruined his oldest son and cost a number of men their lives.

Religion in Bordeaux dominated all authority, even civil authority, which was said to proceed from it. Attendance at important religious services was, for the nobles and rich merchants, mandatory. Piety was mandatory, and the cathedral was a busy place. If the King died hundreds of leagues away, if a battle was won by the King's armies, if an heir was born to the throne, if parliament opened or closed — for every event everyone trooped into the cathedral and an elaborate religious celebration took place. Once, according to letters from Paris, the King and Queen ten days previously had fallen into the Seine. The four leading horses of the King's party were already on a ferry, and the last two and the King's carriage were trying to get on, when the ferry slid away from the shore; the King's carriage went into the water. The King saved himself by swimming, but the Queen went to the bottom. One of the barons swam down, grabbed her by her hair, and saved her. In Bordeaux the entire court went to the cathedral, and a Te Deum was sung.

Now in 1589 the childless King Henri III was murdered in Paris, and Henri of Navarre, a Protestant, became heir to the throne. This was during the series of religious wars that ravaged the country. Henri of Navarre held probably less than one-sixth of France, a city here, a city there. His armies were outnumbered by the armies of the Catholic League, and most cities were trying to remain neutral.

The authority for what comes next is Etienne de Cruseau, who kept a diary from 1586 until his death in 1619. Cruseau was a lawyer and counselor at parliament, and the manuscript of his "Chronique" turned up in Paris in an auction in 1859.

Bordeaux being one of the cities loyal to the new Protestant king, a Catholic conspiracy was put together inside the walls. The King's lieutenant, Maréchal Jacques de Matignon, would be murdered and the gates thrown open to the Catholic League.

But the conspiracy was discovered. A captain and a sergeant were brought to trial before the Grande Chambre, where they identified Jean de Pontac's oldest surviving son, Thomas, as the leader of the conspiracy. Jean de Pontac, who was then 101 years old, was also involved, they testified. The two soldiers were convicted, dragged out, and hanged forthwith, each in front of a different gate of the city, while the assembly returned to the chamber to debate the fate of the Pontacs. Thomas de Pontac fled Bordeaux — he did not come back until a general amnesty was declared more than five years later. Jean de Pontac was too old to run or chose not to, but before the assembly could reach a decision about him, word came that he was dead.

In his diary Cruseau writes: "Jean de Pontac, *greffier civil et criminel* of the court, notary and secretary to the King, yesterday gave up the ghost, having exercised the above offices under the reigns of Louis XII, François I, Henri II, François II, Charles IX, Henri III, age 101 years, suffering neither from gout nor gall stones, in good health, speech and hearing unimpaired up to the last breath, and the richest man in the present city." Two days later Jean de Pontac was entombed in the church of the Carmelites as he had ordered.

Haut Brion and the other domains passed to his second oldest surviving son, the bishop, at 44 the new head of the family; he bore the name Arnaud, after his grandfather, and was already famous in his own right, though he would become more so. Supposedly the bishop had aimed for the priesthood from his earliest years, and this was either a pious personal choice or the only direction in which younger sons could go. He was highly educated, particularly in Oriental languages, and was said to speak Hebrew. He wrote many books and translated others into Latin from the original Hebrew or Chaldean. At 27 he was consecrated a bishop — in those days one bought bishoprics too — and took possession of the See of Bazas, a town thirty-five miles southeast of Bordeaux. Twice as a young man Bishop de Pontac went north, to Blois on the Loire and to Melun outside of Paris, to take part in clerical conventions, and he had audiences with the King during which he denounced ecclesiastical "indiscipline," begging the King to reward with titles, parishes, and money only priests who were virtuous and learned.

He lived in the episcopal palace next door to his cathedral. He compiled an immensely expensive library, one of the finest of the day, that became renowned all over France.

In 1576, in the midst of the religious wars, the Huguenots took control of Bazas. Bishop de Pontac was then 31. The Huguenots roped masses of wood around all of his cathedral's pillars from floor to roof and made a blaze that was expected to cause the collapse of the pillars, the vaults, and the roof. Once unsupported, the facade would fall down as well. This is how cathedrals and châteaux were destroyed during wars and riots in the age before the wrecker's ball. But this first clumsy fire failed in its object. The Huguenots were about to start another when Bishop de Pontac bought the cathedral back from them for 10,000 ecus. This was either his own money — he was enormously wealthy and could easily have afforded it — or else he collected it in donations from the merchants and peasants of the town. He spent the rest of his life restoring the cathedral.

The sick and the hungry came to him in the thousands, particularly during a "plague," the nature of which is unspecified in these documents, that reached this corner of France in 1598. It killed about 14,000 people. In times of plague there was always famine as well, and an estimated 2,000 persons lined up at Bishop de Pontac's door every day, and he fed them.

It is impossible when paging through documents, diaries, and books in an archive not to become sidetracked, and in the course of researching Bishop de Pontac I found myself reading even about the weather: a cold wave struck in 1589, so severe that the river froze over; not a boat could move. A terrible storm the next year flattened trees, collapsed buildings, and blew ships up onto the banks. Hail in 1595 fell with such ferocity that the vines froze and died, and wheat became so dear it couldn't be found at any price. There was such a quantity of poor people throughout the city that no one knew what to do, and a search for food went on through barns and attics.

In 1605 Bishop de Pontac fell ill. He was 60. He had himself carried to the Château des Jauberthes near Langon, in which lived the widow of his late brother Raymond, mother of his nephew Geoffroy, who was his favorite and heir. He lay there dying for more than five weeks, suffering "excruciatingly," according to the documents. The doctors diagnosed kidney stones, but when the various drugs and broths they prescribed failed to ease the holy man's torment, it was decided instead that he was possessed by demons, who could be chased from his body only by song, and so for a time six men stood around his bed singing at the top of their lungs. Servants, relatives, and friends came to his bedside with tears in their eyes. He blessed them all, and died, it is written, "in the odor of sanctity." As he expired a mighty tempest blew up outside, and the winds whistled so strongly through the house that all the flambeaux around his bed were extinguished. Then it began to rain. It rained continuously until at last he was placed in his coffin wearing his gold chasuble and mitre, his red silk gloves. The rain then stopped. He lay with his hands clasped in prayer, and on one gloved finger he wore an enormous diamond of "inestimable" value. His death was counted a public calamity. His will

called for him to be entombed in his cathedral at Bazas. His funeral
cortege was so long the head of it entered the cathedral before the
Bishop's body had even left the château, more than nine miles
away.

Two portraits of him remain, one in the hospital at Bazas and
the other, which was mutilated during the Revolution and restored
later, in the Château des Jauberthes. They show a round-faced,
somewhat portly man with a double chin, a thin mouth, thin
eyebrows to go with it, and a sharp, pointed nose. Today a Rue
Arnaud de Pontac runs alongside his cathedral, and a plaque behind
the main altar commemorates the work of the bishop, and of
Geoffroy and even Geoffroy's son in restoring the cathedral. But
the bishop's once-venerated tomb is no longer there. It is no longer
anyplace, and the cathedral itself is in poor enough condition today
because during the Revolution, 187 years after his death, men stood
out front firing musket balls up at the facade, picking off the statues
one by one, until all were without hands or eyes or heads, after
which they began blasting away at all the noble tracery in stone.
With this job completed to their satisfaction, they went inside to
empty and defile Bishop de Pontac's tomb.

What is difficult for modern man to comprehend is the
amount of wealth amassed in France during those centuries by
some priests and virtually all prelates. Pastors didn't so much run
parishes as own them; bishops owned whole dioceses. It was like
owning a casino. The man who had been ordained had hit the
jackpot. It is equally impossible today to comprehend the reverence, which is another word meaning fear, with which the faithful regarded their clergy — these men in black, after all, were in
a position to give or withhold eternal life. It was the same in many
other countries, and the ultimate result was the same everywhere
too. Once the dam finally burst in France after 1789, and in Spain
and Latin America even in this century, the people turned on their
priests and even on nuns and slaughtered them with unimaginable
ferocity. The fear had turned to hatred so intense that it overflowed
and spilled backwards hundreds of years, so that the bones of men
like Bishop de Pontac were ripped from their tombs and thrown
into the river or the fields, and Bazas was not the only place where

the stained glass was smashed and the statues were pulled down from their pedestals and smashed or, if too high to reach, shot to bits where they stood.

Geoffroy de Pontac, the bishop's successor, 29 in 1605, became the lord of approximately nine domains and manor houses, including the Château des Jauberthes and, now, the Château Haut Brion, but he did not live in any of them. He thought of them as weekend places in the country, if he thought of them at all, and lived instead in a sumptuous mansion in downtown Bordeaux that was the size of a modern department store, for it covered an entire city block. It was called La Maison Daurade because nearly everything in it was either gold or covered with gold leaf. Whatever fell into the hands of this acquisitive family normally stayed there for centuries, La Maison Daurade being no exception: the family lived in it for 200 years.

The year he was 20 Geoffroy both married and bought his way into parliament as a counselor; at 40 he bought the presidency of one of the parliamentary chambers. There were during this period about twelve provincial parliaments in France, and the parliament in Bordeaux broke down into ten or a dozen chambers, each led by a president. The overall head of parliament was the premier president, which office Geoffroy either did or did not buy some years later — the documents I have found are not clear. He died in 1649, forty-four years after succeeding to the bishop's inheritance. According to one document, he was killed in battle fighting for the royal cause during the minority of Louis XIV. If true, this made him a very old man for perishing nobly: he would have been 73. One can pore over documents for days or weeks, sometimes without coming too close to what the truth must have been. And at some point one must stop, even though there may still be other information in there somewhere to be found.

Geoffroy was succeeded by his oldest son, Arnaud, 50, the third Pontac of this name and the fifth generation overall. Born in 1599, he became president of one of the parliamentary chambers in 1631 and premier president in 1653, a job he held for the next nineteen years. With the appearance of this Arnaud the documentary references to the Pontacs become more numerous. The voices of the past speak louder, and there are more of them. Arnaud was without question the most powerful man in Bordeaux in his lifetime. He owned apartment buildings in the center of the city, four important vineyards, including Haut Brion, farmland at St. Quentin, and a château and pine forests at Salles, and he still owned his great-grandfather's tollgate at Belin. He lent money at interest to a good many people, rich and poor, and the archive includes many of the legal papers that he served on such people when they wouldn't or couldn't pay up.

Arnaud lived with a magnificence that eclipsed that of the nobility. He lived far beyond the range of the other bourgeois and merchants of Bordeaux. In 1663 the *intendant* of the province, who was the King's representative in Bordeaux, reckoned that Arnaud de Pontac's yearly income came to 25,000 livres francs. It is impossible to translate this sum into modern money, but the workers in Arnaud's vineyards earned 10 or 12 sous a day on the average, and there were 20 sous to the livre franc. That is, Arnaud de Pontac's yearly income was the equivalent of 50,000 workdays of ordinary men.

The Maison Daurade was now more splendid than ever. It had four domes entirely covered in gold leaf, and the wrought-iron grillwork enclosing its interior courtyard was gold plated. Its furniture and decorations were luxurious. There was a proliferation of tapestries, Turkish carpets, and paintings — in one room alone there hung fourteen paintings and in another thirty-seven.

The English philosopher John Locke journeyed to Bordeaux in 1677. After ten days in Paris he had started south, looking for sunny weather that might cure his persistent cough. Even today one can travel from Paris to the Mediterranean by boat or barge down the rivers and canals of central France, and in those days of poor roads there was no quicker or more comfortable way to do it. Locke played cards aboard the various barges, whiling away the long hours, and each night the travelers stopped at an inn along the shore.

At Montpellier he reached the Mediterranean, where he put up in the back of the town, for the side which gave towards the sea and sea air was considered unhealthy.

In his diary he wrote of the hardships of the tourist in France: "Coarse and stinking lodgings . . . lean, ill-dressed meat . . . a rascally inn, four or five in a chamber."

Only occasionally did he find "good mutton and a good supper here, clean sheets of the country and a pretty girl to lay them on."

He added that he had seen "five acres of poverty for one of riches," that everyone carried pistols, and that there had been several murders. His cough did not clear up.

He visited Bordeaux for the first time in May 1677. "Friday May 14: I rode out & amongst other things saw President Pontac's vineyard at Hautbrion. It is a little rise of ground, lieing open most to the west. It is noe thing but pure, white sand, mixd with a litle gravell. One would imagin it scarce fit to beare any thing." Pontac's wine sold, according to Locke, for 100 ecus the tun: "It was sold some years since for 60, but the English love to raise the market on them selves."

The next year Locke again rode out to Haut Brion. It is possible to speculate that, to attract such a tourist in successive years, it must have enjoyed a tremendous and flourishing reputation. Locke was not after all a farmer.

The rest of what he saw disturbed him: "Talkeing in this country with a poore paisant's wife, she told us she had 3 children; that her husband got usually 7s. per diem. . . . She indeed got 3 or 3½s per diem when she could get worke, which was but seldome. Other times she span hemp, which was for their clothes & yeilded noe mony. Out of this 7s. per diem they 5 were to be mainteind, and house rent paid & their taile (tax), & Sundays & holy days provided for. For their house which, God wot, was a pore one roome & one story open to the tiles, without window, & a litle vineard which was as bad as noe thing they paid 12 ecus per annum rent & for taile L4, for which, not long since, the collector had taken their frying pan & dishes, mony not being ready. Their ordinary food rie bread & water. Flesh is a thing seldome seasons their pots &, as she said, they make noe distinction between flesh & fasting days; but when their mony reaches to a more costly meale, they buy the inwards of some beast in the market & then they feast themselves. And yet they say that in Xantonge & severall other parts of France the paisants are much more miserable than these, for these they count the flourishing paisants which live in Grave."

As a philosopher, Locke's most signal contribution to human thought was the concept of democracy: that self-government might prove feasible provided votes were taken and the will of the majority carried out.

Even though rich, Arnaud de Pontac's life was not entirely without problems.

The market for Bordeaux wines was, as always, dependent on ships sailing to the northern ports. To transport casks aboard a wagon towed north by oxen was theoretically possible, but there were toll roads everywhere, many towns demanded customs duties in and out, bandits infested the wild country in between, and the roads of the day could shake barrels to pieces. The risks and cost of road transport were too high.

However, the northern ports were constantly being closed down by wars. From 1652 to 1657 France and England were at war. After that it took years for the wine trade to build itself up again. In 1663 Bordeaux exported about 44,000 barrels of wine to the British Isles. Four years later the total was up to 68,000 barrels, and by 1672 it was 88,000 barrels. Whereupon France and England declared war against Holland — later turning on each other — and the bottom dropped out of the wine market once more. In 1678 the English parliament prohibited all trade with France.

Worse, there now appeared a number of new beverages: coffee, cocoa, chocolate, tea, and also a new drink that the Dutch made out of hops and called beer. New wines, namely port and sherry, had begun coming out of Portugal and Spain. In the absence of Bordeaux these so-called black wines attained great popularity in England. They made the Bordeaux reds seem rather thin.

Arnaud de Pontac countered by changing the way his wine was vinified, which changed both its taste and its longevity.

The new techniques were the *soutirage* and the *ouillage*. *Soutirage* means to clarify the wine at regular intervals by drawing it off its sediment. *Ouillage* means to keep the barrels topped up so that evaporation does not permit air to get in on the wine and spoil it. Wine so treated can be aged in cellars while waiting to be sold.

There have been many technical refinements since, but the *ouillage,* the *soutirage,* and the aging of wine in cellars were the essential ones, and the Château Haut Brion of those days must have tasted not unlike the Château Haut Brion of today.

In 1672, bypassing his son François-Auguste, who was a great disappointment to him, Arnaud de Pontac stepped down as premier president of the Bordeaux parliament — he was 73 — ceding his office to Jean-Denis D'Aulede de Lestonnac, Baron of Margaux among other noble places, husband of his daughter Thérèse.

On the night of April 26, 1681, the news went forth that the 82-year-old Arnaud was on his deathbed, and it was ordered that the great bells in the cathedral tower should toll, signaling the end of the old man's life, and this was done. According to a contemporary account: "This illustrious premier president had all the qualities which form magistrates of the first order, a solid virtue, a great detachment, a noble soul, kind and affable towards all the poor who came to him to claim justice; he was revered by people of standing, loved by the common people, and universally missed throughout the province. All the messieurs of the city council assisted at the funeral mass which was sung for the illustrious deceased, though without wearing their robes and hoods, inasmuch as several years had passed since Monsieur de Pontac had given up his office in favor of Monsieur D'Aulede, his son-in-law."

According to Arnaud's will, written out in 1677 in his own shaky old-man's hand, all of his affairs were in order, and perhaps technically speaking they were. But more than ten years later his estate had still not been settled, for Arnaud did not anticipate, and his will did not anticipate, the behavior of his son and principal heir, François-Auguste.

François was the sixth generation of this powerful family. He was born in 1636, and when he was 17 his father bought him the presidency of one of the chambers of parliament at the going price, 27,000 livres. At 26 he sold the office, pocketed the money, and disappeared for the next nineteen years. That is, he disappeared from mention in those documents that later found their way into the Bordeaux archives. Archives offer only tantalizing glimpses into the past, and of François-Auguste de Pontac for nineteen years there are none, apart from a single oblique reference — a document that describes Premier President de Pontac as brokenhearted at the loss of his only son. However, François-Auguste was not dead, and suddenly his name reappears in the documents. It is four months after his father's funeral, and the official inventory of La Maison Daurade is about to start in connection with his father's will.

There were two daughters as well. Their father willed them only money, 100,000 livres each. The will ordered bequests to the general hospital, to the Sisters of Mercy, and to the Dominicans for the building of a chapel to include Arnaud de Pontac's tomb. To all of his servants Arnaud willed an extra year's wages; he arranged that his maids should be cared for all their lives. He willed that his library — the late bishop's library — should not be broken up but remain intact.

All the rest was willed to François-Auguste de Pontac.

The widow de Pontac, François's mother, was still alive, but according to the customs of the rich families of the day, none of the estate passed directly to her. Her name was Henriette de Thou. She was the daughter of one of the presidents of the Paris parliament. She would be allowed to take from her husband's estate whatever she had brought into it, and that was all.

And so we see François-Auguste de Pontac, 45, standing in La Maison Daurade beside the notary he has hired. It is 1:00 P.M., Aug. 23, 1681 — the hour and the day on which this great family began to break up. François is waiting impatiently for the inventory to begin. His two brothers-in-law have been officially notified. Couriers were sent to them two days before. Neither has replied, and neither is present. François wants to begin the inventory without them, but the notary does not. Two hours pass. At last the notary agrees to begin.

The inventory is on file in the Archives Départementale de la Gironde. It begins with a statement by the notary that Jean-Denis D'Aulede, premier president of parliament, husband of Lady Thérèse de Pontac, is not present; nor is Jean-Baptiste Le Comte,

Captal de la Tresne, husband of the late Lady Marie-Anne de Pontac and father and administrator of their son. Nor has a representative of either appeared.

So richly cluttered was La Maison Daurade that the inventory took six full days. The most delicate part of it, accosting the elderly widow in her chambers, was left for last. About thirty-three rooms were inventoried, plus various hallways and antechambers. The doors and walls of the suite in which Arnaud de Pontac died were covered with paintings, a dozen or more of them religious, four of the Virgin, sometimes with the child Jesus, sometimes alone. In a painting on the old man's bedstead, Christ was being taken down from the cross. Elsewhere hung paintings of the pope, of the Queen Mother, of the Queen. Over the chimney hung a portrait of the King. The final two paintings were of the dead man's daughter, Thérèse, and of his son François-Auguste, who now stood watching the notary jot down descriptions of all these goods which had recently become his.

There was a chapel upstairs containing as many gold and bejeweled vessels and as many richly brocaded vestments as most cathedrals, and next to it was the room in which lived Pontac's two chaplains.

The inventory of La Maison Daurade stayed resolutely away from François's mother for five days. There she waited in her suite, as if a prisoner. Married forty-nine years, she must have been about 70; she had three years to live.

Her rooms too were hung with crucifixes and religious paintings, including all twelve of the Apostles, and near her bed was a prie-dieu whose tiny closet contained a two-volume life of the saints. The notary counted more than forty books in the old lady's room, all of them books of devotion.

But as he jotted down his descriptions, she became agitated. Those paintings on the ceiling, she said, and these six other paintings here were all given to her by Mlle d'Orléans, a princess of the blood. Here was another painting of the late Mme de la Tresne, her daughter, which also belonged to the old lady personally, because it was given to her by her other daughter, Thérèse, wife of Premier President D'Aulede. That clock over there was hers personally too, having been given to her by the Duke de Vendôme, and that tapestry there was given to her by the Queen Mother, and this set of damask linen, napkins and tablecloths hand-brocaded in flowered patterns — the entire set had been given to her by the bishop of Toulon. Over here was a beautiful desk which belonged to her personally, because it was a present from her son-in-law D'Aulede, and these other paintings had been presents to her personally from the Guise and Epérnon families. Here was a painting given to her by her brother.

The notary diligently inventoried all this, noting that the old lady claimed personal ownership, and gave her the document to sign.

She signed it "de Thou" — her maiden name.

The son had watched in silence. Once outside his mother's quarters, however, François-Auguste became agitated in his turn. Out of respect for his mother, he told the notary, he did not wish to contest in her presence the declaration she had just made. It would not have been good for her health. Nonetheless, in order to protect his own rights, he was obliged to declare that the seven paintings mentioned by his mother, since they were painted on the ceilings and walls, were part of the room and could not be removed. Since they had been given to his mother during her marriage to his father, they formed part of his own heritage and no longer belonged to her. As for the clock from the Duke de Vendôme, this was actually a thank-you present after the Duke had stayed with them in the Maison Daurade. Therefore it belonged to the house, not his mother personally. As for the Savonerie tapestry given by the late Queen Mother, this was in exchange for another tapestry his parents had sent her. Since the original tapestry would have belonged to him, François-Auguste, the tapestry given in exchange for it also belonged to him.

Dutifully the notary copied down this claim too; it was affixed to the inventory then, and is still attached to it today.

That was the start of more than ten years of intrafamily lawsuits. Eventually the courts had to appoint a neutral arbiter, Count de Beaumont, to intervene in quarrels that otherwise could not be solved at all.

François-Auguste kept that notary and other notaries busy for more than a month inventorying all the manor houses and lands he now owned. It was September before they reached the Château Haut Brion in the village of Pessac, four miles southwest of the city, which proved to be as sumptuously appointed as the Maison Daurade.

There was a proliferation of velvet chairs and silk bed canopies, of tapestries and religious paintings — over the fireplace in the grand salon hung a painting of Christ. The inventory lists twenty-three rooms, none of them bathrooms, of course, plus anterooms such as the one off the dining room — this was the bedroom for two lackeys. In another off the master bedroom slept the master's valet.

Upstairs was a game room. It contained a billiard table, cue sticks on the wall, four chairs, and a tapestry.

Madame's bedroom was upstairs, too — both here and at the Maison Daurade Monsieur and Madame slept in different bedrooms on different floors. Those were the days when marriages were arranged among families of property, and if a love match ever came into existence it was an accident. Madame's bedroom was on the western side of the house, for she liked to watch the sunset. The tiny antechamber that adjoined this room was the bedroom for her maid.

On the third floor was the chapel, with its complete set of vestments and vessels, twenty small religious paintings, plus one great painting, a pietà, over the altar. The chaplain's bedroom was nearby with two beds in it. Apparently the Pontacs kept two chaplains in attendance here too.

Downstairs again, the notary trooped through the cook's room and the gardener's room, mean little places crowded with mean, worn furniture. In addition to his bed, the gardener's room contained all his various tools for trimming the endless hedges and the vast lawns by hand.

As soon as all of the inventories were completed, François-Auguste abruptly got married. The bride was 25 years old and from a titled family, but it is not clear that they lived much together.

We next see François-Auguste de Pontac two years later in the London restaurant he owned and ran, speaking English with John Evelyn. It is because of Evelyn's diary that we know what

François-Auguste looked like, how he sounded, and how he seemed:

"Friday, July 13, 1683: I had this day much discourse with Monsieur Pontaque, son to the famous and wise Prime President of Bordaux. This gent was owner of that excellent vignoble of Pontaque & Obrien, whence the choicest of our Burdeaux-wines come and I think I may truly say of him (that was not so truly said of Saint Paul) that much learning hath made him madd: He had studied well philosophy, but chiefly the Rabbines & was exceedingly addicted to cabalistical fancies, and eternal hablador, half distracted with reading abundances of the extravagant eastern Jewes: for the rest he spake all languages, was very rich and handsome person & well bred; aged about 45."

By *hablador* Evelyn meant chatterer. François-Auguste de Pontac talked a lot, and he didn't always make sense.

The restaurant was called the Sign of Pontac's Head. It featured wine from Château Haut Brion, of course, and it was said to be London's first fashionable eating house. Its chef was supposed to have come out of the Maison Daurade; possibly it was the first authentic French restaurant ever established outside France.

That François-Auguste de Pontac, of the richest and most distinguished family in Bordeaux, should go into the restaurant business in London seems incredible. Was he trying to invest money where his creditors — he had many — couldn't get at it? Was he trying to make a name for himself out from under the giant shadow of his father?

On these questions the documents in the archives are silent. I could find no details.

The Sign of Pontac's Head was a fantastic success. More than ten years later Evelyn mentions it again, and long after François-Auguste de Pontac was dead the restaurant was still drawing London's best people: Defoe, Dryden, and Swift all mention it, and around 1715 Swift complains of the high cost of a meal there — 7 guineas. In brief, it had a tremendously long reign as the *restaurant de mode* in London.

If he spoke English so fluently François-Auguste must have spent much time in England. He also spent part of his time in his mansion in Paris, where he didn't always pay his bills. Lawsuits against him were constant. In 1683, the year he met Evelyn in London, he was involved in one suit in Paris, because of nonpayment of rent, and another in Bordeaux, where his brother-in-law Le Comte had the Château Haut Brion sealed. He had to pay Le Comte more than 15,000 livres to have the seals removed. The next year he was sued by his sister.

His principal income seems to have been from the Château Haut Brion, which in 1684 sold its wine at between 400 and 450 livres per *tonneau* — the next most expensive Bordeaux wines were selling for under 100.

Nonetheless, he was spending money faster than it came in. In 1688 he was censured by parliament. In 1690 there were suits against him for nonpayment of taxes and for nonpayment of grocery bills in Paris, and his furniture and other belongings in Paris were seized for nonpayment of bills in a Paris restaurant. A little later came a suit from a shopkeeper, which the shopkeeper won. In 1692 his brother-in-law Le Comte again had Haut Brion seized. The debts of François-Auguste de Pontac to that date totaled 141,227 livres, 2 sous, 9 deniers.

In those days a member of parliament normally employed four to six servants. A president of parliament employed about ten servants, but in 1689 François-Auguste de Pontac, who was neither, employed fifteen people in Bordeaux alone: secretary, valet, wine steward, cook, two coachmen, kitchen boy, doorman, two stableboys, four lackeys, one servant girl. Wages, therefore, came to 1,251 livres. He kept two carriages, spent 450 livres on fine wine, 900 livres on meat, 1,000 on other kitchen expenses, 800 for clothing, 660 for heat. He gave his wife 6,000 livres allowance and donated 400 livres to charity. His expenses totaled 18,000 livres. It was costing him only 3,000 livres a year to run the Château Haut Brion, which in a good year might bring in three times that much in profit.

But these were not good years. The war between England and Holland that had begun in 1688 lasted almost to the end of the century and was a terrible blow to the Bordeaux wine trade. In December of 1688 the King's *intendant* wrote a letter, which is extant, to the effect that the price of wine had dropped by half since last year. About one-fifth the normal number of English ships had come into Bordeaux. In 1693 the same man wrote that only two foreign ships had gone out; they would bring wine only as far north as Rochefort. The harvest will be lost, he wrote, adding that Premier President D'Aulede, Baron of Margaux, had not sold any wine in four years, and had more than 120,000 livres' worth of wine on hand. His vines had been abandoned for several years.

The *intendant* in his letters also described the suffering of the peasants because of the war, urging that the loading tax on wine be dropped. Later he asked permission to authorize commerce with the northern ports by ships flying the flag of Spain, for all the English and Dutch ships were gone.

In 1691 a hailstorm hit Bordeaux, killing cattle and sheep, destroying the vines, causing floods. The following year there was famine, and food had to be distributed to the starving poor.

François-Auguste was unable to sell his wine, and his debts mounted. On Jan. 13, 1694, aged 58, he died. His death excited almost no public notice. He was childless. His estate (and his debts), including the Château Haut Brion and its vines, now passed to his surviving sister, Thérèse D'Aulede, and to the surviving son of his other sister.

Thirteen days later Premier President D'Aulede died too. He was about 74.

With François-Auguste's death the Pontac line ended as a dynastic power in Bordeaux. There were no more premier presidents. The line had lasted six generations, about 200 years. The name would continue, for by now there were many lesser branches of the family, and to this day there are a number of land-owning Pontacs in the region. And the blood of the original Arnaud de Pontac, and of Premier President Arnaud de Pontac, would continue on the female side.

The war then in progress lasted four more years and was followed, after a four-year hiatus, by another: France and Spain against an allied coalition encompassing most of the rest of civilized Europe. Those Bordeaux wines that reached the northern ports at all did so most often as prizes of war. In Bordeaux the wine trade virtually ceased to exist. Vines were untended, and some of the most important families faced financial ruin.

Château Margaux, twenty miles north of the city in the

Médoc, was a ruined fortified castle dating from the Middle Ages. The D'Auledes never lived there, and even those who worked the vines dared not live on that side of the river. The Médoc was not healthy, nor was it safe. For the most part the workers rowed across every day, some of the world's earliest commuters, and rowed back again when it was night. The strip of wine-producing, gravelly soil was about three miles wide along the river. Further inland were swamps that had not yet been drained and planted with pines. The swamps produced insects, and the insects bred disease — a medical concept no one at the time was aware of, though they recognized a sickly place when they saw it. The Médoc was also lawless, being popular with brigands of all descriptions, and the nights were loud with the baying of wolves. Today more of the world's great wines come from the Médoc than anywhere else, but their excellence was just beginning to be discovered.

D'Aulede had built sheds at Château Margaux. At his death they were gorged with unsold harvests. Now the walls could hold no more. Men had learned to keep the great wines a fair length of time by now, but not indefinitely. These Margaux wines went bad and were spilled out into the dirt so that at least there was room for another harvest, which most likely would be unsold in its turn. There are no records of the situation at Haut Brion, but it must have been similar. Though the English by now had opened up trade with the Iberian peninsula and with the new world, with Scandinavia and the far-flung British empire, the Bordeaux wine trade was still totally dependent upon its few traditional northern markets and on the foreign shipping that serviced them.

Now at the beginning of the eighteenth century times were so desperate that a bizarre idea surfaced: if Bordeaux wine could be shipped south to Portugal, and there poured into Portuguese barrels, it could then be transhipped to England and sold not as Bordeaux but as port. It wouldn't taste like port wine, but once in their tankards the English would enjoy it, and Bordeaux would be saved.

So ships set out from Bordeaux to Portugal, and eventually some Bordeaux port did reach England. Other ships from Bordeaux to the north of France and/or neutral ports were captured by British warships. The *London Gazette* of May 12, 1705, announced "the sale by the candle" twelve days later at Lloyd's Coffeehouse in Lumbard Street of 200 hogsheads of "neat, choice, new red Obrion and Pontack prized wine, just landed" — apparently the first auction in London of wine as a prize of war, but not the last. Often Haut Brion, Margaux, Lafite, and Latour were sold at auction together — the famous 1855 classification was still a century and a half in the future, but already the four great names that would head it had begun to move in the same orbit.

When Catherine D'Aulede, 22, granddaughter of Premier President Arnaud de Pontac, married Count François de Fumel in 1682, the marriage contract stipulated that the young man was bringing to the marriage half of his father's goods, plus one-third of his mother's; the girl brought a dowry of 100,000 livres, 60,000 from her father, D'Aulede, and 40,000 from her mother, Thérèse de Pontac.

The young couple quickly produced four children, whereupon Count de Fumel died. The documents seem to indicate that he was murdered in the street. He would have been about 28.

From Catherine the Pontac fortune passed to her oldest son, Louis, who became the lord of Haut Brion, Margaux, and many other places and who married the daughter of the premier president of Toulouse. She brought him a dowry of 150,000 livres. The lifestyle of these dynastic figures did not change much over hundreds of years, and the acquisitive Pontac blood still ran strong through all of them.

Louis de Fumel wrote out his will in the Château Haut Brion on Sept. 21, 1749. After stipulating how much money should be spent on his sepulcher and how much distributed to the poor, he willed the rest to his third son, Joseph, for his oldest son had died young and his second son was a bishop.

This last-named Joseph de Fumel would prove as commanding a figure as any of the Pontacs before him. He was born March 14, 1720, at 19 took a commission in the army, and over the next twenty-five years carved out an illustrious military career. In 1741 began what became known as the Seven Years War: France and Prussia on one side, England on the other. The war was caused by the Prussian King's claims to parts of the Austrian empire.

Young Count de Fumel fought in western Belgium, in south-western Germany, in Provence, in Holland, in Brittany. It was a war that destroyed the Bordeaux wine trade still again, and Bordeaux society with it, but it offered brilliant opportunities for a soldier, and young Count de Fumel commanded a regiment of cavalry as it ended.

The period just after the Seven Years War was one of the most economically prosperous France had ever known. All the port cities, including Bordeaux, reported increased exports and imports. France held Canada, Louisiana, trading ports on the coast of Africa, a large part of India, and the rich sugar colonies of Haiti, Martinique, and Guadeloupe. In Bordeaux a building boom took place. The Place Royale, begun in 1730, was finally finished. The Allées de Tourny was transformed into an elegant, wide boulevard, with gardens and fountains, and it led up to the Place de la Comédie, where the new opera house was soon under construction. People were buying up vineyards and planting vines throughout the Médoc, throughout the Graves. Wine soon became so profitable that foreign wine shippers established themselves and their families in Bordeaux, and before long dominated the trade formerly controlled by rich parliamentary merchants like the Pontacs. The first Lawton came to Bordeaux at this time, the first Barton, the first Johnston, and many others; and today their French-born descendants are still there, bearing the same foreign names and running the same family firms, still working in offices along the Quai des Chartrons.

A second Seven Years War broke out in 1757, and Count Joseph de Fumel commanded cavalry at various battles in Germany. It was a war that settled nothing in Europe, though much in America, where Canada was lost to the French and all of North America swung irrevocably into the orbit of England.

By 1773, aged 53, Count Joseph de Fumel had left active service and returned to Bordeaux, where he became governor of the Château Trompette, the enormous old fort on the river at the northern edge of the city and, later, military governor of the entire province as well.

The harvest of 1788 was a poor one, and it was followed by an unusually severe winter. The river again froze. The peasants were reduced to the last extremities of poverty. Beggars, tramps, and robbers multiplied on all roads. There was famine everywhere, and the city of Agen asked Governor de Fumel for a loan of 6,000 livres to buy wheat. He sent the money immediately, his own money, a gift, not a loan.

In Paris two months later the Bastille was stormed, and the Revolution began. Bordeaux became governed by ninety electors, who asked for an audience with Count de Fumel at the Château Trompette. For three and a half centuries this fortress had symbolized the military sovereignty of the King. The people had always detested it, and they detested it still, exactly as the people of Paris had detested the King's dungeon, which was the Bastille. The electors asked Fumel for guns, and he gave them 1,000 rifles, asking only for a receipt. Next they worried about control of the fort, so he ordered its gates left open all night, and he allowed them to place a guard of twenty-six men inside its walls.

He did not have to do any of this. In a time when relays of post horses constituted the world's fastest means of communication, the Château Trompette and its garrison were under his personal command. He could have given any orders he liked, but had sided with the people against the King.

By September the national treasury was broke, and an appeal went out from Paris for "patriotic contributions." Count de Fumel responded by renouncing his 12,000-livre annual pension, and he also sent to the treasury silver vessels and jewels belonging to himself and his family, stipulating only that the transaction be kept secret; he wanted no public acknowledgment.

But when his gesture was announced to the National Assembly it broke into applause and voted that expressions of public gratitude should be published, and that Count de Mirepoix express the national gratitude personally to Count de Fumel.

In Paris the assembly soon voted that all citizens must sacrifice a quarter of their yearly income to help their country through these hard times. Count de Fumel was one of the first to comply, handing over the sum of 12,000 livres in February 1790.

Because there was again famine in Bordeaux, he also donated 12,000 livres to the city. To the village of Pessac, outside the walls of Haut Brion, which was as hungry, he gave 2,000 livres, and regularly after that he had his workers carry baskets of wheat and rye to the public square to be distributed. He also donated to the subsistence committee of Pessac 100 livres a month to feed indigent families.

The electors still governed Bordeaux, and during the nine months of their reign not a drop of blood was spilled and no uprising threatened the peace of the city. The Paris revolutionaries were astonished at this. Though much of the country was in turmoil, Bordeaux was living in tranquillity, the only one of France's major cities to escape bloodshed.

Elections were announced. Citizens who paid at least 3 livres in taxes per year went to the polls, each in his own district, to name a mayor in a new municipal administration. Voted mayor almost by acclamation was Count Joseph de Fumel. On April 3, 1790, he was sworn in, and afterwards mass was celebrated and a Te Deum was sung.

Parliament, which had governed the city for more than three centuries, was dissolved.

Still not a drop of blood had been shed.

Elsewhere in France other military commanders were hated and feared, and it seemed odd to the revolutionaries in Paris that Bordeaux should place its confidence in a general; it was perhaps with this act that the city became suspect.

Mayor de Fumel, the great-grandson of Premier President Arnaud de Pontac, was then 70 years old and no longer in good health, but he knew he represented stability in an unstable time and country, and he performed his new office as long as he physically could, retiring after a year to the Château Haut Brion. Bordeaux was still quiet.

A man named Saige, who was said to be even richer, replaced him. Most of the men in the new administration were rich merchants from the Quai des Chartrons. But then Bordeaux had always lived by and for commerce. Under the Revolution, nothing much had changed. A few decisions were made that would alter the physical aspect of the city. That was all.

Although priests in Bordeaux were not having their throats slit yet, anticlerical attitudes had become widespread, particularly against the enormous sprawling convents, which were like walled cities within the city itself. And so it was decided that the Carmelite convent out at Chartrons would be turned into a marketplace. The other Carmelite convent within the city, being of even greater expanse, would be knocked down and streets pushed through. Its church, which contained the tomb of the first Jean de Pontac and of other rich and famous Bordelais as well, would disappear. The same thing would happen to the Dominican convent in which lay the bones of later Pontacs. Streets would be pushed through, and public squares and new buildings would come into existence. The last dream of most of the Pontacs seems to have been to lie in an imposing stone sepulcher lording it over the city forever, and they must have felt rich enough to command eternity in this way, but it all ended now. Bordeaux was throwing off its past.

At some point the Maison Daurade was pulled down too.

Bordeaux seemed a happy place. People believed in the Revolution. There was an almost religious fervor to their faith. They watched the city change physically day by day and felt masters of their future, without so far having killed anyone.

Inevitably the Revolution began to run out of excitement. There must be more to freedom than the mere act of casting votes. The mob began to want more.

The mood of the people turned towards incoherence, and then into anarchy. Revolutionary clubs sprang up, most with banal names, though one was called the Club for the Surveillance of Enemies of the Constitution, a title that accurately describes the spirit of most of the others.

Bordeaux had always been a hard, stubborn, single-minded city. Whatever interested it had interested it totally. Now it became interested totally, absolutely, and solely in politics, and even commerce came to a standstill. People crammed themselves into theaters. The show began at 6:00 P.M. but by three in the afternoon the good places were taken. The show was not a theatrical play, not vaudeville, not dance, but a series of political speeches, patriotic parades, and ceremonies of oaths to the constitution, with never an intermission or halt of any kind, lasting till midnight or beyond, every orator applauded, every flag-waving display bringing down the house. The Bordeaux public had accepted politics with a kind of delirium.

But still there was no violence.

Out at the Château Haut Brion, at peace with his country and himself, surrounded by his vines, which he watched change with the seasons, surrounded by his family and by devoted servants, lived old Count Joseph de Fumel. He shared the château with, among other relatives, his daughter Marie-Louise, 45. Most other Fumels had fled the country by now, for they had recognized what was still not apparent to the old man — that very bad times lay ahead.

Three years and one day after the fall of the Bastille in Paris violence at last came to Bordeaux.

For some time priests had been obliged to swear allegiance to the Revolution, but as the years passed quietly many had taken renewed courage and had swung back towards the traditional church, with its rights and its riches. Some priests in Bordeaux had raised their voices to speak against the Revolution, and the mob was becoming irritated. Three churches were closed, and two priests who had fled were chased as far as Cauderan, where they were captured and brought back. The two were standing in the courtyard of the old archbishop's palace when the mob broke through and cut their throats. It was July 15, 1792. This was the first triumph in Bordeaux for the Sans-Culottes, the pantsless ones, the downtrodden, ignorant, poisonous mob of common people. Faith in the Revolution had just become both brutal and exclusive.

In Paris Robespierre had been heard to remark half jokingly that Bordeaux and its province were preparing to secede from France and rejoin England. Ysabeau declared that the merchants there were planning to sell their port to the English and that he had proof. By October 1793, when he and three other men came south to straighten out Bordeaux, the mob was ready to receive them with open arms.

The four men entered the city unopposed and within a few hours commanded it. A letter sent back to Paris read in part: "The Sans-Culottes came out in a mob before us, laurel branches in their hands, and followed along beside us crying '*Vive La République!*' Anxious to complete our work in lopping off the proud heads who would found here an empire other than the one described under our holy laws, we caused to be published on the next day a law ordering general disarmament. Today it is being executed with an incredible zeal, and it will provide a superb collection of arms in great quantity for our dear Sans-Culottes. Among the rifles were some decorated in gold. The gold will go to the treasury, the rifles to the volunteers, and the Federalists to the guillotine."

The people of Bordeaux obeyed these men, and also their successors, with astonishing servility. One of these successors, Marc-Antoine Jullien, a youth less than 20 years old sent to Bordeaux by Robespierre to check out what was happening, wrote back: "They treat the representative of the people as if he were an *Intendant* under the old regime. When he passes in the streets with gendarmes following, people take their hats off, they applaud, some voices even cry: 'Long live the savior of the people!' "

In Bordeaux these men from Paris set up a "Military Commission" directed by seven men, only one of whom had ever had the slightest military experience. The others were a schoolteacher, an actor, a merchant, and three artisans. The presiding officer, chosen by the other six, was Jean-Baptiste Lacombe, 33, one of the most sinister figures thrown up by the Revolution anywhere in France. For his swearing in the former schoolteacher came grotesquely attired in a Henri IV hat two centuries out of date, plus a general's uniform to which he had added an elaborate white collar, a black cravat, a white vest with extremely wide lapels, a tricolor sash, and a dangling saber of unaccustomed weight, which he seemed unable to keep from getting between his legs. The other six men were similarly ridiculously outfitted.

These simple citizens now held life-and-death power over every inhabitant. They could arrest, try, and judge anyone on any charge, enter into any home to search for food or contraband, and sell confiscated goods at once.

Lacombe wore a great deal of long and not very clean hair. He was a tall man with a long, pointed nose and protruding eyes. Born in Toulouse, he had come to Bordeaux eight years previously. In addition to school teaching, he was suspected of being a carriage thief and swindler. He was extremely eloquent, and at his swearing-in ceremony made the following speech: "The blood of our brothers, spilled in torrents since the beginning of the Revolution, demands vengeance. Their cries have finally been heard. The law is about to strike the guilty. . . . As organs of the law, we will be as impassable as the law. No consideration will stop us. And, if within this commission, there exists a man too weak to condemn his own father to death though guilty, let that perfidious man fall himself under the sword of the law."

The Reign of Terror, which had long since come to Paris, had reached Bordeaux.

On the day Lacombe took office, carpenters were already erecting the guillotine on the Place Nationale (today the Place Gambetta). The Military Commission lasted ten months. When it ended there were still 1,569 persons in the prisons. More than 300 men and women had been guillotined. Of these, 49 had been nobles and 54 priests or religious, a normal enough percentage for any reign of terror of that type and quite in proportion to the statistics of Paris, where over 3,000 were executed. What was particular to Bordeaux was that 100 merchants were sentenced to death for being merchants and for "egoism." The sole crime of these people was being rich, and in truth the Military Commission was more interested in their wealth than in their lives. Many bought their way to freedom, coming to agreements with Lacombe in advance of their "trial." The Military Commission in its ten months of life brought in more than 7 million livres in fines, a good deal of which disappeared. The Terror in Bordeaux was not only an excess of idealistic fervor, it was at times a gigantic blackmail.

It is said that Lacombe coveted the Château Haut Brion. This may well have been so. In any case, he needed victims, for the fire was burning hot and using them up fast, and inevitably his eye fell upon Count Joseph de Fumel.

The first knock on the door at Haut Brion came on Dec. 3, 1793. The people's militia wanted not Fumel but his daughter. They had a warrant and they took away Marie-Louise de Fumel. Her mansion on the Rue des Trois Conils was broken into and sacked.

Her interrogation revealed that she had permitted a clandestine religious marriage to take place the previous June in her house.

The bride was her chambermaid, the bridegroom a wig maker. The marriage was pronounced by a priest named Coste, who had refused to swear allegiance to the Revolution and who was still at large.

Under the Terror the law did not directly forbid religious ceremonies, even those celebrated by unsworn priests, though obviously any citizen who assisted at such a mass became suspected of "fanaticism," for which he could go to prison. But he was guilty of a major crime only if he invited such a priest into his house, in which case under the law of March 26, 1793, he was subject to six years in irons. This is the law under whose jurisdiction the clandestine marriage had taken place, and so Marie-Louise de Fumel seemed to be facing no worse than six years in a dungeon. It is true that a second law had come into force on Oct. 21, four months after the marriage and six weeks before Marie-Louise's arrest, under which she could be sentenced to be deported; but the death penalty for such a crime would not become law until April 11, 1794, more than four months in the future, so apparently she at least did not face the guillotine.

Three days after his daughter's arrest, men came for Fumel himself. The old man was taken to Bordeaux and thrown into a cell in the Fort du Ha.

He had been denounced by one of his valets, and there is on file a letter sent to the Committee of Surveillance signed by a man named Barbe, one of the most dreaded zealots of those days: "Republicans, my brothers, I write to advise you that at Haubrion, an unsworn aristocrat says mass for Fumelle. . . . Let me grab this black animal on the spot. *Salut.*"

The letter's postscript identifies the valet: "Jean Lafon, Daubrion, has declared that a priest is saying mass in the house of citizen Fumel. Has made his mark, not knowing how to sign."

The Count de Fumel, sick with the infirmities of years, plus worry about his daughter, had to be transferred almost immediately to a hospital.

News of his arrest provoked outbursts of emotion in Pessac, and two days later most of the villagers gathered at city hall and in concert with their elected officials addressed a long letter to the Committee of Surveillance in Bordeaux: Count de Fumel should be set at liberty at once, or at least allowed to live in the château under house arrest. "We do not fear asking for the liberty of this true father of the poor who, after the last harvest, saved so many people from famine by having distributed without charge twenty-four baskets of grain to the people of our commune. Give him back his liberty, we ask it out of humanity." There followed some thirty signatures. A few days later a second document was forwarded to the committee. A man named Arnaud Pineau declared that his brother-in-law, who had worked for Count de Fumel, had died, leaving four orphans. Fumel had adopted the four and sent them to school. He paid their lodgings and heat and gave each a yearly allowance of 100 livres. Since the arrest of Fumel, wrote Pineau, "the four orphans have not stopped weeping." He begged for the liberty of the prisoner.

These letters had no visible effect, except perhaps to slow the course of revolutionary justice. It was going to be necessary to put together some evidence.

Fumel recovered enough of his health to be thrown back into a dungeon in the Fort du Ha, while an investigating magistrate was sent out to Haut Brion to interview his employees and others. In January 1794 testimony was taken from eighty-two witnesses. This dossier, which exists today, is more than thirty pages in length and tends to prove that the worst Fumel could be accused of was refusing to permit hunting on his property.

The following month the commune of Pessac delivered another document attesting to Count de Fumel's patriotism and his generosity towards the poor of the commune. Fumel himself wrote a letter asking that the seals on the Château Haut Brion be lifted so that he could send someone into the house for funds to pay his employees. He also wrote a petition to the Committee of Surveillance outlining his conduct since the beginning of the Revolution and asking to be set at liberty or, if this proved impossible, at least to be transferred to the Orphelines prison so that he could be with his sister, his daughter, his niece, and his nephews, affording all "the sad consolation of mixing our tears together." This request was granted, but he arrived there too late to see his daughter, for on Feb. 1, sixteen days previously, Marie-Louise de Fumel had been brought before the Military Commission. After waving her chambermaid's illegal marriage certificate before the terrified woman's eyes, Lacombe had written out her death warrant: "The Military Commission, convinced that the accused has given a thousand proofs of her hatred for liberty and that she helped several French citizens leave their native land to go join the most cruel enemies of France, that she has always frequented aristocrats and fanatics, and principally Coste known for his counter revolutionary principles, that she helped one of her domestics receive the nuptial benediction from this traitorous priest, and that she furnished her house so that he could exercise his functions in contempt for the law, that in the certificate of marriage signed by this priest on June 25, 1793, there is mention of the power given to him by the Archbishop of Bordeaux, which demonstrates that both still believe in the counterrevolution, that she urged several citizens to sign this document who, without her, would never have strayed from the principles which are their happiness, that in her testimony she gave evidence of the most profound contempt for all those not devoted to fanaticism and aristocracy. She asked her father to give a certain sum of money to her husband and her brother so that they could emigrate. That by all these reports she must be considered an enemy of the revolution and consequently proscribed by the law of 27 March, 1793. Ordered, in conformance with this law, that she suffer the death penalty, that all her goods be confiscated to the profit of the republic. Ordered in addition that this present judgment shall be printed and posted throughout the city. Done and judged in public session."

The document was signed by five members of the Military Commission, including Lacombe. Marie-Louise de Fumel, Countess d'Argicourt, was taken out of the building, loaded aboard a cart, dragged through the streets to the Place Nationale, and beheaded.

Her father was not going to be as easy to execute. The investigation into Count de Fumel's conduct, which had lasted on and off for months, had failed to turn up sufficient damaging evidence. Instead people were still signing depositions in his behalf. The municipal officers of Pessac attested that never had they seen any man enter the Château Haut Brion who was in any way suspect. The mayor, who was a doctor, testified that because of the old man's health he had been called daily to the château and had never met there any persons the least suspicious. Once he had heard Fumel declare to the chaplain who was teacher to the old man's nephews that he would have to swear the new oath to liberty and equality according to law or else he could not stay in the château. The priest, testified the doctor, had properly conformed to the law.

The months passed.

On March 31 Fumel wrote to the municipality at Pessac asking for a certificate to the effect that he had turned in all his commissions and military decorations. It was brought to him at once.

The old man wrote again to the Surveillance Committee: "Citizen Joseph Fumel, age 74, weakened by infirmities, has been held five months in prison. His detention was necessary without doubt, according to the circumstances, and he is not complaining." The petition went on to outline all the depositions in his favor and also his conduct since the beginning of the Revolution, and it concluded: "The infirmities of the petitioner increase each day, his bad health weakened further by age, by 56 years of long and difficult active service, demand repose, tranquility, and prompt and regular treatment. The petitioner asks with confidence, citizens, your justice and your humanity, that he might be reunited in the country at Haut Brion with his old and infirm sister, his young niece and his nephew, all of them held many months in the Orphelines, and their care and aid being necessary to the reestablishment of his health."

This document, which can be seen today, is signed simply "Joseph Fumel."

It received no response.

May passed. June. At the Place Nationale the ground beneath the scaffold was soaked in blood. The repugnance of the populace was growing. The mob no longer cheered as the merchants and former aristocrats were dragged through the streets to their doom.

On July 27, 1794, Fumel was called before Lacombe's tribunal. Lacombe was in good spirits.

"Name, rank, position that you occupied under the reign of the tyrants," he demanded, according to the minutes on file.

Lacombe had addressed the old man in the familiar *tu,* and with an insolence to which mayors, governors, generals, noblemen — and Count de Fumel had been all these things — were not accustomed.

Joseph de Fumel gave the required answers.

Lacombe cried: "As mayor of Bordeaux, you wished to prevent the sublime élan of the Bordelais who wished to fly to the aid of their brothers in Montauban, who were being oppressed by the aristocracy. You have relatives who have emigrated. You have held conferences in your house which were attended by counterrevolutionaries. There's enough there already to judge you on, but given your great age, we decided we'd have to do an investigation in your case. A *commissaire* was sent by us into the different villages. These investigations show that you oppressed the good people who inhabited your region, that you carried out vexations against those who in the past you called your subjects. Finally, you stood up against the parliament at a time when it seemed at last to be showing itself as a friend of the people, and as enemy of the tyranny of which you were an agent. What do you have to reply?"

"If sometimes there were aristocrats in my house," said the old man mildly, "it was by accident, and not because I knew they were aristocrats. I never had unsworn priests in my house. Here are some documents which prove what my conduct has been since the beginning of the Revolution."

He passed the tribunal a great number of certificates and affidavits.

It was Lacombe's habit to accord each judgment no more than eight minutes. He glanced at a few of these papers, then said: "That's enough. The tribunal has decided."

You can read Fumel's death warrant today: "Convicted on all counts, he must be counted in the class of enemies of the revolution. Ordered according to the law of March 27, 1793, that he suffer the death penalty, that all his goods be confiscated to the profit of the republic, and that the present judgment be executed at once on the Place Nationale."

The document is signed by five members of the Military

Commission, but not by Lacombe himself, who was perhaps shrewd enough to sense that public sentiment was turning against the bloody deeds of his commission.

Joseph de Fumel, 74 years old, condemned to death, was hustled outside and into a cart. The cart moved through silent streets to the place of execution. The old man mounted the scaffold. Standing, he was strapped to the board, which then was tipped over into a prone position, his neck directly under the blade. He made no final speech that was recorded. Perhaps he was too old, sick, and disgusted to care anymore. In any case, he had never lacked physical courage in battle, and did not lack it now.

The order was given. The blade descended.

So perished Count Joseph de Fumel, and there are few more sympathetic figures among all of the victims of the Revolution than he. We do not know what he looked like, and a document, signed in the town of Fumel, the original family seat, by a renegade priest named Paganel on behalf of "the representatives of the people" indicates why. Since "monuments to feudal vanity and power" were contrary to the principles of liberty and equality, and injurious to the French people, the municipality was ordered to enter the Château de Fumel without delay and collect all crests, shields, coats of arms, crowns, banners, portraits, paintings, or other "vestiges of former feudalism that might give insult to a republican"; and on the Sunday following, the citizens of the commune were to gather for "the agreeable spectacle of the public burning of all of the paintings and objects mentioned above."

Similar burnings occurred all over France.

In ordering the execution of Joseph de Fumel, Lacombe may have expected trouble. But he could not have expected as much as he got. From the populace went up cries of pain and outrage. With the murder of old Joseph de Fumel, aristocrat though he was, Lacombe had overreached himself. This was not clear at once. The Military Commission sat for four more days, during which nearly every prisoner to appear was judged guilty, sentenced to death, and immediately executed.

But the seance of July 31 was the commission's last. That night word reached Bordeaux from Paris that Robespierre had been overthrown.

To save themselves, the other leaders turned against Lacombe. He was arrested in his bed and thrown into a cell, where he languished for two weeks. His trial came on Aug. 14. He was convicted of antirevolutionary acts and led to the guillotine, where the mob attempted to break through the cordon to get at him. When his head was in the basket, the mob did in fact break through, and his once-feared visage was paraded through the streets on the end of a pike. He was the terrible blade's last victim in Bordeaux.

St. Laurent du Maroni
A TALE OF JAIL

In French Guiana today the remnants of prisons are all around you. Every village has one, and so do a good number of what must have been only clearings in the jungle. To drive along the few roads is similar to driving past former battlefields — at each new turn you come upon another terrible name and site. Or past the bull ranches of Andalusia — sinister memories crash at you out of the underbrush.

In the last few days I have looked at ruins in the capital, Cayenne, and at Kourou, which is where the new space launching pads are located. At Heatte, where the dirt road ends and a broad golden beach stretches for miles, there is an Indian village — open-walled straw huts — to one side of the road and a ruined prison to the other. Yesterday evening I watched naked squaws preparing dinner, then turned around and stared at roofless walls half hidden by underbrush so thick it was impossible to approach them. Each former building was like an overfull vase, with the jungle growing out the top. Near the peak of one wall the number 1907 was incised in the stone — the year that particular cellblock was built, presumably. France's South American penal colony had been a failure by then for fifty-five years, but the Administration Pénitencière was still throwing up new buildings. In the increasing dusk, clouds of mosquitoes suddenly assaulted us. We strode hurriedly away from the Indian village and drove out of there. The prisoners who once inhabited those buildings couldn't leave at dusk when the mosquitoes came in, and mosquitoes in those days were as deadly as bullets.

Today we are in St. Laurent, a few miles up the Maroni River, on the western edge of the country, which is where all prisoners from France disembarked. They kept arriving until 1938, and the last were not released until 1954 — a few hundred broken men, not all of whom accepted the free ride back to France. St. Laurent today is a pleasant colonial town of 7,000 or so, with a few paved streets and many unpaved ones, and the Maroni, though I had never heard of it until shortly before I saw it, is one of the great rivers of the world, nearly two miles wide here and about 600 miles long.

In the middle of St. Laurent still stands the arched gateway marked "Camp de la Transportation"; I march in under it, as did every prisoner who ever came here. Beyond the arch are guard-rooms which have lately been used as warehouses — they are littered with used oil drums and other such junk — and decaying barracks buildings in some of which entire families of squatters have set up housekeeping.

I push through leaves and find myself in a cellblock: a square courtyard overgrown with waist-high vegetation and rimmed by half-rotted cell doors standing open. Over here is part of a window whose bars were once as thick as wrists, and kept shiny by hands. A few decades of rust have rusted them slim. In places they are as thin as roofing nails. A child could wade through them now. Whether filled with silence, or with milling men, prisons abound with ghosts. They are the ghosts of failure, which make no noise, and the ghosts of suffering, which seem to wail like birds. Vines have entered certain cells like overly curious tourists, nosing around in there before twisting out the barred windows high up, as if gasping for fresh air.

Incarcerated criminals are the most documented individuals alive. I have been inside a number of American prisons. In one of them my guide, a corrections department captain, presented me with each of the thirteen forms an incoming prisoner had to fill out. They came in seven different shapes and six colors: white, orange, blue, yellow, beige, and brown. There were forms for court appearances, for visitors, for medical treatments, cell location, personal property.

Here in St. Laurent the same paperwork was stressed, for in a cell drier than the others and dusty from fallen plaster, stacks of forms stand on the wooden cot that formerly served as some prisoner's bed. Other forms lie thick as fallen leaves, and as dry and brittle, on the floor. The forms have outlived the prisoners and possibly will outlive the prison as well, which must be true all over. Though the ink has faded, they appear still to be legible. As I lift a batch off the cot to read, a snake slithers out from underneath. I drop the forms back onto the cot without reading them and leave the cell.

After separation into categories, the new inmates were dispersed throughout the country to subsidiary camps. All prisons have frequent searches, especially when moving an inmate from building to building or floor to floor. They had searches here too, but the inmates hid money and perhaps a shiv in metal cylinders that were never found. They hid them in their rectums. Today such cylinders would be revealed by x-ray machines. Today in most of the world's prisons convicts use condoms instead. They don't show on x-ray machines and they contain usually drugs.

The only roads inland are the rivers, and now we ride up the broad Maroni for four hours — about fifty miles — in a forty-foot-long native pirogue, a hollowed-out log driven by an outboard motor. On the other side of the river is Suriname, formerly Dutch Guiana. At first there are pirogues all around us, moving people and produce up and down the river and across it: they can be hired like taxis. Then they drop behind us. The water is fast-moving and brown. In some places the banks are high up, and there are villages. We stop three times. The first two times we visit villages inhabited by blacks — known here as Bush Negroes — who are the descendants of runaway slaves of long, long ago. Open huts strung with hammocks. Tree stumps for chairs and tables. It is like being dropped suddenly into central Africa. The villages at this time of day are inhabited mostly by women and children. There are few able-bodied men around. The children are naked. The women wear short skirts tied around their middle.

Nearly all are both barefooted and barebreasted, though one or two wear what appear to be American brassieres — stark white, honest to God, Playtex Cross-Your-Heart quilted brassieres. How did American underwear get this far up the Maroni River, and what made these women want to wear it? We distribute candy to the children out of paper bags. The entire village follows us back to our pirogue.

Finally we step ashore into what was once a penal camp known as the Forestière. Little is left of it. A few feet inland stand some brick pillars and a brick staircase that leads into space.

Prisoners here slept in hammocks until they had built their own prison, and after that they logged enormous trees — some of the hardwood trees above us are fifteen stories high — starting them downstream towards a profit for someone, not them. They were undernourished and there were years when the rules called for them to work stark naked. Possibly they liked this camp. They seemed to have more freedom here: trapped between the vast river and the virtually impenetrable jungle, where could they go? And so they were often allowed to roam around the clearing. Are freedom and the illusion of freedom the same?

The jungle floor is littered with old bricks. I turn some over with my foot. I come upon two stamped "St. Jean," which is the name of still another prison. At one time the rules called for each brick in each prison (all bricks made by prisoners) to be stamped with that prison's name, and today there are men who collect sets of such bricks. Certain of the rare ones are worth money. Our guide picks up my St. Jean bricks. In Cayenne he will attempt to sell them.

No object is too grisly for a collector. One of the prison doctors used to collect the heads of guillotined cons. He had about a dozen in a cabinet, it is said, but higher authorities found out and advised him to get rid of them.

We eat a picnic lunch on a rock, gazing out over the great river. Nearby are anthills twelve inches in diameter, and about as high, with ants working. There is a breeze and the odor of earth and trees is everywhere.

The St. Jean bricks drop into the bottom of the dugout pirogue, and we start downriver. A torrential downpour falls almost at once. The river boils. In seconds we are soaked. Then the rain stops and the sun comes out again.

The heat and humidity in French Guiana are about the same all year round as New York in summer. For the convicts there was of course no air conditioning. There was no entertainment to look forward to at night or any other time. American prisons always boast a library, which is usually a smallish room containing relatively few books and no inmates. There is always a movie theater as well and nowadays many television sets — often one in every cell. In French Guiana recreation was limited to card games, knife fights, and an occasional execution.

Prisoners got only two meals a day, but their contents had been calculated to the last calorie and should have been sustaining. However, the stronger convicts, and those closest to the source, stole extra food for themselves, or they connived with guards to sell it to shopkeepers. Their fellow cons were always hungry.

When discipline was meted out, food was always the first item withheld. Cons sentenced to months or years of solitary confinement on bread and water suffered from scurvy and their teeth fell out. When sent back into the main compound they had little chance on prison fare to recover.

In addition, administrators soon found that undernourished prisoners became lethargic, were easier to handle, and made little effort to escape. Undernourishment, however unofficially, began to be encouraged.

About 1,200 prisoners arrived from France each year, but the total under guard remained constant, about 7,500. Some finished their sentences each year, a few escaped, and about 10 percent, 750 men, each and every year died. That is, two-thirds died before completing their sentences. They died of yellow fever, dysentery, malaria, and a great many other diseases; some died of snakebite, or were shot to death by guards, or were guillotined for additional crimes, or were killed by other cons, or went mad. Presumably some died of despair.

The guards, well fed and living in comfortable villas cons built, died rarely. Some guards were decent men, at least at the start, and some were or became sadists. Most, like the cons, dreamed of seeing France again.

The head administrator lived in St. Laurent in an elegant colonial mansion looking out over the river and worried principally about being embarrassed by and/or losing his job over some sensational escape or riot. The *sous préfet* of French Guiana, a kind of lieutenant governor, lives in the same mansion today. Anyone who walks by can peer into his garden or even walk in it.

Very few men listed as "escaped" ever escaped far. In 100 years some 9,000 men "escaped"; some survived to terrorize neighboring countries and some to write books that were made into films, the most famous of which was *Papillon*. But a con had to get nearly 1,000 miles away — as far as Trinidad or Venezuela to the west or Brazil to the south or east — before he could surface. The one route led through jungle, the other over open sea. Cons lost at sea left no trace, and few lost in the jungle left any trace either, though cons logging trees or pushing through roads sometimes came upon a skeleton stripped clean by ants.

In French Guiana there were three categories of prisoners. In minimum security were the *relégués,* mostly petty thieves sent here because of numerous prior convictions. They lived in barracks and mostly worked camps like Forestière or Heatte. Some even worked as domestic servants in the villas of guards or administrators.

The other two categories were the political prisoners and the *transportés,* the hardened criminals. The worst of the *transportés* were sent to two islands, Royale and St. Joseph's, ten miles off the coast of Kourou, and the political prisoners went to the third island, Devil's.

The three islands lie like pieces of a triangle, separated from each other by 200 yards of water. Each is about half a mile long. Devil's Island is the narrowest and lowest, a kind of inkblot on the sea.

We ride out towards the islands on a rusty old tugboat — a ninety-minute crossing costing about $15 round trip — and we land on Royale. Though decades of grisly publicity would make you think of Devil's Island as the world's number-one hellhole, the pinnacle of man's inhumanity to man, this is false. Royale was the place, or else St. Joseph's. Hardly anyone served time on

Devil's, and those who did almost always got back to France eventually. On Devil's a man's only enemy was boredom.

Today Devil's Island is inaccessible to tourists unless they swim. There is nothing there. It is a place of tall coconut palms and cool breezes. From Royale it can be seen quite clearly. In the underbrush, it is said, you can find the ruined foundations of the five or six stone huts that once stood there, but you must look hard. There were never more than a handful of political prisoners on Devil's at one time, usually only one or two, sometimes none. They had the run of the island. There were no boats tied up for them to steal, and sharks supposedly cruised offshore. They had no workshops, no tools, nothing to build a raft with. Escape was impossible. They were watched by one or two bored guards. They had nothing to do. They sat on a flat, ten-foot-long stone and stared across the sea towards France, 5,000 miles away, while the waves smacked against the rocky coast. Over the decades the stone bench got worn smooth by the rear ends of men waiting for the regime to change. Their island was supplied from Royale by a kind of aerial cable car, which also wafted individual prisoners in and out, a tropical ski lift. The cable has long since rusted away, and today the stone pylons on either shore are in ruins. In his book Papillon claims to have escaped from Devil's, but no one who has ever seen this place believes it. They say no one ever escaped from Devil's, or from the other two islands either. Escapes were from the mainland only.

When prison horror stories are told, Devil's Island reigns alone, though why? There was no brutality there, no mosquitoes, no disease. But Devil's is fifty times more notorious than St. Joseph's or Royale or any of the mainland prisons. Devil's is legendary, a bestseller that, despite being dull reading, caught on.

Among those who know about the French Guiana prisons, St. Joseph's was supposed to have been the worst because of the "reclusion" cells. For crimes such as assaulting another prisoner or attempting to escape, already hard-nosed cons would be sentenced to two or more years solitary confinement on St. Joseph's in cells that measured about eight feet by six and had wooden doors and no roofs. Guards enforced absolute silence. Transgressions were punished by the withholding of food. About 200 cells still protrude from the jungle on St. Joseph's. Up to 200 men at a time went two years or five or ten without leaving their cells, or speaking a single word, or seeing another human being except for the feet under the doors of the relays of guards. Very few survived even two years of this. Any longer and the mind broke, a man began to scream, and when the door was opened on him, months or years later, the guards dragged forth a young madman with snow-white hair.

The torture of silence. In American prisons the torture is more likely noise: voices, radios, television sets, toilets flushing, bars banging, noise that never stops.

Royale could be bad too. About 1,500 men, mostly prisoners but including the staff for all three islands, lived on Royale. There was a church and even, for the guards' wives, a maternity hospital with a wrought-iron gateway and a horseshoe-shaped staircase.

There were also about sixty *cachots*. Men needing discipline were condemned to the *cachots* for weeks or months. Today these *cachots* surround a square courtyard whose roof has fallen in, and all the doors stand open. Each *cachot* is about five feet long and three feet wide, scarcely bigger than the wooden cot it contains. The prisoners' ankles were shackled to the wooden cots which virtually filled the cells, in such a way that they could not even turn onto their sides or get the weight off their buttocks, much less stretch out, and then the stout wooden doors closed on them. The doors were cut to fit exactly so that no light or air got into the cell except for what little might penetrate high up through a barred porthole of a window. Behind such doors men lay in the dank dark, purging their infractions.

Medieval dungeons were worse no doubt, and those American prisons I have seen seem terrible enough today. Every generation has attempted to devise "humane" prisons, or so it pretends, though good order was always necessary, and apparently the result has always been prisons as appalling as the standards of the day would tolerate.

The French Guiana prisons were founded on the mistaken notion that convicts at hard labor would develop the colony and after release would settle there; their families would come over to join them. Others would come too. The inherent richness of the country, the gold and other minerals, the splendid hardwoods, would be exploited.

In any case, France would be safe from these men for a while.

Instead, the sinister reputation of the prisons smothered Guiana's development totally. It was a place with more prisons than towns, more cons and ex-cons than people. Even today there is virtually no economic growth and no more than a few hundred tourists a year. Even food is imported. The population of the entire vast country — it is bigger than Indiana — is still only about 70,000, including naked Indians in the bush. There is heavy subsidization from the Paris government. Without it, the country would vanish back into the jungle.

I look over the other ruins on Royale. The maternity hospital is a shell, but the church is being repaired, and the former administration building is now a hotel. Everywhere vines and trees climb. On the peak of a ruined wall, a large, healthy tree grows two stories above the ground. Its roots come all the way down the wall into the ground. It's not a vine. It's a tree growing on top of a wall.

The hotel is surprisingly clean and attractive. Seven private rooms cost about $25 each per night. Two dormitories cost less. There is also a restaurant, in which we sit down to lunch.

Most of the other visitors to Royale, the waiter says, are young people. They come over carrying sleeping bags and are content with dormitory accommodations, though it splits the sexes up for the night. The fishing and swimming are good here. It is quiet and tropical and cheap and there is always a breeze.

After a quite good lunch costing $13, including wine, there is time for a stroll before the boat back. A path leads under an alley of coconut palms around the entire circumference of the island. There is no beach; smooth black boulders slope down to the sea. Presently we come opposite Devil's Island. Two teenage girls are sunbathing topless on the rocks in the French manner, and behind them, framed by them, is Devil's.

For an instant time shrinks, and cons stand here. What would they make of two half-naked girls in such a place? What would the girls make of them?

Everything exists within its own time, it seems, and can't possibly exist in any other.

Every few years in the National Assembly in Paris the deputies debated about their jungle prison complex. In their passion they shouted, slapped each other's faces, and voted reforms. As late as 1925 major reforms were still being mandated and sent across the sea with the next convoy of convicts; and in 1936 the deputies voted to abolish for good and all what they called "this blight on the honor of France," though not immediately, of course.

In a tin-roofed shack beside the dirt road between St. Laurent and Mana there lives a man named Grich, an *ancien du grand collège,* as they say here. An alumnus of the big college. Grich sailed here in 1935, when he was 23. Most cons in prisons everywhere claim to be innocent, but when I ask Grich what his crime was he answers, "I killed a guy." He is proud of it. Sentenced to twenty years, he served fourteen, most of it pushing narrow-gauged railway cars between the prison at St. Laurent and the one at St. Jean nine miles away. There were no locomotives. Men as beasts of burden. Guards and supplies rode, cons pushed.

Grich was rare. He survived. Today he still looks as fleshless as any concentration camp victim. The morning came when he was given a pair of sandals, a shirt, a pair of pants, and a straw hat and set free. He had no place to sleep. In a few hours he would be hungry. He was given no money, no job. He had no way to get back to France. That was his problem, not the administration's.

Men released from American prisons are given back the clothes they came with. Most times they get no money and no job either. Their problem usually becomes the problem also of the next citizen they walk up behind and tap on the head.

Many cons here were helped by the Salvation Army, which had set up a major outpost for that purpose. Or else they begged. They were not helped by France. Effectively, France was safe from these men forever.

Today Grich captures butterflies during April, August, and November, when they swarm. Some of the most beautiful butterflies in the world are found here — Morphos, Heliconians, and others — and a rare specimen brings Grich a dollar. In a good year his income must total $100 at least, and with what food he grows out back this is enough. His nearest neighbor, Garcia, also sells butterflies. Garcia, a triple murderer, is another *ancien du grand collège* who survived. There are a dozen, perhaps twenty, of these men left.

Chavaniac
THE YOUNGEST GENERAL

The village in the old province of the Auvergne clings to the flank of a hill. Official population is 451. It is not a pretty village. It is the site of no famous battle. It is at the end of a side road which is itself off a side road. The first sign announcing its existence doesn't appear until the motorist is almost upon it: Chavaniac — 1 km. No one I asked had ever heard of it. It doesn't even have a post office. For a long time I couldn't find a map with Chavaniac on it. I knew I wanted to go there before I was ever able to find out where it was.

The province itself is scarcely better known. Though lying just south of the exact center of the country, the Auvergne was and still is isolated, rarely visited by tourists, or even by the French, who treat it almost as a foreign country. That is, they avoid it. They appear to think of it as densely mountainous, which it is not, a place of forbidding terrain and high tortuous roads, which it is not either. At an altitude of between 3,000 and 3,500 feet, it is the general plateau that is high, not the mountains. The highest peaks scarcely exceed 6,000 feet, and there are few of them. Furthermore, they are all widely separated. This is only to be expected given their odd, for France, origin. The Alps and the Pyrenees, which are much higher and more tumbled together, rose up as a result of geological plates crashing together — that's the normal

European mountain range. These Auvergne mountains were once volcanoes. The center of France once boiled. In between eruptions the terrain became covered with jungle. Rhinos and saber-toothed tigers once roamed, leaving behind fossils that were found only recently.

There is no jungle now, and in winter the Auvergne is so cold that eighteen so-called ski resorts have come into existence, some of which maintain only one lift, others many. But the mountains are not high enough, and the skiing is usually mediocre. With one or two exceptions there are no comfortable hotels or inns or restaurants to be found anywhere, and even the superhighways from Paris south bifurcate when they get there, veering off to Bordeaux in the southwest and to Nice in the southeast, giving the province a wide berth.

Chavaniac can be approached from the north via Clermont Ferrand, population 150,000, the Auvergne's only major city — its capital, so to speak — or from the south via Le Puy.

Clermont-Ferrand boasts a cathedral built in the thirteenth century in the classic Gothic style but out of black lava — the only black lava cathedral in the world, presumably. It is indeed black, but then so are most other public buildings in modern industrial cities.

Inside there are two marvelous rose windows to admire and also a remarkable statue of Christ from 1270 that is missing its right arm and the fingers of its left hand — a Christian Venus de Milo. The statue's amputations date from the Revolution. For a year or more gangs of young hoodlums moved through every cathedral in France smashing up the statuary. It was the thing to do in the early 1790s. By knocking off fingers and toes, noses, and sometimes heads, one evened the score with the clergy, with bishops and priests who had lived like kings and paid no taxes for centuries; one evened the score with God. Besides which, vandalism was fun. It was a bit unfair to generations still to come, however.

The rose windows to either side of the transept were safe only because they were too high up to reach. They are not round at all but square, the north window such a dark and unusual violet as to be almost black, the south window a mixture of intense oranges and vivid reds.

Not many notables ever came from Clermont — or from anywhere in the Auvergne, for that matter. In the last many centuries Clermont has sent forth only three sons whose names are remembered today. The first was Blaise Pascal (1623–62), who was a mathematician, an inventor, a physicist, and a theologian — in those days there was room for a man of many talents to exercise them all. Pascal published a book about geometry at the age of 16. He invented what may have been the world's first adding machine. He invented the wheelbarrow, which may not sound like much, but nobody ever thought of it before him. He dreamed up the idea of horse-drawn buses operating over regular routes in the Paris streets and then put it into operation; it may have been the world's first rapid transit system. He established laws of probability and laws of hydraulics — making possible the hydraulic brakes that are on all our cars today, long before cars were ever dreamed of. He also came to the conclusion that air had weight and then worked out the experiment that proved it. He wrote lucid, beautiful prose. He was the author of *Pensées,* a religious treatise advocating personal piety, austere self-denial, and reforms in the Catholic Church.

Clermont's other two famous sons were the Michelin brothers, Edouard and André, who operated a small rubber ball factory at the dawn of the automobile age and afterwards built it into you know what. Today there are Michelin tire factories all over France and the world, but the home office is still right here. So much for Clermont. A factory town; check which way the wind is blowing before you open your window.

The better approach to Chavaniac is from the south via Le Puy. As we drive into its streets I pick up signs to the Office de Tourisme. There is parking space along both curbs. Provincial cities like Le Puy, like Verdun, are still not overrun by cars. Inside there is a counter and behind it a woman whose pleasant face is framed by stacks of folders and brochures. I ask for whatever is available on Le Puy and its region, particularly Chavaniac. She hands over a handful, together with an apology: she has none on

Chavaniac, has never heard of Chavaniac. Well, I tell her, it's twenty-five miles away. I know that much by now, though not much else.

Le Puy's population is 26,000. "Sacred City, City of Art" reads the cover of one of the brochures. The city's decor has been "sculpted by fire and water." The writers of these things really let themselves go. "Enshrined in a framework of volcanic mountains," I read, it is "the most curious city in France."

The town lies in the middle of a vast, saucer-shaped valley out of which jut a number of high hummocks, together with some enormous rock spurs. Hummocks and spurs are both of volcanic origin, and certain of them jut up within the city, including the steepest spur around, which is called St. Michael's Rock — a "needle of lava," according to my brochure. It is a 265-foot-high pinnacle, and a Romanesque chapel occupies its entire summit, sitting on top of it like a chef's toque; the spur is that steep. Spur and chapel are visible from many parts of the town, as is part of the staircase that goes up there — 268 steps in all. A very steep climb. There were no steps when the chapel was built at the end of the tenth century out of blocks of stone quarried elsewhere, and my first reaction is wonder: how did the workmen get all that stone up there? The chapel's steeple is like a minaret, a finger pointing at the sky; its interior is completely irregular, being held together by a complex system of vaults that seem to conform not to any architect's plan but to the contours of the underlying spur.

St. Michael's Rock rises just inside the new circular boulevard that surrounds the city. Closer to the center is a similar spur, slightly lower, slightly less pointed. This one is surmounted by a colossal cast-iron statue of Notre Dame de France. The statue alone is six stories high and weighs 110 tons. It was cast in 1860. A nationwide collection was taken up to pay for it. The iron came from 213 cannons captured at Sebastopol during one of France's now-forgotten wars and was donated by Napoleon III, the first Napoleon's nephew, who ruled at the time.

There is a third spur, or perhaps this one is only a hummock. It is much bigger than the others, and on its slopes was built the original city. The word *Puy* in the old Auvergnat dialect means peak. The cathedral is on top of the hummock, and the streets and

houses spill down the sides. It is not until you reach the bottom
that the modern town begins, the boulevards, the new shops, the
parks and the parking lots. Most French cities are divided in two,
and in this respect Le Puy is no more schizophrenic than the others,
except that here the medieval quarter is called not the old city,
but the high city.

There is no river running through Le Puy, and it does not
seem to be a natural crossroads of any kind. It owes its existence
to these spurs, and not because they lent themselves to defense,
as might be expected, but because they were perfect for shrines.
Many times in the history of human events religion has influenced
men's conduct in untoward directions, and it did so here. The
Romans evidently built pagan temples atop all three of Le Puy's
eminences. Once they left, it was essential, if Christianity were
to flourish, to destroy these temples forthwith, and if paganism
were to be wiped out completely, then churches had to go up in
their place. Once churches had been erected, there could naturally
be a village, which could then grow little by little into a small
provincial city, which is what happened.

In religion Le Puy was born, and it was to religion — to one
of the most remarkable, almost hysterical religious manifestations
of its own age or any other — that it owed its period of greatest
prosperity.

At Santiago de Compostela, in the extreme northwest corner
of Spain, in the ninth century a sanctuary was built over the supposed tomb of the apostle St. James, and for the next hundreds
of years Christians in vast numbers made pilgrimages there, traveling thousands of miles from all over Europe mostly on foot,
often crossing country where there were not even roads. One of
the first to make this pilgrimage was the Bishop of Le Puy, who,
upon his return in 962, began the curious chapel atop St. Michael's
Rock. He may also have sent out publicists to extol his town,
because from then on Le Puy served as one of the principal assembly points for pilgrims coming down from Switzerland and
from the north of France. Most of these people had little money,
but there were an awful lot of them, and they kept coming for
centuries. Generations of itinerant merchants set up stalls in Le
Puy to see to it that what they had they spent. Weapons were

purveyed, fabric, jewels. So many troubadours arrived with their lutes that Le Puy became known as the place love songs came from — the Tin Pan Alley of its day. This flow of money built houses and inns. It built more churches, including very soon the cathedral that adorns the top of the town.

By the twelfth century Le Puy was so prosperous that it attracted also the *cotereaux,* a band of brigands who robbed, raped, and murdered, as a result of which business began to fall off.

It was time for an apparition of the Virgin. This was a frequent solution in those days. She appeared to a carpenter named Durand and ordered a holy war against the *cotereaux.* Since this war was at the direct orders of the Mother of God, honest men came from miles around. It was almost like a crusade. The Virgin's army wore white hoods, presumably to identify themselves to each other as they hunted down brigands. Perhaps this was where the tradition of white hats versus black hats got its start. The crusade was at first — though not subsequently — a success. The white hats strung up every brigand or suspected brigand they caught. According to popular legend, they hung them 500 at a time. Unfortunately they acquired a taste for it and very soon were seen to be, and perhaps were, an armed force in revolt against the King. So royal troops were sent down here, and they massacred most of them.

The Michelin guide rates Le Puy's cathedral at the same level of excellence as Chartres or Reims or any of the other celebrated ones in the north. Now we climb towards it up steepening streets. About halfway up we pass in front of a church that for two reasons attracts me: 1, although not mentioned in most guidebooks, it looks very old; and, 2, its doors are open. You never know what you're going to find inside French churches.

This is a Jesuit church attached to a Jesuit college. It is built in the austere so-called Jesuit style popular from the late sixteenth century on, and it is named after St. Regis. It was already standing when Regis lived in this town beginning in 1625.

Although the Jesuit order was Spanish in origin, the majority of the famous Jesuits, and especially the martyrs among them were, oddly enough, French. At about the time that Regis lived and preached hereabouts Isaac Jogues, Jean de Brébeuf, and other Jes-

uits were in North America converting, or trying to convert, the
Iroquois. Six of these priests, plus two lay brothers, underwent
unspeakable tortures followed by butchery. A little later their col-
league, the Père Marquette, paddled a canoe from the St. Lawrence
into and down the Mississippi, thereby opening up the interior of
the American continent. Unlike them, Marquette died of natural
causes, though not exactly in bed, as there were none within 1,000
miles of him. He died of a raging fever on the ground in a lean-
to shelter under an animal robe. He was 38. The influence of the
French on the formation of the American character, and on the
foundation of the American nation, is much more grand than most
Americans realize.

As for Regis, he was a missionary too, as were so many French
Jesuits at that time. The difference was that he worked in France,
mostly among the Huguenot heretics of the south — Le Puy stood
at the edge of territory entirely controlled by them. Regis was also
a kind of civil rights priest, and one of his present titles is patron
saint of lacemakers. At that time, and to some extent still, Le Puy
was known for its handmade lace. The women of Le Puy had
organized the equivalent of a union. They were refusing to be
treated any longer as servants. Henceforth they would work out
of their houses, and they would control the distribution of their
product themselves. They would sell to whomever they chose.

Previously the wearing of lace had been proof of rank. Now,
because of the industrious women of Le Puy, there was so much
of it around that the price dropped. This meant that more and
more people could afford it. Soon, in terms of class or wealth,
the wearing of lace signified nothing. So in 1640 the parliament
of Toulouse, under whose jurisdiction Le Puy lay, passed a law
that forbade the wearing of lace by commoners. This threw the
women of Le Puy out of work. Noting their distress, Regis went
to Toulouse and managed to get the law repealed. Next he arranged for Jesuit missionaries the world over to make known the
excellence of Le Puy lace. When he died, the patron saint of lacemakers was canonized almost at once. The Jesuit martyrs of North
America had to wait for canonization for nearly 300 years.

The first thing I notice about St. Regis's church is that it is
full of art. Religious art in museums is often not very arresting,

or, rather, it gets overwhelmed by the nonreligious art on display in the previous room and the next one. But when seen in some gloomy and often cold corner of the church for which it was created, in its own setting so to speak, religious art often produces a different reaction altogether. For one thing, one can imagine what the artist went through to get the picture up there: arguing with some pastor or bishop about what his theme was to be, not to mention his eventual fee; then submitting first his sketches and afterwards his finished product, not so much for approval as for censorship; and then holding his breath to see if the painting would be accepted and his fee paid, all this time regretting the conventions with which he had had to work — the halos, the winged angels, and the like. If a painting ever succeeded as art despite all this, it was a fine painting indeed and probably very moving.

In this church there are some magnificent ones, most of them painted on wood, artists apparently unknown. In the choir are portraits of the earliest Jesuit saints and martyrs, and in the chapels even some of the ceilings are painted. It makes me realize anew that France is full of unknown art, unknown treasures. Tourists in America will find much to admire, but they are not likely to come across paintings and sculptures in every country church. Finally I come to three big seventeenth-century paintings — the Crucifixion, the Nativity, and the Apparition of the Virgin to St. Ignatius — all by a local artist named Guy François. Whoever Guy François was, he was very good.

Resuming our climb towards the cathedral, we cross under archways and vaults. As we get higher there are places where the giant statue atop the nearer of the rock spurs suddenly appears looming over us at the end of a street; at the next turning it fills a stone archway framed from ear to ear. The effect is stunning.

The cathedral that rises out of the top of the city is almost 100 years older than its more famous counterparts in the north, and it is therefore of an earlier style, Romanesque rather than Gothic. But it is in no way pure Romanesque, for Byzantine and Moorish elements have crept in, brought back presumably by the pilgrims returning from Spain. So it is different from other Romanesque cathedrals, and it hardly resembles the Gothic ones at all. To begin with, it wasn't built on level ground but on the summit of a volcanic cone that wasn't quite big enough to hold it; as a result, a portion of it hangs out over the void, where it is supported by arcades, and its principal facade stands at the top of a monumental staircase. It was not built of blocks of stone either, but of blocks of lava; the lava hereabouts can be found in many different colors, apparently, and the builders found uses for all of them.

According to one of my brochures the cathedral's staircase that we now climb is "an invitation to permanent, spiritual ascension." Maybe. We are out of breath by the time we reach the front door. Actually there are three great doors, and in the archways over them white stones alternate with dark reds and tans. All the way up to the roof the colors of the facade keep changing. The effect ought to be ugly, but is not at all.

Inside, instead of a vaulted cathedral ceiling overhead, there is a series of cupolas that cover the entire nave. This is supposed to be the building's principal architectural distinction; it certainly looks odd. The columns that support the cupolas are bizarre as well, for they rise not only in many different colors, but also in different styles, some smooth, some fluted, some of great girth, some of small. In places columns of several styles and thicknesses are gathered together like arrows in a quiver, forming in effect a single pillar to support the massive weight above. Many of these columns are surmounted by capitals, the stonework incised here by figures, there by motifs, no two capitals resembling each other.

Near the center of the nave is an enormous fruitwood pulpit, walnut I think, hand-carved by one or several extremely gifted sculptors. Gorgeous chandeliers hang from chains in each bay the length of the nave. They're something like Tiffany lamps, though hung upside down. In the old days candles must have burned inside them.

For a while this cathedral was the repository of the famous "Black Virgin" — a statue carved out of black wood which was believed to have miraculous qualities. A cult grew up around the Black Virgin that survives to this day. The statue itself was brought to Le Puy about 1250 by Louis IX, the King known as St. Louis, who spent the night here, or perhaps several nights, upon his return from the seventh crusade to Egypt, which he led. The Black

Virgin was venerated for more than 500 years until the Revolution, when it was burned by hoodlums. Afterwards, of course, it was replaced, and you can have a look at the replacement today if you care to. The statue and its cult are the subject of two splendid paintings that hang on either side of the nave. Both depict processions in which the Black Virgin rides in state. Both are enormous, measuring perhaps twelve feet by eight. One shows six clerics in cassocks flanking a carriage on which the Virgin rides, while two noblemen stand on either side of the painting looking on. The cassocks are red, with white collars and sleeves. On the other side of the nave the Virgin is being carried on the shoulders of eight men in the same red cassocks. There is a canopy over the statue's head, and she rides in the midst of a procession in which at least fifty faces are visible. All the faces in both paintings are carefully done, miniature portraits in themselves, and perhaps even recognizable to people of the time. There are many more colors than reds and whites. There are black cassocks too, and golden chasubles and copes — how artists must have loved painting church finery. These are vivid paintings, vivid colors, and now above the cathedral the sun must have just come out from behind a cloud, for suddenly it pours through the stained-glass windows onto the paintings, changing all the colors, making tones the artist or artists never thought of. Next the sunlight moves a few feet down the church and falls upon a wonderful wrought-iron barricade eight feet high that guards the main altar. The ironwork in such light becomes dazzling, as intricate and delicate as any of the lacework for which the women of Le Puy used to be so famous.

As we near Chavaniac the country opens up still more, and far ahead we can perceive the supposedly fearsome mountains of France's Massif Central, including the highest of them, the Puy de Sancy. Most of them are perfect domes. Most are totally isolated one from the other. In between them and us is a country of vast cultivated valleys laced by rivers, with here and there rolling hills and patches of forest.

The sign to Chavaniac points to a country lane that begins to wind uphill through trees until suddenly we come upon a château that almost blocks the road. Now many, many French villages have châteaux, relics of some former grandeur, and some are massive or gorgeous or for some reason notorious. This one, although it is the building that has drawn me here, is none of these things. It is not a medieval fortified castle, though there are elements of that in the round, rather squat towers at either end of the front facade. It is not particularly picturesque, nor does it appear elegant; it is no miniature Versailles. It does look comfortable and bright and airy. As we drive into a gravel courtyard, I count nine French doors across the facade on the ground floor, all of them giving onto a terrace, and the same number of large windows above.

By today's standards a vast place. By the standards of 200 years ago, its heyday, it was perhaps only a modest country home. In any case, it was big enough, for it was so far from any population center, and the roads were so miserable, that it attracted few visitors, and no one significant to history came here except for Gilbert du Motier, the Marquis de Lafayette, the château's owner.

In front of the house stand two tall flagpoles, and although one flies the tricolor of France, the other flies the American flag. How odd to come upon it here in this freshest, least visited part of France.

Below the house is a formal garden. Below the garden is a pond, and then comes the valley, which in Lafayette's day was planted in rye. The view is quite spectacular, fifty miles or more. Even as a little boy Lafayette owned most of this land that we can see. He owned most of the village up there behind the trees too. The villagers were not slaves, but they were totally beholden to the child. The women curtsied when he happened to stroll by, and grown men tipped their hats.

In grade school we were taught that Lafayette came from France to the American colonies to help George Washington. He was 19, and the Continental Congress made him a major general. I saw nothing wrong with this idea at the time; 19 seemed awfully old to me. The teacher asked if we had any questions about him, but none of us did, and so in one day he both entered and disappeared from our history courses and our lives. The teacher probably sighed with relief. She would have to work hard to get us to remember Washington's name or Jefferson's or the name of anyone who came later, such as Lincoln or Franklin Roosevelt, who was president at the time, so forget Lafayette. History books focus on a select few. They are not always fair even to history's giants, certain of whom get only a passing mention before the course and the students pass on.

Although Lafayette was arguably the second most important figure on the colonial side after Washington, the rest of his life after he went home is, to most Americans, a blank. He was only 24 then. That later he wrote the French declaration of independence was not, in my time at least, considered relevant. That he instigated the French Revolution, and for a time controlled it; that he was arguably an even more important figure in this second revolution than in the first; that he was forced to pay a heavy price — did not as Americans concern us. History courses prefer men who can be described in one dimension: Washington, for instance, or Napoleon. In many ways Lafayette was more human and worked in broader strokes than either of these men whom he knew so well. History is seldom interested in broad strokes, and heroes had best remain unapproachable. To most people of his day Washington seemed a cold and silent man, and Napoleon inspired awe. Lafayette, however, was loved. He was the darling of the mob on both sides of the ocean, the true hero who could do no wrong, and for as long as this emotion lasted he was accorded adulation on a scale that cannot be overdescribed, and that was almost impossible even then to believe. Certain sports figures today get adulation like that; for them it lasts an hour. For Lafayette it lasted decades. He had only to show his face in public and it started up again.

To one side of the château is a centuries-old stone house that was perhaps the house of his bailiff. At present it holds a cashier's desk (tickets cost 10 francs each), and a number of trestle tables spread with a few postcards, and some thin brochures. But there is no one browsing over this stuff, and no one waits for the start of the next tour. I keep waiting to hear the noise of tourist buses or other cars coming to a stop on the gravel outside, but this does not happen.

Maurice Durand, manager of the château, enters. I have an

appointment with him. He is a small, thin man in his seventies wearing a business suit who, after a moment's small talk, leads us into the château and up a wonderful old staircase. In a round room in the west tower we gaze at a four-poster bed under a canopy; it is obviously hundreds of years old. On the wall is a portrait of Lafayette aged about 30. It was in this room, according to M Durand, that the hero was born on Sept. 6, 1757. A big window faces northwest up that gorgeous open valley, and light pours into the room. The walls are covered in embroidered fabric, and the floor is made of wide planks that have become, over the years, somewhat too widely spaced. The bed seems to me not only old but also shabby, and M Durand confesses that it is not the original. It is "similar" to the one that must have been here and in which Lafayette was born.

M Durand asks me to stand in the center of the room and say "*Bonjour.*" "It will make an echo," he explains.

It takes me three tries to get it right. The first two times my voice comes out too softly, apparently. The third time my "*Bonjour*" does make an echo. Not much of an echo. A little echo. But it is not the type of echo I have come to this place for. I gaze at the bed for a moment and try to imagine a girl lying in it. No sterile hospitals in those days, no stirrups, no painkillers. If she died, she died. The chances of the baby reaching maturity, however healthy at birth, were not great.

Lafayette was the only son and the sole heir in the family, M Durand tells us. He was raised in this château by four women: his grandmother, two aunts, and his mother. His father was a colonel off fighting the English and, like almost every male Lafayette ancestor dating back several centuries, managed very soon to get himself killed in action. He was 27, and the son he had never seen was 2.

Little Gilbert's mother stuck it out here in the backwoods for another year, then fled to Paris, for she was only a girl herself, and there were bright lights in Paris. She left her son behind. His grandmother taught him about his illustrious lineage, and about the glory to be won in battle, and about the hated English, who had killed his father. Priests who lived in the château were his tutors, the first a Jesuit and then, after the Jesuits were suppressed in 1764, a secular priest. The boy was brought up in a kind of lonely splendor — what passed for splendor in the provinces. There were no other little boys of his rank for miles around. M. Durand begins to lead us from room to room. Originally the château was a fortified castle, but it burned down in the fourteenth century, and the present building, built up on its foundations, was finished in 1701, which is about when our Lafayette's immediate ancestors came here to live. In other words, by the standards of those days the château was almost new when Lafayette knew it. It was altered again during the French Revolution, or at least that is when the plans to alter it were drawn up, and this is the version that is on display now. The descendants of Lafayette lived here until about 1890, when the house was abandoned. It remained empty until 1916, when it was bought by a newly formed private group calling itself the Lafayette Memorial Association, which cleaned it up and reopened it as a museum. The association, which still owns it today, is American, M. Durand tells me, but when I begin to question him I receive answers that only confuse me. Its founding force was not an American but a Scot, it seems, and four of the six members of its present board of directors are French. M. Durand is French also; he has been managing the château since 1950. The Scot's motives were, to say the least, peculiar; and the motives of the present board are obscure, for it becomes clear in the course of this conversation that the museum has few visitors and loses money. I am still puzzling over all this as we look into the oldest parts of the château.

At least two of the ground-floor rooms date from feudal times. One must have served as the kitchen. On the walls hang a good deal of cooking paraphernalia from two centuries ago, and in the center of the room is a great old wooden table, very thick. There is a stone fireplace big enough to sit inside of, which is what people used to do when winter days got cold enough. In such a fireplace the cook could, and probably did, roast whole sides of beef, entire pigs.

At the other end of the building is what was called the guardroom. It is small with a vaulted stone ceiling, and the walls, I can see by the window cut through them, are about six feet thick. It does not take much imagination to picture the footman and the coachman, sitting in here with coats unbuttoned, smoking, waiting until whenever their lord might summon them.

The dining room is newer and decorated in the style of Louis XIII, who died in 1643. Its fireplace is tiny: a pretty, carved-stone fireplace, but small. The room itself is small, with vaulted ceilings, and the walls are hand-painted in designs that are quite faded now.

Next comes a wonder of a living room. It must be sixty feet long or perhaps more, and more than half that wide. Huge as it is, it looks comfortable. There are old rugs on the board floors, and the armchairs and settees are arranged in several separate areas, giving an impression of intimacy. The sideboards and tables have been polished to a luster. This room is Louis XV, the style in vogue on the eve of the American Revolution. But nothing here is as elegant, if that is the word, as the pieces that would have been on display at Louis XV's court. This is a country living room in a country house. It is more sober. This is how a rich squire lived. The true Louis XV style has always seemed to me an attempt to make the furniture match the decadence of the rest of the court. The shapes become unnatural, almost bulbous. The brass decorations become gilded, and there are too many of them; the marquetry woodwork is nice, but to me polished walnut catches the light better.

There are paintings all over the walls of this room, many of them portraits of Lafayette, including a number that are very well painted. But as I study them I come to certain conclusions about the artists of Lafayette's time, and presumably of any time — they were not very good at likenesses. In this house there must be twenty or more portraits or engravings of Lafayette at various ages, executed in various mediums: oil, pen and ink, charcoal, pastels. The likenesses do not resemble each other very closely. They agree only on what must have been his salient features: the high forehead sloping back at the same angle as the long, pointed nose. I find myself wishing that a photographer had shown up here or at Valley Forge or somewhere so that we might see what he actually looked like.

The boy Gilbert lived in this house until he was 11, when his mother summoned him to Paris. She had an apartment in the Luxembourg Palace, which today houses the Senate. At the time it was a kind of luxury condo for the nobility. Gilbert was sent every day in a carriage to an exclusive finishing school only a few hundred yards away. Finally there were plenty of potential playmates of his rank, but he was an awkward, rather solemn child, and he was from the sticks, and so they mocked him incessantly.

When he was 13 his mother abruptly died — she was 33 — and shortly afterwards, her father, Gilbert's grandfather, died too, and the whole of the fortunes on both sides of the family devolved upon the youngster. Income from his father's estate at Chavaniac had been about 25,000 livres a year; income from his maternal grandfather's estates in Brittany and the Touraine came to about four times that much. To give an exact equivalent today is impossible. Certainly it would amount to millions of dollars per year. From one day to the next the orphan had become certainly the richest boy in the kingdom and one of the richest persons of any age.

It was his great-grandfather, the Count de la Rivière, who took over his care and made the next decisions. He arranged two things: a commission for Gilbert in his own regiment when he would reach the age of 18; and marriage to Adrienne de Noailles, the second daughter of the Duke d'Ayen. Gilbert was 14 years old. Adrienne was 12. The girl's mother, who had little say in such matters, was appalled and insisted that the marriage could not take place for at least two years. In the meantime, she said, Gilbert should move into the Noailles palace on the Rue St. Honoré so that the kids could meet and get to know each other, and this was written into the contract. So was the matter of Adrienne's dowry. She would bring to the marriage 400,000 livres — the Duke, though he had five daughters, was very, very rich.

Gilbert was here at Chavaniac, a schoolboy on his summer vacation, while all this was being decided. He was living behind one of these windows on the second floor. When he went back to Paris at the end of vacation, he moved into the Noailles palace. He was told that the little girl running around the other wing of the house was to be his bride, and he accepted this, but then a rare and rather wonderful thing happened — the two children fell in love. Puppy love, maybe, but they were allowed — obliged — to act it out. The marriage took place on schedule. Adrienne got pregnant at once, but had a miscarriage. She got pregnant again and at 15 gave birth to a daughter. The 17-year-old father professed himself very proud, though it wasn't a son. Adrienne loved her husband obsessively all her life, at one point even confessing that she loved him "voluptuously." He loved her too, though not exclusively, and wrote her tender love letters whenever he was away, which was often. Many times he talked to her or wrote to her of Chavaniac, of this house in which we stand, of the countryside we drove through today, which he so liked to drive through himself, though not at sixty miles an hour. He was a boy describing his *pays* to his girl. He told her how much he loved it. He promised to bring her here and show it to her, and he did, though not right away, because the American Revolution intervened.

At that time the court at Versailles was the seat of all power, all ambition, all advancement, all glory whether potential or real, and also of any perversion one might care to contemplate. It was the last word in sophistication and taste, in luxury and splendor, in sexual debauchery, in extravagance of all kinds. It was a monument to gorgeousness, to excess. The hundreds, even thousands of aristocrats who flocked there and frolicked there, who curried favor there, had developed a court jargon that was almost another language, and their rituals and even their dress had been carried to such an extreme as to become grotesque. Men wore wigs whose curls hung down their backs. Women's headdresses were sometimes two feet tall. Their skirts were so wide that they could barely get through doorways.

No success in France was possible without first obtaining success at court.

Lafayette's father-in-law, the Duke, was an example of such success. As a courtier he was perfection. He was witty and urbane, sharp-tongued and also obsequious. Sometimes he was all these things at once. He had won appointment as captain of the Royal Guard, the highest office at court. In processions he had a right to walk just ahead of the King himself, which was apparently the most magnificent honor to which any nobleman could aspire.

That is, Gilbert de Lafayette arrived at court under the best possible auspices.

But he was a flop there. He was a gawky boy, very tall with reddish hair. He was not witty. He did not know how to flirt. He was not so much a country bumpkin as simply too young. Casual adultery took place all around him. Who was sleeping with whom was the principal topic of conversation among all age groups. But none of the presumably grand ladies would even look at him. He sat through the endless banquets, the candlelit suppers. He attended the stately dances, the masked balls. One night Marie Antoinette laughed at his dancing. His dreams were solitary ones. They concerned glory. How was he to obtain glory?

By the middle of 1776 the swirling court gossip had changed its tone. Suddenly people could talk of nothing but the Revolution that had broken out in the American colonies. France had been driven off the American continent definitively in 1763. No one much minded in the court at Versailles. No one was burning for revenge. As Voltaire put it, France had lost nothing but a few acres of snow. But now the American revolutionaries were tweaking the English nose, and this was delightful. Dozens of noblemen and pseudo-noblemen sailed immediately for America to offer their services to George Washington, the new hero of the French court.

Gilbert had two intimates. One was the Viscount de Noailles, his brother-in-law; and the other was the Count de Ségur, who was about to marry Gilbert's mother-in-law's younger sister and become his uncle-in-law. All three boys decided they would go to America and find glory. Gilbert spoke and wrote often of "*ma gloire.*" It was not liberty that drew him to America; it was a chance for glory.

By this time Silas Deane, a Connecticut merchant, was acting as American envoy to Paris. He was the one you went to see if you wanted a commission in the Continental army. He gave them out to anyone who asked. All three boys approached Deane. As the highest ranking among them, Gilbert, though only a lieutenant in the French army, demanded a commission as a major general. Deane gave him what he wanted. Why not?

But his father-in-law was furious. The Duke flatly forbade Gilbert and the Viscount de Noailles to go. Ségur's family was equally vehement, and the other two boys immediately dropped out. Being dependent upon allowances, they had no choice. But there was a difference here. Gilbert, who had his own money, could do as he pleased. If he were willing to defy his father-in-law plus whoever else might be against him, he could go to America alone.

But he would have to do it secretly. Everyone, he soon learned, was against him, including the King. Gilbert was such an important nobleman — not so much in his own name but as a member of the Noailles family — that his appearance in the colonies might seem to the British a formal intervention by the French in the colonial revolt.

There was no way he could sail from one of the northern ports as an ordinary passenger. Gilbert's solution was to buy his own ship and to sail for America out of Spain. He moved south under an assumed name, one jump ahead of the King's rider bearing a warrant for his arrest. He had not even said goodbye to his pregnant wife. His ship was not yet even provisioned. Waiting ahead were fifteen other officers whom Deane had commissioned and whom Gilbert had invited to ride to America free on his ship.

In Spain letters reached him. The family was furious. The King and all his ministers were furious. For some days Gilbert wavered, and once he even set out across the border to return to Paris. As he rode away from the ship the other noblemen aboard were certain he would not be back, that the trip was off.

But en route letters from his contemporaries also reached him. The young people at court were wildly enthusiastic about his plan, it seemed, and all the ladies were agog. Gilbert wheeled his horse around, galloped back to the ship, and on April 20, 1777, set sail. He had books on warfare with him, and English grammars. He studied every day. Of the other officers aboard, only one had battle experience — the only one who could be called a grown man, the now famous Johann de Kalb, who was 56. De Kalb was a German serving as a lieutenant colonel in the French army, the highest rank he could hope to reach. He claimed to be a baron, which apparently he was not. The same hopes that nourished most of the other immigrants who were to arrive in America in the next 200 years also nourished de Kalb: that in America a new future might open up for him.

The boys aboard were merely thirsting to be heroes. The ship was fifty-four days at sea, during which Gilbert practiced his English on de Kalb and wrote some touching letters to his wife. He always wrote beautifully and had the instincts of a poet: "Since my last letter I have been living in the most tedious of places: the sea is so sad and I think she and I impart our own sadness to each other."

The plan had been to stop to offload cargo in the French West Indies, but Gilbert feared that the warrant for his arrest might have reached there before him. When the captain said he was stopping anyway, for he owned the cargo, Gilbert bought the cargo from him, and the ship kept on.

He disembarked June 13, 1777, near Charleston, South Carolina, and in the city met Gen. William Moltrie, commandant of the harbor fort, which was built of palmetto logs. Moltrie had his troops drawn up for inspection. Most were barefoot. Some had no coats or hats. Gilbert gave Moltrie enough money to buy rifles and clothing for 100 men.

The French group started north for Philadelphia, 650 miles away. They had some carriages and some horses. The road shook the carriages to pieces. Many of the horses went lame, and Gilbert bought new ones. After thirty-two days they at last reached Philadelphia. It was July 27. They cleaned up at an inn, then rushed over to present themselves to Congress, which was in session. John Hancock, president of the Congress, came outside to see them, took up their commissions from Deane, and told them to come back the next day. But his manner was icy, his lack of interest total.

The next day they were received by James Lowell, who spoke excellent French. He told them that Deane had exceeded his authority, that their commissions were invalid, and that those Frenchmen who had preceded them had all turned out to be louts and frauds. They had best board the next ship and go home. He turned and went back inside.

In the street outside Independence Hall young Gilbert and his group stood stupefied.

Gilbert's English was still rudimentary, almost nonexistent. That night in his lodgings the boy wrote in English to Congress begging to be allowed to serve in the Continental army as a volunteer without pay. Congress would find this offer more surprising than he knew, for most of the earlier French officers had demanded tens of thousands of livres for their services.

In addition Gilbert had with him letters of introduction furnished by Deane and others, and he sent these around to the homes of various members of Congress. Two members soon called on him to apologize for their earlier rudeness. They found him a cool, polite young man and neither arrogant nor greedy, it was written later. All he asked was a chance to get shot at in the Continental cause.

After four days of deliberation, Congress passed a resolution: ". . . that his services be accepted, and that in consideration of his zeal, his illustrious family, and connections, he have the rank and commission of a major general in the army of the United States."

It meant that cooler congressional heads had prevailed. Help from France in the form of money and munitions was urgently needed, and somebody inside Independence Hall had recognized the power of the Noailles family name. Congress's good sense was confirmed shortly afterwards when a letter reached it from Benjamin Franklin in Paris. The young Marquis was "exceedingly beloved and everybody's good wishes attend him. . . . We are satisfied that the civilities and respect that may be shown him will be serviceable to our affairs here, as pleasing not only to his powerful relations in court but to the whole French nation." Of the others who had accompanied Gilbert, Congress kept de Kalb plus one or two young men whom Gilbert selected as aides. The rest were sent home.

The new major general met Washington the next night at a dinner party and afterwards talked to him — tried to talk to him. Washington was always courteous, though cool and detached in manner. He spoke no French, but he invited Gilbert to review the troops with him the following afternoon.

And so they sat on horses while the American army paraded past — about 11,000 ragged, often unshaven, barefoot young men. Gilbert was shocked. Washington saw this, and found himself apologizing. He supposed his troops did not look like much to an officer who had served in the army of France.

"I am here, sir," Gilbert replied, "to learn and not to teach."

Washington, it was said, liked almost nobody, but he liked this teenager at once. He was a formal man. He never called him Gilbert. He never called him anything but "my dear Marquis" — but he invited him to live in his own house with several other young officers. The boy of course was thrilled. This was merely the American way, but Gilbert didn't know that. It was certainly not the French way. No French commander would ever have allowed such intimacy.

Washington liked everything about this boy: that he was so eager to learn, so eager to please; that he was working so hard to learn English — none of the previous French officers had bothered. But the affection that grew between them was frequently tinged on Washington's part by annoyance. This 19-year-old major general kept demanding command of a division, which Washington had no intention of giving him. "What the designs of Congress respecting this gentleman were, and what line of conduct I am to pursue to comply with their designs and expectations, I know no more than a child unborn," he wrote, "and beg to be instructed. If Congress intended that his rank should be unaccompanied by command, I wish it had been sufficiently explained to him. If, on the other hand, it was intended to invest him with all the powers of a major general, why have I been led to a contrary belief?"

Within six weeks occurred the battle of Brandywine Creek, some twenty-six miles southwest of Philadelphia. The British attacked the American army with superior force, and the center division began to crack. Earlier Gilbert had asked to join this division, and Washington had agreed. The boy was there as an observer, but now he jumped off his horse, placed himself at the head of some troops, and urged them to charge. No one obeyed the excited young foreigner, but for a time no one retreated any further either. Suddenly Gilbert took a bullet in the calf. Supposedly the redcoats were twenty yards away at the time. According to one version, Gilbert realized he had been shot only when blood boiled out of the top of his boot. According to another, Washington rode up and saw him ashen-faced with blood spurting from his leg and told him to retire, but he didn't. The soldiers were running away, but again Lafayette managed to stop their flight and to turn them to face the advancing British. About then Washington rode up with a surgeon, to whom he gave the order: "Treat him as though he were my son."

And so the boy spilled his blood on American soil for American freedom, and the glory he craved was at hand. When news of his wound reached France, together with reports of his valor under fire, he was transformed overnight from an awkward youth into the hero of the French court and the French nation. His wound was not a bad one, though many a soldier in those days suffered amputation for less, or a fatal infection, or both. It healed cleanly, and as soon as he could ride again Gilbert went forward with about 300 men to reconnoiter British positions in New Jersey. He ran into Hessian troops who outnumbered him, and a battle started, and he drove the Hessians back half a mile, inflicting about fifty casualties and taking fourteen prisoners. His own losses were one killed, five wounded. "Such is the account of our little entertainment," he wrote Washington. "I wish that this little success of ours may please you." It was the first time he had had men under his actual command, he had shown himself no less brave than before being shot, and he had won the battle, and afterwards Washington at last gave him command of the division he had begged for. He was 20 years old. The childless Washington was 45, and from then on Gilbert de Lafayette seems to have become for him the son that he never had.

Gilbert spent the winter at Valley Forge drilling his troops and writing letters, some of which were surprisingly astute. "I read, I study, I examine, I listen, I reflect," he wrote his father-in-law, "and from all that I try to arrive at an idea into which I put as much common sense as I can. I will not say much lest I speak nonsense. I will do even less lest I make a mistake." In other letters he begged for help for the Americans from the French court: "America is waiting impatiently for us to declare in her favor, and I hope that one day France will resolve to humble the pride of England." Apparently without realizing it, he had assumed the role of intermediary between the Continental army and the court of Louis XVI. The odd thing was that both sides now accepted him in his self-assigned role, also apparently without realizing it.

"With the help of France we shall, though at some cost, carry to victory the cause which I have at heart because it is a just one; because it does honor to mankind."

That winter France recognized American independence, and two months later a treaty of trade and friendship was signed, with a further promise of military alliance. It was spring when the news reached America, and the joyful Gilbert de Lafayette kissed Washington on both cheeks, soundly embarrassing the austere father of his country. But then a smile came onto the older man's face. "You have done more than anybody," he said, "to bring about this great event."

After a year and a half on active duty, and at Washington's recommendation, Gilbert asked Congress for a leave of absence that he might return to France to lobby for more help at court. Congress not only granted his request, but also provided a frigate to take him home. His crossing took only twenty-six days, an amazingly fast voyage.

In France the boy — he was still only 21 — was cheered and feted everywhere he went. The King and Queen applauded him, the populace stopped his carriage in the streets. Cabinet ministers vied with each other to engage him in consultations about America, about foreign policy.

He stayed in France a long time. He impregnated his adoring wife, and when she gave birth to a son on Christmas Eve, 1779, he named the boy George Washington de Lafayette. He bought himself a regiment, the King's Dragoons, and took a mistress, Aglae d'Hunolstein, the wife of a count and supposedly the most sought-after woman at court. He stayed away fourteen months. Surely no one in America ever expected to see him again.

Then he was back. He landed near Boston April 26, 1780, after thirty-eight days at sea, and rode off to meet Washington, who was at Morristown, New Jersey, a trip of fourteen days more. There was a different concept of time in those days; there must have been. As I stand in Lafayette's house contemplating such numbers, I remember that yesterday I was in London; two days ago I was in New York. Lafayette's story makes heroic reading when reduced to a few lines, but count up the days and, by our standards, it is a picture of unrelenting tedium. Fifty-four days from Spain to South Carolina, and twenty-six to go home; thirty-eight more to get back. Thirty-two days on the road between South Carolina and Philadelphia; fourteen from Boston to Morristown. There were freezing-cold months in Valley Forge that were not only without bread, sugar, tea, coffee, or milk, but also without much to do. In his first year and a half in America Gilbert de Lafayette was in action only a few hours, but he seemed satisfied, presumably because the rest of the time his glory accumulated by itself for want of anything else happening or likely to happen that would catch the public fancy. Events moved no faster than the wind could push a ship. One receives the impression that no one ever rushed anywhere, that crowded schedules were unknown. When trying to comprehend historical figures, the hardest part is to comprehend their relationship to time.

Even Gilbert's trips from Paris down to this château, and he made many, took at least a week each, two weeks round trip, and sometimes more.

He reported to Washington May 10, 1780. Behind him now came an army and a fleet, he told him, for the French were involved in the American war to stay. The French general was to be Rochambeau; the French admiral, de Grasse. As soon as they had arrived, Washington assigned Gilbert to them as his personal representative, for they spoke no English. Experienced warriors both, men in their mid-fifties, they were furious. They were being made to deal through a boy.

Washington sent Lafayette south with a division of ragged Virginians to harry the army of Lord Cornwallis. Before starting out, Gilbert de Lafayette with his own money bought his troops hats, shoes, underwear, shirts, overalls — it was a kind of uniform.

In Virginia Cornwallis had five times as many troops, but for six months Gilbert harassed him, the two armies moving back and forth across the state for 1,000 miles, fighting many skirmishes, Gilbert each time skillfully avoiding the decisive battle that would have crushed him. "The boy cannot escape me," Cornwallis declared. But in the end it was the man who could not escape the boy. When in October of 1781 Washington's army and the French troops of Rochambeau at last reached Yorktown, with the French fleet arriving off the coast, they found Gilbert's division already in place. He had somehow managed to confine Cornwallis's army to a narrow peninsula from which there was no possible escape.

Cornwallis surrendered on Oct. 19, 1781. Gilbert waited two more months, then sailed home — another twenty-seven days at sea, plus four more days by road between Lorient and Paris. He had spent most of four years with the Continental army and had spent all of his income for those years, plus 750,000 livres of his capital.

His carriage was acclaimed all along the route to Paris, and when he came through the gates into the streets — Paris at the time was a walled city — the news somehow swept on before him. Everyone was out-of-doors that night anyway, for an heir apparent had recently been born to the throne, and the King and Queen had come in from Versailles to receive the homage of the mob and to attend a reception at city hall, to which Adrienne and the rest of the Noailles family had been invited.

So Gilbert came home to an empty house.

Word of his arrival swiftly reached city hall, and Marie Antoinette called Adrienne to her side and told her she must go to her husband at once. But Adrienne declined, for it was against protocol, so Marie Antoinette loaded her into one of the royal coaches and drove her to the door of the Noailles mansion.

A crowd had already collected there. Adrienne got out of the carriage and at the sight of her husband fainted dead away. Gilbert caught her before she hit the ground and carried her into the house in his arms while the Queen beamed and the mob shouted itself hoarse.

Such adulation continued day after day. When the young couple went to the opera, the entire audience turned to face them in their box, and a soprano holding a laurel wreath offered it to Gilbert amid tumultuous applause. The King commissioned him a marshal in the French army with date of rank from the surrender of Cornwallis. Pamphlets and poems were written about him. Engraved coins were struck bearing his likeness. He dropped Mme d'Hunolstein and took a new mistress, Mme de Simiane, whose husband was both a count and a marquis and who was said to be the most beautiful woman in France, and this liaison was to last years. His wife gave birth to a daughter, and he named her Virginie, after the troops he had commanded and after the home state of his idol.

The revolutionary war was over, but no one knew this yet. Washington wrote how much Gilbert (still "my dear Marquis") was missed and that he had prepared a corps for him when he should return. But peace negotiations had begun in Paris and London, and Gilbert had thrust himself into the middle of them. In Paris he met regularly with Benjamin Franklin, John Adams, Thomas Jefferson. He kept offering suggestions, wanting to help. He kept writing Washington that he could not, under the circumstances, immediately return to combat duty. Finally American independence was recognized, and the peace treaty signed.

"He brought his wife down here to Chavaniac after the war," M. Durand tells me.

It was the first time Adrienne had seen Chavaniac. Gilbert showed her the house in which he had been born and the countryside he had known as a child.

He found that the sheds were full of grain, but it had been a bad season and the peasants were in desperate straits. "Now is the time to sell your grain," his bailiff told him.

"No," responded the hero of two worlds, "now is the time to give it away." And he did. Together he and Adrienne established a free weaving school in a nearby village so that the peasants would be less dependent in the future on every harvest. In his way Gilbert was devoted to his wife. Though Adrienne came from a background even more privileged than his, she had accepted all of his new ideas, and she was the more skilled of the two in putting them into effect.

Gilbert wrote frequently to Washington, once suggesting that they buy jointly a property in Virginia, together with the slaves that went with it. They would educate the slaves to the point where they might be self-supporting and then free them. If the experiment worked it might point the way towards the freeing of all the slaves in America. Washington was against slavery too, but was also intensely practical. "It's all very well to talk of freeing the slaves," he once said, "but who would work our plantations?"

When nothing came of this scheme, Gilbert bought land in French Guiana, together with about forty of its slaves. He was going to try his experiment of freeing the slaves there. He also took up the cause of the persecuted Huguenots.

"He came down here every year for a while," M. Durand tells me. "He brought his wife and children and the servants. It made for a convoy of many carriages on the road."

Chavaniac had the advantage of being close to Huguenot territory, and Gilbert invited the Huguenot leaders into this house and opened discussion with them so that he might better present their case in Paris. He must have entertained them in this living room here. They must have stayed overnight in certain of the bedrooms upstairs — all of which was probably against the law. Gilbert might have been prosecuted. Back in Paris he began to meet with the most influential of the King's ministers, and then with the King himself, pleading for an end to the abuses against the Huguenots. Although sympathetic, these men were afraid of the Catholic backlash, and years went by before anything was done. Finally Gilbert brought the matter before the Assembly of Notables, where certain of his notions, not all, were carried. Protestant marriages were at last to be recognized as valid, and Protestant children were legitimized. Protestant dead at last could be legally buried. By no means did this amount to full-fledged religious freedom, but it was a start, and he did it virtually all by himself.

His contemporaries, and a good many of his biographers as well, never accepted this highborn young man's apparent commitment to the poor, the downtrodden, the persecuted — his commitment to a possibly new and democratic France. Most often he was accused of trying to curry favor with the populace or else of parroting ideas that were not his own but Washington's. But everyone's ideas come from someone, somewhere, and if the recipient is young enough, as Gilbert was, inevitably they take hold hard and in the normal course of events become accepted as his own. By now Gilbert's ideas ought to have been considered his own, it seems to me, as much as any man's ideas are his own, though frequently they were not.

He was a restless young man, constantly on the move. He went to Berlin and was received by Frederick the Great, King of Prussia, and to Vienna, where he dined with the Emperor Joseph. He was appalled by both men, appalled by absolute monarchy in principle. In America he had been smitten by something else entirely; it was to America, his one true love, that he would be faithful for the rest of his life. His wife and children were here at Chavaniac that summer. He rejoined them riding on a white horse. All the villages acclaimed him as he rode through, and in one of them a Te Deum was sung.

Washington had urged him to bring Adrienne to Mount Vernon for a visit. In the summer of 1784 he sailed back to America, but alone. Bells rang and cannons boomed in every city through which he toured. He has often been accused of thirsting for applause, and this tour is offered as part of the evidence. He journeyed through eleven of the thirteen states and was greeted with parades, banquets, speeches, and delirious crowds everywhere. But he also addressed several state legislatures. There was no constitution yet, the new nation was on the point of dissolving before it had ever been formed, and to these legislatures he pleaded again and again for a stronger union: "May we never withhold from government the essential powers of doing good from jealous apprehension of doing evil." He spent two weeks with Washington in Mount Vernon, where they talked sometimes far into the night. Washington was desolate when they parted. "In the moment of our separation, upon the road as I travelled, and every hour since," he wrote, "I have felt all that love, respect and attachment for you with which length of years, close connection and your merits have inspired me. I often asked myself, as our carriages separated, whether that was the last sight I should have of you? And though I wished to say no, my fears answered yes." And of course he was right.

When Gilbert got back to France a present came from Washington: a barrel of Virginia hams.

During the years between the American peace treaty and the outbreak of the French Revolution, Gilbert's mansion on the Rue de Bourbon served as a kind of clubhouse for the Americans in Paris, but many of the younger French noblemen came too, especially the ones who had fought in the war, and so did more and more of the writers and thinkers of France. There were philosophical and political discussions around Gilbert's dinner table nearly every night, and the word on everybody's tongue was liberty. France up to then had been politically quiet; the King had been an absolute monarch who ruled absolutely. But now there began to be increasing agitation for change, and principally it came not from the mob but from the intellectuals clustered around the Marquis de Lafayette. They started it, they propagated it, and they soon lost control of it.

France was certainly ripe for their ideas. The incredible extravagances of the court had finally brought the nation to the edge of bankruptcy. Money, it seems, is not only the root of all evils, but often enough the root of all change as well. Gilbert, who was still so close to the throne that he sometimes rode to ceremonies sitting beside the King, began urging more and more publicly that a national assembly should be called, that a constitutional monarchy on the English model was desired by France. He argued furthermore that installing one would be easy. Goodwill and idealism were all it would take.

A series of local assemblies were now called throughout France. In several different provinces members of the powerful Noailles family either presided over these assemblies or served as the leaders around whom men gathered. The Marquis de Lafayette himself, having just turned 30, toured many of the cities and villages of the Auvergne, where he was received each time with a mixture of awe and love and where he began to woo the lesser nobles and the important members of the bourgeoisie. At that time the word *lobbying* had probably not even come into existence, but that is what he was doing, lobbying for support for his ideas.

Exactly what was he hoping to achieve?

"A sufficient degree of fermentation," he wrote to a relative, "to produce a threat of civil war, though without letting it materialize: in the army, enough of patriotism to worry the government, without causing actual disobedience; in the collection of taxes, a sufficient number of obstacles to lead to capitulation, though not to bankruptcy. The general effect of all this will lead us, by the shortest possible road, to the winning of that constitutional liberty for the attainment of which other countries had not thought torrents of blood and a hundred years of wars and misfortunes too high a price to pay."

In March of 1789, three months before the French Revolution exploded, he was here at Chavaniac again, "quietly preparing myself for the heavy responsibilities which await me," as he wrote to Mme de Simiane. There were those who accused him of preaching treason, for he was clamoring for a meeting of the Estates Général, which, in solemn session, would decide on reforms and vote them into law. The Estates Général, a nationwide congress bringing together the clergy, the nobility, and representatives of the people, had not met in 175 years. To guide the congress when and if it met, he wrote out his Declaration of the Rights of Man, nine points similar in tone to the American Declaration of Independence, by which the absolute monarchy would be converted into a free and constitutional state. He was back in Paris by then, and as soon as he was satisfied with his draft he ran it around to Jefferson's house, and the two men studied it together and made some improvements. Lafayette gave no indication then or ever that he hoped to lead the new France that would grow out of the old one. It was the ideal of freedom that he was married to and that occupied all his devotion. He did not want to be king, or even George Washington.

Louis XVI did call the Estates Général, and with great pomp, processions, music, and speeches it opened on May 5, 1789. But the King had waited too long. By now France was in the grip of a roaring inflation, and in Paris there was a shortage of bread.

The Estates Général met every day. On the night of July 4, Lafayette and his wife went to dinner at Jefferson's house. Many Americans were there, and liberty was toasted many times. On July 8 before the Estates Général, which by now was calling itself the National Assembly, Lafayette made a sensational speech demanding that the King's foreign mercenaries, who policed the city and who it might be argued were all that preserved order, be withdrawn. On July 11 he presented his Declaration of the Rights of Man and was elected vice president of the assembly. His declaration, somewhat amended, was not only adopted at the time, but still serves as the preamble to the French constitution.

Lafayette thought this the greatest day of his life. But the patient —
France — had only three days to live.

The ideas that he had brought back from America, much
misunderstood and, at the end, to be totally perverted, had taken
hold not so much in the country at large as in the city of Paris.
On July 14 an outraged mob stormed the Bastille, and not only
the *ancien régime,* but also most of what the Old World had considered sacred and precious, was over. The next day huge crowds
surged back and forth around city hall, cursing the Queen, cursing
all aristocrats. But it cheered wildly for Lafayette when he appeared. The disturbances continued all that day and into the night,
and the National Assembly was frantic: it met and elected a new
mayor of Paris, and it proclaimed Lafayette commander of the
city's militia. But the riots continued.

"As soon as the idea of my commanding the Parisian militia
had been mentioned to me," he wrote his wife the next afternoon,
"it suddenly conquered everyone: it became essential for me to
accept; it has become essential to stay, and the people in their
delirium of enthusiasm can be moderated by myself only. I wanted
to go to Versailles; the leaders of the city declared that the salvation
of Paris demanded that I not leave it for an instant. Forty thousand
souls are assembled, the fermentation has reached its highest degree, I appear, and one word from me makes them go home. I
have already saved the lives of six people who were being hanged
in the different quarters, but this furious, drunken people will not
always listen to me. As I write you, 80,000 persons surround City
Hall, claiming that they are being duped, that the troops have not
been withdrawn, that the king was supposed to come. As soon
as I go away, they go mad. If I leave for more than four hours,
we are lost. I reign over Paris, but it is over a maddened people
urged on by abominable plots. In this very moment they are
uttering dreadful shouts."

On July 20 he dined with Gouverneur Morris, who urged
him to take command of most of France, but Lafayette refused.
"He tells me," Morris wrote, "that he has commanded absolutely
100,000 men, has marched his sovereign about the streets as he
pleased, prescribed the degree of applause he should receive, and
could have detained him prisoner had he thought proper. He

wishes, therefore, as soon as possible, to return to private life."

Two days later Lafayette watched a councillor of state and the man's son-in-law hanged from a lamppost before his eyes. He immediately tendered his resignation as commander of the militia, which had been renamed the National Guard, but deputations rushed forward begging him to stay. He was eloquent, they told him, he was known for his virtue. He was the only man who could save Paris, save France. So he withdrew his resignation.

It was proposed in the National Assembly that all aristocrats voluntarily surrender all privileges. Lafayette immediately seconded the motion. Then he wrote to Mme de Simiane: "Here I am at the very center of a great adventure, and the only thing I really want is to get out of it, free from all reproach of having indulged any thought of personal ambition, and, having put everything to rights, to withdraw into obscurity with a quarter of the fortune which was mine when I came into the world."

He helped organize the new civic government, arranging for an elected council. He set out regulations governing the National Guard, stipulating that guardsmen would wear a tricolor cockade — this was the start of blue, white, and red as the colors of the French flag. He was offered a yearly salary of 120,000 livres; he refused it. Men, particularly the Americans in Paris, wondered what would become of him, what use he would make of such power. With amused irony he replied: "I rather think that ingratitude will save me from the embarrassment of being rewarded." Marie Antoinette is supposed to have said, "Monsieur de Lafayette will save us from the mob, but who's going to save us from Monsieur de Lafayette?"

For a year following the storming of the Bastille Lafayette kept order, more or less. On July 14, 1790, the first anniversary of French "independence," a great outdoor celebration was organized at which Louis XVI swore to observe a constitution that did not yet exist, and tens of thousands of adoring persons surrounded Lafayette, chanting his name.

Many of the other aristocrats understood where the Revolution was headed, and Lafayette's father-in-law, the Duke d'Ayen, was among them. They got their money out to Switzerland or somewhere, then followed. The Revolution had not ended. Passions were as inflamed as ever, perhaps more so. The various factions of revolutionaries were beginning to turn on each other.

In the center of all this stood Lafayette, tall, virtuous, noble in both senses of the term, and the mob began to turn on him too. He was still an aristocrat at heart, it began to be whispered, and scurrilous pamphlets appeared. One of them was hawked on the streets of Paris under the title "Confession of Marie Antoinette to the People of France." In it the Queen claimed that among her lovers was a cardinal, a brother of the King, and "my dear Lafayette." These same pamphlets now usually referred to Lafayette not by title but by family name. They called him "Motier."

The King and Queen were under virtual house arrest, but on the night of June 20, 1791, together with some servants, they boarded carriages and slipped secretly out of Paris without being observed by members of Lafayette's National Guard, who were supposed to be "protecting" them. The royal flight was discovered the next morning, and the King and Queen were arrested at Varennes in eastern France three days later and brought back. By then the mobs filled the streets again, and there were mutterings against Lafayette, according to which he had not only permitted the King's flight but organized it.

The days passed, but Paris continued to boil. Three weeks later came the second anniversary of the storming of the Bastille, and a mob gathered on the Champ de Mars to demand that Louis XVI be deposed. A monster petition circulated to be signed by all, but the signing turned into a riot, and the mayor of Paris requested Lafayette to bring in his National Guard and suppress the rioters by force. Someone took a shot at Lafayette, apparently missing him by inches, and with that the National Guard opened fire on the mob. Twelve rioters were killed, the government lost any lingering support it might have retained, and Lafayette's reputation plummeted. The pamphlets called him murderer. However, he hung on three more months, until the new constitution was at last finished, published, and signed by the King, and until the National Assembly, formerly the Estates Général, having decreed that none of its members could serve in the forthcoming legislative assembly, or in the executive branch of the government either, dissolved itself. That is, nobody with any legislative experience would be left in power. The Revolution was at an end, Lafayette declared, and resigned. He would retire here to Chavaniac, he declared. The gesture won him back a good deal of his lost popularity. The National Guard presented him with a gold-hilted sword, a medal was struck in his honor, and he started the long journey by carriage south to Chavaniac. But he was obliged to stop in every village he passed through "to receive enough civic crowns to fill a carriage," he wrote.

Twenty-seven months into the Revolution, he settled down in this building in which I stand. He did not even bring a secretary. From now on he would be a farmer. He did have an architect with him, for he wished to redo the château, modernize it, and make it comfortable. He was 34. His public life, he believed, was over. He was out of it now, and that's what he wanted. Perhaps, he said, he would write his memoirs of his two revolutions, his fight on two continents for liberty for the common man.

Of course the Revolution was not over. The guillotine had not been invented yet. The worst had not yet begun. Lafayette, had he stayed quietly in Chavaniac, would probably have been safe from the horrors that were coming. But he did not stay. Within three months war had broken out in the north, his country was in danger, and he was asked to head one of three armies. Leaving his wife and children behind, he returned to Paris.

And that, I realize, is the end of Lafayette's story as far as Chavaniac is concerned. To follow it further I will have to go north, as he did.

This living room is certainly not as he left it. The colors would have been vivid rather than faded and the upholstery new rather than shabby. There would not have been this odor of mustiness in the air. The room is handsome and some of the antique pieces quite lovely. However, there are not enough of them. The room is half empty. Of course, to buy additional pieces in the open market would cost hundreds of thousands of francs, money that the Lafayette Memorial Association apparently does not have. The windows face southwest, making this a bright, sunny room, and the doors give onto a small formal garden with gravel pathways delineated by sculpted bushes.

Upstairs M. Durand opens doors into a number of bedrooms. There are also one or two bathrooms obviously added in this century; the bathtubs are claw footed. Telephones, running water, and even electricity came very late to rural France, in some cases not until well after World War II.

At the end of the corridor is the library. It is full of handsome old books, many of them original editions of Lafayette's own writings, and on the walls are more engravings and miniatures of Lafayette and his family, and framed documents in his own hand, or signed by him.

After that M. Durand leads the way through three small museums, two of which seem to me completely inappropriate. The first is a room devoted to memorabilia from World War I: uniforms, German helmets, photographs of World War I generals who by now have been thoroughly discredited by all students of that war. It is a room that does not seem to belong in this château, but before I can ask M. Durand for an explanation he has led us into a dark corridor lined with brightly illuminated alcoves behind glass. In each alcove is represented a scene from Lafayette's life. The actors are life-size wax effigies wearing crude and ill-fitting facsimiles of uniforms. It is possible to decide which figure must be Lafayette or which one Washington, and so forth, but only if you look hard.

In the third and final museum are glass showcases in which are gathered mementos from Lafayette's life, and certainly this room, unlike the previous two, belongs here, but the principal emotion it evokes is disappointment, even sadness, for the most important of the treasures these showcases once contained are gone, never, presumably, to be seen again. They are represented behind the glass only by photographs.

In Lafayette's day lockets containing locks of hair were often exchanged as gifts between loved ones. The lockets themselves were likely to be of gold and were sometimes encrusted with precious stones, and this showcase here until a short time ago contained a number of such lockets — locks of the hair of Benjamin Franklin, George and Martha Washington, and Lafayette's wife. In addition there was a gold snuffbox which had belonged to Washington and a set of matching pistols which Washington willed to Lafayette on his deathbed. But in the summer of 1985 burglars broke into the château. They seem to have been looking principally for weapons, especially antique weapons, as if they had a market for them. They stripped the World War I room of several — no great loss it seems to me, since the same items are on display more fittingly elsewhere — then came into this room here and took Washington's pistols. Apparently they stole the snuffbox and the various lockets too only because they seemed to be gold and would be easily disposable.

They were caught six months later and tried a year after that. There were six of them in all, most in their early twenties, although one was 45 and their fence was a 33-year-old book dealer. They were convicted not only of the break-in here, but also of having stolen two machine guns from the war monument at Solignac sur Loire; plus a number of helmets, sabers, and other such antiques from a collector in Le Puy; plus pillaging 160 telephone booths throughout the region; plus having machine-gunned both the doorway of a local nightclub and the car of the man who owned it.

Not a nice group. A search warrant turned up part of their loot at the house of one of them, a 23-year-old so-called student, but the pistols of Washington were not there, nor was the snuffbox, nor any of the lockets.

Held in preventive detention while awaiting trial, the accused were threatened with heavy sentences unless Washington's pistols turned up. However, they remained mute. Ultimately the court did not punish them harshly at all, and the longest sentence meted out was two and a half years. Most got much less, fifteen months for one boy, a year for another, three months for a third. The other two got suspended sentences plus probation. France's prisons are overcrowded too. Nowhere in the free world, it seems, are voters willing to spend money to build new ones. It appears likely now that Washington's pistols will never be found — whoever has them probably doesn't even know what they are — and the centerpiece of this small and rather impressive room will remain the curling color photograph of what they used to look like. The Lafayette Memorial Association was founded by a Scots financier named John Moffat, M. Durand explains now. It was Moffat who saved the château. I had noticed his dates incised over one of the doorways: 1879–1966. When his brother was killed in action in 1914, Moffat became part of a group doing propaganda for the Allied cause. The principal goal of this group was somehow to coax the United States into the war, and it was decided to find ways to remind Americans of the debt they owed to Lafayette and to France. One idea was to enlist about thirty American pilots in a special combat unit called the Lafayette Escadrille. These Americans shot down over 100 German planes. They lifted their flimsy machines into the air above the trenches day after day until they either died in dogfights or were killed in ordinary crashes while trying to land or take off. Those planes crashed rather a lot, even if you didn't shoot at them. Only a few of the young Americans, five or six, I believe, lived out the war.

A second idea was to buy Lafayette's ancestral château and publicize that, and in 1916 a Frenchwoman was sent to look it over. She found it half ruined. The roof leaked, some of the floors sagged, the staircases were unsafe. The peasants on the estate hadn't been paid in three years. The association bought it anyway.

After 1918 Moffat and his associates began to put together the collection of antique furniture, paintings, and other art objects which are in the rooms today. Most were bought from local antique dealers, and some had perhaps come out of the château originally. Moffat, meanwhile, lived here for months each year. He came in summer, he came at Christmas.

When he died he left an endowment that was supposed to keep the place in operation, and for a time it did. But the area is too isolated, it offers tourists few other significant attractions, and there are no fine hotels or country inns or restaurants anywhere around. There were never many visitors, and still aren't, and Moffat's endowment is no longer enough. Government subsidies would help, but as a private museum Lafayette's château is ineligible; nor does it qualify for any part of the Ministry of Tourism's publicity budget. As a result its existence is almost as much of a secret in France as in America. The château, M. Durand confesses, as we stand beside my rented car, is passing through *"une situation difficile."*

As we drive away he waves after us.

What will happen to Lafayette's château? Well, the French government might take it over and continue to run it as a museum, or it might be sold to private developers as a hotel. Maybe they would call it the Hotel Lafayette. Maybe they would keep the Lafayette motif throughout. Or maybe they wouldn't.

A dense forest has come down over the road. It's as dark a forest as I've ever been in. We go through a number of logging villages, each with a sawmill, each reeking of newly sawn wood.

There is a gigantic Gothic abbey in La Chaise Dieu, about nineteen miles north, so that's where we stop for the night. Our hotel is called Au Tremblant. From our window we can see the mountains opposite, whole hillsides yellow with autumn.

This hotel is clean, basic, neither better nor worse than expected. Our room is newly redecorated. There is a new sit-down tub in the bathroom, replacing a bidet, no doubt, and new imitation oak headboards on the beds. They have wallpapered the ceilings as well as the walls — the loudest, busiest wallpaper imaginable.

We go down to dinner, and the dining room has been done over too: new Formica paneling on the walls to match the new Formica tabletops, the new Formica veneer chairs, and the new Formica bar in the corner. In rural France you often see this. People decide to modernize. They sell off all their beautiful old pieces, convinced they're worthless, getting almost nothing for them, then they buy the loud wallpaper and the latest advances in Formica, and whatever new plumbing can be crammed in. We imagine the owners here hugging each other in delight as the workmen leave. They tell each other they've made a beauty out of something old and ugly.

In the morning we walk toward the abbey. The village smells of wood smoke and cows. There is dung caked to the streets. We pass cows in stalls under the houses. On the floors above the cows live the people, and this is on the principal street of the village.

The village square slants downhill, and the entire high side of it is the facade of the great abbey.

La Chaise Dieu today is a village of less than 1,000 people. I don't imagine there were ever any more than that, even in the early fourteenth century when the abbey was built. There are monumental churches like this dominating villages all over France; nonetheless, it is always a surprise to come upon one. They are all so huge, and the surrounding houses so small in comparison even now — at the time that these great Gothic structures went up, even in the years Lafayette would have gone through here, the rest of the village would have been huts with thatched roofs.

Inside there are a number of interesting sarcophagi. Marble bishops, dressed in marble robes and miters and grasping marble staffs, lie out on top of the lids of their tombs. However, many of these effigies have been vandalized. During the Wars of Religion there was a battle at La Chaise Dieu, one of the few the Protestants ever won. On Aug. 2, 1562, they bashed down the front doors and walked up and down this row of tombs knocking off fingers, feet, noses. On some of the lids entire faces are gone.

In addition to its sheer size, this church is notable for the row of sixteenth-century tapestries that hang along the nave. The Annunciation is depicted, the Epiphany — almost the whole New Testament. Many of the faces are as vivid as any portrait painted during the same period. The darker colors are still strong, especially the hair and the beards of the men, the blacks and dark reds. The lighter colors are much faded, and the skin tones are gone completely. Light from the high windows has been pouring down onto them for more than 400 years. It's amazing that any color is left at all. They're quite splendid, although difficult to see. A young Dominican monk in a gray cassock shows us through. He carries a heavy-duty flashlight and shines its beam on the tapestries, illuminating one sainted face after another.

Le Vernet
A CAMP IN THE PYRENEES

The Pyrenees: a chain of mountains 270 miles long and 60 thick extending across the bottom of France from the Atlantic to the Mediterranean. At this wall France ends and to an extent so does Europe. On the other side begins the high, arid plateau of Aragon, terrain that foreshadows Africa. The language and the culture have been influenced by Africa. A Spaniard is not a Frenchman.

These are rude, abrupt mountains two miles high, and in France in their shadow the villages are isolated. Most are poor. They are laced with fast-moving streams soon to become rivers, and the air is cold and damp. The slopes are heavily forested. Higher up, the trees give way to meadows that are frequently in the clouds. The meadows are tilted steeply on their sides and from so much moisture are of an exceptional greenness. They are dotted by sheep, who are watched often enough by a shepherd wearing the tiny black beret of the region; he sits on a stone and holds a staff as in the Bible. Above the meadows rise crags and peaks — rock that is most often brown or rust colored, not gray. And of course at the top of this world for most of each year there is snow.

In 270 miles, with the exception of the roads along both coasts, there are only eleven widely spaced places to cross. Certain of them are fifty miles apart, and most are closed all winter by snow. There are foot passes, of course. Pyrenees folklore is rife with tales of smugglers and smuggling, particularly in the Basque country on the Atlantic side and near the tiny principality of Andorra in the center. Free trade is a relatively new concept in Europe.

So is peace. During the wars the frontier posts were always kept closed and border guards were nervous. Afterwards came years of scarcity and want. Wars were good for smugglers. Over the high passes they moved people as well as products, whether spies or refugees or escaping airmen made no difference, no questions asked. The wars' aftermaths were even better. A knapsack full of sewing machine needles could make a smuggler rich, never mind jewels or gold.

That era is over. The era of the romantic smuggler is certainly over. Today's travelers cross in cars by the tens of thousands, principally via the four-lane toll roads along both coasts. Such smugglers as still exist lead Spanish terrorists across the high passes to and from hideouts in France, or else they run drugs. In either case, not the stuff of folklore.

Nowhere in France is more lonely than certain valleys in the Pyrenees. In peacetime they seem perfect for sportsmen: the hunters and fishermen, the bike racers and skiers.

Beginning in 1939 they seemed just as perfect for something else entirely, something France seems to pretend never happened: the French version of concentration camps. The camps are never mentioned today. The worst was at Le Vernet, a place not noted in any guidebook I have seen and difficult to find even on the most detailed map. We will come back to Le Vernet in a moment.

Today's hotels, where there are hotels, stand with the mountains at their backs. Most are unpretentious, though comfortable enough and very cheap. There are eagles in the sky here and, some say, condors. In addition to deer, boar, chamois, and other ordinary forest game there are also bears that sometimes come down to forage close to the villages or even within them. There are many mountain lakes. There are trout in most of the streams, and salmon come up the Adour and into a mountain torrent called the Gave d'Oloron, where they are fished near a village called Navarrenx.

In most ways Navarrenx, population 1,100, is typical of the Pyrenees. Surrounded by mottled stone ramparts half covered by moss, it stands on a cliff above the noisy torrent. There are turrets at the corners of the walls. A narrow stone bridge dating from the thirteenth century reaches from the opposite cliff across the river to the town.

The only thing different about Navarrenx is the salmon. The Gave boiling past is about sixty yards wide. The salmon swim upstream against the heavy, churning current. They find deep pools in mid-channel and lie up there to rest and spawn. The water is melted snow which has run down off the mountains. In most seasons it is very cold. In April, which is when Navarrenx stages a so-called world salmon-fishing tournament, it is icy cold. The fishermen stand in the river in hip boots, or even chest deep in waders extending up to their armpits, and before long are half frozen. They cast with poles about ten feet long. All kinds of bait are used, even orange peels at times, but most men favor spinners and spoons. There is a sinker on the line too, and the anglers cast thirty or forty yards out into the churning river. They let the bait drift downstream, and sometimes a salmon grabs it.

I watched this tournament one year. It rained every day except the last one. It was very cold, and I walked along the banks and licked the rain off my lips and talked to the fishermen. The salmon being yanked out of the Gave were a yard long and as thick around as my thigh. The winning catch weighed 23.8 pounds, and we ate fresh salmon at the hotel every night.

One other thing about Navarrenx: it serves even today as the metropolis, if that is the word, for the village of Gurs, which is about three miles down the road. There were many concentration camps, and Gurs was the site of one of the biggest. Some camps were for men, some for women, and a few were coed. Gurs was a women's camp. The barbed wire, it is said, extended along the road for almost a mile. Through it the women could be seen moving about. In summer many wore shorts. Most wore kerchiefs around their heads. They kept themselves and the camp very clean. There was always laundry drying on lines, and even on the barbed wire itself, women's underthings and such, in many colors. Everyone who saw this remarked on it.

The ski season in the Pyrenees is somewhat briefer than in the Alps, which are both further north and higher. Most of the skiers here are day-trippers from nearby towns and from Toulouse, the biggest nearby city. The stations — Barèges, La Mongie, Superbagnères, and one or two others — are well equipped and the trails well maintained. The skiing is most often respectable, but there are no luxurious hotels or restaurants or shops. The Pyrenees are not chic. This is local skiing. The international set skis elsewhere.

The roads in these mountains are often both steep and high, and usually they are narrow — perfect for bike racing. They are also mostly empty, which is even better. It means they can be closed to ordinary traffic for hours without much protest while the race and its caravan of cars, trucks, and motorcycles goes through. The Tour de France, by then about half run, spends two or three days in the Pyrenees each July. The Tour's itinerary changes slightly year by year, but among the brutally steep climbs it must always seek out are two favorites. One is the Tourmalet, the other the Envalira.

Tourmalet Pass, 6,935 feet high, is closed by snow seven months each year. The rest of the time its scenery delights the few picnickers who happen by and the many devotees of the bike-racing cult who know its evil reputation and come to see for themselves if it is really that tough. Ten miles north of the Spanish frontier, it is a road that doesn't really go anywhere.

Envalira Pass is even higher, 7,900 feet, the highest in the Pyrenees. It takes the riders four and a half hours to get up there over intervening passes. On a summer's day the temperature may have dropped from 100 degrees to 60. From Envalira Pass the riders plunge down the other side over roads as steep as roads ever get. The finish line is at Andorra, twenty miles ahead and below. The fastest riders make it in under twenty-four minutes.

Andorra, nestled in these 10,000-foot peaks, is an independent principality left over from feudal times. Measuring about twenty miles by thirty, it is a kind of miniature Switzerland, and a free port. Its only industry is tourism. There are eighty lakes and countless trout streams. It is a lovely place. The air is cold and exceptionally pure.

It is full of hotels. The Tour riders are fed and sent to bed.

In the morning they pedal back over Envalira Pass the way they have come, and the race goes on.

The Romans discovered and exploited thermal springs in the Pyrenees and quarried marble and then went away. After them came various Visigoth and Iberian tribes and especially the mysterious Basques, whose origins no one knows to this day and whose language resembles no other. The Basques martyred St. Sernin near Toulouse in A.D. 250, established themselves in what are now the Basque provinces of France and Spain, and resisted Christianity until the ninth century.

About 719 the Moors came up through Spain and crossed the Pyrenees, and in 778 Charlemagne drove them back in a battle that resulted several hundred years later in the famous *Song of Roland,* the earliest epic poem in the French language. Roland was a Breton count commanding a rear guard of Charlemagne's troops at the pass of Roncesvalles near St. Jean Pied de Port. According to the poem, 300,000 Saracens attacked Roland, who, having perceived that victory was lost, did two things. First, he swung at the side of the mountain with his beloved sword Durendal, aiming to break it, for such a mighty weapon must not fall into the hands of the infidels. It was the equivalent of a modern naval captain opening the petcocks to avoid capture of his ship — the concept hasn't changed in all these years. But so powerful was Roland and so sharp was his blade that he sliced the mountain nearly in two. There are guides today who solemnly show tourists Roland's cleaved cliff at Roncesvalles, and also at Gavarnie, which is about sixty miles away.

Roland's second act was to summon the aid of Charlemagne and the main body of troops by blowing a blast on his horn — French children are taught that this was the type of horn called the *olifant.* Roland blew so hard he burst a blood vessel in his neck and died. Heeding his call, Charlemagne came at a run and threw himself on the remaining Saracens, praying to God for time to do for them all in one day. In answer to this prayer, God stopped the sun in the sky.

Such is the *Song of Roland.* In actual fact Roland encountered not Saracens but a tribe of Basque warriors who rolled boulders and tree stumps down on him and his men where he had foolishly grouped them together, crushing them to death. Or so historians tell us.

Which in no way lessens the impact that the *Song of Roland* had on history, for in France it influenced much of the literature that came after it and also much of the killing. It might even be thought of as one of the world's first and most effective recruiting posters, for its publication occurred during the time of the crusades. Thousands of young men, hearing it, decided they wanted to emulate Charlemagne and Roland and kill Saracens, and they joined up and started out for the Holy Land.

After Charlemagne went away, the Pyrenees broke up into dozens of feudal holdings, whose rulers most of the time warred with each other. Henri IV, King of Navarre, became King of France in 1589, bringing to the crown his personal domains in the western Pyrenees, but interest in the region did not survive him. There was an abortive drive in the eighteenth century to develop the region economically, and then came the Victorian English to put Pau, Biarritz, and certain other stations on the map once and for all. But these places are on the flat and on the fringe.

There was always a slight cultural leakage along both coasts. On the Mediterranean side today you will sometimes come upon road signs overprinted in Catalan with spray paint; and on the Atlantic side every Basque village has its fronton, its whitewashed houses, and its curious small churches with wooden galleries halfway up both walls to keep the women separated from the men. But there is no cry for "independence" in either place, and the 250,000 French Basques — there are five or six times as many in Spain — do not mount terrorist attacks against policemen and police stations as their Spanish counterparts do.

The rest of the Pyrenees remained over the years as empty, as unexploited, as ever. And why not? France is a country with, in effect, but a single important city: Paris. All roads led there, all power emanated from there, and the Pyrenees were as far from Paris as you could get and stay in France. Paris, which never cared about the region, knew it was there, however, and in 1939, once the decision was made that concentration camps were needed, it seemed the perfect place to put them. This most neglected corner of France could be made to serve for something at last. And the worst of the camps was at Le Vernet. I first heard of Le Vernet from an American living in Nice. I had just come to France. He was in his late thirties — much older than I was. He was married to a Frenchwoman and living, I realized later, on his wits, changing money on the black market, smuggling cigarettes, writing adventure yarns for the men's magazines that flourished at the time. He had fought as a volunteer in the International Brigades in the Spanish Civil War. Le Vernet was where many of his comrades had finished up, and I received the impression that he had narrowly missed Le Vernet himself.

He was, it seems clear to me now, a fervent communist; communism, for people like that, had been and still was a religion. He had fought in Spain to free the world from the fascists and the capitalists, to him they were the same, and his youthful idealism by the time I knew him seemed to have turned into a hatred for all governments past and present, not only for the fascist regimes in Italy and Germany that had helped Franco win in Spain, but also for his own government, which had stood by and done nothing and now recognized and aided Franco; and for the government of France, which also had done nothing to help and which afterwards had established concentration camps such as Le Vernet in which to pen up not only the Spanish survivors but all the rest of the unwanted debris of Europe as well. France, as he saw it, had matched Hitler camp for camp.

So I sought to find out more, at first in libraries and afterwards in conversation with people who at least had lived through that period as adults, which I had not. But if books existed on the subject I was unable to find them, and those men I questioned either had no information or were unwilling to give it. Perhaps I realized even then that I would go looking for the camps one day, whatever was left of them, particularly Le Vernet. Perhaps I realized also how difficult they would be to find. There were not going to be any signposts.

It was not a quest that preyed on my mind. It was simply there, and whenever I was in the neighborhood of the former camps, whether talking to salmon fishermen or watching bike races or just hurrying through, it would make itself known. Finally one year we were driving from Bordeaux to Nice, taking our time, stopping at every antique shop we passed, but getting closer all the time to that part of the Pyrenees where I supposed Le Vernet to be. By then I had acquired considerable information on the camps. However, Le Vernet was still not listed in any guidebook I had seen, and I still could not locate it on any map.

We were at Massat when I began asking for directions. The village is high up and the air was cool. The road went no further. Beyond were the mountains, impenetrable here, and beyond that was Spain. We drove around the village square and pulled up beside an old woman. Though it was summer she wore a black shawl, a black dress to her ankles, black stockings, and sturdy black shoes which looked nearly as old as she was and which conformed, obviously, to her corns.

If you want information in the villages of France, find an old woman. They know everything, and they love to talk. This one was leaning on our windowsill, her head inside the car, and her grin displayed her few teeth.

She had never heard of Le Vernet. She had never heard of concentration camps hereabouts at all.

As for antiques, she said, this village had been cleaned out. The *chiffonier* was a spy for the two antique dealers in Foix, and the one in Tarascon as well.

A *chiffonier* in the French villages is roughly a ragman. He pushes a handcart through the streets or drives a small truck. He buys up old newspapers, empty bottles, old clothes. This way he gets into the houses. Most of the people in villages such as Massat are closed in on themselves, and their houses are closed up tight. Even sunlight can't get in past the closed shutters, but the *chiffonier* gets in, looks carefully around, and if he sees anything he sells the information to antique dealers.

We should head straight for Tarascon, the woman told us. Her daughter ran a butcher shop there and would steer us to antiques. Though we said we were not going to Tarascon, the old woman insisted we copy down the daughter's address. Foix was good, the crone added, but watch out for one of the dealers, he's a Spaniard.

The road down out of Massat runs beside the boiling Salat, which is more than a mountain torrent but not quite a river this high up. Where it passed in front of a restaurant, we stopped for lunch and we sat out on a terrace under the trees listening to the roar of the torrent and ate fresh grilled trout, and drank a cold rosé wine. Asked about Le Vernet, the waiter said he didn't know but he brought the proprietor over. Neither man was familiar with a village of that name, however. The sun filtered down through the trees and the white flesh of the trout came off the bones cleanly and we ate them and drank the wine and then continued down the mountain road beside the torrent. We passed a number of other restaurants and inns. All had signs out front: fresh trout.

At Foix we came upon the shop of the "Spaniard" on the Rue du Four d'Amant. His name was Abdel Kader Slami, which did not sound Spanish to me. He had one showroom and, across the street, a room jammed to the rafters with old furniture. We could hardly get in, there was so much. Slami had old carriage lamps to sell and a very old hand-hammered caldron. He had old *sabots,* wooden shoes, some still clotted with dung and grass. You could shine these up and hang them on the wall and put flowers in them, he told us. For a few dollars you would have a lovely decoration. He had old pewter silverware and old brass lamps and door fittings and such. He could not tell us the whereabouts of Le Vernet.

The oldest thing in Foix, older than any antique shop, and dominating the town, is the feudal castle, which dates from before 1002, the year that the Count of Carcassone left it to his son in his will, a document that still exists. The castle squats atop a magnificent spur of rock in the fork where the Arget and Ariège rivers join. This rock spur looked to me 300 or 400 feet high, and the castle surmounts all of it, leaving the town of 10,000 to cluster about its base. We approached Foix on a winding mountain road, there was a sharp turn, and then the castle's three great towers suddenly filled the valley and the world. The three towers are each of them high, each different in shape. They are widely separated. Between them and below them are the ruined walls which once guarded the fortress. The castle does not in any sense dominate the horizon, because the mountains all around are much higher than it is. It dominates only the town below it and the two rivers rushing by below it, plus the eye and emotions of travelers coming upon it for the first time.

At its best visiting antique shops is a little like visiting museums, except that there are no catalogues, the artwork changes constantly, and one never knows in advance what treasure might be waiting just behind the door. At St. Lizier we entered the shop of Marie-Louise Rivère. She and her husband had once owned a shop in Paris. Now her husband was dead, and she had moved her shop back to St. Lizier, where she was born.

She showed us a seventeenth-century traveling altar about five feet wide, four feet high, and a foot and a half deep. It must have weighed 500 pounds, and in the old days, whenever the local lord went on a trip, his chaplain, who was possibly a bishop, followed on a mule, and footmen slogged along behind, carrying a traveling altar like this one by the handles. Its two doors opened out to disclose the actual altarpiece inside. The doors bore the likenesses of saints inside and out, painted almost in the manner of Russian icons and worthy, I thought, to hang in any museum in the world. The panels to either side of the doors were painted too, as were the sides of the piece and even the back.

Mme Rivère led us down into her cellar, where she had stacks of armoire doors, all of them carved, all in lustrous walnut or oak. The cellar was crammed with pieces she had no room to show upstairs.

She had no need to bribe *chiffoniers* to find new stock, she told us. Instead, because she was so respected in the region, families who found themselves obliged to liquidate a palace or a château in which no one lived anymore (for the young people had gone to live in the cities, in Paris if possible, but at least Toulouse) would sometimes summon her and sell her everything the place still contained. Much of what she was showing us now, she said, had come out of the Thévenin château over by St. Gaudens. Much of the rest of it had come out of similar private collections. Nonetheless, her prices, by the standards of Paris and especially by the standards of New York, seemed ridiculously low.

However, she did not know the whereabouts of Le Vernet, and she was unaware that there had ever been concentration camps in the region.

We took the time to wander through her village. The cathedral, across from her shop, was completed about 1080. It is basically Roman in architecture, but about 1350 an octagonal steeple was added, giving it an almost Moorish look. There is a twelfth-century cloister with charming arcades and delicate lovely columns. Inside it was dark and cool, and there were some wonderful twelfth-century frescoes. St. Lizier, though a backwater now, had been an important city under the Romans, and it was still important in the centuries when the counts of Foix were big men in the neighborhood. Later the town was owned totally by a succession of bishops, and the palace they built for themselves in the fifteenth and sixteenth centuries is two or three times grander than anything else in the town, including the cathedral. Though now a psychiatric hospital, parts of it are open to visitors.

At Pamiers we found a shop run by a couple named Dubois. Monsieur, his wife said, was out on the road hunting pieces. At Varilhes, same story. Monsieur would not be back for a week. He was out in his truck. He was knocking on farmer's doors. He was listening in bars for information on who had died recently, which widow might want to sell something. His life, his wife told us, was difficult and trying.

Even unpretentious shops such as these are often enchanting. In one of them we saw a foot-long barrel — not an ordinary barrel made from staves but one hollowed out of the bough of a tree. The ends had been stopped up and encircled with brass, and in the middle was a hole for a cork. Such homemade barrels were what peasants used for carrying their wine up into the hills each day, and this one had been polished to a shine, whether by some bored shepherd or by time itself no one now could say. Next to it stood a wooden bucket also hollowed out of the bough of a tree. The bucket was about six inches in diameter and about a foot and a half deep. Its outside was smooth and had been polished until its texture was like leather. The wood was from a crespal tree. It both looked and felt like leather. It would make a lovely vase to keep flowers in, or keep anything in. It would make quite a conversation piece, although originally it was only a pail into which peasants milked cows.

All this antiquing, this asking of questions, occupied us for a number of days. The country was lovely. It seemed to us almost empty, no traffic jams, no smog, and sometimes we would stop and look across a valley at a ruined château or stop just to breathe the pure air and listen to the silence. Or we would stroll through old stone villages or stop for lunch on a terrace above a torrent.

It was in an antique shop that we at last picked up the trail of Le Vernet.

This particular shop was owned by a man named Alain Krausz. I was only the second American he had seen, he said. The first was a dealer from New York or maybe Philadelphia or some place like that, who had come by in a rented pickup truck and after thirty minutes, without speaking or understanding a word of French, had gone away with every clock Krausz had. Krausz was a specialist in antique clocks, though short of stock at the moment, he said, as we could see.

Oh yes, Le Vernet was only a few miles further along. We couldn't miss it. No, he knew nothing about any former concentration camps.

We drove north as directed, but by the time we came to Le Vernet we were within twenty miles of Toulouse, population 354,000, and no longer in the Pyrenees at all, and I was surprised. We drove in and out of Le Vernet's few streets and then off into the countryside for several hundred yards in each direction, expecting to see the remnants of a stockade or the camp cemetery or at least a monument, but there was nothing. The only cemetery was in the village, and it was not very big. I got out and prowled among the gravestones looking for a heavy concentration of deaths during those years or for foreign names. But I found no such graves.

Back in the village we sat outside a café and ordered drinks and engaged the waitress in conversation.

She was a girl of about 20, and she looked entirely mystified. What camp? She brought the owner over, who acted just as mystified. Camp, monsieur?

He said he had lived in this village more than ten years.

The camps had been an embarrassment to the administration even at the time and in retrospect had shamed all of France. But had some kind of national pact been agreed upon? Were the young people of these villages to be brought up with no knowledge of the camps? Were the inquiries of strangers to be turned aside? Was the memory to be forced to die?

The camp at Noé was the only one he knew about, the owner said. His finger located Noé for me on my map.

It was about twenty miles south and west. Trying for a short-cut via back roads, we fetched up against the banks of the Garonne, and there was no bridge, but the map indicated a ferry, and we drove along the bluff above the river until we found it. It was being pulled back and forth by cables. It was bringing over pic-nickers and swimmers and, looking at it, I didn't have to ask if it took cars. Ours would have sunk it. We sat on the bluff and watched the river for a time. People were swimming or sunbathing on the bank. A rope hung down over the river from a tree, and some boys were swinging on it. The Garonne is one of France's four great rivers. Every French schoolchild learns about the Gar-onne, the Rhône, the Loire, and the Seine, and here we were looking at the same river that runs through Bordeaux. It was already almost as wide here as there, although it starts only a few miles higher up in the Pyrenees, at the confluence of a number of mountain torrents.

But finally we drove into Noé, and I stopped beside another old woman in black and asked about the former camp here. She said nothing was left of it except for a portion of the village cemetery which had been given over to prisoners who had died in the camp.

Since she seemed knowledgeable, I told her about our un-successful trip to Le Vernet, near Toulouse.

"Le Vernet *en Ariège,* monsieur," she said. There were two Le Vernets, it seemed, and we had gone to the wrong one. But she didn't know where the other was.

In the meantime we looked over Noé.

There are hundreds of villages like it in the Pyrenees. They are small and old and some are half abandoned, and I concluded that most of the people who inhabited them were so isolated and so insular that they knew nothing at all about villages two valleys away, unless a relative had moved there, much less about former concentration camps within them. To Paris such valleys must have seemed the perfect place for camps. The mountains would choke off all protest. The problem was settled. The country was saved.

All these camps — and there were others in the Alps, in Brittany, and elsewhere — came into being principally out of fear, though there were other contributing factors: chauvinism, anti-Semitism, political opportunism, even the indecisiveness of muddle-minded bureaucrats. Their immediate cause was the arrival of tens of thousands of Spaniards who crossed the border into France in 1939 because they were on the losing side and feared a massacre by the victorious Franco. These were men who had been engaged in killing and violence for the three years that the civil war had lasted. They couldn't go to hotels, for they were destitute. Worst of all in the world that existed in 1939, they had no papers. Many of them were believed to be Anarchists and Communists, and some no doubt were. They had to be put somewhere. The safest thing was to lock them up. And so camps were built near various Pyrenees villages, and the Spanish rabble was stuffed into them.

For some time Europe had been seething. It was like a gigantic anthill; the ants were running in all directions, and not just out of Spain. There were refugees from Stalin's Russia, from Mussolini's Italy. There were refugees from lesser-known purges in Hungary, Rumania, and Poland. Hitler had built camps and filled them with Jews, gypsies, homosexuals, and petty criminals of all kinds, not to mention political opponents such as democrats and Communists. There were no ovens or gas chambers yet, but it was as if everyone knew there would be. Germans who could afford it were running for the frontiers.

Among all these various refugees were many who had been in camps or jails in other countries, often in several other countries, for months or years already, for no one wanted them. France didn't want them either, but let them in. France has always let everyone in, though of course they were not allowed to work.

Many of the refugees were trying to get to America, but this took time. Some had money. Others lived by selling off piece by piece whatever valuables they had been able to smuggle out of Germany or wherever, particularly jewelry and rolled-up paintings. And of course some, once in France, worked illegally, were caught, and now had criminal records. All refugees were of course obliged to register with the police and most, particularly the formerly monied classes and those with the new criminal records, were careful to do so. They put their addresses down. These were the ones it would soon be the easiest to arrest.

By the time war with Germany was declared, France had absorbed 3.5 million refugees, almost 10 percent of the total population. Sympathy for these people, such as it was, disappeared overnight. Their status had changed. They had become enemy aliens, possible fifth columnists, saboteurs, secret agents, spies. France was in a panic, and police, gendarmes, security agents, and even soldiers were sent out to round them up. Most times the arresting officers banged on doors at 7:00 A.M., not only because people were more likely to be home at that hour, but also because a subject caught in his underwear or befuddled by sleep was less likely to resist — although there was not much resistance left in these people in any case. Most of them had long ago learned to sleep with emergency belongings in a small suitcase beside the bed, and if nothing had happened by 8:30 A.M. then all was clear until the following day.

The prisoners were kept packed into guardrooms in station houses and *préfectures*. In most cases no provision had been made to feed them, though those that had money were usually allowed to send out for food. At night they were told to sleep on benches or the floor. In Paris during the days and weeks that it took to process them all, some were taken to prisons at night, while others were herded down into basements and coal cellars. In the coal cellar under the Paris *préfecture,* the available space was about ten feet wide, all the rest being filled with coal. About eighty men and women were locked in there for the night without food, water, blankets, toilets, or, of course, space. The air, one prisoner later wrote, was "thick with our exhalations and with coal dust." Sick old men were coughing their lungs out and the women were hysterical. By the end of the next day about half of the eighty had been processed. The remainder were forced back into the cellar for a second night.

As the number of prisoners grew they were housed, if that is the word, under the grandstand at the Stade de Colombes, which was France's biggest soccer stadium at the time, seating about 40,000; or under the grandstand at Roland Garros, where the results of a recent Borotra-Cochet tennis match were still posted on the scoreboard. Sports stadiums were good; they were surrounded by fences and could be easily guarded, they had running water and toilets, and there was room for exercise, though of course water flooded down through the seats whenever it rained, there were no beds or blankets, and as September turned into October it began to get cold in Paris.

Finally, as processing was completed, masses of these "enemies of France," many of them elderly Jews and almost all of them passionate antifascists, were moved in buses and boxcars and sometimes third-class railroad carriages to concentration camps that had been hastily expanded, or hastily built, and that were in all cases remote. Families were casually split up, the husbands herded one way, the wives the other. Spouses and lovers said goodbye to each other for the duration, if not forever.

Some of them were brought here to Noé, which appears to have been one of the benign camps. In any case, I never heard of it before the day I first saw it, although by then I knew a good deal about the camps. As the old lady had told us, there is nothing left now except the few gravestones in the cemetery, though these are eloquent enough, and as I walked among them, they told the story of Noé: that it was a mixed camp containing women as well as men; that the prisoners kept there had some money and were granted some privileges, if only the privilege of paying for their tombstones; that not all were Jews, for some of the stones bore crosses.

The refugee graves are in a kind of alcove surrounded by the same continuous wall as the rest of the cemetery. There is no entrance gate from the street; entrance is via a gate into the alcove from the main part of the cemetery. However, the main part, which is overhung with handsome trees, was, when I was there, well cared for. The refugee section, measuring about thirty yards by sixty, was barren except for tombstones and weeds. Several times a year those weeds were mowed, or they would have been higher than they were. Otherwise no care was taken of the refugee cemetery as far as I could see. Why should there be? No one came there anymore.

I stopped at the grave of a Count Maximilien de Bissingen, a German, Sept. 27, 1895–July 2, 1941. Near him lay Gertraude Liselotte Nawratski, born in Berlin Oct. 10, 1919, died at Noé Aug. 23, 1943. Who was Gertraude Nawratski, who died here at 24, and what threat could she have posed to the French state which imprisoned her in this camp for the last years of her young life?

The next gravestone read: Hermann Strauss, *Docteur en Médicine*. He died aged 60 on Sept. 2, 1942. He was a Christian, for there is a cross incised on his stone. If he was both a Christian and a doctor, then why was he a refugee in France? He must have kept many of his fellow inmates alive, and his death must have thrown the camp into despair.

According to the dates on the gravestones, almost no one died during the first year of the war. Presumably the prisoners were living on expectation; perhaps the war would be a short one. It wasn't, of course, and the counts, doctors, and young girls who had been sent to camps like this one were left to idle away the years one day at a time, until finally illness brought them down, or malnutrition or the end of hope. The French state was kinder to them dead than alive — a portion of the village cemetery was given over to them, and if they had any money left, it was allowed to go for a tombstone.

In a sense, captives here in the Pyrenees were luckier than some others, for the region fell under the jurisdiction of the Vichy government after France capitulated; thus they were not at first molested by the Germans. But after the victors occupied all of France in December 1942, the Gestapo came south and went through the camps, taking the people they wanted most first, leaving the Gertraude Nawratskis for later. In some cases sympathetic French commandants allowed refugees to escape, but never on a large scale and usually not at all. Mostly the prisoners waited there at the barbed wire, watching the snow line move up and down the mountains, until the Gestapo got around to them.

The Gestapo, my research had indicated, went to Le Vernet first.

From Noé we drove back to the Hotel Eychenne, at St. Girons, where we were staying. Our balcony was hung with vines and flowers — all the hotel's balconies were. The view was south towards the high mountains, which, this late in the afternoon, were not visible, for a low fog was dropping down into the valley. The sun was gone and it was cold and presently it began to rain. We had an aperitif in the bar, which was entirely paneled in old armoire doors. Then we had dinner in the hotel restaurant, which rated one star in the Michelin guide.

It rained the next day too. I went for a stroll through the town. The population is 9,000, and it is not a particularly pretty town, though the Salat, which pounds and boils through the middle of it, is a very impressive mountain river. The fog hung low all the time and we could not see the mountains from our window. The flowers attached to our balcony dripped water down into the courtyard below, and the mountain meadows that sloped upwards into the fog looked sopping wet. I had bought a detailed map of the region while I was out, and I spread it on the bed and followed the Ariège River towards its source in the mountains, and at last my finger found Le Vernet. The next day we drove there.

The village itself is dusty and lost and far back from the road, but a railroad line runs past it, and on this railroad those Jews and political exiles whose dossiers were marked with the word *undesirable* arrived under heavy guard to be penned up. They were men only. They had been arrested under the *loi des suspects*. They weren't charged with anything. To the frightened French bureaucrats who sent them to Le Vernet they were "dangerous to public order," for some were Communists and some had fought in Spain and some were criminals who had spent time in French jails for the crime of working. But others were only terrified old Jews sent to Le Vernet by mistake. There were Czechs, Poles, and Swiss with German accents sent to Le Vernet by mistake. The Hungarian journalist Arthur Koestler, who had covered the Spanish war and who was accredited to a British newspaper, was sent to Le Vernet by mistake. Among the other prisoners were an Austrian opera singer, a Yugoslav violinist, several doctors, a lion tamer, and a

German rabbi who had lost his right arm in the German trenches in World War I. France was going under, and knew it, and in her panic mistakes were unfortunately common.

When these newest refugees got to Le Vernet, they found it already crowded with refugees from Francisco Franco.

The village square was unpaved then — it was still unpaved when I saw it — and the local peasants worked the surrounding fields. But 2,000 prisoners arrived at the camp in the first three months of the war, and before long the population of the village and the camp rose to 17,000.

Some of the men sent to Le Vernet had already served time at Dachau and elsewhere. Some said conditions at Le Vernet were worse.

The camp occupied about fifty acres of hard, stony ground on which nothing grew except, here and there, tufts of grass. Until winter came there was always dust blowing about; in winter the ground froze like iron. The camp perimeter was delineated by a deep moat and then by three rows of barbed-wire fencing. Within this perimeter the camp was further divided into three sections, each separated from the others by more moats, fencing, and barbed wire. Section A was for aliens with criminal records — illegal working usually. Section B was for aliens with political records, and Section C was for all others. The men were housed in wood and tar-paper barracks that were long and narrow, measuring ninety feet by fifteen.

Inside in place of beds or bunks were upper and lower sleeping platforms that ran the length of the barracks on both sides, leaving a two-foot aisle down the middle. Two hundred men were assigned to each barracks. They slept 100 on each side of the aisle, 50 men on the lower platform, 50 on the upper, feet toward the center, twenty-one inches of space per man. About an inch of straw had been spread on the boards. There was no other bedding. There was no stove, no lighting, no glass in the windows. No blankets were issued. In theory all these men had been told to bring blankets and luggage when routed from their beds in Paris or wherever. But in fact many were picked up in the streets or in cafés or train stations and shipped to Le Vernet with only the clothes they wore. It was September then. In the Pyrenees winter came early and lasted a long time. There were barracks in which 200 men shared fifteen blankets.

Each new batch of prisoners was marched on the double from the train into the camp, where their skulls were shaven — first things first. Rules were explained to them. The rules were strict, and even minor infractions were punishable by eight days of "prison," the first day without food or water, the next three days on bread and water only.

Each man was assigned his twenty-one inches of straw-covered wooden sleeping platform.

They were assigned tools, principally picks, shovels, and sledgehammers, and set to work building roads and maintaining the camp. They worked from eight to eleven, and from one to four. All of them were refugees who had made it as far as France, meaning they were not of the laboring classes. No clothes were issued to them. They worked in the clothes in which they had been arrested until these became rags and fell off. There were four roll calls per day, each lasting half an hour. During roll calls they were obliged to stand at attention. Some days it was raining or windy or icy cold or all three. Moving or talking was punishable by prison.

There was water, but no soap. They were never able to get clean. There were no eating utensils. They were fed eleven ounces of bread per day. For breakfast they got black coffee. For lunch and dinner they got a thin soup, which they ate out of cans scavenged from the garbage dump. The soup had chickpeas floating in it, but no meat or fat.

The only toilets were holes in the ground. Winter came on. Frigid winds blew down off the Pyrenees and the temperature dropped to five degrees above zero Fahrenheit. The men worked in the rags they wore and in shoes that no longer had soles. The barracks were still unheated. There were still no stoves, no lighting, no glass in the windows. There were still no blankets.

A detachment of prisoners was obliged to parade to the colors each morning and to salute the French flag as it was raised over the camp.

There were some brutal guards who beat prisoners half to death and some officers who watched and did not care. As France collapsed it was easy to believe that these filthy and desperate men were responsible and were only getting what they deserved.

Improvements were instituted. There began to be three ounces of boiled beef in the soup at noon, though of a quality so poor it was difficult to eat. Inmates over 55 were separated out and moved into barracks that had stoves.

Men began to die. A number hanged themselves from the rafters with their neckties.

In April of 1941 there was a riot in the camp, and prisoners were killed by guards, perhaps as many as 150.

The cemetery is about a mile north of the village and about 200 yards off Route 20 back in a wheat field. It measures about forty yards by forty, delimited by concrete pillars set ten feet apart and still hung with the remnants of rusting barbed wire. There is a monument in the center bearing the words *Aux Étrangers Morts Loin de Leur Patrie*. Some of the letters are missing and presumably will never be replaced. When all of them are gone, so will the memory of the camp be gone. The day I was there the stele was decorated by a wreath of plastic flowers whose ribbon, also plastic, bore the legend *A nos camarades morts en captivité*. The wreath had been there a very long time already.

The cemetery is flat and was overgrown. The soil is stony, and great, smooth stones were lumped in mounds on top of each grave, and these mounds poked up through the weeds. After the war some of the bodies were removed, and so there were also numerous grave-shaped holes, none of them more than two or three feet deep now.

Not a single one of these graves was marked, as far as I could see, although the farmer I later met in the fields said that there was a small plaque on each of them with a number and that on file in the *mairie* in the village was a name to go with it, together with the date of death. Maybe so. I couldn't tell how many graves were in there. The whole thing was too overrun with weeds, brambles, and wild rosebushes to count them. Various stunted cactuses grabbed at my trouser legs as well. There were all kinds of wooden crosses, only two or three still standing, most of them lying among the weeds, and not a name, not even a letter, on any of them that I could see, nothing.

There were originally a number of stone and stucco buildings here, as well as the barracks. The farmer who bought the land in 1950 knocked down all but two of them, keeping one as a barn and one to house his tractor and other gear; the rest of the land was now under cultivation, except for the cemetery itself.

The farmer came at me across the field carrying a pitchfork and when he was close said, "Don't be alarmed at my pitchfork, for me it's just a tool."

So I asked about the camp, but he didn't know much. He told me the village road mender came out once a year before the *Jour des Morts,* which is Nov. 1, and cut down all the weeds and cleaned things up a bit, and that occasionally people came by.

A few years ago, the farmer said, somebody came out and dug up a rotting coffin and took it away. Apparently the men who died at Le Vernet were buried in wooden coffins. It's hard to know, when men become uncivilized as they do during a war, in what ways they become uncivilized. If it's true that the dead had coffins, this is slightly incomprehensible. The authorities were unable to provide, or willing to deny, food, clothing, heat, blankets, medicines, and most of all liberty, but not coffins. Why?

Apparently Le Vernet was the worst of all the French camps. Certainly it had the worst reputation. No one can tell you why conditions here were so bad. This is all long ago. When France finally fell, the farmer told me, and the Gestapo was on its way, the prisoners at this camp were not liberated, except for whatever Spaniards were left. The farmer said this was a mistake, for those Spaniards went around preaching anarchy and made a great deal of trouble in France. The Gestapo got the rest.

By this time the farmer had determined that I was American. He immediately wanted to talk about America, and what Americans thought of France. I got him back onto the camp, and he admitted that there had been a great deal of misery on this spot, but he wasn't terrifically upset about the whole idea.

We had to have a long conversation standing there in his field staring at the few strands of rusty barbed wire, the few gray and weathered crosses. He wanted to know all about America and to grumble about French politics.

Le Vernet may always have its legend, but from now on any

information on the place will only be more or less true. Accurate stories nobody is ever going to get again, nor on the other camps either. They're nothing that France was proud of, nothing that anyone wants to remember, and the German camps, ultimately, were so much worse. Le Vernet was just a place of misery, of innocent people kept in captivity for no good reason for years and years, some of them badly weakened by torture or malnutrition before they ever escaped to France, and who then had lived in Paris or elsewhere on dwindling money, eating badly, getting no medical attention; and who now were penned up again, no gas chambers, no ovens, but concentration camps still again.

In the car we were silent for a time. The valley is flat and often treeless. Le Vernet and the villages nearby are all outstandingly ugly. There is a brick factory around there somewhere, and the villages are all made out of bricks. They are among the ugliest in all of France.

Nantes
A BRITTANY DIARY

Tuesday, May 23

From London across the channel to Brest. Whitecaps on the water below, plane swirling about. The plane is small, fourteen passengers, two props. An adventure these days. Brittany as it comes into view is fierce cliffs, as I expected, miles and miles of them, but surprisingly beachy too. Clouds blow in and out. Sometimes I can see nothing. The beaches are in front of the cliffs or tucked into them. Some are a few yards wide, some several miles at a sweep. We come in over the continent. No trees. Here and there atop the cliffs is a villa, a lighthouse, each one isolated, wind scrubbed. Inland we cross over farm country, losing altitude, the earth green and brown. Thin roads. Brittany one of the poorest regions of France, especially this most distant part of it, but from the air pretty and rural. Its number-one export is its young men and women. No one wants to stay. A small airfield appears; the pilot lines it up. We land, step down from the plane, rent a car, and only then discuss where we might drive to.

This is a vacation in a part of France we do not know. We have no fixed itinerary, no reservations ahead. Once when I worked for the paper out of Paris I was assigned to write a piece about how Brittany would vote in one of de Gaulle's upcoming referendums. I thought it was a stupid idea and said so. I was told to do it anyway. I was told to drive out to Rennes, capital of the department, interview the préfet and a few others, and write the story as ordered. I had been traveling a lot that year and was tired. I was very unhappy, but P. said she would come with me, we would make a holiday out of it. So we drove to Rennes, where I did the interviews and filed my story — which New York never used, by the way, so I was right — and afterwards we went sightseeing, stopping at whatever interested us all the way back to Paris. Anyway, that's the only other time we've been to Brittany, and we did not come this far out.

After studying the road map we turn out of the airfield and drive west toward Pointe St. Matthieu, which is the furthest west Brittany goes. France's elbow jutting out into the Atlantic. Land's end, though not called that here. This is what we should look at first, I argue. My arguments sound exceedingly wise to me. See where something ends and perhaps understand it better, I argue. The theory is perfect, is it not? P. gives an indulgent smile. After that we'll drive south, stopping wherever we please. The town where Gauguin painted might be interesting, and the ports that had the submarine pens, and much else. We'll visit whatever cathedrals and castles we come upon, including the one in which Henri IV signed the Edict of Nantes.

Beside the road the broom and gorse are in bloom. The windows are open. It is cloudy and the air smells of rain. The houses here are different from elsewhere in France, painted white and gray with stucco walls, steep slate roofs, dormers. Flat, wide chimneys at either end. Suddenly the sun comes out. Whole fields turn gold. Other fields blue with wildflowers.

Clouds blow in again. The coast is further than we thought and it is lunchtime, so we stop in a village called St. Renan in the Breton equivalent of a fast-food joint. Instead of a McDonald's or Burger King, it is a wonderful stone and timbered room. Blue and white tablecloths. Flowers on the tables. We eat the Breton equivalent of fast food: a *galette,* plus a green salad. The *galette* is a buckwheat crepe the size of a pizza but very thin; the sides are folded over its contents — mine is ham and tomatoes — to form a square. For dessert we eat a *crêpe aux pommes chaudes,* a hot apple pie using a crepe for pie crust. *Galettes* and crepes are all around

you in Brittany. Bretons drink hard cider with meals, not wine.
We down an entire bottle. It's somewhat fizzy, brut, not a bit
sweet. The owner assures me it's only five degrees alcohol, less
than half the strength of wine. But as we leave the restaurant I
can feel it.

We come to Pointe St. Matthieu, a place of desolate cliffs
with the sea beating at them far below. The sea is engaged in
breaking up the cliffs — has been for some time — even as the
cliffs imagine they are splintering the sea. Atop the extreme point
of the cliff are two lighthouses, one old, one brand new; with, in
between, a ruined abbey from the sixth century. A bit further
along there are some German blockhouses, gunless now, from
1944, and next to them some French telephone relay towers, spin-
dly and high, from 1988. The new lighthouse throws a beam that
is visible, supposedly, thirty-seven miles out to sea. How far could
the blockhouses throw a shell? The telephone towers throw out
signals that can't be seen and don't come down for the next 3,500
miles.

Bretons were seafaring men historically: fishermen, pirates,
explorers. They worked always with this rocky coast at their
backs. The most famous was Jacques Cartier out of St. Malo, who
opened up French Canada. There were Breton fishing vessels on
the Newfoundland banks from as early as 1540. Most of the later
New World voyages went out from Normandy, usually from
Honfleur or Dieppe, because Normandy was closer to Paris, and
Paris was where the money was. But the sailors were mostly
Bretons.

The blockhouses are not up forward on the cliffs as you might
expect but are set back in fields. Why? The Germans in them
waited for an invasion that never came — here. Maybe some got
transferred to Normandy in time. Lucky them. Many of the blockhouses lie half buried under huge earthen mounds. An earthen
cushion to dim the impact of incoming shells. The ceiling would
last longer and the men's ears wouldn't ring so much. But over
the past forty-five years the turf has crept inexorably downwards;
by now the eyes of the blockhouses are half closed. In time they
may become covered over entirely, and after that forgotten, to be

exhumed by some incredulous archaeologist 1,000 years from now. What will he think they were for?

There are villages out here along the cliffs. We begin to drive through them, one resort village after another. Most stores look closed and the houses look shuttered tight. These villages come alive only in summer apparently. We are driving south. Villages with very clean streets, not a bit honky-tonk. Where there are villages that means a beach below. Immense, flat beaches down there, but almost deserted. Tidal beaches — the tide this afternoon is out. On one a young couple stands near a child digging in the sand. On another a man bundled up runs with a dog. We're a month ahead of season. In July and August these beaches will not lack for half-nude girls. In my day to get that a good look at a girl you had to seduce her, or else go to a strip joint. Now even in prim old Brittany, staid old Brittany, thousands of them prance about — the same girls who, during the village fetes, will wear the costumes of yore and *coiffes* in their hair.

The sky is low. The wind blows. Cold sand and a colder sea. Even to imagine sunbathing makes one shiver. About four o'clock we come to Morgat, formerly one of the most popular Brittany resorts. We stop at its best hotel, the Villa d'Ys, and are shown to a room by the proprietress. When she has gone I check out the bedside lamps. As expected, twenty-five watts. No soap in the bathroom. No heat in the room — nor in the rest of the hotel either, I assume. Well, Brittany these days does not attract millionaires. But from our window there is a lovely view of still another empty beach and roadstead and of cliffs beyond. The tide is either coming in or going out. I watch it for a while and can't tell. That's because Brittany tides are enormous, up to forty feet in places. Their movement seems imperceptible, until suddenly they leave behind or cover up these vast beaches. We go downstairs. In the lounge we order hot tea and watch the French Open on television.

After dinner we decide to take a look at Cap de la Chèvre, which is supposed to be a particularly rugged cape. We get into the car and drive. The road climbs through picture-postcard Brittany: silver road, gray sky, green bushes to either side, trees bent

by the wind. Here and there houses huddle together. It's past 9:00
P.M. but still daylight. On top of the cape the landscape becomes
austere, perpetually windswept, a treeless moor. We pass a number
of parking lots — empty now but in season filled with caravans
and campers. A van is parked in one lot even tonight.

At the end of the cape are more German bunkers and gun
emplacements and also a French military signal station. New.
Signs don't say what it's for. They say keep out. The sea below
froths. Huge chunks of cliff have broken off. They extend out a
ways like the hulks of wrecked ships. It is as if they drifted out
to form islands. At our feet slabs of a half-built monument lie
about. The stones that will be put together to form the monument
are already engraved: "To our naval aviators lost at sea." Too cold
to read further. The wind is enough to blow the eyeglasses off
your face. It's 10:20 and still not dark.

Wednesday, May 24

Raining. We decide to go on anyway, and I pay the bill. In
response to my questions the proprietress says her hotel, all the
big Morgat hotels, dates from around 1900. This is the only one
still functioning. The others have been taken over by the Assurance
Sociale for welfare families, or are boarded up, or serve as something else. Morgat doesn't have much need for the hotels of the
past. The available clientele today is young and poor or old and
poor. People who sleep in their vans or on the ground. People
who don't spend money.

Morgat was once a great and famous resort, the proprietress
says. The Peugeot car family had the big house. All the Brittany
resorts were prosperous. If you were a Paris businessman you
liked to send your wife, kids, and a maid or two to hotels such
as hers for the summer. This was the way you proved how much
you loved your family. You yourself summered in the city with
your mistress. The same was true all over France. But these days
the wife has no maids. In the old sense, the husband has no mistress. Together they probably have a summer house in the country.
Or go someplace more exotic and with better weather than Brit-

tany. "The season here is too short," the proprietress complains. An understatement. A way of saying that the Morgat of long ago did not have to compete with southern Spain, the Caribbean, Africa. For Morgat, for Brittany, prosperity is not around the corner.

At Pointe de Pen-Hir we come upon the most spectacular cliffs yet. Also the most fortified. A veritable Maginot Line 300 or more feet above the lashing combers. A fort more than a bunker. It's hundreds of yards long and all bashed about. Bashed when? By whom? A bombardment we never heard of? A diversion, perhaps? The ceilings are six feet thick: beetling brows over huge, toothless grins.

Only a few tourists are up here today, but we overhear two speaking German. Their compatriots left these concrete master-pieces everywhere. When they see them, what do they think? They are in their twenties. They weren't born then. They can tell them-selves it's got nothing to do with them. They can stare down at the sea, which batters the continent with the force of a thousand wars.

There is a footpath along the edge of the cliff. It's marked as such by low signs. It's right on the edge. I begin to walk it. Ahead of me the rocky coast disappears into gray mist. Wind blows the drizzle almost sideways. I can't tell exactly where the path ends and the void begins. The sea is crashing down there. I go back to the car.

Our next stop is at Locronan — even for Brittany an excep-tional village. The road comes through the square, which is cob-blestoned and lies on a slant. It's surrounded on three sides by sixteenth-century stone and timbered houses. Steep slate roofs that glisten in the rain. Arcades: under the arcades, shops. The square's fourth side is the village church, one of the oddest in France: it is actually two churches built a century apart stuck together. Inside they intercommunicate. Nice stained glass, but not at its best today, given the gloomy weather outside. Some primitive poly-chromed statues of saints.

The locals consider the second church, though it is substantial, to be only a chapel. The chapel was built at the same time as most of the houses, the mid-1500s. The church predates both by 100 or so years. It has a great square tower that is handsome in its proportions but slightly too big for it; the chapel has a steeple. Church and chapel are both more or less Gothic in design, but it is not the Gothic one sees elsewhere in France because it took Gothic two extra centuries to get this far out into Brittany. By then austerity of line was gone; the style was no longer pure. Brittany's Gothic churches are often highly embroidered, almost feminine in ornamentation. There was no reason for local architects to copy the rest of France anyway. Brittany wasn't French until 1532. It was ruled by its own duke, had its own language, which was of Celtic origin and akin to Welsh, not French. There are separatists today, one tends to think of them as fanatics, who preach that Brittany should break off from France, become independent. These people want to bring back the old ways, the old language. Some are violent about it. Bombs have gone off. Not many: a tax collector's office, a police garage. It is not a movement the populace has embraced with open arms. Nonetheless, Bretons do feel they are different from other Frenchmen, and most of them would prefer to go on feeling that way, if possible.

As we continue driving there are many stone crosses beside the road, or at intersections with other roads, and we pass a number of "calvaries" as well. A calvary is a crucifixion scene carved in stone. Most of them are life-size or bigger and very old. Usually they stand in front of or beside the church in a village that reeks of cows and manure. The stone face of Christ on his cross may be fifteen feet in the air, perhaps more. Grief-stricken stone mourners cluster about the base. Most calvaries date from the sixteenth century. The carvings may be crude, the work of the village stonemason of the time, but the impact is considerable. It's impossible not to stop to look at them.

By supper time we have reached Quimper, population 60,000, where we check into a hotel, then walk across the bridge into the town. We look for a restaurant but don't see one. What do people do here? Women with their string bags and baskets are out shopping for dinner. The cathedral looks stunning, but is closed. The shops are closing. We come to a second river, narrow as a canal. It mirrors the houses that hang out over it, the trees, the flowers in window boxes. One house has a protruding half turret, and

below it is the river. Quimper is famous for its faience. The principal faience shop is still open. There are people inside looking
over the pottery. We go in. The stuff is pretty, though rather
thick. The prices seem very high.

Thursday, May 25

Early morning. Tourist buses are already parked outside the
cathedral. People stand in groups waiting for their guide to give
them permission to go in. They look eager. Obedient too. I go
past them and except for two or three worshipers have the place
to myself. The Quimper cathedral has confused more people than
any in Christendom. The tourists outside are in for a surprise. The
nave in here is not straight. It curves off to the left. The whole
church curves. It is possible to think you must be drunk. Perhaps
the architect was drunk. More likely the builders — it was started
in the thirteenth century and finished in the fifteenth — encountered some problem: ground water, boulders. Rather than deal
with it, they went around. Very strange. Nothing else of note that
I could see.

The best Quimper faience is made by Henriot, supposedly.
Admission to the factory is 12 francs. We go there but have to
wait, the receptionist tells us. A group of thirty is due on the hour.
When their bus comes we can go in with them.

We begin waiting. The group of thirty is soon ten minutes
overdue, then twenty. The receptionist is adamant. We must continue to wait. So we leave.

A short distance away is the Keraluc factory. Since they are
only number two, there is no admission fee, immediate entry.

Inside the potters work with loaves of slate-gray clay two feet
long and eight inches in diameter. To make a dinner plate a kind
of wire cheese slicer comes down and separates an inch-thick slice
from the loaf. This goes into a mold, where it is pressed and
trimmed by machine. Out comes a slate-gray dinner plate. By the
time the plates reach the decoration section, four women in smocks
in the corner, they have been printed with an outline drawing of

whatever the motif is to be. The women overpaint the outlines with their colors.

Yes, by today's standards this counts as handmade, but why does it cost so much? Faïence de Quimper is not fine china. If you bought a service for twelve you wouldn't be able to lift the box; any more than that, you would need a truck to get it home. The designs are primitive, the colors are washes rather than colors. I don't deny they are attractive, even lovely, but why so expensive?

Back in the car we steer towards Concarneau because in the guidebook it sounds interesting. The original city was the small island in the harbor called the Ville Close. We cross over on a footbridge. It's three or four streets surrounded by massive ramparts dating from the fourteenth century. The city long ago spilled over onto the two banks, leaving this walled island to the curio dealers and foreigners. Concarneau may be the only city left with an actual ghetto — an enclosed space to confine a specific group, in this case tourists. Germans. Scandinavians. Whatever. We walk along. The sun has come out. The only language not heard is French. Lots of art galleries with, on the walls, harbor scenes, nudes. Bright, garish colors to please people from countries even further north than Brittany who might come here and think this place Florida. We have lunch.

Pont Aven: still driving south. Plenty of tourists and galleries here too. Art better. When Gauguin arrived in 1886 this was a thriving art colony already. Having decided to become a painter, he wanted to be where other painters were. In the town museum a photo blowup from that time shows ten artists sitting around a café table outside the pension in which most stayed, including him; the pension is a dentist's office today. The artists stare straight out at the cameraman under his black cloth, motionless for the required ten seconds, or whatever it was.

Many were Americans. In all there were twenty artists or more. Some had considerable talent and their names are known today, especially Bernard and Sérusier. But only Gauguin among them can be said to have made it big. The biggest possible. How did he do that? Why him among so many? It is too easy to say he was a great painter. That's not enough. Someone has to discover an artist in the first place, so as to put him out there for audiences to find. Audiences have to learn to like his work, and most times they don't have time or are dazzled by something else or don't even look. Plenty of great artists in all the arts are never discovered, never recognized. Conversely, plenty of artists recognized as great are not.

Also in the museum is a blown-up photostat of a letter Gauguin sent his wife, whom he had abandoned. He was perhaps not the entirely free spirit that, from his publicity, one imagines. At least at first. He is regarded as the best painter here, he writes, but it doesn't bring in money, he is living on credit. The letter sounds faintly apologetic. He knew what he had done to his family. He wasn't a monster. Gauguin's time in Pont Aven was before he worked with van Gogh in Arles, before he sailed to Tahiti. He went away from here and came back. He went away again and came back — four times in all, I think, four extended stays in Pont Aven — a man, as the French say, who had lost the pedals and was trying to find them again.

The town museum is short on art from the period, and there are no Gauguins at all; how could there be? What is a Gauguin worth today, $10 million? More? But there are many photo blow-ups of him and his family, of the other artists, of the town as it was then, and they are fascinating. One shows the women of the day in their black dresses and sometimes *coiffes* doing their wash in the Aven, standing amid great, smooth boulders in water up to their knees. Beating the linen senseless on the rocks. Their great-granddaughters have washing machines. The linen lasts longer, the women too.

Friday, May 26

Spent last night in Les Moulins du Duc. The hotel is one of the Relais et Châteaux chain — a loose association of country inns or châteaux that have been converted into hotels. There are about 150 in France, which is where the idea started, and many more in the thirty-seven countries into which the association, begun in 1954, has spread. Some are more elegant (and more expensive) than others, but all are comfortable and some are stunning: handsome buildings in handsome settings, antique furnishings and paintings, huge rooms, futuristic bathrooms, perfect service. Their restaurants are all splendid too. Almost all are small.

Hotels that want to belong must undergo a year or more of incognito inspections, must pay money. It isn't very much money, apparently. A few thousand dollars. For this they get listed in the association's guide, half a million copies of which are distributed worldwide, some sold, some handed out.

Les Moulins is at Moëlan sur Mer, a village not listed on most maps. Unlike some of the others, it's not an ancient castle but an inn in a forest with outbuildings scattered around a dammed-up river that makes a private lake. Like most of them, it's in an isolated spot. Above all else, association members seem to be selling silence, which in our world becomes increasingly rare. Our room was a rather luxurious cabin in the trees. The window looked out at the ducks on the lake.

For dinner we ordered the least expensive menu. Is this the best way to test the qualities of a chef? Ordered fish salad to start, and leg of *mulard* and apple tart for dessert.

All of which may not sound like much. But —

The first course was both hot and cold: cold salad greens doused in walnut oil and wine vinegar, then overlaid with hot fried filets of *rouget, lotte,* and *sambre* — I don't know the names of these fish in English. The hot and the cold set each other off amazingly well. There were many kinds of greenery in the salad, and the hot fish filets were similar in their chewy texture but each one subtly different in flavor.

A fine start. Then came the leg of *mulard* — not a duck from the pond, I was assured — with its accompanying vegetables, which were arranged like paints on an artist's palette. The cooked mushrooms sat each one on top of a dab of purée of turnip. The tiny round roast potatoes came in a little latticework potato-chip basket. The Frenchman eats first with his eyes, it is said, and this was a chef who believed it. As wine I chose a more or less unknown, more or less local St. Nicholas de Bourgueil, and drank it chilled; it's as pleasant a wine as Beaujolais but has never caught on.

The baked apple tart was served hot under an elaborate sauce composed mostly of Calvados, which is apple brandy. Beside the tart were thin slices of fresh apple covered with a caramel and Calvados sauce. The chef was marrying apple to apple to apple, and he was successful.

Met him later. I didn't ask to. The *maître d'hôtel* led me into the kitchen, I don't know why. I congratulated the chef, he beamed, and we talked awhile. His name is Xavier Gabart. He's 36. A heavy-set man, pleased to talk about his art. The chef here a few years ago was a Japanese, he said. Very strong. Michelin gave the inn one star. But he left and was replaced by a Frenchman, who managed to lose the star and a good many customers. Now Gabart was starting almost from scratch. I promised to write the Michelin guide in his behalf. Probably three or four such letters constitutes a landslide and will get him his star. People don't realize. When I used to work for the paper, three letters on something was a lot. Wrote an extremely controversial article in the old *Saturday Evening Post* once, circulation five or six million, and got eighteen.

The dining room was on a terrace looking down on the smaller ponds and islets that the river forms below the hotel. It was pleasant to dine and look out the big windows and watch the light fade.

Among the other diners were several Americans. None of them spoke French and they had trouble ordering. What were they doing here? How did they find this place so far from the great cities to which Americans go? This morning I passed one on the path. He said good morning. I said *bonjour* to him, I don't know why, and kept walking.

Now we are in the neighborhood of the submarine bases the Germans built, the first of them at Lorient, a big port town, 65,000 people. We can see the pens as we drive out onto the dockyard. They are as big as airplane hangars, which is a surprise, but why? Subs may lie flat, but conning towers and gear are high, and the roof above is no ordinary everyday roof — it is concrete twenty-five feet thick, two and a half stories. The pens are surrounded by a chain-link fence, and there is a gatehouse with a gendarme guarding it, which is normal, for it is nominally a military installation. There may be French subs in there now. Visitors are allowed in, but only if they are French, which I hadn't known. Not having a French passport, I am turned back. From the gate I can see only the back of the pens, and I marvel again at their size. They are higher than apartment houses.

A guide has come out, thinking he was about to make a sale. Instead he stands beside the car and gives part of his spiel. He's disappointed he can't take us in. Bald little fellow. An ID card hangs from his sweater. The roofs were built in layers like plywood, he tells us, but with air spaces between layers to absorb shock. Most of the German fortifications throughout France were built by German troops or engineers, he says, but 15,000 Frenchmen working around the clock built this one. There were no days off or vacations, and if you claimed you were sick they mixed you into the cement. So he says.

Vast fishing yards next door. Trawler after trawler tied up at docks. All of them rusty. Until the subs came in 1940, Lorient for its entire history was a fishing port. We look down at nets of nylon rope, and at rusty cables by which they are dragged in full over sloping fantails. Cranes, waiting trucks. Great plastic baskets full of fish. And rust everywhere.

Having driven inland, we stop for lunch at a restaurant that stands across the river from the château in Josselin. From our table we look up at it across the river. Three enormous round towers on our side. Great high wall. It was a medieval stronghold once. Intimidating then, only beautiful now. It seems to grow straight up out of the river. We sip our wine and watch the colors play across it as the weather changes: sun, clouds, sun showers, clouds again. We admire it for over an hour over lunch, then I pay the bill and we cross the river to go into it, only to discover that it's closed today. Come back tomorrow or next week, the concierge tells us. Never, more likely. Unfortunately.

Well, there is another château inland that I have heard of, the château of Trécesson, so we drive there. From time to time the sun comes out. The sky is piles and piles of clouds of all colors. Fields of buttercups beside the roads. Wet, head-high ferns. Queen Anne's lace in big round bushes. We find the château easily enough but can't get in there either. Trécesson turns out to be privately owned, visitors not admitted. We get out of the car and study it. In photos it looks to be made of red brick. They're not bricks but flat stones of reddish schist, stained with yellow lichen. A mauve château. Very odd. It was built around 1440. A moat. Many towers, some of them round, some six-sided. A kind of causeway crosses the moat, and there are outbuildings for farm machinery, hay, animals — at present Trécesson is a working farm, and the glorious château serves as the farmhouse. A woman with her hair pulled back and wearing rubber boots invites us into the dirt courtyard for a closer look. She has excellent manners and in no way resembles a farmer's wife. The *châtelaine*, then. That's what *châtelaines* look like today. It's nice of her to offer us this closer look. She does not invite us into her house though.

At tea time we stop at Rochefort en Terre, another village more or less unchanged since the Renaissance. Timbered slate-roofed houses, curio shops, tourists. Some of the buildings are unchanged inside too, the bar we drink our tea in for one: stone fireplace, paneled walls, gargoyle moldings. Others, like the pharmacy next door, are more modern. The pharmacist, or perhaps someone before him, has ripped out all the polished wood and put in plastic.

At St. Nazaire we reach the estuary of the Loire and drive out onto the dockyards. Warehouses, cranes, parked ships. Rusty cables lying about. St. Nazaire is another submarine town; this dockyard was the site of one of the most famous raids of the war, and for that reason I want to see it.

It is evening now, no one is about. The dockyard is untended. This enables us to drive all around staring. How huge this installation is! How long a kilometer is if you're running under gear, carrying explosives, ducking bullets!

St. Nazaire is the center of French shipbuilding. Is and was. The *Normandie*, the biggest and fastest liner in the world, some said the most beautiful, was built here in the thirties; and the *France*, which was just as beautiful and even bigger and faster, in the fifties; not to mention innumerable cargo vessels and warships.

This dockyard is unusual in that it is not at sea level and is not open to the sea. It is instead an enormous man-made basin —

two interconnecting basins actually — high up above the river. Basins that can float ships of tremendous size, even many at one time. Two great man-made lakes high above even the highest tides. Ships sailing upriver from the sea get up here in what may be the world's biggest lock. They float up as if on an elevator. During the war German submarines did the same, though using a smaller lock off to one side that is to this day overhung with an immense thickness of reinforced concrete: U-boats slowly rising in the lock — or descending loaded with fuel and torpedoes — had been incredibly vulnerable to bombing raids. Once this concrete carapace was in place above their lock they were safe. We stare at this covered lock tonight, at the marvelous thickness of the roof, at the sub it currently houses — a decommissioned French one, sinister looking for all of that; tourists clamber through it each day upon payment of a fee. As soon as the planes had left, the U-boats, if they were coming in for refitting, simply motored across the basin and into one of the fourteen pens on the other side; or else, having descended to river level, they headed out to sea. The pens are of course still there and will be presumably forever. From this side of the basin we can see into them. A row of huge concrete garage sheds, impossible ever to remove or destroy. They do not appear quite as massive as the ones at Lorient, but they are substantial. They could hold twenty or more U-boats at a time. Today they serve only as warehouses and workshops.

St. Nazaire is about four miles up river. On the night of March 22, 1942, British commandos came in from the sea to attack this place, which was aswarm with German troops, ships, and guns. Their object was to destroy, if they could, the locks that controlled access to the basins, particularly the biggest of them, which could be used as a dry dock for repairing the battleship *Tirpitz*. They planned to ram the outer face of this lock at river level with a superannuated destroyer loaded with explosives on a delayed fuse, then jump ashore from the destroyer and from the seventeen small, slow motor launches which had brought most of them this far and were all they would have to take the survivors, if any, home again; and once they got up here they would attack all the other locks too, and also all the pumps and hoists and Germans they could find.

That winter was the low ebb of Allied fortunes in the war. Defeat was everywhere. A success was needed, whatever the cost. Something that could be made to seem spectacular even if it failed. So thought the politicians. Churchill was enthusiastic; he was always enthusiastic. Mountbatten was chief of planning; it looked like mass suicide to him. People conceive these things on the basis of flawed intelligence, without ever having been there. They plot them on maps. On maps distances look short, everything looks possible. How did the commandos even get up here onto the basin from the Loire so far below? Standing here tonight, seeing how vast this dockyard is, it is amazing that they reached any of their objectives at all. With the first shot every square foot of the place was immediately floodlit. There were hundreds of Germans shooting at them. It was an impossible raid.

Their destroyer did ram the biggest lock, wedging itself into the machinery. It did explode there the next day, killing 100 or more incredulous sightseers who had come to look at it, some of whom were certainly Germans. The lock and the dry dock it represented remained out of commission until 1946. The *Tirpitz* was never able to use St. Nazaire; vital as this was made to seem, it might never have done so anyway. The commandos also managed to blow up some important nearby machinery, all of it rare, expensive — all of it French, by the way, and after the war it was years before the French could replace it. The great lock included.

Most of the commandos' motor launches were discovered and sunk in the Loire before they ever got this far. The men floundered in the water and were blown up there, or burned there, or drowned there. Only a few commandos got ashore. It had been hoped that they could smash enough locks to empty the basins entirely. Put St. Nazaire out of the war as a repair base for ships and as a U-boat base too, at least for some months. But those who actually landed were too few in number, and the target locks were and are all widely separated — the distances, when you stand here and imagine men running under floodlights, under fire, planting limpet bombs out of knapsacks, are truly amazing. In addition there were five locks to attack, ten doors in all. The commandos never got near most of them.

Worse, there was no way for them to get home. They tried

to fight their way out through the back of the town during what was left of the night; except for two or three who escaped overland to Spain, the survivors were taken prisoner to live out the rest of the war in camps. Of the 611 men who took part, 169 were killed and many more wounded, some dreadfully. Only a handful made it back to England more or less intact, more or less on schedule.

All this was given out to the public as a great triumph, and by the standards of that war and that time perhaps it was. The raid was its own war in miniature. Glorious destruction. Heroic death. There is a monument to the raid out on the boulevard beside the sea, and I stand looking at it. In the cold light of almost five decades later it seems to glorify behavior that could just as easily have been counted insane.

Like all of Brittany's coastal cities, St. Nazaire — except for the indestructible U-boat pens — was totally flattened during the war. Now we drive up and down its streets trying to find what must be its center, and can't. A strange, low, new city, not a bit pretty anywhere, totally dominated by the basins and shipyards off to one side.

Saturday, May 27

From St. Nazaire we cross the bridge over the Loire. The bridge is a stunning thing, extremely modern, not American-looking at all: a mile and a half long and enormously high — over 200 feet above the river. Out in the middle we feel like we're in an airplane. It's a suspension bridge, but with a difference. Its two towers are steep inverted V's, not the traditional arched stanchions, and its cables are not anchored at either bank in massive doses of concrete. There is no need to anchor them; each tower supports an equal weight of roadbed in each direction; each is stabilized by the very weight it holds. Together the two towers support the entire span and at the same time are stabilized by it. Very impressive.

Brittany ends at the Loire. We are on the south side now and the villages change, the houses. The slate roofs become orange tile. We stop for coffee in a bar in a small shipbuilding town. It's midmorning but the bar's already crowded with men drinking beer, drinking *marc*. Out front in a small dry dock under an awning, a steel trawler is being built. Across the river is the Brittany side: bigger shipbuilding towns, factories, refineries. It looks like New Jersey over there. On this side it's bucolic, cows in the fields, expanses of wildflowers growing in all colors.

To get to Nantes, population 250,000, Brittany's biggest city, our destination all along, we cross back over and plunge into the maze of traffic of every major French city. Cars everywhere, car exhaust. Cars double-parked, cars on sidewalks.

Unlike the coastal cities, Nantes escaped the war more or less intact, and the ducal castle, to some extent the goal of this entire tour, still looms over the town. It was begun in 1466, but April 13, 1598, is its important date — the day Henri IV signed the Edict of Nantes, ninety-two articles, the first comprehensive document in the history of the world, so far as I know, guaranteeing total freedom of conscience, plus what seemed then to be total freedom from religious persecution as well. All this in a world that had been slaughtering heretics and unbelievers for centuries, with France at the head of the list. It was France who fathered the crusades, those noble endeavors whose goal was to massacre Moslems; when the Albigensian heresy broke out in its own southwest in the thirteenth century, the nation mounted an additional crusade to kill all the Cathars there and lay waste their towns, and when one soldier asked the presiding bishop how he was to tell the heretics from the Christians, the reply came back, "Kill them all, God will know his own." No one knows how many people that crusade butchered, only that the killing and pillage and burning went on for twenty years.

The wars of religion of Henri IV's time were merely the latest manifestation of the religious hatred and intolerance that the French church sponsored and that Frenchmen held dear. Between 1562 and 1589 there were eight of these wars and in between were isolated assassinations and massacres without number.

For French Protestants there was no escape. Several hundred sailed to uninhabited Florida to form a colony where they could worship God in their own way. Pedro Menéndez de Avilés, the so-called father of modern Florida, came upon them there — they were there before he was. He tricked them into surrendering. They had his word of honor as a Spanish gentleman that they would be safe. When all had come over and laid down their arms, he ordered them butchered. Towards Protestants a Spanish gentleman's word did not count, and God wanted them dead. They were speared, knifed, their throats were cut, every single one, and that was the end of French attempts to colonize Florida. The incident caused a diplomatic crisis between France and Spain, but it quickly blew over. Deep down nobody cared very much — the victims were only Protestants.

The St. Bartholomew's Day massacre, ordered by Charles IX, followed in August 1572. It killed nearly every Protestant in Paris except for the King's brand-new son-in-law, the future Henri IV, married only three days to the royal daughter when it started. Perhaps as many as 10,000 were killed; the bodies piled up in every turning of the Seine for miles downriver.

All of this Henri IV ended here in Nantes. "Those who follow their consciences are of my religion," he said as he signed, "and I am of the religion of those who are brave and good."

By then, to solidify his hold on the throne, he had become Catholic. "Paris is worth a mass," he is supposed to have said. He was a practical man as well as a tolerant one. He was a skillful general. He was a womanizer who left bastard children all over France. He was always short of money and he was not entirely selfless — he was responding that spring of the Edict of Nantes to an invitation from the leaders of the city. If he would come here and somehow end the bloodshed and misery, the city would pay him 200,000 ecus — to an impecunious king a lot of money.

He reigned from 1589 to 1610, when he was assassinated. Someone jumped into his carriage and stabbed him several times. The Edict of Nantes did not survive him very long — Louis XIV revoked it in 1685, and the Protestants got persecuted all over again.

The ducal castle is splendid and impressive — from the outside. It's surrounded by great walls, a moat. But inside it's a disappointment. Only three rooms are open to the public, and none is the one this visitor — any visitor, I would think — has come to see: the room in which the edict was signed. Perhaps Henri himself was unaware of the landmark quality of the edict.

Perhaps the French are not impressed still. There is no copy of the document on display anywhere in the castle, and no room has been singled out as the centerpiece of the castle. It may have been signed in one room or another. The guides say that nobody quite knows. It might not have been signed in this building at all but in the palace of one of the King's pals across town somewhere, a palace that no longer exists.

Rain falls all afternoon. In our hotel room we watch the tennis from Paris. Dinner in a *brasserie* on the Place Royale. Wonderful oysters, called *creuses* here, succulent, very fresh.

Sunday, May 28

High mass in the cathedral. The whitest cathedral in France, it is said, perhaps the world. The granite used elsewhere in Brittany runs out when you get this far south, so the architects used a local stone that is not only white, but also relatively light in weight, meaning that they could let themselves go and did. The vault is soaringly high, 123 feet, about 8 feet higher than Notre Dame de Paris. It makes for an absence of gloom which is as pleasant as it is surprising.

Also the cathedral is full, every seat taken, another surprise. France is nominally a Catholic country. Nominally. In a recent poll by the newspaper *Le Monde*, 81 percent considered themselves Catholic, but 52 percent said they did not practice; 80 percent said they would not take the church's position into account when making major decisions in their lives. Another significant statistic came to light during the most recent Plenary Assembly of the bishops of France: 1,160 priests ordained in France in 1945, 116 in 1985.

On sale in the back of the cathedral are color postcards. One shows the cathedral roof ablaze in the night some thirty years ago — the entire roof — probably not the only time in 550 years this happened, merely the only time it was photographed.

We go outside into a rainy morning, our last in Brittany. Church bells have begun tolling from steeples all over the town. We walk through the rain listening to them, all ringing at a different rhythm, all on different notes. They toll all around us.

Avignon
THE PAPAL IMPRIMATUR

It is night. The street is narrow, the sidewalk narrower still. The narrow houses press together flank to flank, and a strip of dark sky shows between their overhanging brows. A medieval town in our time. Then the street ends and I am at the ramparts. They are as high as the houses that face them and of great girth. The houses are not new, but the walls are older; they have been there since about 1350. In some places the stones have eroded slightly from the rains and winds of centuries; otherwise they are unchanged.

These walls are several miles in circumference, solid and high all the way around. They girdle the city. Around 1792 an effort was made by the revolutionaries to dismantle them to sell the stones. It was not possible. The workers gave up.

At regular intervals the walls become swollen so as to support guard towers or else turrets for bowmen. In between they are crenellated. In places bushes and even small trees sprout from the top. Here and there, inset into the inner sides, the streetlights show arched rooms that are almost like caves; guardrooms once, probably.

There are fourteen gates in the walls these days, double the original number. Having reached one of them, I pass outside the fourteenth century into the late twentieth, which, for the time being, is the most modern age there has ever been. I stand at the edge of a road. Fast headlights go by in the night. Beyond the road is the dark river and, extending out into it, the famous bridge, which is even older than the walls. It took ten years to build and was finished about 1185, the only bridge over the Rhône this far down, the marvel of the age. Partway out was built a two-story Romanesque-Gothic chapel. Call it a church. A Gothic church in the middle of a river. In those days people put them anywhere. The church is still there, and tonight it is floodlit, and it divides the current that pushes by it.

The bridge once had fourteen arches, some reports say twenty-two. It went all the way across and was meant to last forever. It lasted intact barely forty years before Louis VIII, King of France, decided that the city was insolent and needed to be punished. Since the bridge was its pride, he punished the bridge. What kind of man would destroy a bridge?

It was rebuilt afterwards, but other wars came. Floods too. It got shorter and shorter. Nowadays it is the length of four stone arches. A bridge that doesn't bridge. It goes out into the middle of the river and stops. Louis also tore down 300 houses and the original town walls that had been built by the Romans. What did he care? Avignon belonged at the time not to France (meaning not to him) but to the counts of Provence. Later one of the counts sold it to one of the popes, a story in itself.

But when the first popes lived here beginning in 1309 Avignon was Provençal. It was a town of 6,000 whose mud streets reeked of uncollected garbage and unpunished crime. It was a miserable and dispirited collection of hovels, and the mistral then as now blew straight down the Rhône valley twelve months of the year. It was incredible that the popes came, even more incredible that they stayed. They did more than stay. They established the center of the world here.

On a more personal level they built a monumental palace for themselves and filled it with treasure. The bishops and cardinals in favor with one pope or another built only slightly lesser palaces and did likewise. These were holy men and they knocked down buildings or requisitioned buildings; either way they threw the inhabitants out. Afterwards they added so many embellishments that the eaves of one house nearly touched the eaves facing it.

Below the houses the streets filled up with merchants and petitioners, with jugglers, fire-eaters, and whores, with clerics and monks and all too often their concubines. Avignon became richer and more populous than Rome. There was a curfew at night because of all the murders. So many people crowded in that bubonic plague, the Black Death, passed through regularly. In 1348 it killed 60,000 and the population was reckoned as 100,000 afterwards, or about 10,000 more than the much-expanded city holds today.

Avignon's wealth regularly attracted one or another of the so-called free companies — armies of roving brigands. The present walls are the popes' work and are, relatively speaking, new. They were built to keep such armies out, but didn't always work. Around 1365 a man named du Guesclin at the head of 30,000 men camped across the river and demanded tribute — 200,000 gold florins and absolution for all his troops. The then pope, Urban V, levied a head tax on the inhabitants and sent out the ransom. Du Guesclin sent it back, saying he wanted the pope's money, not the people's, and not to forget the general absolution. The pope and his cardinals did as ordered. Dragging their wagon of gold, the 30,000 men rode away.

I go back inside the walls, walk along narrow streets, and a few blocks later come to the Palace of the Popes. Its facade is absolutely white with floodlights, something the popes who lived here never saw.

It stands on the Place du Palais, which is not so much a square as a great cobblestone esplanade sloping upwards. The Palace of the Popes occupies most of one side, and a number of more ordinary buildings occupy the other; the Petit Palais — the bishops' palace — blocks off the upper end. The Place du Palais did not exist when the popes lived here, or at least not in this way. The houses in those days came up almost to the walls, and the popes sold whatever space was left to merchants for their stalls. From the popes' windows there wasn't room to spit without hitting someone below; there were said to be no open spaces anywhere in the city.

The first time I came here the bishops' palace did not interest me, for I did not then know what was in it or how it related to the popes either, and the Palace of the Popes I found impressive almost exclusively for its size. It is huge. It is bigger than huge. To take in its entire facade one has to pan one's eyes like a camera. This single building covers two and a half acres. One of its towers is seventeen stories high. It must once have been the greatest building in the world, two or three times higher and wider than any other castle or château ever built, the Empire State Building of the day. Its straight, flat, windowless walls seem to go up and up.

Inside, the impression it gives is no different. During that first visit we moved through one vast empty room after another. The ceilings are 35 or more feet high. One room is 170 feet long. One hundred and seventy feet. One room. In another we could see by the markings on the walls where, at some point in history, this single room had been converted into three rooms, one on top of the other, each of them with ten- or twelve-foot ceilings. The Palace of the Popes is not a place to evoke intense, poetical emotions, and certainly not religious ones. Rather it evokes almost consternation, plus a good many questions to which, at the time, I had no answer. Who were these men who lived here? How did they keep such rooms warm, and themselves warm? How did they get hot food to the table? How did they like climbing all those stairs? What made them think they needed to accord themselves, or could enjoy according themselves, so much space?

Inside the palace we wandered around for a while, not understanding it in the slightest, then came out into the sunlight again, and there were musicians playing on the Place. The musicians I enjoyed much better. There was a small crowd around them. They were playing medieval folk songs on stringed instruments. They wore medieval capes. They were either students or in the employ of the municipality, and it was very nice and we listened to them, and from time to time we gazed across at those enormous walls.

It was a Sunday afternoon and presently we walked down to the Place de l'Horloge, which is one of the most pleasant squares in France, with its handsome surrounding plane trees and its dominating fourteenth-century clock tower — jacks still pop out sounding the hour. Under the trees the café tables were out and we sat down and a waiter came out and we ordered aperitifs and sipped them and talked about the palace and about what life inside must have been like.

Across from us was the opera house, which dates from about 1880. I saw that the ticket window was open, so I walked over and bought two tickets for the performance that afternoon. Then we had lunch. The opera was to be Massenet's *Don Quichotte,* which neither of us had ever seen. Going to the opera on a whim on a Sunday afternoon seemed to us rather grand, and I mention what follows precisely because Avignon is not La Scala or Covent Garden or the Met, which is where the attention of most opera lovers (and opera singers, as well) is concentrated.

In the small opera houses of France — Avignon, Nice, Strasbourg, Bordeaux, and many more — there are usually two performances a week, Friday night and Sunday matinee, from December to May, expenses underwritten by the municipality (meaning the taxpayers), and today's singers would play to a house only three-quarters full, we saw as we entered, which explains how we were able to buy tickets at the last minute in the eighth row of the orchestra.

The building inside and out is ornate, almost baroque. Its auditorium is horseshoe shaped in the Italian manner and seats 1,300. It is not as beautiful as Nice or Bordeaux, but it is very nice.

Don Quichotte is an opera rarely given in France and almost never anywhere else. Even recordings are rare. Except for the obligatory windmill-tilting scene and its general premise, the libretto does not follow the Cervantes story too closely. Rather, it follows a play by one Jacques Le Lorrain, a cobbler's son who was born in Bergerac in 1856 and who at about the age of 25 came to Paris to write poetry. Poets were no more in demand then than now. He went hungry, wrecked his health, and wound up as a cobbler himself. At 47, ill and despairing, he left Paris for the south — but he had left behind his play, his variation on the Don Quixote theme, which a producer suddenly discovered and to the poet's astonishment decided to put on. To the poet's further astonishment it was an immediate hit. The dying man rushed back to Paris to see it performed, had himself carried into the theater by his friends, and shortly afterwards expired.

In his story, as in the opera, the fair Dulcinea promises to become the Don's *bien aimée* provided he can recover a necklace stolen from her by bandits. He and Sancho Panza go to the bandits' lair. The terrified Sancho bolts. The old man, after being bound, beaten, and mocked, commends his soul to God. His soul, he sings, *"n'est pas méchante."* The bandits kneel before him as if to a saint. They also hand over Dulcinea's necklace. Back at the tavern Don Quixote presents his prize and asks Dulcinea's hand in marriage. She has to tell him she is not quite the saintly young girl he thinks. Everybody laughs at him, at which point Sancho Panza, in defense of his master, jumps in with the best song in the show, *"Vous commettez tous un acte épouvantable."* In the final scene the old man dies in his servant's arms.

It was all quite moving, though not necessarily in a musical way. The Orchestre Lyrique de Région Avignon-Provence, which was formed in 1982 and which consists of fifty-nine mostly young musicians, was under the direction of Robert Martignoni. The Dulcinea was the Bulgarian Eugenia Dundekova, of whom I had not heard. She seemed to me by far the best singer on the stage. She was quite young, rather pretty, still only slightly plump, with a lovely mezzo voice, and it seemed possible that she had a big career ahead of her. Pierre Thau sang Don Quixote. Denis Léandri was Sancho Panza. Both acted well and sang well enough. That is, I kept wondering throughout how the music would have sounded if sung by better singers than they all seemed to be.

Except for Dundekova all the singers were French and a number were from Marseilles. All were unknown to me and, so far as I know, unknown outside of France. Like all opera singers in France, they were technically civil service employees. That is, opera is government subsidized; the government employed them in opera houses — here this week, in Nice the week after, in Bordeaux the week after that. Even in Paris sometimes if no foreign star was engaged. As *fonctionaires* job security was assured. Vacations, sick leave, and, ultimately, old-age pensions were guaranteed. Show business to them was not nearly as risky as performers in other countries usually found it.

French conductors, singers, dancers — even chorus members — are civil service protected also. Some of them get to have civil service mentalities; they have tended at times to judge civil service work rules more sacred than their art. They cannot easily be fired or even retired. New talent can't get in because there is no room.

It is a system that has failed for forty or more years to produce great conductors, not to mention great voices, in numbers sufficient to command the attention of the operatic world. Why is a performance of *Don Quichotte* so rare? Because there is virtually no one of stature to champion French opera at home, much less abroad. As a result an entire tradition (with a few exceptions) is being underplayed or not played at all, and much of it is in danger of disappearing completely. Even in Paris the repertory is predominantly foreign. The many gorgeous French operas, meanwhile, are largely ignored.

Like all French cities, Avignon is oriented politically and commercially north towards Paris, but on hot summer days the populace heads the opposite way; thousands of cars move towards the Mediterranean, some ninety minutes south. The goal of many is Les Saintes Maries de la Mer, in the Rhône delta.

It was dusk by the time the opera let out. What to do next? Well, we needed a place to sleep, and we thought of Les Saintes. We had heard it was a very strange town, that the beach in front of it was stranger still.

Unfortunately it was night before we got there, so we could not see the beach, and most of the hotels, since we were out of season, were closed. Also, whether open or closed, they all looked in our headlights like fleabags. Finally we picked one.

In the morning we at last were able to look over the famous Saintes Maries de la Mer. It is white and old and has a bullring. It seemed almost Spanish.

What it is famous for is gypsies. They gather from all over

Europe for their big festival in late May, which each year is like a Lions Club or Rotary Club convention, except completely different. The conventioneers do not wear name tags, they live not in hotels but in their rickety caravans or their broken cars or under their carts, and there are always plenty of knife fights. At this time of year (it was April) there were a number of gypsies on hand, either early birds or else left over from the year before, and we had to give money to several. Those we ignored trailed after us for blocks with their hands out.

The town church, which dates from the twelfth century, fascinated us for a while, for it has no windows low down and only a single door. It is what is called a fortified church. Whenever trouble occurred, the entire populace used to take refuge inside it. Pirates or invading armies would land and the town would be empty except for the church, and the invaders would assault the single door. A lone strong-armed swordsman would have been standing in the doorway, I suppose. He would have been expected to hold them off. Being the local champion must have been quite a burden.

As for the beach, we discovered it from horseback. Dozens of stables line the road coming into the town. After lunch we hired horses, which is what tourists do in Les Saintes. It was a warm, sunny day and we walked them along the dikes and the edges of the lagoons past all the nesting flamingos, and then at last out onto the beach.

It was like no other beach I am acquainted with. In the brilliant light that came off the sand and the water, we galloped the horses over the sand, and it seemed to me that this was the flattest beach and the flattest country I had ever seen, flatter than Kansas, flatter than anywhere. The slope down into the water is so gradual as to be imperceptible, and there are no dunes, no higher ground anywhere. The beach was enormously wide — enormously long too: it goes on mile after mile — and it was interesting to imagine galloping along here in summer when the whole flat beach would be populated by weekenders from Avignon, from Arles and Marseilles too, and by vacationers from all over France and Europe. The sand is absolutely covered, I am told, with bare bodies, nearly all of the girls and even women nowadays in France topless, and a good many of the sunbathers male and female entirely naked.

When we started home the Rhône delta, which we had not been able to see the night before, continued to amaze us. Five miles back from the sea the elevation was still only about four feet, and in the flat scrub pastureland grazed the short, stubby Camargue horses such as we had just ridden, or else herds of wild bulls. It is a quiet, almost soundless place, full of sun and flatness and birds and space.

The Avignon papacy was the result partly of civil disorders in Rome, partly of an implacable quarrel between King Philip IV of France and Pope Boniface VIII of Christendom. It started when the French King tried to tax the French clergy, which was sending enormous amounts of money month after month to Rome; he wanted to keep some of that money in France.

The pope, who claimed to be ruler of the spiritual and temporal worlds both, reacted by issuing a bull excommunicating any monarch who would dare even to propose such a tax.

Which made the King angry. In Paris he jailed a papal nuncio and had the pope's bull publicly burned while a fanfare blared on royal trumpets.

Which made the pope angry. In Rome he issued another bull, *Unam Sanctum,* which maintained that to be saved the faithful must believe themselves subject in all matters to the pope. And never mind any kings.

King Philip was certainly not going to stand still for this. In Paris he summoned the Estates Général, the same assembly of nobles, clergy, and bourgeois that nearly 500 years later would bring down France, and ordered it to debate the following propositions: that Pope Boniface in Rome was a heretic; that he was a criminal; that he was not the true pope; that he must either abdicate or be deposed by force.

When Pope Boniface scoffed at such nonsense, men in King Philip's employ went into Italy, where they scaled the walls of the pope's palace and, after ravaging his private apartments, threw the aged Vicar of Christ on Earth into a cell, leaving him there three days without food. Soon afterwards the old man died. His successor quickly died as well, possibly poisoned, and at the conclave immediately following, the cardinals decided they had best elect King Philip's choice, namely Bertrand de Goth, the cardinal-archbishop of Bordeaux. This they did, and the new pope took the name Clement V.

France at this time dominated continental Europe. England had a king but was isolated; Spain and Germany had not yet coalesced as nations. Italy was dozens of squabbling city-states, most of them in revolt against the papacy which attempted to govern them. Rome itself was perpetually ravaged by riots. In Rome no pope was safe, especially not a new French pope, but where to go? Well, King Philip wanted Pope Clement on French soil; this was perhaps a condition for Philip getting him the job, and Clement was homesick for France anyway.

He went back. He was crowned at Lyon on Nov. 14, 1305.

He would be the first pope to reign at Avignon, though not right away. For four years he wandered around France living in various bishops' palaces, sponging off the local faithful, a virtual prisoner of the French King. Finally he wandered into Avignon and stayed. He reigned there five years. The city had the river, which was a highway, and technically King Philip did not own it. A pope could be more or less free there.

There were no other advantages. Pope Clement found mud houses, stinking mud lanes. The mistral blew all the time. Only the wind made breathing the noxious fumes possible. The pope moved into a local convent which became the de facto papal palace, but kept a second palace at Carpentras, sixteen miles east, which he seemed to prefer, saying the water was better there. He built nothing at Avignon, and it was at Carpentras that he fell mortally ill. He died on a litter on the road a league or two out of the town. He was trying to get home not to Avignon but to Bordeaux.

At Carpentras the twenty-three cardinals went into conclave to elect a successor, but fought over whether the papacy was to return to Rome or stay in Avignon. They argued so long and so fiercely that the palace in which they had convened was attacked by a mob led by the dead pope's nephew. The mob turned mur-derous, its swords and pikes cut swaths through the merchants at their stalls outside the palace and through the servants and guards at their posts inside. The cardinals fled out the back door, and the dead pope on his bier was abandoned. The mob stripped the corpse of its jewels, its rich robes, and set the place on fire. The nearly naked first Avignon pope went up in smoke.

After that the papal throne stayed vacant two years, until finally the cardinals were sealed for forty days into a room at Lyon. According to one story the food sent in was progressively diminished, forcing the cardinal-voters to settle on a pope or starve. At last they named a "compromise" candidate, an "interim" pope, a French cardinal less than five feet tall who took the name John XXII; since he was already 72 he would surely not reign long.

He was to reign unfortunately eighteen years.

From Lyon he came down the Rhône in a barge and got out and walked through the streets of Avignon to what is now known as the Petit Palace, the bishops' palace, which was where he would reside. The Palace of the Popes had not been built yet, and he was not the man who would build it. He was said to be a frugal, abstemious man personally, a man of piety who ignored creature comforts; in eighteen years he never rode a horse or mule. He was also a canon lawyer and a theologian, which gave him a special abhorrence of heresy and heretics. Torture and burnings at the stake were the way to solve the heresy problem, he believed. And he was chauvinistic — nine of the ten new cardinals he created were French. And he was good to his family — three of those cardinals were nephews.

He was not loved. He was particularly hated by the Italian cardinals, for they knew he would never take the papacy back to Rome, and there were a number of attempts to poison him. This made him extremely nervous at table. But not everyone was as careful as he, with the result that at one dinner party one of his cardinal-nephews fell dead at his feet. A prime suspect was the Bishop of Cahors, who of course had to be punished. First the skin was flayed off him. He was stripped of his episcopal immunity, so to speak, then dragged through the streets and given over to the mob, which tore him apart with red-hot pincers. The pieces were thrown on a pyre in front of the palace.

Most of all Pope John was a miser. For eighteen years he piled up money. The papal treasury contained 70,000 gold florins on the day he was elected, 17 million on the day he died, plus 7 more millions worth of jewels, crowns, and other precious objects. For eighteen years he spent almost nothing; he merely amassed, and he thought up clever new ways to do it. He sold offices, he sold promotions — if a man at the top died, everybody down the line moved up one notch, and they all paid. He sold appointments to livings that brought in regular stipends — a single cleric might hold 300 livings.

He invented expectatives, which meant the appointing of someone for a price to a post or episcopal see that was not yet vacant; and reserves, which meant to reserve to himself an office when someone died — they had paid for it but couldn't pass it on; and the *annate,* which was the first year's revenue of anyone granted a benefice or living.

During his reign almost anything could be arranged for a fee. There were fees for the legitimization of a child, fees for dispensations, fees for the commutation of vows, fees for monks who desired to live as hermits, fees for laymen who wished to enter holy orders but were crippled or deformed or blind in one eye or squinted. These were specific sums written down. It cost a man more to become a priest if he were blind in the left eye than the right.

There were fines for sins, also all written down. Sin was worth money. To get absolution you paid. Your cost depended on the "degree" of your sin. For instance, fornication came in varying degrees, whether by priest or layman, whether with nuns or female relatives or young boys. A nun already guilty of fornication who nonetheless wished to become an abbess paid so much extra. Priests could receive permission to live in concubinage upon payment of a certain sum. Murder cost a specific amount depending on the identity of the victim — dead bishops cost the most. One could buy absolution in advance for "accidental" murders committed in the future.

And the money piled up. An eyewitness described what he observed every time he went into the apartment of the pope's chamberlain: bankers and money changers, tables loaded with gold and silver. Another told of men with rakes raking up the gold florins. Petrarch, who was there, called Avignon "mother of all the vices."

"Ungodly Babylon," he wrote, "where shame is king, from whence by now every virtue is banished."

The pope's cardinals became fabulously wealthy, as is attested by their wills, still on file. One of them owned twenty-one houses, another fifty. One cardinal had 637 servants, including musicians, singers, buffoons, and men to care for his hunting birds and Arab horses.

There were said to be 240 retainers around Pope John, almost clinging to him, no doubt. At 90 he at last died. He lay in a gold cope studded with gems, wearing his tiara. When he was exhumed 425 years later to be moved to a chapel, someone decided to have a look at him, which is how we know how short he was and what he was wearing.

The Palace of the Popes had still not been built. The bishops' palace in which John XXII lived is now one of the newest and also one of the most memorable museums in France, for it houses several hundred paintings and sculptures dating mostly from the time of the popes and the antipopes at Avignon. There are a few artists from a slightly later time, Crivelli, Veneziano, Carpaccio, and Botticelli, for instance, but these are the exception. Many of the artists belonged to the Avignon school, which is not this well represented anywhere else in the world; some of their paintings must have been commissioned by the resident popes and cardinals themselves; and if by chance they once hung in these very rooms, then they are back now for a second time.

Most of them — not all by any means — constitute what is thought of today as medieval church art. There are diptychs and triptychs and altarpieces, and in the center of one gallery hangs a great wooden cross on which is painted a crucifixion. The artist was Lorenzo di Bicci, who died in 1427, and this crucifixion rivals in style and perhaps even in excellence the famous Cimabue in Florence that was damaged in the flood there some years ago. There are innumerable annunciations and presentations and crucifixions and Virgins with Child, meaning an incredible profusion of gold-leaf halos, miters, chasubles, all of which when illuminated by unobtrusive but effective modern lighting give, surprisingly, an impression of luxuriance and wealth. But there are also landscapes, battle scenes, scenes from mythology, and portraits. These artists were the giants of their time, and all of their works, whether religious or secular in nature, are in quite wonderful condition and they are wonderfully displayed. Furthermore, this old, old building is perfect for them. The walls are three feet thick, and where windows have been cut through there are stone benches in the bays. The floors are wood or blocks of stone worn smooth by years, or orange and reddish-orange tiles — the colors of the rooftops of Provence — that are as irregular in thickness and shape as in color. The ceilings in most cases are supported by narrow medieval beams ten inches deep and set no more than ten or twelve inches apart. There are narrow spiral staircases leading from floor to floor, and in some cases narrow stone doorways barely as wide as a man's shoulders leading from gallery to gallery.

There are at least sixteen major galleries, and in the last one on the second floor hang two paintings by Louis Brea from about 1510, and gazing at them, I marvel once more at how good he was. They measure about five feet high by two feet wide. One of them, *The Circumcision of Christ,* is especially striking, for in addition to the baby and the rabbi with his long gray beard, his unusual headpiece, and his knife, there are seven other figures looking on, seven faces, seven splendid portraits. It is painted mostly in varying shades of brown, a color not much used by other painters of the time — an intensely satisfying picture.

The entire collection seems to me extraordinary, as does its setting, and the story behind it is bizarre. Most of it — and much more besides — belonged originally to one Giovanni Pietro Campana, born in 1808 into a Roman family that had grown prosperous in the marble business. As a young man Campana went to work as a director of Rome's official pawnbroker agency, which was also a repository for Vatican funds and which he built into a bank. As a banker he was so successful that at one time he was lending money to the Ministry of Finance. He had all sorts of brilliant ideas, and the bank got richer and richer, and he was decorated by the pope and others.

One of his ideas was to lend money using works of art as collateral. A panel of experts would judge the value of the work and up to one-third of this value would be lent. But the year was 1849, the world did not yet prize art objects very highly, and many of those Campana took in were never redeemed. So that idea failed and the law was changed, making it a crime to lend money against art.

By then Campana himself had become passionate about collecting, and he began to push this passion to lengths probably never reached by anyone before or since. He collected paintings, statues, bronzes, bas reliefs, gems, ceramics. He opened his personal archaeological digs all over central Italy and even Greece. He kept multiple workshops cleaning and restoring art almost around the clock, and he stored his collections partly in warehouses, mostly in a number of second-rate palaces that he owned in various parts of Rome. He catalogued almost nothing, and the history and provenance of nearly every object that came into his hands was lost forever.

By the time he was 30 his collection had a worldwide reputation and he himself was a celebrity. By 1845 he had achieved the title of marchese. He and his wife, the Englishwoman Emily Rowles, lived in opulence; at the same time they were known and loved for their charitable works.

Suddenly in 1849 there was a surprise audit of the pawn brokerage, and the till was found to be empty. There was, it seems, no liquidity left at all. More than a million Roman ecus had disappeared, spent by Campana on works of art. He was arrested, tried, and sentenced to twenty years in the galleys. He was then 41 years old.

At first there was sympathy for Campana — he was perhaps a man rendered blind and sick by his addiction. He hadn't stolen the money exactly, he had merely spent it all. But the investigation showed that he had operated quite carefully. Under fictitious names he had pledged each of 218 paintings against separate loans and then each time, with the loan in his pocket, he had gone out and bought the painting in question. He had advanced himself not one-third of the value of the paintings he wanted to buy — and even this was now illegal — but the entire purchase price. Even worse, this "collateral" was not in the possession of the pawn brokerage, but was hanging, all 218 paintings, in Campana's house.

It happened that Emily Rowles Campana was a friend of Napoleon III, Emperor of France. A very good friend. He had lived in her house in London when she was a girl. He had been in exile at the time and, according to rumor, had wanted to marry her. Now she went to him for help. She asked the French Emperor to somehow get her husband out of an Italian jail.

This Napoleon, sometimes called Louis-Napoleon, was the nephew of Napoleon I. The first Napoleon is much better known to history of course, but this one lasted longer on top of France, twenty-two years against sixteen, eighteen years as Emperor against eleven.

He was born in 1808 (the same year as Campana), at which time his father, Napoleon's brother Louis, was serving as King of Holland. When Uncle Napoleon got deposed, so did all the brothers and others whom the great man had established on thrones here and there as kings; the boy Louis-Napoleon was brought up therefore in Switzerland, Germany, and England, a dreamy young man who from the age of 24 conceived the idea that he was the legitimate heir of the late Emperor, and would be Emperor in his turn. No one took him seriously. At 28 he turned up in Strasbourg and attempted to convince the garrison to march on Paris with himself at its head. He was arrested but was considered such a joke that the authorities chose not to deal with him severely. Instead he was put on a ship to America.

So he wrote a book called *Napoleonic Ideas* which presented his late uncle as a champion of human rights and himself as heir apparent. In 1840 Uncle's body, by then nineteen years dead, was brought back to Paris from St. Helena for one of the most grandiose funerals in history; and Louis-Napoleon, 32 years old and living in London, made his way across the channel to Boulogne, where he tried to instigate another uprising. Again he was arrested and jailed, but this time he was sentenced to life imprisonment. After six years in jail he escaped, got to London, and for the next two years lived in Emily Rowles's father's house on Camden Place.

France since his uncle's downfall had been run by a series of not very notable kings, and in 1848 the most recent of them fell to a more or less bloodless revolution. Louis-Napoleon hurried back into France and managed to get himself elected to the new constituent assembly, where his speeches were so bad and he cut such a poor figure that the other deputies considered him a lightweight and a fool. But some strong-eyed men began to surround him, seeing the chance for themselves, and before the year was out he ran for the presidency and on the strength of his name alone was overwhelmingly elected. During the next four years he managed to gag the press, suspend the right to public meeting, and suppress the dissident voices in the National Assembly, and in 1852, when he was 44, he proclaimed himself Emperor, brutally put down the Paris mob that opposed him, and then set up a nationwide referendum so the voters could grant their approval. They did so, again overwhelmingly.

So he was well established as Emperor when Emily Rowles Campana went to him in an attempt to save her husband.

Louis-Napoleon's reign was not particularly repressive. Gradually civil liberties came back. He ruled until the Franco-Prussian war of 1870, which he more or less instigated. The Prussians crushed the French armies in three months. They surrounded the last of them at Sedan. To the very end Louis-Napoleon remained a dreamer — he was with his army inside the town and there were no helicopters available to get him out as France surrendered. The Germans took prisoner 100,000 soldiers and the Emperor of the French. He went back into exile, back to the Rowles house on Camden Place, where he died three years later.

His name is all around you in France today. He seems to have given whole towns what they needed, or thought they needed. He is credited with having made Vichy the world's preeminent spa, he gave the funds to restore the Château Henri IV at Pau and the cannons to make the great bronze statue of the Virgin at Le Puy. Nice and Savoy became French again. Paris at his orders was practically rebuilt.

And he is responsible also, more than 100 years after his death, for the new museum here at Avignon.

The Roman authorities were trying to sell the Campana collection to a foreign government for enough money to refloat the pawn brokerage and the bank. They hardly cared about Campana personally. They needed 7 million francs. They were desperate. By allowing the authorities to believe that he might purchase the Campana collection, Louis-Napoleon was able to get Campana's sentence commuted to banishment for life. But in return he was obliged to send secret emissaries down to Rome to appraise the collection and perhaps bid for it. To have sent the superintendent of the Beaux-Arts and the two chief curators of the Louvre, which the Emperor might ordinarily have done, would have caused too much comment. He sent instead a painter of modest talent who was a friend, and a professor unknown in the art world. These men succeeded beyond anyone's expectations. They got the entire Campana collection, 860 monstrous cases containing 11,835 objects of art, for a bit over 4 million francs.

Back at the Louvre the superintendent and the two curators were livid when they found out what had been done behind their backs, and they spent much of the rest of their lives plotting to denigrate and destroy the collection.

Louis-Napoleon seems to have had some idea of establishing a separate museum for it that might even have been named after himself — after all, London's Victoria and Albert Museum had opened in 1857, only four years ago. But he reckoned without the wrath of scholars scorned. The superintendent and the two curators — the loudest seems to have been Curator of Paintings Frédéric Reiset — spoke with one voice in the name of the Louvre. The Louvre wanted no such museum in Paris. The Louvre didn't want the Campana collection — as a collection — anywhere. It wasn't good enough. Who was the Emperor to pretend that he knew more about art than the Louvre? A few of Campana's best pieces should be incorporated into the national collection. The rest, since the Louvre didn't need or want them, should be dispersed to provincial museums throughout the country.

The Emperor was not intellectually secure enough to struggle very long against this kind of thing; he appointed a committee to argue for the collection, and the Louvre finally agreed to accept ninety-seven pictures.

Which caused a scandal in art circles. Ninety-seven was not nearly enough, declared Delacroix and Ingres, who were probably the two most famous French artists of the day. Many others agreed, and in the end the Louvre was forced to keep 303 pictures. For a time these were displayed apart in the so-called Museum Napoleon III. When in 1870 the Emperor fell, the Louvre curator, still Reiset, purged the collection. At first he threw out 141 Campana paintings; a bit later he dumped 40 more. He operated apparently with extreme malice, for he consulted no one and he distributed the paintings out into the countryside to villages that were sometimes so small, as one commentator noted, that no one knew where they were except the local mailmen. Paintings went to Nérac (population 4,300), Mirande (2,700), Varzy (1,900), and the like. Reiset even broke up altarpieces, dealing out triptychs like cards: Laval, Caen, and Melun got one-third of a triptych each. Another was broken up among the Louvre, Ajaccio, and Toulouse. He broke up four-piece ensembles, sending two to Nantes and two to Rennes; two to Le Havre and two to Dijon. In the end the Campana paintings had been spilled all over France, and hardly anyone even knew where they were.

Then for three-quarters of a century they were forgotten.

At the end of the Second World War there was created in Paris a new agency called the Direction of the Museums of France; its inspector general was a man named Jean Vergnet-Ruiz, who, as a university art professor, had given a course called "The History of the Great Collections." He had fallen in love with the Campana collection without, of course, ever having seen it. Now he was in a position where he could possibly put it back together again. It was too huge to put all of it in any one place. He would have to break it down into periods, then find towns that would like to have each of the parts, provided they had the buildings to put them in, after which he would have to track down and demand the return of the paintings themselves. Someone suggested to him that Avignon would be perfect for the medieval art contemporary with the time of the popes, and the Petit Palais in which one of the popes had actually lived would be an equally perfect building.

By then the former bishops' palace had been a school for 130 years. It did not become vacant until 1952, which is when it was acquired as a future museum. It was not in good shape, and funds had to be sequestered to restore it and after that to put in the sophisticated lighting, temperature controls, and security devices that a modern museum requires. Meanwhile the paintings themselves had to be located and in many cases restored. It took more than thirty years, by which time Vergnet-Ruiz was dead, as were most of the men who had helped him. They were never to see the glorious collection as it is displayed today.

At this point it is necessary to speak of still another palace relating to the Avignon popes.

It predated the massive Palace of the Popes and it stood not in Avignon itself but across the river on top of a barren plateau, where it served as the popes' summer home. A town came into existence around it and was named for it: Châteauneuf du Pape. The plateau was windier and cooler than down on the plain, and there were fewer petitioners banging at the doors. A pope could get away there, relax, think, make some practical decisions. One or two of these men may even have used Châteauneuf as a place to pray. However, trying to commune with God was long, and for the most part popes had too much else on their minds.

It was at Châteauneuf that the new pope, Benedict XII, faced the next great crisis of the crisis-ridden medieval papacy. John XXII had just died. Benedict had hardly sat down upon the throne. That the crisis bedeviling him was theological in nature made it, in those days, no less real.

Not long before he died, having concentrated until then almost exclusively on hoarding money, the 90-year-old Pope John had lapsed into theology. After much thought and prayer (so he said) he had concluded that the saintly dead did not ascend immediately into heaven, and he announced this. It was a theological bombshell, and he dropped it on the world. They did not see God immediately after death. No one did. They had to wait for the end of the world first. Even the saints would have to wait for the end of the world. John was pope and this he had decreed, and you better believe it.

Christendom reacted with consternation.

With this one insight, this one decision, John had destroyed two of his own and his successors' most lucrative sources of income. For centuries the faithful had been praying to saints to intercede for them before God, each prayer to be accompanied by an offering; and they had been buying indulgences to gain quick admission to heaven and avoid spending time in purgatory. But why pray to saints who were nowhere near God, who were sitting around someplace waiting for the end of the world? And why buy indulgences if quick admittance to heaven was impossible?

Europe was outraged. In Germany men wanted the old man prosecuted as a heretic. Avignon was no less in shock. The bishops and cardinals remonstrated with John, but it did no good. Under intense pressure he held firm. He seemed determined to kill the golden goose.

Then he died. The new Pope Benedict, together with his cardinals, retired to Châteauneuf for four months to try to think out what to do — how to restructure their ruined business. Finally the solution came to them, and Benedict issued a papal bull. It said that Pope John, shortly before he died, had in fact come to his senses and had written out a bull of his own that retracted his bombshell, sucked it back up into the bomb bay, so to speak. Those who died in a state of grace did indeed go straight to heaven at once, did see God at once absolutely, and could be prayed to. Indulgences worked and were good value for the money.

Unfortunately, Benedict's bull continued, God had called Pope John to his reward before he could put his seal on his bull. However, John's bull was not lost. Benedict had found it beside the dead man's bed and was publishing it now as part of his own bull. Both the late Pope John and the newly elected Pope Benedict hereby reaffirmed all the original doctrine concerning the matter. Anyone who believed differently was a heretic and would be punished as such. There. The crisis was over. Whew!

One day we drove over to Châteauneuf du Pape for a look at whatever might be left of this "summer home" of the popes.

Not much, it turned out: a single wall. These days Châteauneuf du Pape is far more famous for its vineyards than for its connection with the medieval papacy.

The papal wall dominates the plateau and could be seen from far off as we approached. It is quite a wall, six or seven stories high in places, for the Avignon popes did not think small, and I parked and stood looking at it for a while.

But my attention was divided between the towering unsupported wall and the vineyards that almost touched it in places. A wall this old and reaching so high up is a marvelous thing, I suppose, but such vineyards as surround it seemed more marvelous yet, and even as I walked out onto the surface of the nearest one, I had trouble believing it. I was amazed at the way it looked, at the way it felt under my shoes.

All the wine books report that the Châteauneuf vineyards are stony, an adjective that failed to impress me when I read it, for the soil of every wine-growing region I have seen is stony. But as applied to these vineyards here stony is simply not a big enough word. I stood on and peered across a solid blanket of big, smooth stones with row after row of vine roots sticking out of them. There was no dirt visible at all, just rounded stones. Some were the size of coconuts. Some were like pie plates. Some were the size and shape of American footballs and must have weighed ten pounds apiece. And there was no dirt to be seen. When I tried to walk further out into the vines, I could barely maintain my balance as the stones shifted and rolled underfoot. It was inconceivable to me that vines or anything else could grow in such a place, but acres and acres of them stretched away before me. And no dirt anywhere.

It was the popes themselves who first ordered vines planted here, close to the walls of their palace — how and why, now that I had seen the terrain, was beyond me. How did they ever imagine it could be done? How was it done? And now that wine was grown here commercially, how did men plow? How did they plant?

Avignon, with the huge bulk of the Palace of the Popes standing out above the rooftops, was in plain view eleven miles away, though the outlines today were somewhat softened by smog. When the popes were in residence at Châteauneuf the couriers used to gallop back and forth with the ordinary dispatches; more urgent decisions were transmitted by flashing mirrors across the void.

I returned to the towering wall of the former palace. After

the popes returned to Rome there was no one to use this huge building. Not many people lived over here. Gradually it fell into ruins. For centuries builders used it as a quarry. It was ravaged during the religious wars beginning in 1552. The Germans blew up most of the rest of it in August 1944 as the American armies, following their invasion of southern France, came up the Rhône. As buildings go it did not have an easy life.

The wind was blowing hard against my face, and I mused for a moment about the vines all around me, and about the wine. Wind in the Rhône valley is of course a constant. Clearly it is the wind and the stones together that give the wines of Châteauneuf their character and their alcoholic power. Often the summer sun is blisteringly hot here, but the stones hold the moisture in the ground — there must be dirt under there somewhere. The stones store up heat all day and at night throw it back up at the grapes so that they ripen even in the dark. The wind thickens the skins, and when rain does come it dries them off quickly.

Châteauneuf today, apart from the papal wall, is an undistinguished village of 3,000 with about 3,000 hectares under vines all around it, more than any other town in France except St. Emilion. There are three plateaus — two others in addition to the one I am standing on — with slopes and valleys between. The plateaus are vast flat terraces covered with stones to a depth of up to two feet. According to present geological theory, these stones were broken off the flanks of the Alps during the last ice age and were pushed down here by glaciers. When the Rhône River came into existence, it was many times larger than it is now and kept rolling them along. The big ones settled on these high plateaus about 400 feet above sea level.

Each of the plateaus is dominated by a single property, one by the Domaine de Mont Redon, another by the Domaine du Vieux Télégraphe, and the third by the Château des Fines Roches. As the land slopes down from them, dirt begins to be visible among the stones, and the soil down on the flat looks almost normal for wine terrain.

That afternoon Daniel Brunier of Vieux Télégraphe drove me out onto his vineyard in a small car. The car pitched and rolled on the stones like a small boat in a rough sea. Plowing, Brunier said, was done not by the growers themselves but by specialized firms. When a plot was to be replanted, this meant deep plowing to bring dirt up to the surface. The shoes of the plows dug two feet into the ground, and the tractors that pulled them often had caterpillar treads. Even so they moved along in lurches and jerks. Sliding from side to side on the stones, plows wore out fast. There was a special tool for planting too. A new vine shoot looks something like a thick pencil. In other parts of the wine world men sometimes ram a finger into the earth, put the new root stock into the hole, and then pack the dirt around it. But here a kind of two-handed crowbar was used to make the hole, then sand was taken off a truck that followed the planters, and packed around the new root. Nonetheless, Brunier said, the survival rate was about 95 percent, the same as elsewhere.

Châteauneuf du Pape has never had the reputation of Burgundy or Bordeaux, nor commanded their prices, and as I wandered from one vineyard to the next buying bottles to take home, I kept asking why this should be so, in view of the wonderful wines it is capable of producing.

A number of reasons were given.

To begin with, there were only two or three merchant shippers in the town. Most of the selling has always been done by shippers in Burgundy, who naturally gave precedence to their own wines. Often the Châteauneuf wines never reached the market at all but were dumped into lesser Burgundies to raise their alcohol content and color. This is illegal, but it has been done.

Nor does Châteauneuf's reputation even such as it is go back very far. Its principal grape, the grenache, came here from Spain only about 1865. Then came the phylloxera epidemic, which wiped out almost every vineyard in France. Richer areas kept replanting, and eventually a cure was found. Most of Châteauneuf did not replant, for the cure was more than twenty years coming and they could not afford it. Château Beaucastel, for instance, possibly the best of the Châteauneuf wines, was not replanted until 1909. Instead men lifted the stones out of the fields by hand — not the plateaus, of course, only those fields less dense with stones — and tried to plant wheat, peppers, and other unsuitable and therefore miserable crops. Embankments of stones, some of them nine feet high, surrounded many of the fields until 1945, when bulldozers belonging to the victorious American army were commandeered to push them back where they belonged.

Back in Avignon, I stand outside the Palace of the Popes, peering up at all those towers and walls, feeling their weight, their thickness. It is hard to overdescribe the power that this place once represented. It was the most powerful place in the world — not power over men's warlike nature or their catapults or their embryonic cannons, but over their fear: their fear of eternal damnation. However many kings may have walked the earth on any given day, there was only one pope — at least at this point in our story — and he lived in Avignon high up in this tower here, or that one over there, and he was the one who controlled the doorway to hell.

He also controlled the international bureaucracy. In that century there was no other international authority. In a sense the popes controlled international jurisprudence, international banking, and to a considerable extent international trade. The pope's clerks and scribes, his permissions and rubber stamps were vital to the ordinary functioning of most of western Europe.

This two-edged spiritual and commercial sword the Avignon popes wielded bluntly. For instance, Gregory XI, the last pope to reign at Avignon if you forget the two antipopes, once excommunicated Florence. It was a complicated quarrel. When the papal legate led an army against Florence, Florentine troops invaded the papal states. Pow! Excommunication. The whole city. Pope Gregory XI did it with a stroke of the quill from this palace here at Avignon. It meant that the people of Florence might die without receiving absolution, that their babies might die unbaptized. That was the spiritual side, and it had people tearing out their hair. The commercial side was as bad or worse. Florentine merchants overnight were the same as outlaws, and other Christians were forbidden to trade with them. Vital necessities such as firewood, clothing, and even food did not come into the city; money owed Florentine merchants need not be repaid, and their property could be confiscated wherever found.

*   *   *

Visitors to the palace today see the "old" part of it first, the half built by the third of the Avignon popes, Benedict XII (1334–42), the one who inherited all that money from John XXII. It was enough money to construct the biggest building in the world, which was perhaps what Benedict set out to do. The guide leads the group into the consistory, which, some of the tourists seem to think, must be the vastest single room in the world. Wait until they see the great audience chamber a bit further on, which is almost twice its size.

The consistory is empty. Not a stick of furniture. The guide chattering statistics tells us the ceiling is thirty-six feet high. Our heads are all hanging back, and we are staring straight up, most of us trying to visualize human beings living in rooms as cavernous as this one. Hanging on the wall are portraits of the nine men who reigned here at Avignon, only the last seven of them in this building, the final two of whom were declared afterwards to be antipopes — making them to me at least the most interesting of the lot. The portraits are well enough painted, but if they bear any resemblance to the actual men it is an accident; they were made in 1839 by an artist named Henri Serrur working off engravings dated 1684.

Pope Benedict, builder of this half of the palace, was another compromise candidate, for the cardinals, most of whom were French, wanted someone who would not go back to Rome. Supposedly he was tall and red-faced. He was a nephew of his predecessor, and of course it was Uncle John XXII who had promoted him to cardinal in the first place. He came from the Pyrenees, where he had made a name for himself as an inquisitor.

Here in Avignon he ordered the Angels' Tower built first. It is a great square thing, 35 feet to the side, almost windowless, 150 feet high. It took two years to construct. As soon as its lead roof was hammered down on top, Benedict took up residence in an apartment in its upper reaches, moved the dead Pope John's treasure in with him, and there he stayed amidst the noise and the rising dust while the rest of the palace went up around him.

The guide leads our group upstairs towards his apartment. The staircase is stone, and as it spirals steeply upward it is barely as wide as a man's shoulders, meaning that attackers could not hope to get at Benedict in any numbers, if at all. We climb in single file, and I keep banging my elbows on the walls — the staircase is that narrow. Benedict was not a young man and he too had to go up and down these stairs from time to time, and I wonder how he liked it.

He had been a Cistercian, and he wore a white monk's habit even as pope. He was at least in theory a reformer. In one of his writings he described the clergy as having flung themselves into fields of license, "pursuing their untamable passions . . . they wallow in the slough of lust." He forbade priests to carry weapons and ordered them to shave off their beards. He tried to stamp out nepotism as a basis for appointing prelates. And he ordered the scores of bishops and monks who now nearly swamped the city to go back to their sees, back to their monasteries. In seven years he built more than half of this palace as it now stands. Then he died. The building he left behind him had walls from six to thirteen feet thick and on average they were sixty-five feet high. They rose up straight and flat and awesome into the sky.

The next pope, Clement VI, whose real name was Pierre Roger, didn't like the gigantic new construction that Benedict had left him. Too austere. Not big enough. God's Vicar on Earth deserved better. Benedict had been a baker's son. Clement came from a rich and noble family. He was used to luxury. He thought a pope should live like a king. He called in the builders again.

The rooms on his side of the palace are even vaster, and in their day were certainly more gorgeous, than those on Benedict's side. As soon as Clement's masons and carpenters had moved out, his decorators moved in, the sculptors, the tapestry weavers, the fresco painters. Matteo Giovanetti de Viterbo was one of the principal artists. Some say Giotto worked here too, some say only his pupils; whoever the artists were, they covered almost every wall with frescoes.

The ceilings were especially handsome. They were supported in some cases by carved and decorated beams, in others by groined stone vaulting. The beams and groins are still here of course, but of the frescoes not much is left. The centuries wore them out, sometimes slowly, often enough brutally. From the Revolution until 1906 the palace was used as a barracks. For over 100 years troops and sometimes horses moved in and out of these rooms. The soldiers built their fires either in the fireplaces or else on whichever floors or against whichever walls they pleased. At some point they learned how to chisel entire faces out of such frescoes as were not already ruined, and to sell them to art dealers as antiques. Today's tourists are left to gape at faded frescoes with chunks of wall hacked out of them.

In his sumptuous new palace Clement VI held court. All of the old abuses were back. He appointed as cardinals one brother, five cousins, and two nephews, one of them a boy of 18. Women were seen in his private apartments and so, it was said, were young boys. The best-preserved frescoes in the palace are in Clement's study and in his bedroom. The study walls are decorated with scenes of stag hunting, falconing, fishing. The bedroom measures thirty feet by thirty and its wonderfully ornate ceiling is twenty-five feet high; not exactly a cozy room. Its walls are painted with forest scenes all leafy and serene, the trees full of squirrels and exotic birds. These rooms are where Clement lived, and there is not a religious motif anywhere.

Downstairs he gave galas and banquets for hundreds of people at a time. Kings and queens came, and ambassadors without number, and the nobility and the famous of many lands. The court blazed with talent. Petrarch and Boccaccio were there, along with astronomers, geographers, mathematicians, sculptors, musicians, painters.

The streets were as foul and stinking as always, and crowded with people trying to get into the palace: with bankers and money changers; with monks of every conceivable sect, some of which were not only bizarre but possibly heretical; with prostitutes and sideshow freaks, including an armless woman who could sew with her toes. "Woe to your people, Jesus Christ," Petrarch wrote of Avignon. "This same Christ they buy, they sell, they traffic in, they tie a bandage over his eyes. . . . I will not speak of adultery, seduction, rape, incest; these are only the prelude to their orgies."

Petrarch, Pope Clement must have thought, was becoming a real pain in the ass.

In 1348 Joanna, Queen of Naples, Countess of Provence, and

owner of Avignon, came here. The pope wanted to buy the city from her. Joanna was five months gone with child, and she had probably murdered her husband two years previously. She wanted absolution, and permission for marriage. Her trial took place in the great hall of the palace. The pope kissed her on the lips, acquitted her of all guilt, then bought Avignon from her for 80,000 florins. And built walls around it.

Pope Clement was not all bad. The plague when it struck was widely blamed on the Jews, who were accused of having poisoned the wells. In some places numbers of them were massacred, but not in Avignon, where Clement put them under his personal protection, at the same time promulgating two bulls exonerating them of all blame. In addition he set up hospitals and bought a field in which to bury the dead. He distributed food and tongue-lashed members of the clergy who attempted to flee the city, admonishing them that their job was to care for the sick and the dying. He himself kept bonfires burning day and night around the palace, as it was believed this would keep the plague out.

He reigned eleven years, then died — of venereal disease, some said. His funeral was splendid. Fifty priests celebrated masses for nine days, and he was carried from Avignon up to La Chaise Dieu in the Auvergne near where he was born and with great pomp laid to rest in a tomb in the monastery there.

The Huguenots broke into this tomb in 1562 and, we are told, used his skull for a football.

In 1352 Innocent VI became pope. He found the treasury to be empty, and most of his nine-year-nine-month reign was spent trying to tax foreign churches and otherwise begging money which, for the most part, no one would give him. It was a time of great disasters. In Italy the papal states were at war one with the other and not sending taxes. Bands of brigands, meanwhile, pillaged Provence. In 1359 the Rhône overflowed and laid waste the countryside. Between March and July 1361 the plague struck again and 17,000 people died in Avignon, including 100 bishops and 9 cardinals.

Innocent died the next year. The winter that followed was so frigid that the Rhône froze over, and he was not buried until spring, when the King came down for the event.

Pope Urban V, who came next, was from Marseilles. He was the first of the Avignon popes to return to Rome — temporarily. He was a Benedictine, a stern man from a stern order. He wore his monk's rough habit even to bed — he slept not only in his clothes, but on bare boards. He had a wooden room built for himself inside one of these echoing palace chambers, and this cell was his house. He confessed himself every day. He too attempted reforms. He was against the keeping of exotic hunting birds, prize horses, and too many servants. He was against luxury, pomp, simony, drunkenness, debauchery, and hair-splitting canon lawyers. He was against concubinage, especially by the clergy.

When he had been pope not quite five years, leaving behind the papal zoo, the papal wine cellar, and the papal treasure walled up in a room in the palace, Urban left for Rome. His twenty-three galleys rowed out of Marseilles on May 19, 1367, and after several stops landed him in Italy June 3; his silk tent was set up in a field and he said mass. The papal party went on by road towards Rome but at Viterbo was besieged by a mob. The pope and his cardinals took refuge in a castle the papacy owned there while the mob rioted. The riot lasted three days and was put down only when seven men were hanged.

After an absence of sixty-three years, an incumbent pope (together with 2,000 of his troops) entered Rome. He stayed three years, during which the French cardinals around him ached for France. So did he. Italy was an impossible place. The people rebelled against every restraint. In 1370 the Perugians formed an alliance with the Romans, and they drove Urban back to Viterbo to the same castle where he had been besieged before. He decided he'd better return to Avignon, even though St. Brigit of Sweden, a renowned mystic of the place and time, told him he would die if he did. He thought himself more likely to die if he didn't. He and his party piled into thirty-four borrowed galleys and eleven days later rowed into Marseilles. He was as glad to see Avignon again as it was to see him; in his absence business had been slow. But St. Brigit had perhaps been working from good information, for Urban died three months later — a death that would weigh heavily on the mind of his successor, Gregory XI.

Gregory was 41 and a nephew of Clement VI. He was the

nephew Clement had made into a cardinal at 18. He still wasn't a priest and now had to be hurriedly ordained. He was said to be short, grave, timid. Also he burned with the true faith. He was a dedicated believer in torturing any heretics who fell into his hands: Moslems, Jews, Cathars, whatever; not to mention individuals possessed by demons. He tried and failed to mount a crusade against the Turks.

He was also the man who excommunicated Florence, ruining many merchants, causing untold anguish, and this had results no one could have foretold.

When Florence sent ambassadors to beg his forgiveness and to implore the lifting of the terrible ban, he refused to receive them. So the desperate city sent a holy woman from the neighboring town, the woman known to history as St. Catherine of Siena, who, upon reaching Avignon, began to have trances and ecstasies in plain view of everyone. Most of the cardinals considered the famous nun a complete fraud, but the people were much taken by her. So was the pope. She began to speak to him not only on behalf of Florence but also on behalf of Rome. He was needed there to restore peace in Italy, and to save the church. God had revealed all this to her personally during her ecstasies. The pope must return to Rome.

Mindful of what had happened to his predecessor who had ignored the advice of one of these saintly women, the timid Gregory began to pack the papal bags. Hearing this, the King of France was furious. So were the cardinals and even the pope's parents. On Sept. 13, 1376, together with fifteen cardinals (six other cardinals, refusing to follow him, remained behind), Pope Gregory departed for Rome, where he soon died.

Avignon's day was by no means over.

It was by then March 1378. With Gregory stiff on his bier the Lords Banneret, who governed Rome, demanded that a Roman pope be elected, and mobs filled the streets. There were four Italian cardinals, twelve French, but the French votes were split. When the conclave could not decide, the mob set fire to the apostolic palace. The terrified cardinals conceived the idea of dressing an aged Italian cardinal in papal robes and showing him at the window. This may or may not have been a valid election. Once it was done the most fearful of the cardinals bolted out the back door. The next day those that remained, being still afraid and, they claimed later, acting under extreme duress, elected a second pope, the cardinal from Bari, who took the name Urban VI.

Urban, who would listen to no one, who could not be talked to, turned out to be mad, or so the cardinals came to believe, and they fled to Fondi, which is halfway to Naples, where they went into conclave again, declared Urban null and void, and elected Robert de Génève, who was either their second or third selection that year. Calling himself Clement VII, the new pope took the papacy straight back to Avignon. There he established a court nearly as brilliant as Clement VI had done thirty years before.

That was the start of the great schism which was to last thirty-nine years, some say forty-four. Clement VII is regarded now as the first of the antipopes. This was not the case at the time, and even today his claim seems legitimate enough. He was recognized by the French King, by the French clergy, and, after careful investigation of the circumstances of the two elections, by the theologians of the University of Paris. Avignon, meanwhile, was crowded again and bustled, as prosperous as at any time in the past. It was again the center of the world.

For ten years the other pope wandered around Italy, welcomed nowhere, not really the Roman pope, for he did not live in Rome. He could find no place that suited him, and he tried to settle down in one town after another: Genoa, Lucca, Pisa. He returned to Rome only to die. Immediately the Italian cardinals elected another Italian pope, and the papal schism was maintained.

Year by year the world, it seemed, became more complicated. There was war in Italy; the kingdom of Naples was on fire. Raymond de Turenne, Lord of Les Baux, terrorized Provence, and for a time the Avignon pope fled his palace to hide in the fortified castle at Beaucaire on the other side of the river. Finally in 1394 he too died. He had lasted sixteen years, and the schism with him. He never thought of himself as antipope, and never imagined that history would either.

A new antipope was elected twelve days later, though if his predecessor was legitimate or if the cardinals who elected him were legitimate, then he was too. This one's name was Pedro de Luna and he was, unfortunately, a Spaniard. There were tremendous pressures on him to refuse the papal crown or to agree to resign, so as to end the schism, for the Western world needed a functioning papacy. It was absolutely essential. But de Luna refused.

A Frenchman would have found much more support in France. The French King, Charles VI, turned against de Luna. So did the doctors of the University of Paris, because when they sent emissaries to Avignon, he refused to see them.

De Luna, who took the name Benedict XIII, was known as tough, opinionated, obstinate. He was from Aragon and had the armies of Aragon behind him. He was elected for this very reason — he could back his claim with force — and because the French cardinals knew he would hold out, which he did.

He had the Duke d'Orléans, who was the French King's brother, on his side, and the King of Aragon, and he closed himself up in the Palace of the Popes together with his brother Rodrigo, who had brought troops and catapults from Aragon, and from the top of the walls these catapults began to bombard Avignon with boulders.

The French King sent troops to lay siege to the palace. They were commanded by Marshal Boucicaut, who later was captured by the English at the battle of Agincourt and who died in England in captivity. But Boucicaut could find no way to breach the massive, virtually impregnable palace walls, and the pope's booming catapults were too high up to stop.

Boucicaut sent sappers to tunnel under the walls. The pope's men caught them and they died. He piled a bonfire against Trouillas Tower and kept it blazing for three days and nights. It didn't bring down the 170-foot-high tower. It didn't do anything. The Cardinal of Ostia came with cannons; he built towers and put his cannons on them, but cannons were new and few men could work them. In any case the walls were simply too thick.

Realizing that the troops inside the palace had little food, Boucicaut decided to starve the pope out. But de Luna had supporters in the town who did not want to lose the papacy to Rome, and he sent out secret agents to try to organize a popular uprising in his favor. This conspiracy was discovered and its leader tried and decapitated. His body was then cut into sections and displayed in different parts of the city, his right arm here, his left arm there, his legs, his head, his entrails still elsewhere. Nice.

The pope's partisans went to Paris to negotiate. The results: the Spanish troops would leave the palace, except for a 100-man bodyguard, and food would go in. In exchange Pope de Luna agreed to renounce his tiara if the Roman pope would do the same. While all waited for a reply from Italy, de Luna was able secretly to bring back the Spanish soldiers, this time with food to hold out, if necessary, for years. Simultaneously renouncing the signed protocol, de Luna proclaimed himself still pope and began once more to bombard the rooftops below his walls. Houses fell, churches fell, even the cathedral steeple fell. He seemed resolved to stay pope even if it meant obliterating the city. From time to time he sent his Spanish soldiers out of the palace in search of groceries, which they stole, usually despoiling the countryside as well.

There came more attacking armies. Some were led by French noblemen or even cardinals. Some included irate citizens of Avignon. On March 13, 1403, Pope de Luna escaped to Spain, leaving behind his brother and the Spanish troops to hold the palace until he could come back. He never did, but his brother and the troops stayed on until 1410, seven more years, and the palace was in deplorable condition when they left it.

In all, Avignon had felt the papal presence for 101 years.

In conclave at Pisa the cardinals deposed both popes and elected another; so now instead of two popes at large in the world, there were three, all launching pronouncements and interdictions against each other. At Constance nine years later the cardinals tried again, and this time it took: Martin V was recognized as pope in most of Christendom, though not in Aragon, where de Luna/Benedict XIII hung on to the age of 95. He finally died, and his claim with him, in 1423.

To govern Avignon, which it still owned, the papacy began to send cardinals and archbishops one after the other for four centuries. Which was odd, because when it became clear that this time the popes were not coming back, the merchants and petitioners, the jugglers and whores, the scrambling monks and priests all left. The population dropped to less than 6,000 again. Avignon became an empty provincial town full of buildings that were too big for it, ruled by prelates with too much rank. Not until the revolutionaries marched in and "annexed" it in 1791 did Avignon leave papal control and at last become part of France.

Traves
AN SS MAN IS AMONG US

The noise woke the villagers. It sounded like gunfire. Coming from the woods where only one house stood. Firecrackers, they nervously told themselves. A crime like this, though expected, could not be happening — not in Traves, population 350. Whereas firecrackers made sense. Because it was past midnight, not July 13 anymore but July 14, Bastille Day. Firecrackers must be exploding all over France.

But it wasn't firecrackers. Above the woods the sky was bright because, exactly as promised, the house was on fire. The villagers came up close and watched it blaze. Some wore raincoats over their pajamas. The flames turned their faces red.

Morning came. Gendarmes and firemen, combing the smoking rubble, found guns, spent cartridges, and a charred corpse. A little later hordes of journalists arrived. The headlines when they appeared were lurid:

SS MAN EXECUTED
Joachim Peiper Assassinated

The son of a Prussian army officer, Peiper was born in Berlin Jan. 30, 1915, and at 18 joined the Hitler Youth. The year was 1933 — he must have been one of the charter members. From there he went into the SS and at 21 was commissioned a lieutenant.

The SS was not then the sinister force it was to become. The letters SS stood for Schutz Staffel, which means roughly Protective Brigade. Originally its members fulfilled the same function as the U.S. Secret Service — they protected Hitler and other important political figures. By 1938 Peiper was aide-de-camp to Gestapo chief Heinrich Himmler. Then war came, and the SS broke into two parts. One branch provided the black-uniformed concentration camp guards. The second, known as the Waffen (military) SS, Peiper's branch, was an elite corps of combat troops. He saw action in France and, after France fell, on the Eastern front. He became one of the greatest war heroes in Germany and from the age of about 25, which was when his combat exploits first became known to the popular press, was a celebrity. Germans called him *schneidiger* — daredevil. In Russia once he pierced the enemy lines in a captured Russian tank, drove up to a divisional headquarters, and kidnapped a number of Russian generals.

He grew into a bold, audacious commander, so wily in battle that he was credited with being able to "think Indian thoughts." He won Germany's highest military decoration, the Knights Cross with laurel leaves and swords, and was frequently wounded. One wound, though it healed, would leave a furrow the length of his right leg from heel to buttocks.

With Italy out of the war and the Americans coming up the boot, he was sent into the mountains above Venice, where he pacified the villages one by one by bombarding them. When two of his men, driving through Boves (population 4,700), crashed into a house and were taken prisoner by partisans, he ordered the village elders brought to him. If his men were not returned at once, he told them, he would destroy the village.

Forty minutes later the men were freed, whereupon Peiper, according to some reports, ordered the village burned down anyway. This was done, house by house, and thirty-four civilians died.

That was in September 1943. By D-Day the next year he was in Normandy, a 29-year-old colonel at the head of "Battle Group Peiper," the first Panzer Regiment of the Sixth SS Panzer Division, trying to throw the invading armies back into the sea. He fought the Americans hard for six months as the German army was pushed backwards into Belgium. Just before Christmas 1944 came the Battle of the Bulge, the last German counterattack. Battle Group Peiper spearheaded it, quickly taking prisoner more than 500 American troops and 90 Belgian civilians. In the Ardennes Forest near Malmédy men of Battle Group Peiper machine-gunned them all. Many had their hands tied behind their backs. When Peiper was prosecuted later, this number was reduced to the 71 American soldiers whose identities and deaths could be confirmed.

He was arrested in Austria in 1945 and charged with the Malmédy massacre. Together with seventy-three other officers and men, including three Waffen SS generals, he went on trial at Dachau on May 14, 1946, before a nine-man U.S. military court. Most of the prosecution's evidence was directed personally against Peiper, who testified in his own defense that he was under orders from his superiors and from the Führer to conduct the battle "stubbornly, with no regard for Allied prisoners of war, who will have to be shot if the situation compels it."

Given the unwieldy number of defendants — so many that they had to wear numbers around their necks — the trial was quick, less than two months. On July 11 a 19-year-old private was acquitted. All seventy-three other defendants were convicted, and less than a week after that the sentences came down. The three generals got life, twenty years, and ten years respectively. There were prison terms for twenty-seven other men. Peiper and forty-two of his subordinates were ordered hanged.

As his sentence was read, a flashbulb exploded in Peiper's face, and he laughed harshly. He asked the court to be shot as a soldier, and this was granted.

But legal maneuvers kept him alive until 1951, when another American military court, citing technical errors, commuted his sentence to life. As to the guilt of the accused, no doubt existed, the court noted.

Peiper's life sentence ended just before Christmas 1956 when, on the unanimous recommendation of a mixed clemency board composed of three West Germans, an American, a Briton, and a Frenchman, he was paroled. He was the last of the Malmédy defendants to go free. He had been in jail altogether eleven and a half years.

Most war criminals, once walking the streets of Germany again, quickly changed their names — why ask for trouble? But Peiper did not, and he went to work for Porsche in Stuttgart. He was still a decisive man, still an army officer to the core, and soon he was chief of promotion — whereupon the union council protested, and Porsche had to dismiss him.

He got a job at Volkswagen, where he trained sales personnel, and he lasted there for a time. But by the early sixties there had been an "economic miracle" in Germany. Germans wanted only the best jobs, meaning that most of Volkswagen's assembly-line workers were impoverished Italian immigrants — and now word passed through the factory that Peiper had been guilty of atrocities in Italy. Again the union, dominated by the Italians, demanded that Peiper be fired. And he was.

The past kept tracking him down, but still he would not hide or change his name. By 1964 two Italian Communists had traced him to Stuttgart, where they filed a formal complaint against him for the massacre at Boves. The pretrial investigation lasted years. More than 100 witnesses were heard. "Boves was not a massacre but a battle," Peiper kept insisting. "War is war." At length the court believed him, and the case was dismissed for lack of evidence.

But afterwards Peiper took his wife and his two hounds, Tim and Tom, and moved to Traves, telling friends that German society was bankrupt; he did not want to live there anymore.

He had first come to Traves in 1962. He found a spot beside the Saône River and made his camp and sat and brooded. The river there is about twice as wide as a man can throw a stick, with overhanging trees on both banks. It seemed as slow and lazy as the nearby village itself. The next summer he camped in the same place, and the next. The land wasn't worth much. It was too heavily wooded, and it pitched too steeply down towards the water. Peiper bought about two acres and with his own hands began to build his house. It took years.

When the house was finished, he applied for a French residence permit. According to the Common Market treaty, such permits were almost automatic. Peiper's application, countersigned by Ernest Rigoulot, Mayor of Traves, specified only that he owned a house and land in Traves and wished to retire there. It mentioned neither his past nor his present. The application was routinely approved. The year was 1972. Peiper, 57, was now a permanent refugee in the country Germany had raped three times in seventy years, most recently with the aid of Peiper himself.

The German idea of paradise has always been to live *wie Gott in Frankreich* — like God in France. Peiper had a job translating war histories for a publisher in Stuttgart. "It is very suitable work in a quiet place," he wrote to a friend, "and I understand something of war." His years in Traves, in the woods by the river, seem to have been the only peace he had ever known as an adult. Later, when the trouble started, he commented: "I've had four years of happiness here. Four years in a life — that's a lot."

Traves is about ten miles from Vesoul, population 18,000, the nearest town of any size, and about eighty miles from the German frontier. The village is on no main road. In this rolling country, pastures alternate with woods. Herds of cows move along the lanes towards ancient stone barns. Generations of villagers lie buried in the Traves churchyard. The steeple bell tolls out every hour on the hour all night long, just as it has for centuries. There is no hotel and only one café, Mayor Rigoulot's, which is also a small grocery.

Peiper was rarely seen in Rigoulot's café, for his work did not pay much and he had little money. His wife visited him from Munich from time to time. His children and grandchildren visited him in summer. All the villagers knew him. "We knew the whole family," Rigoulot said later. Peiper spoke French, though with an accent. He had a rowboat and liked to row on the river. He had his books, he liked to listen to music. He was quietly growing old. Yes, he was a German, but the war ended long ago and Traves had not suffered terribly anyway. There is a war monument in the village, but the names chiseled into it are from World War I. There are no names from Peiper's war.

One day he went into Vesoul to buy chicken wire for a cage for his dogs. So that the order might be delivered, he left his name and address with the hardware clerk, Paul Cacheu. Cacheu was a tall, stern-looking man with iron-gray hair and horn-rimmed glasses. Like the other clerks he wore a gray smock to his knees.

He was the proud owner of a copy of the so-called Brown Book, a listing of all alleged Nazi war criminals published by the East German Communist Party. Peiper's accent and bearing were such that Cacheu looked him up in the Brown Book at once. He found his name and crimes listed on page 103. Cacheu was not a Communist himself, so he later told me. But he went straight to the party with the news.

An investigation was undertaken by Pierre Durand, ace reporter for *L'Humanité*, the party newspaper. It lasted most of a year and the result, published three weeks before Bastille Day, occupied most of a page under the headline "Who Protects War Criminals in France?"

And so Traves learned of Peiper's past. As did everyone.

Even as the *L'Humanité* article appeared, communist youths from Vesoul were standing in the road at the entrance to Traves handing out tracts which read:

> Citizens of
> Traves
> A War Criminal
> SS Peiper Joachim
> Is Among You

On the roadbed someone had painted

PEIPER SS

in letters three feet high. Anonymous death threats against Peiper began to be received by Mayor Rigoulot, by the prefect of the Haute Saône department, and by other officials.

From the Communist Party and from French veterans' groups came formal protests demanding Peiper's immediate expulsion. There were demonstrations in the streets of Vesoul. A veterans' delegation demanded to see the prefect, and he received them. A Communist group made the same demand, and he refused.

"The movement against me comes as a complete surprise," Peiper wrote a friend in West Germany. He went to the police, who agreed that he had a problem and that the attacks seemed well coordinated; they suggested he return to Germany for a time.

"They also think it likely that someone would burn down my house behind my back."

There were journalists in Traves every day, following up on what was developing into a top-notch story. They found no one in the village to speak out against Peiper except for an old woman dressed all in black, who said that Peiper's dogs scared the sheep. One villager was quoted as saying, "He's paid his debt to society. Anyway, he committed no crime in France." Mayor Rigoulot said testily, "If we want him to leave we're quite capable of telling him so ourselves."

So the journalists went looking for Peiper. He did not have to meet them, and his small house — there were three rooms downstairs plus two mansards under the red tile roof — was virtually inaccessible. Indeed, it could scarcely be seen in the woods, for it was separated from the road by two pastures belonging to farmers, and both were surrounded by barbed-wire fences. Peiper himself had had to buy access to his own land. One approached it only by opening and then closing again a series of barbed-wire gates. One had to avoid the cow patties, and shoo the cows aside.

If Peiper had remained out of sight, then the news articles might have been less inflammatory, and the so-called Affaire Peiper might have died out. But the former combat soldier met the journalists, like all his problems, head-on.

"If I am here," he said, "it is because in 1940 the French were without courage." It was not a statement to endear him to the French. He was tall and stood straight. He was six foot one, still slim and fit, his face tanned, his white hair cut short. "I thought France was a democratic country that respected human rights."

He denied the Italian massacre and gave various versions of the Malmédy one: That he had had no troops to spare to guard the American prisoners and so had left them to be picked up by the infantry, which had massacred them. Or that some of the GIs had tried to run, and in the confusion a German tank had opened fire, so that all the prisoners got killed. Of course both versions could have been correct, as there was not one massacre of prisoners at Malmédy, but two within a week.

Always he declared: "I was in command. The ultimate responsibility was mine. I have paid. I have paid dearly." The journalists asked how soon he was leaving France. But he had nowhere to go. He was too old to run anymore, and Traves, his house on the river, was all he had. Journalism is not a highly paid profession in France, nor always a responsible one. The same is true in many European countries. At the same time it is fiercely competitive. The Peiper story, properly written, would sell a lot of papers. Properly written it would also arouse every extremist in the country.

And so Peiper's two hounds were turned into fierce attack dogs who obeyed his every guttural command. (The night of the crime they ran off howling and were not seen again for days.) The farmers' barbed wire became Peiper's barbed wire, lines of defense of what was virtually a fortified bunker. *L'Humanité* professed to hold photos of Peiper, binoculars in hand, watching the Boves conflagration, but it did not print them. As for Peiper himself, the headlines referred to him almost always as the Butcher of Malmédy, or else the Butcher of Boves.

Peiper sent a series of letters back into Germany, and the magazine *Stern* later printed excerpts:

"I now have continuous visits from journalists. The atmosphere is that they have caught me in my lair after a long hunt. . . ."

"Out of the friendly and peaceful paradise almost overnight a state of siege has developed. This position I will defend to the bitter end."

Though his phone was unlisted, it rang all the time. If he did not clear out by Bastille Day he would be executed and his house destroyed, the callers told him. Some of them claimed to represent the Avengers. Eight men wearing white hoods and calling themselves the Avengers had given a press conference in Paris's Grand Hotel months before. At that time it was not yet public knowledge that Peiper was installed at Traves, and the Avengers did not mention his name. They did describe themselves as sworn to kill unpunished Nazis.

A photographer with a telephoto lens took up position across the river and began photographing Peiper's every move. "He be-

haves similar to an Indian slithering from cover to cover," Peiper
wrote.

And then: "Once again I have received an ultimatum from
the Red Brigade. They will set my house on fire."

Mayor Rigoulot went to see him and begged him to leave
until the whole thing blew over. According to Rigoulot, Peiper
replied:

"I can't leave. They'll burn down my house."

Rigoulot says he answered: "I know they will. But they'll
burn it down whether you go or stay." Rigoulot was one of those
who thought Peiper had aged ten years in the last three weeks.

"They won't try anything if I'm in the house," said Peiper.

"Save yourself, man," said Rigoulot.

"The war ended thirty-one years ago," said Peiper. "No one
can hate that much after so long."

But of course he was wrong. At seven o'clock on the eve of
Bastille Day he telephoned a friend in Breisgau. He had sent his
wife away; his family was safe across the border by now. And he
had just received a final anonymous call. They were coming for
him tonight. Fine, he had told the caller. I'm ready for you.

The friend thought Peiper sounded happy and full of life.

As darkness fell, he released his dogs from their kennel. He
loaded his shotgun and his revolver. He waited in the night with
guns.

When news reached Germany that Peiper was dead — with an
empty pistol beside him and three spent shotgun shells on the
terrace — it was remarked that this was typical of him, shooting
until the last.

No one knew then nor knows now what happened. Two
guns, a number of spent cartridges, and an unexploded Molotov
cocktail were found. Apart from this the police had very little to
go on. There were apparently no witnesses — none that the police
would admit to anyway, or that the press ever tracked down —
and therefore no way of knowing if Peiper was attacked by one
assailant or many. Nothing was left of the house but the four
walls. The fire had been an inferno that had consumed all other

evidence. The corpse was so thoroughly cooked that it had shrunk to a length of about thirty inches and could not be definitively identified even by its teeth. The legs and one arm were gone completely. The news accounts that reported all this were devoured all over Europe. In most countries readers were only titillated. In France and Germany, however, the fear and hatred of more than thirty years ago were instantly reawakened. Wounds thought to have healed bled again, and l'Affaire Peiper polarized both countries. Extremist groups surfaced promising violence. One bomb exploded harmlessly. Another was found and defused in time. In Traves, which had no police force of its own, death threats against the mayor and others were received, and gendarmes had to be brought in to guard the village at night. The French Communist Party, which had provoked the crime in the first place, was disavowing violence and screaming for government action: "We were using l'Affaire Peiper to alert the public to the dangerous pro-German policies of President Giscard d'Estaing. That was all we had in mind." If this were true, then the Communists got much more than they bargained for. Emotions seemed aroused almost to the virulence of thirty years ago, both on the right and on the left. There were outbreaks of anti-Semitism in France: vandals attacked the Paris B'nai B'rith office, while in Marseilles a synagogue was profaned. In Germany former Nazis were said to have gone into hiding.

As the German press turned fearful and defensive, the French headlines became ever more aggressive. An article in *France-Soir* listed the names of a number of important Nazis now doing quite well in West Germany, calling them "the bloody priests of the Third Reich." The paper seemed to be calling for a crusade, if not a war. Three hundred Nazis who had been condemned to death in absentia in France still lived quietly in West Germany, it claimed; and there were 30,000 of them throughout the world, all members of a secret organization called the Spider. There was another sinister neo-Nazi organization called the Black Orchestra. A secret treasury contained $40 million, and there were "safe" houses for fugitives in twenty-two countries. *France-Soir* was the largest-selling evening newspaper in France.

The *Frankfurter Allgemeine* saw l'Affaire Peiper as the start of a concerted campaign against the German Federal Republic. So did the *General Anzeiger* of Bonn, for whom the campaign was led by "certain forces who, thirty years after the end of the war, refuse to leave in peace this unhappy chapter in the Franco-German past."

France and Germany, after decades of cooperation, were being pushed hard in opposite directions, and because the police could find no trace of the assailants the pressure only grew.

In Paris a voice telephoned the right-wing daily *L'Aurore.* "This is the Avengers calling. The Affaire Peiper was us. Our vengeance will reach not only those Nazis hiding in France, but also those who believe themselves untouchable in West Germany."

But were the Avengers the real killers? Was Peiper really dead?

In cases of this kind French law is strict. There are no press conferences. Prosecutors, magistrates, and police commanders may divulge virtually no information whatever, which leaves a void.

Into this void steps, inevitably, one or more unscrupulous journalists to embroider upon existing details, to invent new ones. And why not, knowing that from the French criminal justice system there will never be either confirmation or denial? Most often the system ignores the existence of the press — the eyes and ears of the people — altogether.

In the Peiper case even the autopsy report was not made public, and so the rumors grew in size and power.

The corpse had a bullet hole in its throat, or it had no bullet wounds at all, death being due to smoke inhalation. Also, the corpse could not be Peiper because Peiper was supposed to have a gold tooth and the corpse did not seem to. Which meant that the former soldier, though 61 years old, had lost none of his combat skills. Having killed one of his assailants and scared off the others, he had dragged the body inside and had set fire to his own house. Even now he was starting a new life somewhere under a new name, just as Hitler might have done. Being still alive, Peiper was no doubt still engaged in whatever mysterious business had brought him to Traves in the first place. Which was what? Well, in Hanover it was common knowledge that there was an

SS group, hardened Nazis who hoped to rise again; Peiper was the head of it and had phoned them instructions every night from Traves.

Or was he secretly a Communist agent? Nearly two months after the fact one Paris paper devoted nearly a full page to this notion. After Peiper's release from prison the Soviet KGB had turned him from Nazi to Communist, and had set him down in Traves. Why? Was not Traves only twenty miles from an important airdrome, and also only eighty miles from the frontier? It was an American CIA agent attached to the American Embassy in Bern who had unmasked Peiper and who had put the information into the hands of his actual killers.

The most grisly rumor of all had Peiper hacking the legs and arms off the assailant he had killed and burying them elsewhere, for they did not bear his own war scars. The rest he poured gasoline on and set on fire.

There was nothing funny about this nonsense. It kept the case in the headlines — and kept the crazies aroused — for months.

In Paris the office of the International League Against Racism and Anti-Semitism was defaced during the night — "Peiper will be avenged" was sprayed on the walls. Then two homemade firebombs were set off that blew out windows and caved in a door.

Three days later still another anonymous phone call was received in Traves. The voice said the Avengers would burn ten houses during the night.

A squad of gendarmes invaded the village. They searched for explosives under virtually every bed, but found nothing. However, a village fair scheduled for that night was canceled, and a good many nervous villagers slept elsewhere. A similar search was conducted in Vesoul, where a device of some kind was found and defused. The police would give no details.

In Cologne the Union of the German People, an ultra-right group, organized a ceremony to the memory of Peiper. That same week an SS reunion in Bavaria drew not only thousands of German veterans, but also about 100 Frenchmen, mostly Alsatians, former members of the SS Charlemagne Division. All these men were in their fifties now, some much older, and a portion of them were set upon by young toughs claiming to be gypsies, were beaten with clubs, and a minor riot ensued.

At the hardware store on Vesoul's Rue Paul Morel, I talked to the clerk Paul Cacheu, who had set the whole sad business in motion. "It was unthinkable that such a man should try to live in France," he said proudly. He certainly sounded proud to me. "We were five years under German boots here." He did not regret the mess he had caused: "I'd do the same thing again." Peiper was still alive, the clerk stated, and now had an additional murder on his conscience. "Nine people out of ten believe he stage-managed that fire. He's made his getaway and has escaped justice again."

This appeared to be the Communist Party line in France — the point being that only the Communists were strong enough and vigilant enough to save France from Peiper and fascism.

Was Peiper alive or dead? With the emotional climate growing ever more heated, the police caused the news to circulate that the corpse was indeed Peiper. But they would not say how they knew, and so were not believed.

To my surprise the Vesoul prosecutor charged with the case, Marc Dreyfus, agreed to my request for an interview. Perhaps he hoped to get a more balanced story published abroad than he could ever get from a French reporter at home. He outlined the police theory. Peiper was attacked by a gang of young hoodlums — youths who were not even born when he had committed his crimes. They threw Molotov cocktails against the house, which caught fire. Possibly they did not even mean to kill Peiper. He drove them off with his guns, ran back into the house to save valuables, was overcome by smoke, and died. Scientific tests on the corpse were continuing; Dreyfus was confident that it would soon be identified without question.

I found that I believed him.

As for the assailants, they could have come from Vesoul or Dijon or Paris or anywhere, Dreyfus said. He doubted they would ever be caught.

I believed that too.

The prosecutor sounded distressed — not so much by the crime as by its aftermath. L'Affaire Peiper was not over. The case had become a symbol not only to French Communists, but also to France's extreme right, which had desperately needed one after thirty years. Perhaps the symbol was strong enough to support terrible future events; no one yet knew. To Dreyfus such symbols were dangerous. This one would last a long time, he thought — until the last SS veteran was in his grave at least.

So I went back to Traves, lifted the barbed wire away, crossed the two pastures past the cows, and went down through the woods towards the river where the house was. I was looking for something, but I don't know exactly what. Clues of some kind, perhaps. Not about the crime. About Germany, about France. Clues that of course were nowhere to be found. As a house it barely had walls. It had no roof. I went in through a doorway that had no door and contemplated the litter of bricks, cinder blocks, and charred beams, the broken wires, the metal frame of a bed, the ruined stove. Peiper's bed, Peiper's stove. I stepped on something and picked it up: a frying pan, its handle a blackened rod. The wreckage of a man's life. I stood in the midst of it. There was nothing else here.

Les Baux de Provence
DRINKING AN 1806 CHÂTEAU LAFITE

Climbing, the road twists back and forth on itself and then comes up over the escarpment and the village is visible out at the end of its white crag. I get out of the car and gaze across at it for a moment. I haven't been here in a long time. From this distance it looks desolate, jagged-edged. It looks unchanged. The wind is blowing my hair around. The wind always blows in Provence. It is wind that makes the air so clear and the colors as brilliant as they are this afternoon. Les Baux was the site of a singular experience in our lives, but we have never come back until now. As I restart the car I wonder how we could have stayed away so long. And I wonder what, after so long, we will find.

There was no bullring at Arles. The *corridas* took place in a 2,000-year-old stone arena left behind by the Romans. There was no bullring band; music was by the Arles Philharmonic, and the toreros — usually the top names from Spain — marched in to the toreador song from *Carmen*. The bulls were from Spain too, and sometimes were defective. Bulls that the Spaniards could not sell to each other. The arena was not as big as Rome's Colosseum, but it was similar in type, better preserved, and it held 15,000. It was usually full, people sitting and standing even on top of the arches behind the highest tier of seats.

What the French public liked best were showy and vulgar stunts. We did too, being new to bullfighting. Spain would have been better, but we had two little kids at home and not much money. We were living in Nice then. Spain required an expedition whereas Arles could be had overnight. Sometimes after the bullfight we would drive to Les Baux to spend the night. Les Baux was partway home, and we would walk through the streets, what was left of them. It was the most dismembered village either of us had ever seen. It hadn't been lived in for 300 years.

The ruins were spectacular. There were decorated windows and doorways with nothing behind them, balustraded staircases that led nowhere, vaulted and groined ceilings in rooms that were missing entire walls, carved fireplaces dominating mounds of rubble. The stonecutters who worked here had been artists. We may have been young, but we could see that. The late-afternoon sun did gorgeous things to the old stone. Sometimes the village was empty except for us. Other times we might encounter one or two other tourists or a stray dog. We walked along gawking at roofless shells, at hulks that had once been palaces.

At first we didn't know the story. Then we learned it.

Les Baux dated from the true Dark Ages. At the time of its splendor its population was about 6,000 — a big city then — and it ruled over seventy-two neighboring villages and towns. Its language was Provençal, in which much poetry and many songs were written. Its people were said to be independent and proud. One of its rulers around 1380 was Raymond de Turenne, who plundered the surrounding countryside and became famous for cruelty in a cruel age; his château was set on the edge of the cliff, and his favorite distraction was to force his prisoners to leap off his battlements into the void. Their hesitations and anguish, it is said, would make him laugh. Later Les Baux belonged to the counts of Provence, but it remained the richest and most important city around.

When in 1486 Provence was absorbed into France, Les Baux was absorbed too — unwillingly. Thereafter, we are told, it affronted the crown with rebelliousness and disobedience. By 1632 Paris had had enough, and Richelieu sent an army. At his orders they lined up their cannons and pounded the proud and gorgeous city to pieces. Its inhabitants, before being sent to live elsewhere, were obliged to pay the costs and a fine of 100,000 livres as well. Except for one or two shops, Les Baux was never rebuilt, and the ruined city I first saw looked much the way Richelieu's men had left it.

Our first night there we dined at the restaurant called the Baumanière. It was down in the valley, not up on the crag with the ruined village, and it was already famous. It had been started in 1946 by an insurance executive from Paris named Raymond Thuillier, who was then 50 years old and had never run a restaurant before. He came south with a woman named Miquette Moscoloni, to whom he was not married but who thereafter would serve as his hostess. He bought an old Provençal building. It dated from about 1675 and was half fallen in. In summer it was hot in the valley. There was nothing else down there but the hot wind combing through the clumps of lavender, the isolated olive trees. The valley was known to the few locals hereabouts as the Vale of Hell.

"Every moment of the day has its own special light, every rock and stone its shadow," Thuillier wrote of the site later. "In this valley the rocks seem to play, to dance about. The region of Les Baux opens itself only to those who truly want to seize it, to love it in all its diversity, including its wild sometimes bitter sides."

He and Miquette put the vaulted rooms back together again and filled them with antique furniture, fine crystal, fine silver, fine linen. They placed fresh-cut flowers everywhere, opened the doors, and hoped people would come this far for a meal. The nearest population centers were Arles, twelve miles away, and Avignon, twenty. The war had just ended. France was virtually destitute. There were not many cars, and gasoline was hard to find.

Midlife crisis? The term, as far as I know, had not yet been coined. At least Thuillier was the son of a restaurateur, for his mother had run the Buffet de la Gare in Privas. In France such root stock is considered important. Thuillier himself was an amateur cook. His mother had taught him a few things. He had dabbled at it. He had written a book about insurance, thereby dabbling at the literary game. He had dabbled at painting too,

which was how he had discovered Les Baux in the first place —
he had come to Provence to paint, almost like van Gogh or Gauguin, except that he was on vacation and they were not. Now he
intended to become a restaurateur, to remake his life — "not by
whim or to satisfy some caprice," he was to write, "but rather to
allow a passion I had inherited to bloom. Something that had been
lying dormant in me finally was ready to awaken, and it proved
to be my true calling."

Thuillier the important insurance man had important friends,
and Georges Pompidou, who much later would succeed de Gaulle
as president of France, came down to represent the National Tourist Board at the inauguration.

Within eight years the Michelin guide had awarded the Baumanière first one, then two, then its highest accolade, three stars.
Nowadays there are usually twenty, sometimes more, three-star
restaurants in France, but at that time there were four in Paris,
only six in the provinces. The Baumanière was the only one even
reasonably close to Nice.

We went there because we had been to the bullfight. We knew
nothing about the Baumanière's history, had never heard Thuillier's name. And when we had taken our places in his vaulted
dining room what impressed us most was his wine list, especially
the oldest and most expensive bottle on it, an 1806 Château Lafite.
We wondered what such a wine would taste like. We wondered
who could possibly afford it, for the price was 30,000 francs —
$60. We knew little about wine. Hardly anyone did in those days.
But though we closed the menu on the 1806 Lafite, ordering I
think a beaujolais, we talked about it wistfully. Perhaps someday
we would be rich enough to come back and drink it. What would
a wine that old taste like?

From time to time we stopped at the other three-star restaurants of the day, the Hostellerie de la Poste at Avallon, the Pyr-
amide at Vienne, the Petite Auberge at Noves. Three-star
restaurants were no more popular than rare wine, so none of them
cost all that much. Besides, I was usually on assignment, meaning
that the paper would pay a set sum towards my dinner and lodging.
However elaborate the wine lists of these other places, we did not
find the 1806 Lafite on them, nor anything else nearly that old.

We moved from Nice to Paris, where we tried the Tour d'Argent, Maxim's, Lapérouse, and the Grand Véfour, three stars all, and they didn't have it either. I had begun to study wine and had started a cellar.

In time we moved back to America to live, but we made repeated trips to France, sometimes stopping at the Baumanière. Each time we would search the wine list. The 1806 was still there, still $60.

I was working now principally for magazines, whose assignments were my solution not only to earning a living but to satisfying whatever interests came upon me. Magazines could get me to places I wished to see, introduce me to any powerful or interesting person I was curious to meet.

I made an appointment to see the editor of *Esquire*.

In France a wine is felt to be alive, I told him. It is born, matures, and later dies. I had conceived the notion of getting his magazine to buy me that bottle of wine. In exchange I would write an article about it. If a wine should hold all or even most of its color, bouquet, and taste for upward of a century or more, I told him, then it became more than a great wine. It would be opened with reverence. It would be lifted to the lips with trembling fingers in a room so hushed as to resemble more a bullring than a restaurant, at the moment before the bull was put to the sword. The comparison was apt, I continued, for the result would be to kill this wine, to destroy this object of veneration.

I looked at the editor, who was peering at his hands. For a moment I thought I had oversold him.

His head rose. "Sounds good to me," he said. "Go ahead and do it."

So I wrote to Thuillier, whom I may have seen but had never met or spoken to. "I think," he wrote back, "that this wine is still perfect enough to appreciate it, judge it, and love it, but you mustn't forget that it was born before Waterloo. However, I don't think the drinking of it will be a defeat, much less a disaster."

I began to research the wine as best I could, and also Thuillier. Who knows what Bordeaux weather was like in 1806? But for the wine to last this long, if in fact it had lasted this long, conditions must have been close to ideal: mild weather during the flowering in spring; sufficient rain all through June and July; little or no rain during August and September, lest the maturing grapes swell up with water; and none at all during the two-week harvest, which would have begun about Oct. 1. We know that fine weather existed all across Europe that fall, enabling Napoleon to crush the Prussians at Jena.

The 1806 harvest was allowed to ferment on its husks for two weeks or more. Nowadays it would be drained off into casks after a few days, producing the "modern" wine esteemed by the public for its lightness and by winemakers because it matures quickly, can be bottled quickly, and the money banked; whereas the 1806 Château Laffitte (as it was then spelled) was for a decade or more so austere as to be undrinkable, not to mention unsalable. No wine ever made again would last such a length of time. Of course it was not certain that this one had either.

Because the vintage was possibly going to be a great one, a few bottles were buried in sand in a stone tomb in the château's cellar for future use. The decades turned into scores of years, and the wine remained undisturbed. It was unlikely that any of the men who put it down imagined that the future would extend two-thirds of the way into the next century. The bottle we would open would have had three owners: the château, Thuillier, and me. Thuillier had owned it since 1954 when he got his third Michelin star. I would own it an hour.

We reached France, drove much of the day across Provence, and were trembling a little when we presented ourselves to Thuillier. This was partly fatigue, mostly nervous anticipation. He was 70 years old, thin, energetic, with a quick step and a warm manner. By now I had read much of what he had written about cooking, which he considered an art form: "What is art in general if not the harmonious and subtle expression of all that can be conceived of the grand, the beautiful, the sublime by the human mind for the pleasure of the senses? *La cuisine,* par excellence, addresses itself to one of the most delicate and difficult senses to satisfy: taste."

And again: "Relishing a fine dish requires as much attention and culture as appreciating a sonata or painting. To practice the art of fine cuisine requires broad knowledge, real patience, long hours, and a poet's soul, sensitive to beauty. You have to have a feeling for appropriate harmonies and a sense of nuance in order to create a dish and give it life."

I was a bit awed by him. He was an artist, and in his field a superstar. He was twice as old as I was as well, and I sought to reassure him that I knew something about wines and cared about them. I did not want him to think that his only bottle of 1806 Lafite would be drunk by ignoramuses as a kind of gastronomic joke. But he smiled and patted my hand, and I had the impression he understood what I was trying to say. He suggested an aperitif on his terrace, which was surrounded by masses of geraniums and roses. Then perhaps we would want to see the bottle on its shelf in the darkest and quietest part of his cellar.

The trip to the cellar did little to quiet my nerves. The bottle — our bottle — lay alone on its shelf. Nearby were other old bottles, none this old. We stood in a clean, well-lighted corridor lined with raw pine shelving, some of which sagged from the weight of bottles, the way cheap bookcases are sometimes bowed by books. It was a cool, moldless, unvaulted, beamless, unromantic, entirely businesslike wine cellar.

The, well, enormity of what I proposed to do began to build up in me. It felt presumptuous. To be there at all felt presumptuous. This was one of the problems of magazine writing. Subjects were usually glad to see you; the resulting publicity figured to help their businesses, advance their careers, did it not? You were, in effect, an invited guest. Nonetheless the relationship was an artificial one and, ultimately, you hadn't been invited at all; it was you who had invited yourself, and the result sometimes was this feeling of discomfort.

Emerging into the waning sunlight, I told Thuillier that, if he agreed, we would drink the 1806 Lafite at luncheon tomorrow. We were too tired from the drive to do it justice now. But what I meant was that this whole idea would take a little more getting used to.

Thuillier smiled, and again seemed to understand what I was not saying. As for tonight's dinner, he promised to prepare it for us personally.

He served us first a *rouget à la nage,* one of his newest creations.

The *rouget* is a Mediterranean fish about the size of a brook trout but thicker, with reddish-orange skin. The flesh seems to be flecked with orange too; it comes away in chunks and has a strong taste and a chewy texture. Over it was a sauce that was principally butter, but with spices mixed in which gave it a variety of tastes all at once, all of them so subtle that we couldn't determine what they were, though we talked about it.

After this came Thuillier's most famous dish, a *gigot d'agneau en croûte,* which is a tiny (two-pound) leg of lamb with the bone removed and replaced by a stuffing composed of finely diced lamb kidneys, Madeira wine, mushrooms, thyme, rosemary, and tarragon, the whole covered with fine-rolled puff paste glazed with egg yolk and then baked for only fifteen to twenty minutes. This was served with a gratin of scalloped potatoes. With it we drank a 1953 Château Lafite-Rothschild, chosen because 1953 was the year the cork had been changed for the last time in the bottle we would drink tomorrow. I guess we imagined that this gave the two wines, separated in time by 147 years, some rapport. We finished the dinner with an exceedingly light and flaky wild strawberry *tarte* with whipped cream and tiny cups of strong coffee.

The Baumanière had about fifteen rooms in the main building, but recently Thuillier had bought and done over two ancient farmhouses a little way down the valley. In one of them we had a two-room suite furnished with antiques. The closet was closed by old armoire doors polished to a gloss. French windows opened onto some of the biggest roses I had ever seen and formal paths defined by hedgerows of lavender. We absorbed the scent of lavender every time we breathed.

In the morning the maid brought *café au lait,* together with croissants from Thuillier's kitchen that were as light and flaky as the *tartes* the night before, and a morning paper, and she threw back the shutters to let in the sun.

We had made a date with the sommelier, René Boxberger, to open the 1806 Château Lafite at eleven-thirty, immediately after he would have eaten his own lunch with the staff.

Too nervous to wait, we got up to the main building fifteen minutes early. Boxberger, a friendly, burly man 56 years old, wearing the leather apron of his trade, was pacing back and forth.

No, he hadn't eaten yet. He wasn't hungry, he said. He asked when we would open the wine. We noted that he had cut himself three or four times shaving. He was at least as nervous as I was.

He got the bottle up from the cellar. It was hand blown, somewhat lopsided, and the glass was impregnated with air bubbles. Its shape was one no longer used in Bordeaux, being wider at the waist than at the base. Thuillier guessed that in its long life its cork had been changed twice. "I have some other bottles which are almost 100 years old," he said, "and their corks haven't been changed at all yet." He speculated that the cork was changed for the first time about 1900, and a label affixed to the bottle. When the cork was changed again in 1953, a strip bearing this information was affixed below the label and joined to it by the château's stamp.

With the bottle in a silver cradle, Boxberger knocked the wax off the cork. Inserting his screw, he yanked nervously at the cork, and half of it came out and the rest stayed in there.

Together with Thuillier, the *maître d'hôtel,* and most of the waiters, we stood over the bottle watching Boxberger work. We were all tense. He worked at the remaining segment of cork but succeeded only in pushing it further into the bottle. He went to fetch instruments resembling tiny forceps. At last, triumphantly, he got it out.

He held it up for all of us to see. He was ebullient now. He sniffed it. He passed it around. We all had a sniff.

The bouquet it gave off was strong, robust, all the things it should have been. It smelled not unlike the cork of last night's bottle. It meant that the wine in the bottle was still sound.

But what would it taste like?

Boxberger decanted the wine, poured a generous dose into a big, crystal glass. He swirled the wine to air it, then filled his mouth. The rest of us waited for the verdict with our jaws hanging slack. All the while staring into the glass, he gargled the wine, then swallowed it, chewing all the while. He masticated that wine drop by drop it seemed, slowly, all the way down. I had always wanted to see this done by an expert. It was an excellent show.

Boxberger stared thoughtfully into the glass. He frowned, he smiled. Still we waited. "It doesn't quite leave to the palate what it promises to the nose," he said finally.

In truth it was the strangest bottle of wine I have ever drunk. It had the bouquet of a mature, confident wine, and its color had gone off only slightly from its original ruby red. Though not vinegary at all, it tasted thin, almost like a new green vintage that wasn't ready yet. And yet in the background at all times was the robust taste of the great wine which had once been there.

"It's like an old man who's still in pretty good shape," said Boxberger, "though of course he can no longer run the 100 meters in ten seconds."

I thought of it more in terms of an old baritone whose voice was gone, but who nonetheless could still bring out certain notes that were as beautiful as ever. The former great taste was still in there somewhere; one moment it was on your tongue, the next it was gone.

Luncheon started with *foie gras aux truffes* with hot toast, after which came another of Thuillier's creations, a *poularde à l'éstragon,* chicken boiled in a closed *cocotte* so that it comes to the table with the skin still white and the meat inside very tender. It was served with rice, and over this was spooned a cream sauce tasting principally of tarragon. We had not been allowed to see the menu; Thuillier had decided for us in light of the very old wine we were to drink.

It tasted best with the *foie gras,* its voice coming out in one final absolutely strong, perfectly pitched note, and it seemed to me that I could tell exactly what it had tasted like 100 or so years ago when it was such a great wine, so absolutely sure of itself, that it must have thought, if wines can think, that it would live forever.

All this time people stared at us from neighboring tables, the way film stars get stared at in restaurants. Our waiter stared at us too, so that I said to him, "Would it amuse you to taste this?"

"Oui, Monsieur," he said almost fervently. "A wine like that one tastes once in a lifetime."

"Get a glass," said I.

He took it into the kitchen to sip, and after that our table was surrounded by waiters, as happens in certain poor restaurants where they are hoping for tips. Here it was not tips they wanted but a taste of that wine, and we gave some to most of them. At times the floor was nearly empty; they were all in the kitchen tasting.

Towards the end, though its bouquet was still a pleasure to sniff, the wine began to lose its taste altogether. It got thinner and thinner. It made us think of a feeble old man about to breathe his last, and P. said to a final waiter: "Won't you please have some? It is dying fast and soon it will be too late." We wanted them all to taste it because their curiosity was so great and because it amused us to imagine them impressing patrons for decades to come: "That reminds me of the 1806 Lafite I had the pleasure of drinking once. . . ."

But all day our strain and excitement had been intense, and as we drove away from there, rolling through the villages of Provence in the sun, we both were exhausted. I felt as drained as sometimes after a great football game or a great theatrical performance, and presently I laughed and said to P., "I'm looking forward to the wine we'll drink with dinner tonight. It will be a one-year-old rosé de Provence costing $1.75, and no one will stare at us while we drink it."

And that is what we did.

I wrote my article, which duly appeared, and Thuillier sent a complimentary letter; no one ever suggested he wasn't an excellent businessman. It was one of the few wine articles published in the American press that year, for the boom in wine was not to start until six or seven years later. I took my fee and bought a case of 1959 Château Margaux for under $6 the bottle; and other cases of 1961 second and third growths for $4 the bottle or less.

Once the boom did start, it exploded. Knowing about the great wines, collecting them, serving them became proof of sophistication. Wine-drinking clubs sprang up overnight. Regular wine columns appeared in newspapers and magazines, and wine prices rose exponentially. Ten years after our experience a bottle of 1806 Lafite went on the block at an auction in New Orleans, and an oilman from California paid $14,200 for it. The next year a second bottle, or perhaps the same one, fetched an almost identical price, $14,450, at Christie's in London. At an auction in Chicago in 1979 still another bottle (or was it still the same one?)

went for $28,000. Perhaps we shouldn't have drunk ours. Perhaps we should have taken it home. For my article and the accompanying photo I was paid $600.

Gastronomy too became the rage. As the old chefs began to die off they were replaced by younger, more imaginative men who claimed to have invented a *nouvelle cuisine;* men who, as soon as they had acquired their Michelin stars, put their names up over their restaurants in giant letters, left assistants in charge of their kitchens, and set out all over the world making personal appearances, like film stars. In major cities they cooked for groups of so-called gastronomic journalists, or even a single journalist if his paper was important enough, charging no money. More often they cooked for banquets of sixty or more rich people and banked fees. In either case they collected reams of publicity and at home their restaurants filled up with tourists, some of whom were trying to set records — it became chic back home to brag about having dined in ten three-star restaurants in nine days, or the like. The old chefs had been unknown thirty miles from home, sometimes less; the new ones were international celebrities, and the prices on their menus rose exponentially too.

We had planned to stop at Les Baux the following summer but something came up, and the next year was not possible either, and after that we were never in the neighborhood or did not have time. Or perhaps subconsciously we merely wished to preserve a memorable experience by not trying to repeat any part of it. The years passed quickly, and we never came back.

Until today, and I drive across the saddle of the mountain toward the village out on its massive crag of rock and start to turn into the parking lot, which is more vast than I remember, but a man comes out of a booth beside the road and stops me. There is a parking fee of 10 francs, it seems, even on a blustery November afternoon like this one when there are no other cars in the lot. So that is the first surprise, though not the last. "Complain to the mayor," says the attendant as he hands back my change. The mayor since 1971 has been Raymond Thuillier.

So I walk through the streets of the village and there isn't a ruin left. It's been completely restored. I don't recognize any of it. People are living here now. There is glass in the windows and doors in the doorways. The church is a church again. I walk past one handsome building after another. In most cases the workmen appear to have used the original stones, picked them up off the ground and put them back in place. It's been beautifully, artistically done. It takes a bit of getting used to, however. There are lots of new shops, restaurants, galleries, tearooms. They look expensive. In a souvenir store the clerk tells me that the population of the commune has almost doubled since I was here last, from 253 to 433. All this is thanks to the mayor too, or so a shopkeeper tells me. Thuillier was 74 when first elected and he will be 91 in two months' time.

I walk all the way to the end of the village, where the final street used to open onto a stony plateau, where the view, I remember, was one of the most fabulous in France. But I am stopped by a barrier that is new and am obliged to pay 12 francs more before I can get out onto the plateau and walk to the end of it. Well, the view is still there. On a clear day, and today is clear, there is a vast panorama. One can see all the way to the Rhône delta and the Mediterranean about twenty-five miles away.

We drive downhill from the once-ruined village towards the Baumanière.

The place looks much the same, I note when we come to it. The parking lot seems bigger, and there is a boutique now in one corner; you see such boutiques at all the famous restaurants these days. They sell the famous chef's jams and honeys, his *foie gras* and sausages, the cognacs and wines he has lent his name to, and especially his cookbook or books. On sale in Thuillier's boutique is one thing more, his paintings. They are mostly Provençal landscapes somewhat in the Impressionist style, horizontal swaths of rather subtle color, that are quite pleasing. The one in the window, which is of good size, is on sale for about $1,000.

We check in and are shown to our room.

On a table in this room — in all the rooms, I imagine — is a thick and luxuriously printed brochure about the Baumanière and of course Thuillier. There are many beautiful photographs and Thuillier is eulogized on page after page, and the various stages of his career admiringly recalled. Some of the writers extol him

as Raymond des Baux, as Raymond l'Accueillant — like one of
the medieval lords of Les Baux of hundreds of years ago — as if
to say: from them he is descended. He is the man who brought
Les Baux back to life. He created his incomparable inn, which not
only delights the world but gives employ to 130 people, 18 of
them cooks. He owns a second restaurant called Le Cabro d'Or
a bit further down the valley; he even made the Vale of Hell come
alive. His books are praised, and his paintings, and the table linens
he has designed, which are used in the restaurant and can be ordered in the boutique. The various celebrities he has played host
to are listed, among them Harry Truman and de Gaulle and various
famous French entertainers, even the Queen of England, her husband the Duke, and Prince Charles. Thuillier himself has described
the Queen's visit in one of his books, *Les Grandes Heures de Baumanière*. The Queen and her entourage were here two days, ending
with a gala banquet for thirty-six people. The Queen's visit may
have been Thuillier's high point.

I did not write ahead to say we were coming because I did
not know what kind of shape Thuillier was in and because I was
afraid he or someone might suppose we were hoping for a free
meal. Now we come into the restaurant to dinner and he is standing near the entrance wearing a white chef's smock as always,
though no toque (he was never one of those theatrical chefs), and
horn-rimmed glasses, looking frail, and I ask if he remembers the
day we opened and drank the 1806 Château Lafite.

He begins to talk about the wines he served the Queen of
England. A big smile comes onto his face and he adds: "Ah, but
that's another story."

His smile remains in place as I continue to try to talk to him,
but he says nothing further, and presently he moves off, taking
very small steps.

The Baumanière today is run by Jean-André Charial, the oldest of his grandsons, who was born in 1945 at about the time
Thuillier left Paris to start his new life. Charial never intended to
become a chef; after secondary school he entered one of France's
top commercial colleges and came out and started to make money.
But at some point Thuillier must have made a deal with him,
because he went back to school, this time in the kitchens of France's

greatest chefs: Bocuse, Chapel, Haeberlin, the Troisgros brothers. He also underwent training programs in reception and management at the Plaza in Paris and the Waldorf-Astoria in New York, before coming back to Les Baux permanently fifteen years ago.

I talk to Charial after dinner. He is a tall, solidly built man with a mustache. He says he has heard about that 1806 wine, but has never served anything remotely that old himself. "Somebody ordered a 1900 Lafite one night." I ask about Boxberger. Eight years ago at 70 he retired, Charial tells me; he died just last year. Thuillier has come up in the course of this conversation. He stands listening to us. He smiles throughout, but does not speak.

After shaking hands all around, we go back to our room to bed, and in the morning we drive away.

The oldest wine on the Baumanière wine list today is an 1870 Château Lafite-Rothschild. Other very old vintages are also represented: Lafites from 1877, 1883, 1888, 1890, 1900; and Château Margaux from 1916 and 1918. These wines are listed apart from the others, and no prices are given. I assume they are not really for sale. Although I might have asked Charial what they cost, I did not do so. I chose not to know. Let whatever mystery is left be left.

There was of course no Château Lafite from 1806. To be young and to drink such a wine in a place like this is an experience not to be repeated by us, not to be repeated by anyone. There is nothing more to say.

A Tour of France
LIFE AND DEATH OF A RIDER

Jacques Anquetil died yesterday. I am in Bordeaux, having just landed. The news is front page on all the papers. "The End of a Giant." "Death Takes Master Jacques." France is about to go through an orgy of grief. The hero is dead, and there is no successor. The headline writers have forgotten that the hero was not much loved in his prime. To my surprise I feel shock and grief myself, though we shared very little in life: a few days each summer for four or five years, some glorious scenery, the sun and wind in our faces. He was a bike racer and I was one of the followers in cars. I never even really talked to him. I used to stand with the reporters clustered around him each morning in some mountain town and listen to the interviews. The bike-racing world seemed to me terrifically exotic. I watched the way he answered, confident but not boasting, pleased with himself, with what he knew that day would bring. He looked as unworried as a little boy and as happy. He was very young, of course. So was I. He was bursting with health.

My eyes would roam from his legs to his chest and back again. I would stare at him as if he were a girl. It made me feel peculiar, but I did it. I was trying to understand where all that power came from. His legs were shaved smooth like a girl's and in the early morning were sleek with oil; his handlers worked hours on those legs each day. He had thick thighs, as all bike racers did, and muscles that bulged over both knees, and calves that bulged smoothly. Some riders' legs were grotesque, full of knots, laced with popped-out veins, but his were not. I never saw him in a suit of clothes, but he must have had to buy his trousers custom-made, extra-wide. His chest was thick; his heart, I had read, was overlarge and beat only forty or fewer times per minute.

Presently the signal would sound and 100 or more superbly fit young men would straddle their bikes and begin to move. They wore garish jerseys and spandex shorts and caps with the bills turned up. Their arms, legs, and faces were the color of cinnamon. They would pack the streets of the town, wall to wall, the mass of them moving without noise, without seeming to move. The reporters and photographers would run for their cars and motorcycles, and the whole caravan would get under way.

As the town opened up the mountains would appear ahead, snowcapped even in summer, and the road would start to climb. The day's finish line would be somewhere beyond those snowy peaks, perhaps seven hours ahead. For seven hours they would not get down from their bikes. From time to time along the route handlers would run out and sling musette bags of food at them, usually quarters of roast chicken plus a mush of rice mixed with broth and orange juice, which they would eat by the handfuls while rolling. They would eat one-handed or even no-handed, tossing chicken bones over their shoulders like Henry VIII, thrusting handfuls of mush into their mouths. They would urinate while rolling too, peeling back the tight, mid-thigh shorts as far as possible and letting fly, sending the spray ahead and sometimes, depending on the wind, riding into it.

The pack would be moving at the beginning at around twenty-five miles per hour, the sun flashing on whirling spokes. Somewhere in the middle would be Anquetil, perhaps already wearing the yellow jersey of race leader, idling along, not paying much attention, knowing that if he wasn't leader yet he had only to wait. The mountains would break the pack into tiny suffering fragments. The mountains terrified everyone, though not him. The others thought him indomitable, and surely he came to see himself that way too. It was where his quiet smile came from, the aura he carried with him wherever he went. It was a physical thing. His chest was indomitable. His legs were indomitable.

But now, well before his time, he is dead.

Three days have passed. I am in Pau, which the Tour de France comes through most years, its last overnight stop before climbing up into the Pyrenees. Anquetil has been much on my mind. He still dominates the newspapers and, at night in the hotel, the television news. His funeral was yesterday in the cathedral at Rouen. The place was full of dignitaries. President Mitterrand sent a tribute, as did Prime Minister Chirac. He was buried in the family tomb at Quincampoix, a nearby village, beside his father. The father was a small farmer, and Anquetil at the end was a big farmer. To both of them Rouen was New York, the big city. The father never got beyond it, but the son did.

I have spent part of today looking into the château in which Henri of Navarre, the future Henri IV, was born a Protestant in 1553. In its gift shop I came upon collections of his letters. One tends to imagine that nothing remains from so long ago except buildings, paintings, and some heavily restored furniture. But letters remain as well. World leaders wrote letters then, same as now, which were published in book form then, same as now; and collections of Navarre's 400-year-old letters are on sale here.

It was hard for me to concentrate on him or his castle. I kept brooding about Anquetil, presumably because the newspaper photos and television images mostly show him the way I remember him, either hunched over the handlebars, pedaling hard, sweat streaming down his face, or else standing beside his bike smiling. We moved back to America about when he stopped racing, and I never saw him again. In my head he never got any older, whereas I did. For me he is still a young athlete. A lot of my contemporaries are dead, all of them violently. Anquetil is the first to die of so-called natural causes — as if the terrible operations he underwent were any less violent than a car crash or a shooting.

The first time I came to Pau with the Tour, Anquetil was not here. He was having a fight with the organizers and had not entered. Although he had already won the race once and was only 26, they were giving out the story that he was finished. They were touting a new star, Roger Rivière, who was riding in his first Tour and was certain to win, for he had recently broken one of Anquetil's world records.

Unfortunately Rivière did not win. Coming down out of the mountains at great speed he went off the road and fell sixty feet into a ravine. Bike racing is a dangerous sport. A helicopter got him out. His back was broken, and he never raced again. He was on painkillers so long he became addicted, and at 40 he was dead.

Anquetil entered the next four Tours and won them all. One he led from first day to last. Another he won in the final few seconds on the twenty-third day after 2,833 miles of pedaling. The night before he had seemed beaten at last, it was thought inconceivable that he could snatch victory from defeat this time, and when he crossed the line in first place no one could believe it.

Bike racers come in four categories. There are the sprinters, who win flat stages in the closing yards because they are fastest. Often ten, a dozen, twenty men jam narrow roads sprinting, elbows out, toward finish lines. Some days elbows or bikes get tangled up and there are mass crashes.

There are the climbers. When the race gets very high up most riders can barely breathe. The few good climbers are mostly physical freaks: they have abnormal heartbeats and lung capacity and will gain twenty minutes or more in a day's stage.

There are the downhillers, men with enough nerve or control or stupidity to ignore braking during the plunge down from the peaks. Downhillers crash as often as sprinters, with much worse results.

And there are the rollers, men who can keep up, whatever the terrain, day after day after day. Anquetil was considered a roller, and therefore boring. He pedaled just fast enough to win, and no faster. He avoided dangerous final sprints, he came down mountains carefully. He studied each race carefully and made his move at a time and place of his own choosing.

The result: during most of his career he was not popular. He was called a regularity machine, a computer. "Jacques," one of his coaches told him, "you are strong enough to win in the mountains, to win at the sprint. If you would just go all out a few times, people would recognize you as the great champion you are."

Anquetil looked at him coolly. "Any more suggestions?"

One year, offered an enormous sum in starting money, he entered the Tour of Spain. In Barcelona on the eve of the race, as a late Spanish lunch dragged to a close, he rose to speak.

"You all know why we're here," he told his nine teammates. "The job of you men is to help me win."

The coach then announced the team's objectives. Number 1 was overall victory for Anquetil. Number 2 was to place the rest of them as high up as possible. Number 3 was to win stage victories each day. One of the possible stage winners was Rudi Altig, a young German new to the team. Altig spoke almost no French but well knew the fundamental rule of bike racing. The star wins the race. On this team the star was Anquetil.

The next morning under a baking sun the seventeen-day, 1,747-mile race started south out of the city. Anquetil, who had promised to relinquish all prize money to his teammates if he won, pedaled serenely in the pack.

Out front Rudi Altig was leading the attack, and he won three stage victories. The stars of the other teams knew Anquetil would never let Altig win the race. They were watching Anquetil only. When Anquetil moved, they would move, and all would pedal past Altig and the rest.

Anquetil was, as he claimed later, neutralizing the race. For two weeks none of the stars budged, while his teammates won nearly every day's stage and in overall standings once held the first seven places.

It was a boring race. Everyone complained. Anquetil's team was too strong. Anquetil had destroyed the Tour of Spain. In the final days he would call in everybody, sprint out in front, and win easily.

The trouble was, Altig's three stage victories earned him a minute's bonus each time, and he was more than four minutes in front of Anquetil, his "patron."

Anquetil began muttering about the German's "loyalty." Could he be trusted to come back when called? The coach wasn't sure. He advised Anquetil to burst out of the pack, win a stage victory by a crushing margin. This would show everyone, Altig included, where the power was. It would get back some of the four minutes. It would prove who was boss.

Anquetil replied, "If I had listened to advice all these years, either I'd still be racing in obscure regional events or I'd be in an asylum." He decided to husband his strength for the time being. Altig would tire. Altig, a second-rate racer, would never risk a double-cross.

The race had wound down the Mediterranean coast to Malaga, had turned north towards the finish line in the Pyrenees. At Madrid a few days from the end, Anquetil's blond wife was waiting to cheer the presumed winner on. He paused long enough to order French champagne sent to the finish line. No true Frenchman, he joked, would consider toasting victory with Spanish champagne.

Three days from the end Altig still led by four minutes. That day's stage, fifty-one miles against the clock, suited Anquetil perfectly. The racers would go off alone at intervals. There would be no pack, no elbowing for position, no dangerous final sprint. Altig and the others were ordered to do well, but to save their strength to "protect" Anquetil in the final two days.

In a fifty-mile dash Anquetil could expect to beat any racer in the world by five minutes. But that day it rained hard. The surface was slick, he worried about skidding off the road and losing a race he considered won, and he did not do his best.

Whereas Altig, disregarding orders, taking fantastic risks, beat Anquetil's time by one second.

The next day, grim faced, Anquetil gathered his teammates around him as windbreaks and attempted to sprint far ahead of Altig. He and his men pumped hard over the mountains all day, but the German, though isolated — no one talking to him — held on.

So the morning after that, one hour before the start of the final stage, Anquetil abandoned the race and his substantial second-place prize money. He claimed to be sick. A doctor was summoned to the hotel to examine him: "Let's get this farce over with," Anquetil told him.

Just then Altig was observed tiptoeing past the open door.

He had his shoes in his hand. He came in and said sheepishly, "Well, so long, Jacques."

Anquetil said nothing.

Altig then made his way to the starting line and victory in the Tour of Spain. He could not stop grinning. He kept saying, "What's Jacques mad about? The strongest racer won. The strongest was me."

Two years later Anquetil went back to Spain, raced to a big lead on the first day, and then simply held it to the end. He did not increase his lead, he merely watched carefully and sat on it, taking no chances whatever.

There is something to be said here about France and sports. The country has had very few sports heroes over the years, and almost none in team sports. Lycées and universities are for study; they do not field official teams. Team sports are not taught even in grade schools; team play is not learned. Children sit in classrooms virtually from dawn to dusk. If there is a schoolyard and they are let out from time to time, they invent their own games, which, even when the children are very young, are likely to be political. "I was a Communist when I was 7 years old," a friend told me once. "There were only two gangs at my school, the Communists and the Fascists. You had to occupy territory. Ours was the bench at one end of the schoolyard. The Fascists had the other end. The object was to raid their bench and throw them off."

This kind of thing is what has formed the French personality, it has always seemed to me. The Frenchman is independent. He does not get along very well with others, having never learned how as a child. He does not easily invite others into his home, apart from family. Politically he is all over the lot — there are fewer political tendencies now than in the time of de Gaulle and before, but there are still a great many. There is great resistance to trying for a consensus.

And the Frenchman admires most a certain type of sports hero: an individual, not a team player, about whom there is something excessive. Maurice Herzog, a government minister during much of Anquetil's career, was such a hero. He scaled Annapurna in the Himalayas, the first 6,000-meter peak ever conquered, but he paid a terrible price. It cost him most of his fingers and toes.

He was a sports hero to stir French souls. Another was Jean-Claude Killy, who in one Winter Olympiad won all three Alpine gold medals. Killy had charm, a sports car, and great girls. Anquetil's life, and especially his love life, was a good deal more complicated than that.

Meanwhile, the country sometimes got ecstatic about losers. When a Frenchman finished second in the Olympic 1500-meter run, it was his name, not the winner's, in headlines, together with the citation: *Vice-Champion Olympique.* There was another bike racer in Anquetil's time, Raymond Poulidor. The mob loved Poulidor, who was not a thinker. He went from catastrophe to victory and back to catastrophe time after time. He was by far the more popular of the two, and in starting fees, endorsements, exhibitions, and other contracts he earned just as much money. They pedaled head to head in eighty races, of which Poulidor won three.

Anquetil won the Grand Prix des Nations nine times, Paris-Nice five times, the Tour of Italy twice. He was called to the Elysée Palace and made a chevalier of the Legion of Honor by de Gaulle personally. One year he won the Criterium du Dauphine, an eight-day, 1,200-mile race mostly in the Alps, crossing the finish line at Avignon after six hours of pedaling at 6:58 P.M. After a bath, a plane ride across France in the dark, dinner, and an hour's sleep sitting up in a chair, he was at the starting line of the 400-mile Bordeaux-Paris, the so-called marathon of the road. It was 2:00 A.M. The start was illuminated by floodlights. He pedaled all that night, all the next morning, and on into the late afternoon, more than fifteen hours, without having been to bed in two nights, and he won that race too.

Yet to his countrymen Anquetil lacked, their word for it, panache. Except in death, of course.

I am in Monaco looking over some new condominiums that have been built facing the Mediterranean on reclaimed land just below the palace. With their pastel walls, their balconies, their big windows open to the sun and the breeze, they look almost like villas stuck there side by side. From every window the view is stunning, a combination of mountains, sea, and town.

The Mediterranean is quite deep. It took twenty years of truckloads of rock and dirt to build the sea floor up to the level that we are standing on. Now that's panache! If you drive along the autoroute a few miles inland you can see where all the landfill came from. Entire mountains lie slain.

I find this panache business impossible to understand. If Anquetil lacked it, then who on earth has it? It was here in Monaco that he provided an image I have not been able to forget.

That day's stage started 150 miles to the north at Briançon, pop. 10,000, a desolate walled town in the most economically depressed corner of the French Alps. Its houses huddled under rooftops of rusty corrugated iron. It had steep narrow streets. Main street, plunging down to the valley floor, was at that time split by a gutter, nearly a canal, ten inches wide, ten inches deep, that was filled to the brim with fast-moving water. It was a street that bike racers negotiated carefully.

The day had dawned hot and bright. In the early light 102 riders pedaled out of Briançon, passed through two shabby villages, and then started climbing. To either side the country was barren. Gray stone mountains shouldered the sky. Their flanks were like deserts tilted sideways.

Ahead was Vars Pass, 7,000 feet high, the first dreadful climb of the day. For eleven miles the road wound steadily up, and the single pack split into two packs, then ten packs, then 102 suffering individuals. The countryside was a bit prettier here. The steep meadows were green, many of them deforested timberlands with stumps sticking up.

Vars Pass is a legitimate road and about what bike racers are used to in mountainous terrain. It was followed by a twisting, dangerous plunge down the other side to 4,000 feet. Then came a short, flat straight with a mountain torrent boiling white on one side of the road and the smell of pine in the air.

The strung-out pack started up to Restefond Pass which, at 9,200 feet, was the highest road in France and perhaps Europe. It had been opened only three years before, cutting, for any motorist brave enough to use it, nearly 100 miles off the drive from the Alps to the Riviera. It was not really a road. In places the pavement was about seven feet wide, a thin tarred surface disintegrating in spots. Even the good sections lay under loose gravel.

At first there were meadows with sheep grazing, and then fields that were blue or red with wildflowers. Too soon the road was above the timberline, and above that came the gray world where even grass did not grow. The racers leaned out over the handlebars, standing on their pedals, and the sweat poured off their faces.

Vars Pass had been steep. Restefond was steeper. There was no guardrail. The edge dropped away at sixty degrees or more. The Tour vehicles were in first gear, climbing steeply, carefully up the narrow ledge. The racers climbed carefully too. Also slowly, tortuously. Higher and higher.

Now there were steep banks of snow on the high side of the road and sometimes on the downhill side as well. One was ten feet high on both sides. Though the date was June 30, the race sliced through winter. The riders raked handfuls of snow off the wall as they passed. They rubbed snow on their faces, thrust it down inside their jerseys. Though it was old gray snow, some of them ate handful after handful.

Fans who had come up earlier had scrawled slogans into the gray snow. Enormous white letters read "*Vive Darrigade.*" And a bit further on "*Allez Poulidor.*"

There was nothing in Anquetil's name.

Poulidor came up in the first group. Anquetil was there too. Poor Darrigade, strictly a sprinter, was still ten minutes down the mountain.

The climb seemed endless and as high as the blazing blue sky. It was fifteen miles before at last the pass was there, widened into a parking lot, and 1,000 fans cheered as the riders came abreast of them, and then went over the edge.

The plunge down to the Mediterranean lasted 100 miles with only two shorter but still brutal climbs to mar the way. The bulk of the pack was many minutes behind the handful of men who were the leaders. After seven hours and twenty-seven minutes in the saddle, this small group rolled into the Monaco soccer stadium and looked around at the waiting crowd.

Anquetil was there, as was Poulidor. So was Tom Simpson of England, who won the Milan–San Remo classic that year. Simpson was an authentic sprinter and a future world road-racing champion. The stands were crowded. The racers began to lap the cinder running track. The finish line would come after one complete lap. No one was sprinting yet. The men were standing up on their pedals, moving easily, watching each other, jockeying for position.

I was rooting for Simpson, with whom I had spoken a good deal lately. He was 26 and had a wife and two daughters. He was funny, irreverent, always laughing. He butchered the French language but was funny in French too.

I did not think Anquetil would try to win. Sprints were dangerous. The running track was soft in places. He had just come seven and a half hours through the Alps and the Tour did not end here. He and it had fourteen more days to go. None of the men sprinting could threaten his overall control of the race. He did not need to exhaust himself any further today. He did not need any extra glory.

Suddenly the heads went down. The elbows came out. The final sprint began. It was Simpson leading, then Anquetil, then Simpson again. It was just those two side by side with everyone else several feet back. Simpson was no doubt the faster, but in force of will no one else was in Anquetil's class. Simpson had left a bit of speed behind him in the mountains and Anquetil did not intend to lose. At the finish line it was Anquetil by a nose. I could hardly believe my eyes.

Later, much later, the rest of the pack came into the stadium and there was a victory ceremony for Anquetil. And later still I wrote my story and cabled it to New York. I too had been taken up by the anti-Anquetil propaganda. I too thought he lacked panache, and, besides, my man had lost. So I ended with the line, "The real star of the day was Restefond Pass." But it wasn't.

The stadium in which Anquetil won that day is gone now,

replaced by a new one built, believe it or not, on top of offices, shops, a sports complex, and a four-level parking garage holding 1,700 cars. A stadium holding 20,000 people. The field is dirt on which real grass grows, but it's three flights up from the street. How's that for panache?

Simpson was said to have panache too. Three summers later, on the thirteenth day of the Tour near the summit of the terrible Mont Ventoux, he began to wobble, then to zigzag. Then he fell off his bike and died. He was 29. The autopsy disclosed stimulants in his bloodstream.

There were always doping scandals in bike racing. As Simpson had told one interviewer, "The public demands super performances of us that are possible no other way."

All the great riders dope themselves regularly, admitted Anquetil, and everyone knows it. Some riders took regular injections of caffeine, he said. He himself had once followed what he called a strychnine treatment; he did not describe it any further than that. Not long after Simpson's death he set a new world record for miles pedaled in an hour, but when he refused to submit to a doping test afterwards his record was disallowed.

With his money he had bought a mansion — some called it a château — near Rouen. He had bought land. He raised cattle. By the time he retired at 35 he owned vast fields of grain. The very next year Eddy Merckx, a Belgian ten years his junior, won the Tour. He too was to win five in all. Before long people were saying that Merckx was the greatest racer ever, that Anquetil would never have been able to stay with him, had never been in his class.

I am in Vichy. The weeklies are now on the newsstands, with Anquetil's photo on the cover of many of them. The *Paris Match* has devoted an entire issue to him. The reporters, like France itself it seems, have decided now that he had panache all along. And as I read the stories, which contain details of his domestic life with which I was previously not familiar, I am amazed that this realization took so long to sink in.

I was out this afternoon looking over the famous thermal springs here. One bubbles up in the center of town inside a glass house, filling what is almost a swimming pool. The air inside is humid, and people sit around fully dressed clutching plastic glasses, waiting until it is time for their next dose.

The many springs more or less surround the town. Some pour out of fountains. Some boil out of the ground at temperatures as high as 141 degrees. Some reek of sulphur or other odorous gases.

Last night I had dinner with Jean-Louis Bourdier, who is both a medical doctor and deputy mayor of this city of 25,000. The idea of "taking a cure" or "taking the baths" may sound old-fashioned, but people still do it, though not as many as in the past, which greatly worries Bourdier both as physician and politician. Most of his patients now are middle-aged women. That is, his clientele as it dies out is not being replaced. If nothing can be done to attract new people, then not only will the doctors here suffer, but so will shopkeepers and everyone else.

He was already a doctor and surgeon when he became interested in thermal medicine, he said. He did a year's extra study. His treatments depend as much on diet, rest, exercise, and a twenty-minute mud bath each morning as they do on drinking the water, which he prescribes in surprisingly small amounts, a typical treatment being the one he wrote out for me on the back of the menu: eighty grams from Parc spring before breakfast, fifty grams from Chomel spring at noon and again at 6:00 P.M., forty grams of Hôpital at 12:30 and 6:30. Eighty grams is less than an inch in the bottom of a glass. I received the impression that these waters react on the human system principally as a purge. He cautions his patients to drink no more than the dosage prescribed because the sometimes malodorous waters these particular springs provide is very strong — not at all the bottled Vichy one buys for the dinner table.

There are over 500 spas in Europe, over 150 in France, but in the old days, meaning pre–World War II, this was the one that drew the biggest, most well heeled crowds. Its very name conjured up thermal springs. But since 1940 it has conjured up something else entirely. We live in a world where image is everything. We attach labels to places as well as to people, and Vichy, like Anquetil, has been saddled with a label difficult to live with and impossible, or so it has seemed, to shed.

It was certainly a prosperous place once. It is a nineteenth-century town, quite beautiful with its handsome houses, big trees, and shady streets. Its parks and promenades are immaculately clean, full of gravel pathways lined with benches and iron chairs. There are smart shops, some of them with wood-paneled walls in the style of 1880. There is a small, rather charming casino, baroque rooms illuminated by chandeliers dripping with 500 pounds of crystal each.

In those days Vichy attracted high society from Paris and the other major cities and from the colonies in Africa and Asia as well. The people from the colonies, it is said, were all drunks. The natives did the work out there, and they had nothing to do but sip ratafia, or whatever, all day. They would come back to France for three months' home leave and spend half of it taking the cure at Vichy to clean out their systems. It worked. The effects were thought to be miraculous. An immense number of hotels were built.

It was the hotels that attracted the government in 1940 as France fell, just as it is the hotels that have brought the Tour de France here for one night most summers ever since. A lot of people had to be (and have to be) housed on short notice, not just government officials and their families but the foreign embassies as well, and Vichy had 5,000 or 15,000 hotel rooms — I have seen all sorts of numbers printed; in any case, a lot. Paris was occupied. France was divided into two zones, with Vichy as capital of the "unoccupied" one. Its hotels were taken over and the collaborationist government set up.

That was on July 1. On July 10 the National Assembly transferred all its powers to Marshal Pétain, the ex-hero of Verdun, who was well over 80 and in his dotage. Terrible decrees began to be promulgated in Pétain's name by the frightened men around him. The citizenship of people naturalized since 1927 was revoked. Jews were forbidden public office; later they were made to wear a yellow star; later still they were rounded up. Hundreds of thousands of other Frenchmen were deported to Germany as forced labor. Pétain met with Hitler. Prime Minister Pierre Laval, who was shot after the war, was photographed shaking hands with Hitler. Vichy France came to sound almost indistinguishable from Nazi Germany.

It is this stigma that Vichy has been trying to shake ever since. In November 1942 the Germans invaded the unoccupied zone and all pretense of independent government was over. But by then it was too late for Vichy's reputation.

I walked past some of the old hotels today. The Thermal housed the ministry of defense; justice and finance were at the Carlton; foreign affairs was at the Parc, as was Pétain himself; the Portugal was taken over by the Gestapo. Most of these places look somewhat shabby, and a number have dropped down in category, but they still function as hotels, even the Portugal, but not the Parc. Once Vichy's most elegant and splendid hotel, it has been converted into offices and apartments, presumably because after the war no Frenchman would stay there anymore. An organization dedicated to the rehabilitation of Pétain's name occupies his old office on the third floor.

An immense effort is under way to rehabilitate Vichy's name as well. "We spend a fortune on advertising," Dr. Bourdier said at dinner, "but all anyone can remember is 1940." Vichy would like to become known as a vacation town for young people, he said, and in truth it boasts splendid recreational facilities: opera house, theater, many cinemas, race track, golf course, tennis courts, squash courts, horseback-riding trails, archery range, a flying club at the airfield for pilots and sky divers. Some years ago the Allier was dammed below the town, creating a vast and rather beautiful lake for water-skiing and rowing and sailing regattas. There is even a downhill stone-and-concrete slalom course for kayak racing. Push a lever and you create the Colorado River. Imagine a bobsled run filled with white water. It is an engineering marvel and spectacular to behold, but a waste of money, it would seem to me, in terms of attracting tourists. Vichy's one major tennis tournament fails to attract name players. Its only major event is the Tour de France, during those years when it serves as finish line one night and starting line the next morning.

The Tour does not mind that the Hotel Parc is gone, nor that the other hotels have become run-down, for at some of its over-night stops, Briançon for one, accommodations are far worse. To the Tour, Vichy is fine, big enough for the racers to wander around in for an hour before bed, with enough telephone lines for the reporters, big enough for reporters and organizers alike to buy a drink and a decent meal.

The reporters who ride with the Tour are in most cases terribly overworked. They bound along in open cars, usually in full sunlight but sometimes in drizzling or pouring rain, for nearly 3,000 miles. Most of them do not get a day off during the twenty-two or twenty-three days the race lasts, unlike the riders, for whom a single day off some years may be scheduled. They do not get a proper lunch all that time, and they are not, like the riders, 25 years old. The mountain driving, as their cars skirt photographers' motorcycles, mechanics' trucks, and packs of wobbling bikes, with a sheer void on one side, can be extremely dangerous.

And each night they must write and phone in their stories. After the few stages each year when I would accompany the Tour, I would file a story approximately 700 words in length. Whereas most of them had to write at least three that long: the results of the day's stage, a profile of its winner, plus whatever sidebars their editors and readers might demand. Some of them wrote under several names, their own on the lead story and pen names on the rest, making it appear that their paper had sent more reporters than it actually had. Some wrote enough copy every night to fill an entire newspaper page, and after the writing they would be on the phone dictating for hours.

These were the men who wrote that Anquetil took no risks, that he pedaled like an insurance salesman, that he lacked panache.

Given the pressure under which they worked, they had little time to acquire or purvey gossip about any of their subjects, even a star like Anquetil, which perhaps explains why they felt about him as they did and why some of what I have been reading all week comes as a surprise. Sports figures in France are not film stars. They are not hounded by paparazzi or the sensationalist press. In any case, Anquetil was a private, proud young man. He deflected questions, told reporters little about himself.

He was married to a woman known in the bike-racing world as La Dame Blanche. Organizers and handlers did not like her. She often accompanied him to races and sometimes stayed with him throughout, moving on from hotel to hotel. In bike racing this was not done. Riders, like boxers or tenors, were supposed to be celibate. They were not supposed to leave their high notes in bedrooms. There were dark hints about this that never reached the public. When Anquetil lost it was her fault; she was a bad influence. Anquetil ignored them. Or rather, he listened long enough to reply, "Here's the program I would advise on the eve of a race: pheasant cooked with chestnuts, a bottle of champagne, and a woman." He seemed to drink more wine and champagne, even whiskey at times, than his handlers liked. He loved to play cards, particularly bridge, and would stay up nights into the small hours if he could find people to play with.

La Dame Blanche, Janine Boeda when he met her, was the wife of the doctor in Rouen who treated him once when he was sick. Evidently the baby-faced bike racer — he was 22 — caught her eye as he entered or left the consulting room. She went down to Nice as the Genoa-Nice road race finished there and ran into him again. She had platinum-blond hair and two children. They were married the next year. She claimed to be 29 at the time but looked older. Although Anquetil had won his first Tour he was not yet the champion he was to become. But his handlers had great hopes for him. As they saw it, La Dame Blanche had just killed off their meal ticket.

But Janine turned out to be the most devoted wife any bike racer could wish for. She would drive the car behind him hour after hour as he trained, would work the stopwatches during indoor races, would wait hours in velodromes for the day's stage to come in. After thirteen years of marriage they had a daughter, their only child.

Anquetil was 53 when he died, which would make her now at least 60. The funeral pictures reprinted in these magazines show her grieving, surrounded by middle-aged ex-riders: Poulidor, Darrigade, some others. She is now an old lady, and the pictures are not kind to her. She was alone at the end. For the previous three years Anquetil had been living with a much younger woman to whom he was not married and who had just given birth to a son, his first.

I stand at the top of the Puy de Dôme, at 4,800 feet the steepest of the extinct volcanoes of the Massif Central. From up here on a clear day one can see, it is said, one-eighth of France. But today — we are in November — I can see very little. It was raining down on the plain. Up here the rain has changed to snow.

The Puy de Dôme is perfect for the Tour, which takes place, of course, in summer. It represents not so much a lung-busting climb, for its altitude is moderate, as murder on a man's legs. The last two and a half miles climb at a pitch of twelve degrees, which is a steep slope indeed.

In the years when the Tour comes this way, the Puy de Dôme confronts the riders for hours before they get to it. Usually its summit is the day's finish line, meaning they must get to the top when already close to exhaustion. As they climb, the road spirals around the mountain so that, leaning out over their handlebars, they can see all the surrounding cities: Vichy, Clermont Ferrand, Le Puy. They can see halfway to Paris, the end of the race, only about 250 more miles due north.

The year that Anquetil tried to win his fifth Tour he came up this mountain with Poulidor head to head on the next to last day, and Poulidor beat him. Neither was fresh, but Poulidor was still in control of his bike, whereas Anquetil's smooth, limpid style was nowhere to be seen. He wobbled from side to side, could barely make the pedals go round. He had already won the Tour of Italy that year, a race every bit as long and grueling as this one, and there had been only two weeks off between races. He had now come twenty-one more days to these steep slopes, and he had nothing left, nothing at all, and Poulidor beat him. Poulidor finally beat him. Vast crowds lined both sides of the road, and all of France watched on television. Anquetil had been taken at last. The popular Poulidor was about to win his first Tour.

To interviewers who crowded around him Anquetil mumbled, "Never in my life have I suffered the way I suffered today."

Heads turned in the direction of Paris, as if the order of finish were visible from here. The next day in Paris Poulidor would win the Tour. All of France believed it. Poulidor believed it. Anquetil did not believe it. The next day he called on reserves from somewhere and after nearly 3,000 miles won by twenty-one seconds.

Earlier this year he was found to have stomach cancer. There were two terrible operations. He had delayed the first to be able to fulfill a contract; for the past eighteen summers he had provided expert television commentary during the Tour. He went into the hospital in August and came out and was more or less normal until fall. He told everyone he would beat this thing. After the second operation he knew better.

Many old riders went to see him. Poulidor sat beside his bed holding his hand. "I suffer," Anquetil told him. "It's worse than the Puy de Dôme."

It brought tears to Poulidor's eyes.

"I'm on the edge of the hole," Anquetil said. "I have one chance in a thousand."

Not even that. He died Nov. 18, 1987.

Paris One
THE BEST-LOVED LOVE STORY

Unlike other world capitals, Paris did not just happen. Most of what is most impressive and most beautiful about it was state ordered and state paid for, built according to the conceptions (or vague ideas) of a succession of heads of state: mostly kings or their consorts, sometimes emperors.

Thus, François I about 1525 razed the old Louvre, a fortress, and started the present one, a palace. He started the Tuileries too — the royal gardens were at first the royal stables. Henri IV ordered the Place des Vosges, which was to have identical buildings on all four sides; he wanted it called the Place Royale. His Queen built the Luxembourg Palace. The Palais Royal, with its theater, its eight courtyards, its great interior garden, was built by Cardinal Richelieu, the King's prime minister, and left to the King in his will.

Again and again royal personages launched their royal whims, which ought to have put a hex on this or any city, but somehow did not; the royal meddlers meddled well. The Invalides was conceived by Louis XIV, the Sun King, who was also responsible for the Place Vendôme and its original centerpiece, a gigantic statue of himself and his horse. Place Louis le Grand, he wanted it called, but the name did not stick. Neither did the statue, which was destroyed during the Revolution by the mob. Similarly, the Place de la Concorde, one of the most imaginative and beautiful uses of space in the world, was ordered up by the succeeding King, Louis XV, to be called Place Louis XV, of course, and surrounding a similar central statue of himself. At the Revolution this statue too was pulled down, and the name changed; in addition the guillotine was set up there. The Place de la Concorde, which today is crowded with traffic, became crowded with people cheering heads held aloft by the hair.

Statues have had a remarkably hard time in Paris. Louis XIV's Place Vendôme statue was replaced by a void. Later, Napoleon ordered a gigantic column constructed there with himself dressed as Caesar standing on top of it. This lasted until its creator went into exile at Elba, whereupon Caesar got yanked off the column, and Henri IV, by then 200 years safely dead, was installed in its stead; when Napoleon suddenly if briefly reappeared, Henri IV vanished. During later regimes two more statues went up and were toppled by the mob, the column too. Finally, under the Third Republic the column was restored, with a replica of the Napoleon/ Caesar statue standing on it, which is still there today.

Meanwhile, the center of the Place de la Concorde remained vacant while various ideas were rejected. Nobody wanted to keep replacing all these statues. Finally Louis-Philippe installed the present obelisk, a present from Egypt. Being thirty-three centuries old it was unlikely to stir political passions.

Louis XV also built the church that was to become under the Revolution the Temple of Fame — known today as the Pantheon. Having fallen ill, the King offered a bribe to God: cure me and I'll build you a church. The first Napoleon commissioned the Arc de Triomphe, and the Place de la Bastille, and much else; the second one, Napoleon III, between 1852 and 1870, with the help of his prefect Baron Haussmann, ordained the redesign of nothing less than all of Paris. On the Ile de la Cité alone 25,000 people were expropriated and their houses, most of what remained of medieval Paris, were razed. The slum problem, to Haussmann, was not a problem: he obliterated them, and his royal master concurred. In one slum district a barracks had to be constructed to house a force of 2,000 men to keep order. From the Place de l'Etoile, now the Place Charles de Gaulle, Haussmann sent forth seven new streets, making twelve in all. Elsewhere he had hills decapitated or leveled. The tree-lined *grands boulevards* came into existence, dislocating or trampling everybody and everything in their way. Their sidewalks were made enormously wide, permitting sidewalk cafés and street kiosks and room for thousands of strollers.

Even in our time the tradition continued. François Mitterrand, President of the Republic, commissioned the glass pyramid in the courtyard of the Louvre and the futuristic new opera house in the Place de la Bastille, and his name will be linked to those structures for generations to come. There were no riots, but the screams of outraged traditionalists were heard around the world.

About 60 percent of present-day Paris was built during the Haussmann/Napoleon III years. Rooftops had to resemble each other and were virtually all the same height. Facades were made uniform along entire streets, around entire squares — this idea, original with Henri IV at the time of the Place des Vosges, was pushed about as far as it would go.

The new Paris was more stately than ever. It offered innumerable vistas up streets and avenues, often ending in triumphal arches or monumental domes or else in public squares dominated by noble public buildings. The beauty of Paris was and is restrained, almost austere.

One other building went up during those years. Located at one of the city's busiest intersections, it was not in any way stately, not sober at all, but was instead huge, garish, extravagant. In the *Arabian Nights* sense it was perhaps even fabulous, meaning difficult to believe, designed as much to stupefy as to please. The letters across its facade read: ACADEMIE NATIONALE DE MUSIQUE. The building is known abroad as the Paris Opera, but locally these days as the Palais Garnier, in honor of Charles Garnier (1825–98), its architect. Certainly it was the crowning achievement of Prefect Haussman and Emperor Napoleon III, the crown jewel of the restructuring of Paris, and although it is today one of the most famous and most visited of the guidebook attractions, nonetheless it shattered then and shatters still the architectural symmetry of the city.

It came about because opera had become very big in France, as big as in Italy or Germany, perhaps bigger. French lyricism demanded a French-style opera house; the one was magnificent, so the other had to be too.

As often happened, and still happens, each time new public buildings are planned, every architect in the country was invited to submit designs; 171 did so, and in 1861 Garnier's was selected. He was 36 years old.

From the beginning the architect thought big. Napoleon III was the one he had to please, and emperors like bigness. And gaudy: emperors are not always known for good taste. Garnier's opera is the biggest theater in the world. Not that it seats the most — it doesn't nearly. It occupies the most space. Try to walk around it some day. The walk is long.

The opulence begins at the sidewalk, for the lampposts are bronze nymphs or nerieds — naked ladies in any case — holding lamps above their heads. The main entrance faces the Place de l'Opéra. An ordinary-size theater, Garnier reasoned, would look lost at the end of the broad Avenue de l'Opéra amidst all those other large buildings; so he designed one to hold its own, a kind of gigantic ruby set in a ring.

From the outside the building is so huge, so ostentatious that it startles. Inside, it startles no less. It is hard to think of art or architecture in there at all. The eye darts around and one thinks instead of money. This place is a monument to almost unimaginable amounts of money.

One cannot decide where to look first, whether down on the mosaic floors or up at ceilings as baroque as a Byzantine cathedral. There is marble everywhere. The foyer in which one stands, the grand staircase one climbs, all the columns, arches, and halls one can see — all seem built entirely of marble. And not just any marble. It occurs in a painter's palette of colors: white, gray, black, red, rose, ocher, green. Every quarry in France, it is said, was ransacked just to find all the colors, and each time I enter this building I am amazed by them. Who would have guessed that marble existed in so many?

Upstairs there is a grand ballroom and a bar and various other public rooms, all of them richly, ornately decorated. Opera goers were and are surrounded by satin and velvet, by paintings and mosaics, by gold leaf. There are vast frescoes and huge mirrors in frames, two of which are twenty-three feet high — how did they ever get such vast pieces of glass in here in one piece? There are dozens of niches in the walls, each containing the sculpted marble bust of some famous musician of the past, and they are good busts.

Not only has money been squandered, but so has space. The ballroom, which occupies the entire front of the building, is sixty yards long and is entered through doors two stories high. It is illuminated by ten chandeliers in two rows, and each of them must weigh half a ton.

Around the corner is the bar. It's not really a bar, merely a smaller ballroom used as a bar between acts. Other gorgeously appointed rooms and rotundas are only slightly smaller. They are connected by equally gorgeous halls, and they almost entirely surround the auditorium, which, if you will permit the analogy, is like the pit in a peach.

All this space is certainly not needed to attract audiences today; on the other hand, parcels of it can be and are rented out to firms for receptions and cocktail parties. My own Paris publisher hired one recently to celebrate publication of the autobiography of an aging ballerina. Since I happened to be in town that day, I was invited. Surrounded by admirers, the ballerina sat autographing her book, while a press agent and I, champagne glasses in hand, explored the otherwise empty building. "This place," she remarked before we had even reached the auditorium, "calls for a long dress."

The auditorium is as elegant and luxurious as the rest, but by opera standards small. It seats only about 2,000, not much more than half the capacity of the new opera house on the Place de la Bastille, or New York's Metropolitan; and some of the seats in the side boxes are, as the French phrase has it, *sans visibilité*. Patrons must stand, lean far forward, and crane their necks to see anything of the stage at all. At orchestra level there are only thirteen rows of chairs, with eight more rows to the rear on a slightly elevated dais. The chairs are red velvet and very plush. Above, supported by the inevitable marble pillars, rise the boxes, four tiers of horseshoe-shaped balconies with gold leaf fronts. The ceiling is a single vast painting by Marc Chagall in yellows, blues, greens, and reds, allegorical figures floating disembodied in space — a bright painting, modern, distinctly of our time. The chandelier that hangs from the middle is said to weigh seven tons. It fell one night in the last century and killed a woman, and that was a surprise. One would have thought it would kill fifty.

This was never a very practical opera house. The backstage area is scarcely roomier than the auditorium. There is almost no storage space for scenery. For more than 100 years entire productions have had to be trucked back and forth to warehouses across the town, which did them little good. Nor was there ever sufficient rehearsal space.

The golden age of French opera. The most popular opera of all time is French: *Carmen*. And Gounod's *Faust*, first staged in 1859, is probably in the top five. In New York in the repertory of the Metropolitan Opera it ranks fourth in performances after *Carmen*, *Aïda*, and *La Bohème*.

During the years that the Palais Garnier was conceived, built, and first used, nearly all that was new in opera came out of Paris, and French composers — Bizet, Saint-Saëns, Massenet, Offenbach, Delibes, Lalo — dominated the operatic thought of the world. *Carmen* appeared in 1875, *Samson et Dalila* in 1877, *Les Contes d'Hoffmann* and *Hérodiade* in 1881, *Lakmé* in 1883, *Manon* in 1884, *Le Cid* in 1885, *Le Roi d'Ys* in 1888, *Werther* in 1892. This is to mention only those operas still performed outside of France. During this same period Wagner produced only *Parsifal* (1882), Verdi only *Otello* (1887). Italian *verismo* composers so popular today did not come into prominence until later than that; *Manon Lescaut*, the first of Puccini's successful operas, was first produced in 1893.

Garnier's opulent auditorium was and is a perfect setting for the French operatic tradition, and at times in this hall I have imagined that 100 years of French music, some of it heard here for the first time, still hung above me under the vast dome.

And yet very few of the best-known French operas were premiered in this house. Many of them were not heard here in their own time at all, and some have not bęen heard to this day. Even *Carmen* had to wait until 1959, except for two galas, one in 1900 (the second act only) and the other in 1907 (the entire opera). This was because France had two operatic traditions, not one, and though equally successful, they were considered separate: there was l'Opéra, and then there was l'Opéra-Comique. The first was devoted to grand opera in the heaviest imaginable sense; works were four or more hours long, usually ended tragically, and were filled with spectacle, including the mandatory ballet. Even Verdi's *Otello* had to have a ballet before it could be put on here. The old man — he was nearing 80 — must have wanted the production very much, for he sat down and wrote a ballet for Paris that is rarely or never performed elsewhere.

The Opéra was also exclusive. It liked to feature works by foreign composers: Mozart, Rossini, Donizetti, and Weber in the early decades of the nineteenth century, after which it discovered Jacob Meyerbeer, the German who dominated its repertory for the next fifty years. Whatever was foreign was best; something of the same spirit survives to this day, and this has always surprised me, for the French seem so intensely chauvinistic in everything else. However, all those foreign operas had to be translated into French first, of course, and until fairly recently it was in French that the French singers sang them.

French composers seem to have had a tough job breaking in, though Halévy made it with *La Juive* beginning in 1835, and Gounod with *Mireille* in 1864. *Mireille* was such a success that in 1869 the management, having declined Gounod's brand-new *Romeo et Juliette* in the interim (it was forced to open at the Théâtre Lyrique), agreed to restage his *Faust,* which had been a flop at the Lyrique ten years before; *Faust*'s worldwide popularity dates from then. The managers of the Opéra could make or break careers, and knew it, and were choosy. Saint-Saëns' *Samson et Dalila* premiered in Weimar and did not reach the Opéra until thirteen years later.

The Opéra-Comique was six or seven blocks away, fronting onto a delightful little square. The present theater, dating from 1898 and known as the Salle Favart, is elegant and ornate as well, though of course much smaller, seating only about 1,400. The

Opéra-Comique was founded in 1715 to present light musical entertainment. As it evolved over the next 130 years, its shows came to resemble certain of the American musical comedies of the 1930s. Characterization was virtually nonexistent. Plots were mostly froth, often based on mistaken identity or on babies mixed up at birth. Endings were happy. There were pages and pages of spoken dialogue, but all big scenes and climaxes were sung.

The songs, often quite florid, did demand accomplished singers. Usually there were only two important characters, soprano and tenor. The soprano had to be a "première chanteuse de roulades," what is today called a coloratura; she had to be an acrobatic singer. So did the tenor, described as a "tenor léger," whose music not only lay very high, but also was as full of runs and trills as hers. It was similar to the music sung by the castrated male sopranos of the past. The *castrati* were gone by now, but audiences still wished to hear men who could sing like boys, and Opéra-Comique tenors had to learn to do it. Arias sometimes soared to high D, an altitude few tenor voices can reach. The solution, obviously, was to float such music out of the head in falsetto. Since orchestras were still small, the falsetto voice could easily be heard. There is just such an aria, "Assis au pied d'un hêtre," in Adolphe Adam's *Le Postillon de Longjumeau* (1836), the only one of these *opéras-comiques* still reasonably accessible, at least in recordings. Adam, who also wrote the ballet *Giselle,* was the rage of the Opéra-Comique. He wrote nearly fifty operas in twenty-two years. He died at 52 in 1856.

But in the latter half of the nineteenth century, France's golden age, opera changed. Orchestras got bigger. Singers had to sing full-voiced to be heard at all. A Frenchman, Gilbert-Louis Duprez, was apparently the first tenor ever to sing a full-voiced high C. It was a sound audiences loved instantly. Overnight falsetto singing and head tones became passé. Meanwhile, a new Paris theater, Offenbach's Bouffes Parisiennes, had begun to present musical farces and satires; patrons in search of triviality and silliness went there, not to the Opéra-Comique.

So Opéra-Comique got more realistic and more serious, even tragic, even somewhat sordid — which is the adjective early critics applied to *Carmen,* whose tenor, Don José, is not a king or general but a corporal. He deserts, becomes a smuggler, murders Carmen. Carmen herself works in a cigarette factory, knifes another girl, throws herself at a bullfighter, is little better than a harlot. Critics and public were scandalized. *Carmen* was not, however, a flop. It was played thirty-seven times the first season and was carried over into the next season's repertory. By then audiences were beginning to get over its sensual characters and lurid story and were enchanted by the music.

There was still some spoken dialogue in *Carmen,* not much, and in the famous operas that followed there was less and less, until finally there was none. By 1890 l'Opéra and l'Opéra-Comique were virtually indistinguishable except for the snobbism — and perhaps the money. The Opéra-Comique, though less prestigious and with a smaller house, may have paid more. Certainly Jules Massenet (1842–1912), the most popular composer of all time in France, must have been in a position to force his works into the Opéra, had he so wished. But he did not usually do so. Only seven of his approximately thirty operas premiered there. Mostly he preferred the Opéra-Comique, which paid him 12 percent of box-office receipts each time one of them was performed. The most profitable was of course *Manon.*

L'Histoire du Chevalier Des Grieux et de Manon Lescaut, possibly the best-loved love story in French literature and one of the most enduring in any literature, began life in 1731 as a short novel, only 50,000 words, by a defrocked priest known as the Abbé Prevost. It was for its time a salacious story and it was by a salacious man, which may have accounted in part for its immediate success. His purpose in publishing it, wrote Prevost piously, was to warn readers away from uncontrollable passion by showing where it could lead.

Antoine François Prevost (1697–1763) was born into a solid bourgeois family, was educated by Jesuits, entered the army, was charged with bigamy, and fled to Holland. He returned to France, entered a Benedictine monastery, and stayed seven years, but left without being released from his vows, which was at least a civil offense at the time and perhaps a criminal one. He appears to have been a part-time swindler and con man, a frequenter of immoral

women, a debtor, perhaps a forger as well, for he spent most of
the rest of his life either on the run or in jail. He wrote about fifty
novels, only one of them still famous today, the one that led during
the next 160 years to all the varying stage versions of *Manon,* or
Manon Lescaut, or *The Maid of Artois* — five operas and a ballet so
far, by Halévy and Scribe, by Auber and Scribe, by Balfe, by
Massenet with Henri Meilhac and Philippe Gille, and by Puccini
with a whole troupe of librettists. Finally, Massenet himself, unable to keep his hands off perfection, added later in life a one-act
opera called *Le Portrait de Manon.*

Prevost's novel is written entirely from the point of view of
Des Grieux, the young nobleman who is ruined by his passion
for the beautiful but poor and flighty Manon. When Prevost's
story opens they are aged 17 and 15, respectively. They meet at
a country stage stop; he is on his way home, she is about to be
put into a convent by her family because she is "too fond of
pleasure." They run away to Paris together. His father cuts him
off. He becomes a card sharp, a thief, and finally, to free Manon
from jail, a murderer. Manon, who loves only pleasure and luxury,
becomes a cheat and thief herself, not to mention the kept woman
of a succession of rich old men. From beginning to end no matter
what she does Des Grieux's passion for her never flags. Manon
loves him too, in her fashion.

In Prevost's novel the two characters are of equal importance.
Not so in the stage versions that followed, which first softened
the sharp edges of the original story and then focused mostly on
Manon. This is particularly true in Massenet, who gives Manon
five arias to sing and Des Grieux only two. Her music dominates,
or seems to dominate, the love duets as well. When the opera had
what may have been its definitive production of this century at
the New York City Opera some years ago, the role was sung by
Beverly Sills, and it made her an international superstar overnight;
it did nothing much for the American tenor Michele Molese, who
sang Des Grieux, even though his performance was quite as brilliant as hers.

Very few composers of the day could live off their music. Massenet could. He conducted all his own business and his operas

made him, by the standards of the late nineteenth century in France, rich. Yet he did not behave as a rich composer might. Rather, he was the consummate professional musician, and though success followed success, he was at his desk each morning by five o'clock in summer, six in winter. He not only worked day after day, year after year, no matter where he was or how he was feeling (or how anyone around him was feeling), no matter what else sought to occupy his mind, time, or emotions; but also he spent most afternoons either at the theater or at the conservatory, where from 1878 to 1896 — at the height of his fame, at the height also of demands on him — he served as professor of counterpoint, fugue, and composition to almost an entire generation of French musicians.

Apparently he was a bland kind of man. He once broke down in tears when a rehearsal went badly, but ordinarily there were never any tantrums. As a teacher he never tried to force students to write like Massenet; instead he encouraged each to find his own voice. He had an eye for the ladies, especially two sopranos. He wrote operas for them and forced them on impresarios, but it is possible that these relationships were platonic. Possibly he remained faithful to Mme Massenet. He was not witty. He never offered biting or malicious comments at soirées or dinners. Delicious repartee was unknown to him. Instead, upon entering a room he would seek to praise or flatter everyone in it to whom he was presented. His autobiography, though written by another, does the same and is not very interesting. In places it seems inaccurate as well, as if he had never bothered to read it.

Some of Massenet's operas in whole or in part are as bland as the man himself appears to have been, or at least they have sometimes seemed so. Certain critics, resenting the immense success of even his lesser works, have disparaged him and them. He was sweet, he was saccharine. He was called "Mademoiselle Wagner" or "the daughter of Gounod" at times. But there is some genius in everything he wrote, and *Werther* is certainly very fine, and no one ever knocked *Manon,* which is a perfect opera in the same way that *Otello* is perfect, or *La Bohème.* It is the story of a desperate love, and there is not a wasted word or note in it. "I would give the whole of Bach's *Brandenburg Concertos* for

Massenet's *Manon* and would think I had vastly profited by the exchange," Sir Thomas Beecham, the most admired British conductor of this century, once wrote.

Though later he was to share billing with Gille, the principal librettist of *Manon* was Meilhac (1831–97), who was one of the most successful men of the theater of his own or any other time or country. In the forty-one years of his active professional life, he wrote perhaps 200 pieces, perhaps more, sometimes alone, more often with one or more collaborators: vaudevilles, comedies, operettas, ballets, musicals, plays, and of course operas. In 1875 he had four shows produced, one of them Bizet's *Carmen,* and in 1884, the year of *Manon,* he had seven. He must have written with lightning speed. In addition to *Carmen* and *Manon,* he wrote the librettos to *Kassya* by Delibes, and to eleven of Offenbach's operettas, including all the most famous ones: *La Périchole, La Belle Hélène, La Vie Parisienne, La Grande Duchesse de Gerolstein.* He wrote the librettos to many other operas by composers who are forgotten now: Jules Cohen, Grandval, Deffes, Lecocq, Planquette, Salvayre. He was evidently a very funny fellow and writer, and his comedies were regularly performed at the Comédie-Française; one of them was later turned into *The Merry Widow* by Franz Lehar. In 1888, when he was 57, he became a member of the Académie Française, one of the so-called forty immortals, the highest honor possible for a French literary man.

He wrote with a dozen or more collaborators, sometimes with several simultaneously on different projects, but his favorite from 1861 to 1881 was Ludovic Halévy. It was with Halévy that he wrote ten of his eleven Offenbach shows and *Carmen* and much else, but the partnership broke up after twenty years. Halévy began to write novels. Meilhac stayed on in the theater, and at first he was alone.

It was at this point that the impresario of the Opéra-Comique proposed that he and Massenet do an opera together based on a story called "Phoebe." Meilhac, who was eleven years Massenet's senior and every bit as successful, perhaps more so, seems to have handed over a script that Massenet didn't like.

In confrontations, Massenet was not at ease. They were sitting in Meilhac's library. How to break the news to the dramatist?

Suddenly Massenet caught sight of the Prevost novel on the shelf over Meilhac's desk. "Let's do *Manon* instead," he found himself saying. When the two men met for lunch the next day, according to his autobiography, Massenet found the first two acts under his napkin.

There is some doubt among scholars that this is the way it happened. The first two acts could not have come into existence overnight; Meilhac was fast, but not that fast. Perhaps it was not two acts but only an outline. Or had Meilhac already started on a *Manon* as a straight play or as an opera for another composer? Did he give it to Massenet instead? If so, was it for the money or the prestige or perhaps just for the fun of working on an opera with Massenet? Was he perhaps even thinking of posthumous fame, knowing that a *Manon* with Massenet would still be filling theaters 100, perhaps 1,000 years later, when all his plays would long since have disappeared?

It is amazing that details such as this, so important in the history of the musical theater, could be so totally lost in not much more than a century. But a good many other details have been lost too, chief among them the personality and fame of Meilhac. The dramatist over the years has got precious little credit for *Manon* or for *Carmen* either. Most operatic reference works barely mention his name. The best that anyone seems willing to concede is that he "inspired" Massenet. As in: "Inspired by Meilhac, Massenet surpassed himself." Indeed he did.

Obviously *Manon* was a collaboration, and it may be impossible now ever to know who contributed what. But it all began with Meilhac. He was the one who decided what to keep of Prevost's story and what to discard and what scenes to invent. He was even the one who brought in Gille after Massenet had begun composing, to make whatever small changes the musical phrases might require, while Meilhac went on to something else. *Manon* is written in rhymed verse, and as poetry its lines are so akin to those of *Carmen* (written with a different collaborator) that one tends to credit Meilhac with all that is best in both.

What seems sure is that Meilhac's libretto somehow touched Massenet, who thereupon conceived the notion of building the score around motifs, one for each character except for Manon, whom he saw as a "mixture of sadness and gaiety," as he wrote, who gets two. "These motifs run the length and breadth of the opera and are reproduced from act to act, shading off or coming into prominence, like the play of light in a picture, according to the situations. In this way my characters keep their personalities distinct until the end." Yes, and he also wrote for them all, not just for Manon and Des Grieux, one hit tune after another.

Massenet began work in the autumn of 1881 in Holland. A wealthy Dutch opera lover had invited the great man to the Hague after promising to install him in a room once occupied by Prevost himself. Massenet appears to have started writing at the St.-Sulpice scene, which is Act III, and as he wrote he slept every night in Prevost's very bed. The writing continued in Brussels, where he conducted the premier of his opera *Hérodiade* on December 19, and in Hamburg and in Nantes after that, and then he was back in Paris again.

The Manon of the Meilhac/Massenet version has become a beautiful, winsome young girl, charming, entirely fascinating, though a bit empty-headed. She is no longer a thief or cheat, nor is she particularly wanton. She loves Des Grieux the best, but cannot resist luxury. All men find her beautiful, and she revels in this, and since she is young enough to imagine that her allure will last forever, her downfall when it comes is all the more tragic.

As for Des Grieux, he is young too, and head over heels in love with her. When she throws him over because he cannot give her the clothes and jewels she craves, he becomes a priest: "I want to put God between the world and me," he sings, but he cannot forget Manon and this fugitive sentiment is followed by one of the great tenor arias in all of opera, "*Ah fuyez, douce image . . .*"

But Manon, when she finds out where her ex-lover is, goes straight to St. Sulpice seminary to get him out: "He does not have the right to forget Manon." And there she seduces him before our eyes, her hands all over his cassock as she sings, "Is this not still my hand, is this not still my voice, am I not still Manon?" Until finally Des Grieux breaks down: "Manon, I can no longer struggle against myself. My life is in your heart, my life is in your eyes. Come, Manon, I love you."

In the opera Des Grieux is no thief or cheat either, and certainly not a murderer. When in the end Manon is to be deported as an immoral woman, he bribes her jailers to release her. Sick and haggard, she dies in his arms while begging him to forgive her for all the grief she has caused him. But there is nothing to forgive, he sings. There are few passions like his in all of opera, or even in literature, though it is a phenomenon that occurs often enough in real life.

The entrance to the Bibliothèque de l'Opéra, one of the more unusual of the world's libraries, is on the Rue Scribe side, about halfway along, in what is almost a separate building, though glued to the opera's wall. Its portico supported by columns, its windows and doorways heavily decorated in stone, it is huge and gorgeous in its own right. Its dome is higher than the main roof of the Opéra itself, though not as high as the Opéra's own dome, of course. This incredibly ornate appendage to the building was meant to serve only as the emperor's carriage entrance. Semicircular cobblestone ramps form a parenthesis leading up to it from both sides from the sidewalk. They rise between balustrades, pass under archways, and join each other inside the building one flight up from the street.

In the preparation of this study I visited a good many libraries both in France and America before coming to this one, hoping to find answers to my more persistent questions over the years — about Massenet, about Meilhac, about the opera itself. *Manon* is a work of extraordinary control and immense power. As far as Massenet is concerned, where did such control, such power, come from? What was different about his life as he wrote *Manon?* Was it Meilhac? Who was Meilhac? I had not found any answers previously. If the Bibliothèque de l'Opéra did not have them, there was nowhere else I could think of to look.

Lacking a carriage, I go up the ramp on foot to the point where the Emperor would have descended from his imperial coach. He was meant to step through a huge and rather florid rotunda — which would serve as his private bar between acts — and then along a hall and into his box, where he would salute the audience. As soon as he had sat down, the performance could start. However, this ritual was never observed. Long before the building ever opened, His Majesty was out on his royal ass.

Today the rotunda seems less florid than the Emperor would have found it. The library occupies almost all of it and looks well used. The shelves line the curved outer walls. The reading tables, busy with scholars bent over old scores, occupy most of the parquet floor under the high dome and under still another central chandelier massive enough if it fell to flatten most of them.

Here in the Bibliothèque de l'Opéra is most of what is left of the French operatic past, and especially of its golden age: manuscripts, photographs, monographs, books — even ledgers showing box-office receipts. Best of all, here are hundreds of original scores by Massenet, Gounod, Saint-Saëns, Berlioz, and all the rest, and although some are fragile and off limits, others can be examined.

I fill out the card requesting Massenet's handwritten *Manon* score and sit down to wait. Presently it is brought to me: five rather thick leather-bound volumes. I begin to leaf through the first one, noting the composer's crabbed handwriting but unable to concentrate on it, for my head has filled up with his tunes on the page. It seems to me a special experience; I am half overcome by awe.

But soon I feel a bit disappointed as well. This is not the early draft I was hoping for. Massenet was a writer like me, and I was hoping to see his false starts, mistakes, corrections.

His other scores on the shelves, I find when I look, are not early drafts either. Massenet did not show such drafts, it seems. It may be that he did not really write them either; that is, he appears to have been a composer who did not correct very much. I have been told that Mozart's manuscripts are much the same, whereas Beethoven's are so heavily corrected as to be almost impossible to read.

So there is no Massenet manuscript to study that might somewhat resemble what I am looking for. In the five thick volumes on the table in front of me, the final orchestration of *Manon,* there are almost no corrections to be found, apart from one or two places where he has neatly pasted part of a page — a few bars scissored out of a virgin piece of music paper — on top of what he had originally written.

I have read that when each new score was finished he would have it printed and bound, would add some flattering inscription, and then would present it to whatever impresario he happened to be wooing, together with instructions as to how he wanted the show produced. Most impresarios of the time considered themselves qualified to tamper with scores, with lyrics, with whole scenes. All the composers complained of it in all the countries. With *Mireille,* Gounod was obliged to remove the death scene and substitute a happy ending. The letters he wrote about it sound like he was in tears.

Massenet, being so popular, was stronger than that. The leather-bound score presented to the impresario informed one and all that this score was fixed. The edifice was standing. Nothing could or would be changed.

After that, even when productions took place in other capitals, Massenet oversaw every detail. It would be the composer himself at the piano for the cast run-through. He would decide even what jewelry would adorn the soprano's costumes. He would never attend opening night, however, but would pace up and down in the street outside, even sometimes in the snow.

For most of a century scholars have pored over his scores looking for hints as to who he was, how he worked, what he felt, imagining as I have that they could learn something from his corrections, and from the notes he scrawled most days in the margins, for he used his working scores almost as diaries. And as I peruse the *Manon* score now I am annoyed at my own presumption. I have come here today supposing that all those scholars, not understanding how a writer's mind works (a composer being no more than a different kind of writer), might have missed something. Instead, just like them, I find virtually no corrections to extrapolate from; and although the diary notes are there in the margins in Massenet's handwriting, they are sometimes illegible and at best don't tell very much — "Paris, five A.M., hot" being a typical entry. In fact the *Manon* score reveals almost nothing about the man, except for what I may be able — no pun intended — to read between the lines:

— That he did his day's stint and then at whatever point he happened to be, stopped. When writing *Manon* he stopped right in the middle of the great third-act tenor aria and then calmly started up again the next day. Of course the second part of the aria only mirrors the first, and he knew exactly what came next.

— That the day of the week meant nothing to him, for he worked Saturdays, Sundays, and holidays without distinction. He got impatient if something broke his concentration. For instance, he worked on these pages here on July 14, 1883, which was not only the national holiday but a Saturday, starting at 6:00 A.M. ("air pure," he wrote in the margin) but breaking off sometime during the day, only to return to his desk in the evening. "I hear all the military musicians returning from the 14th of July review," he wrote in the margin seven pages into the day's stint. "What noise . . . for nothing." In all he wrote fourteen pages that day, then was back at his desk at 6:00 A.M. the next day, which was Sunday.

— That the closer he got to the end of an act, the faster he worked and the more days he went without a day off. But then this is true of nearly every writer in whatever form. Concentration becomes total. The work becomes more real than life. One is almost in a trance. It is as if someone else is setting the notes down, perhaps God.

All in all my picture of Massenet remains nearly as bland as before, so I turn to the second part of my quest: Meilhac. As an art form, music is intellectual, almost mathematic. The emotion is not in the music but in the words. It is the words, Toscanini once said, that make you cry. I expect to find Meilhac manuscripts here, perhaps *Manon,* perhaps *Carmen,* why not? And perhaps a biography, certainly a profile of some kind. The man was after all one of the giants of his age.

But my disappointment is even greater. The card index barely makes mention of Henri Meilhac. I ask one of the curators for help, for the filing systems in libraries can be incomprehensible at times; but she can find nothing significant either: two studies of his work by contemporary critics turn up, nothing more. I begin to search through the shelves hoping to stumble on something. At length I do. In an encyclopedia published in Tours about 1900, I find his enormously long bibliography and beside it his photo.

He was a heavy-set fellow, bald on top, and he wore a mustache and a goatee. But a man's photo doesn't tell much about him, and his bibliography tells little more.

That's all there is. I can find nothing about his likes or dislikes, his work habits, his family. I can find none of his scripts. Some of this material might be there somewhere, if not in this library then in another, but I can't find it.

So I turn to the two critical studies of his work. How strange that a man of such accomplishments should be represented in the archives only by his critics. One of these critiques was published in 1893; the other, undated, about 1896. The first, by a man named Hippolyte Parigot, is unkind enough. Once, Parigot writes, Meilhac had touched a nerve, had made all Paris laugh, but times were more serious now, public taste had changed, and Meilhac's brand of comedy no longer amused. Meilhac, although still active as the critique was written, was to Parigot a has-been.

The second critic, Jules Hûret, speaks of Meilhac's "lamentable puerility, the irremediable dreariness of his burlesque inventions, which for some reason people found funny . . . but given a change in public taste, his work had neither the strength, nor sincerity, nor the acuity of observation that distinguishes major talent . . . his characterizations are so thin that they have now irremediably faded."

Admitting that for forty years Meilhac "had known how, with the complicity of critics, to make people laugh, to impose on public taste his own sense of reality," the critic comes at last to Froufrou, one of Meilhac's most popular comedies, which he dismisses as "an inexplicable parasitic accident with its almost sincere emotion and its infantile psychological incoherences." Meilhac was still alive to read and be pained by this. Carmen and Manon are not even mentioned.

All of which tells me nothing about Meilhac that I had been anxious to know, and the dramatist, had he watched me a century later reading these critical estimates of him, unable to find anything else, would have been mortified. There is a moral in this, I suppose. A career, as they say, is not over until it's over, critics could be on occasion just as vicious then as now, and for all Meilhac's successes and renown, life had not been perfect for him either.

Paris Two
THE GESTAPO OF THE RUE LAURISTON

The trial of Pierre Bonny and Henri Lafont lasted from Dec. 1 to 12, 1944, and two weeks later they were tied to posts and shot, not the last of the *épuration* then shaking France like the ague, but a milestone. *Epuration* means purification, as any dictionary will tell you, but in newly liberated Paris, and in newly liberated France, it meant purge, bloodletting, the settling of accounts. The occupation had lasted four years. People were angry. Legally, quasi-legally, and illegally, perhaps as many as 200,000 accounts got settled in a few months. The exact number no one will ever know.

Lafont was 42 years old at his death, Bonny 49. They were an unlikely pair. Lafont was the more charismatic, Bonny the shrewder. Lafont's fingerprints always showed, Bonny's rarely. Lafont was a career criminal who had lived mostly in jails from the age of 16. Bonny had been in jail too, but he was by profession a policeman — he had once been known as France's number-one cop. In occupied Paris Lafont flaunted his wealth, his power, his connections; whereas Bonny's lifestyle hardly changed. It was as if he were still a detective, nose to the grindstone, just getting by.

In Bonny's past there was much to be proud of. Only 19 at the start of World War I, he served in the trenches under fire, was decorated for valor, and was promoted to corporal. Taken prisoner in 1916, he made two escapes but was recaptured. He was being moved deeper into Germany when, during a halt, he went under the train and off into the trees, after which he walked twenty-four straight nights towards the frontier, hiding in hayricks in the daytime, living off whatever fruits and vegetables he could find or steal.

After the Armistice, he passed the test for detective in the Sûreté National. He was never a uniformed patrolman. In France it is considered that detectives and patrolmen are not the same, that different talents are required. Men coming off the street take the test for one branch or the other.

Thereafter Bonny was attached to Sûreté headquarters on the Rue des Sussaies; he lived in Paris and filed reports there but, like all Sûreté detectives, had jurisdiction over the provinces only, for Paris had its own police force. The Paris force, about 15,000 men, was closer to the national newspapers than the Sûreté, closer to the politicians too, and so got much more publicity, had much more political clout. Though the Sûreté had double or more the number of men, it was considered the lesser service. Its detectives could solve complex crimes in the provinces, but unless some scandal was attached, no one heard about it or them. Lesser Paris cases, meanwhile, got headlines. The rivalry between the two services was intense. They competed for funding, for prestige, usually refused to cooperate, and sometimes sought to discredit each other.

Nonetheless, the Sûreté was a proud name in Bonny's day and afterwards; but in 1969 it ceased to exist, as did the Paris force, and the two were combined into the Police National, a single agency of over 100,000 men which, with help from the Gendarmerie, polices the entire country. The Gendarmerie is a branch of the army. It functions only in communes of less than 10,000 population; it had and has little political clout at all. Nor do the handful of other police agencies: customs, border police, et al.

At the time of which I write, detectives attached like Bonny to Sûreté headquarters were sent into the provinces to give aid or direction to local detachments whenever important crimes occurred. During Bonny's early years a good many such crimes were economic in nature, or had an economic basis, because France, which was still cut in two by a vast zone of shell holes and corpses, was also still studded with warehouses crammed with American Expeditionary Force materiel, which the American army had simply sailed away from. These warehouses attracted swindlers and thieves. They provided Sûreté detectives with many investigations, and also with the possibility of payoffs.

In Paris Bonny lived at 2, Rue du Théâtre across the street from the Citroën factory. His apartment consisted of two rooms. He and his wife had the bedroom, and in the second room, which counted as dining room–living room–kitchen, lived his son and his mother, who slept on divans. The kitchen sink was the family bathtub. There was cold water only. There was no toilet, only a kind of outhouse down in the courtyard. Inside was a shallow basin in the floor. It had two cleated footrests and a hole in the middle. This standup toilet served the entire building. In Paris between the two wars, such an apartment was what a man on a detective's pay could afford. Like most cops everywhere, Bonny was short of money; like many of them, he was perpetually on the lookout for windfalls.

He was tall for a Frenchman, with an elegant build. He wore a small mustache. He liked smart clothes and was known to colleagues as the Boulevardier. They considered him a funny fellow and at weddings and banquets often urged him to perform a skit of his own invention imitating Caruso and mocking grand opera.

Bonny's informants were the envy of the Sûreté. A detective is only as good as his informants. He must find them, nurture them, convince them to trust him, teach them to cooperate. It takes determination, and endless time. He must protect them from arrest by his colleagues and from assassination by their own. Bonny understood this early.

He understood the underworld as well, the so-called *milieu,* Corsicans mostly. What were the allegiances? Who controlled whom? Bonny became a student of crime. When a big one was committed, he knew where to go for answers, whom to lean on.

At some point he got mixed up with politicians, especially the most venal and corrupt among them. He learned who had power and how much. But he appeared not to learn, or to learn too late, what is apparent to many detectives at once: that to "own" a politician is not necessarily wise, because at the same time you own him he also owns you.

Bonny began to catch and to break important cases. When on an investigation he devoted every waking moment to it. He was relentless. Nothing, once he was close, could make him stop. He began to get his name in the papers and even was awarded the Silver Medal, one of the most important Sûreté decorations. In addition he won bonuses for breaking big cases, a Sûreté tradition. But the bonuses were never as great as he hoped.

He was promoted to the next rank up, *inspecteur principal.*

There were occasional allegations of misconduct. It was charged that he liked to drive through the Bois de Boulogne at night trying to catch couples "in full adultery," as the French phrase has it. Together with another young detective, who was also accused, he would bundle the half-undressed couple into his unmarked car and then, according to the allegation, begin whining about how little he got paid, how he needed tonight's arrest bonus just to live. Finally the victims would get the hint, and money would change hands. The adulterers would jump out and bolt for the nearest metro. Most detectives in most countries collect allegations, which in themselves prove nothing. Indeed, most are completely unfounded, and perhaps these were. The offense might never have happened. The offending detective might have been someone else.

Later allegations were of a political cast. Once he was accused of intercepting the American mistress of an important married politician as she arrived by ship and planting on her a sachet or two of cocaine, which customs found. The woman chose to go back to America rather than jail, which was the point of the exercise, and the boudoir scandal that might have brought down the politician, and perhaps the government, was averted. This happened, if it happened, about 1924.

Before long it was clear that Bonny, a lowly *inspecteur,* had access to high reaches of government. As he saw it, he had acquired important friends — except that they weren't friends, and they began to be afraid of him.

In 1928 he was accused of arranging for an Austrian named Volberg to avoid being deported, for which he was said to have accepted a suit and an overcoat. For an extra sum he offered to procure for Volberg an identity card, according to the allegation. Bonny went on trial before the Sûreté's Council of Discipline, but when no trace of the suit or coat or money could be found, he was acquitted.

Bonny charged that he had been set up by his political opponents. He did not name them, and there were no countercharges. Everyone fell silent.

He took the exam for promotion to *commissaire* three times, the maximum allowed, and failed it three times, meaning that *inspecteur principal,* the equivalent perhaps of sergeant, was as high as he would go. After the third failure he charged that his scores were altered by right-wing commanders who hated him because he believed in the politics of the left. Bonny was becoming a militant, even virulent, socialist, or at least so he pretended.

The commanders, who did not like to hear such charges, for the moment waited.

In 1934 came the Stavisky-Prince case. Stavisky was a big-time swindler, the biggest; and Prince was the magistrate who investigated him. Stavisky contributed money to politicians' campaign funds, gave them presents, invited them to fabulous banquets and balls. He gave them stock in certain of his swindles, then used their names to attract the gullible. He became rich.

Bonny was on to him early, and even arrested him, but the arrest stopped the flow of money and so was not allowed to stick. Bonny shrugged and looked the other way; these things happened.

Finally Stavisky's financial empire collapsed. A scandal was about to explode, and all Paris knew it. A dozen or more politicians and police commanders were compromised. The newspapers were on to it. They printed rumor and innuendo every day, while the politicians quaked. But Stavisky had disappeared. Where was he? What would he say when caught? Would his arrest bring down the government?

Stavisky was tracked to a rented house in Chamonix, and a high police official was sent to arrest him. Stavisky, so the story later went, asked for a moment alone before being dragged back to Paris in handcuffs. While the top cop waited outside his door, he shot himself.

Or was he executed on orders from above?

The thirties was a bad time for French politics. The political world was more than just venal. In the National Assembly sat deputies representing every imaginable political coloration: fascists, communists, socialists, radicals, centrists, and every tone in between. Freemasonry was a political force. There was a group — almost an army — known as the Cagoulards, led by supposedly responsible men and dedicated to the overthrow of the government by force and the installation of a right-wing dictatorship. The heavily armed Cagoulards planted bombs. They attempted to assassinate the Jewish premier, Léon Blum.

The hatred of French politicians one for the other, their inability to forge any kind of consensus, their inability finally to govern, neither began nor ended with the Stavisky case. The *affaire* and the killing of Magistrate Prince — or suicide or whatever it was — that followed Stavisky's death only exacerbated the inability of French politicians to get along with each other. This was to continue into 1939, leaving the government, France itself, unprepared for war, unable to resist the Germans.

With Stavisky dead, perhaps officially murdered, the government was in turmoil, as was the country. Who had accepted bribes from Stavisky? Who had killed him? So many ministers, deputies, senators, prefects, magistrates, began to seem implicated that there were riots in the streets with the police firing into the crowds and killing more than thirty people. The government fell and was replaced by another, which also fell. Who had killed Stavisky? Who had ordered it? Accusations flew. Careers were ruined. Politicians attempted suicide or were arrested and jailed. Again the government tottered.

Bonny was called in by someone — top ministers, it was said — and told to find out everything. All by himself. A mere *inspecteur principal*. It was an assignment that made and makes no sense, unless it was a setup from the start.

Bonny was a painstaking, slow-working detective in some respects, a man of extreme lucidity; he also appears to have been self-important, easily flattered, and not nearly as shrewd in this instance as in the past.

Or else the script was written out in detail by men far above him in rank, so that he thought he had only to follow it to achieve a career breakthrough, perhaps a monetary reward, and the national applause he believed his qualities deserved.

What he did was to arrest Stavisky's wife and charge her as an accomplice in his swindles. She would become frightened, he reasoned. She would spill all she knew, naming names. This in fact happened. Jean Chiappe, she blurted out, was one of those heavily involved with her husband. Chiappe was an ex-director of the Sûreté, an ex–secretary general of the ministry of the interior, and the incumbent prefect of the rival Paris police force. He was a powerful right-wing politician and no man for an *inspecteur principal* to tangle with.

Bonny perhaps imagined he was operating under the protection of someone even stronger than Chiappe. On the word of the wife, he sent forward official police reports denouncing Chiappe; he also appears to have denounced him to the left-wing press, whose editorials and cartoons made Chiappe seem not only a crook but ridiculous.

Bonny was removed from the case and slapped with the same charges of corruption — accepting a coat and suit from Volberg — that he had beaten seven years before. He was suspended from the force to await trial.

The mysterious death of Stavisky was followed now by the mysterious death of Magistrate Prince, who was believed to be carrying a briefcase containing all the evidence he had amassed in the case. He had announced that he was about to make this evidence public. He was killed by an express train and was in pieces when found. The briefcase was intact, but empty. The official investigation ruled Prince's death a suicide. He was supposed to have half chloroformed himself, for the residue was found in his lungs, and then sat down on the tracks to await the express. There was a bloodstained knife nearby that apparently had nothing to do with anything.

Prince's death caused another national uproar. No one believed this "suicide," and one last piece of dangerous evidence, Stavisky's checkbook, was still out there somewhere. If it could be found, its stubs would tell whom Stavisky had paid off, and how much, and when.

Bonny, though suspended and awaiting trial, went looking for the checkbook. He did what any good detective would do — he contacted all his informants, called in all his markers, followed all leads. He met with criminals, with politicians. He asked his questions. Finally he found whoever it was who had the checkbook — the man's identity was never clear. He wanted money for it. Bonny went back to the Sûreté for the money, which was given to him. He bought the checkbook, vouchered it, and sent it forward.

This exploit caused a sensation. His picture was in all the papers. The headline writers called him France's number-one cop. His disciplinary trial was hastily convened, and he was exonerated of all charges.

The checkbook almost immediately disappeared from police custody, never to be seen again.

In some government ministries vast sighs of relief rose up. In others the reverse happened. Who knew who was playing what game? In France during those years political circles included police circles. The Paris police were said to be solidly right wing, the Sûreté solidly left. The upper echelons of both were not only venal, but also thoroughly beholden to politicians and political parties.

As for Bonny personally, the pot was still boiling, and the risks to his career had passed beyond all imagining. Apparently he never saw this, or never believed it. As France's new top cop, he was ordered to get to the bottom of the Prince case.

An article by Georges Simenon, a police reporter for *Paris-Soir* back then, had hinted that the *milieu* was behind Prince's death. This sounded good to Bonny, and he announced that Prince's death was murder, all right, and he blamed it on the *milieu*. He then arrested the three top *caïds* in France.

Having "solved" the case, he got another round of praise from the press. However, he had no proof whatever. The *caïds*, all from Marseilles, had rock-solid alibis, and the *juge d'instruction*, who in France performs the functions of prosecutor and grand jury both, was obliged to dismiss the case.

Meanwhile, the informant who had led Bonny to Stavisky's checkbook had been arrested by other detectives on orders from other higher-ups and had been charged with murdering Prince. Bonny began running around trying to save his informant. Within forty-eight hours he had found enough witnesses to prove the charge absurd. He had merely defended his informant as would any cop in the world, but to the country at large it made him seem in league with the underworld.

Everyone now turned against Bonny. An elected deputy from Marseilles charged him with having planted cocaine on the American woman years back, even as the Volberg case was brought forward for the third time, but now with a witness attached, the tailor who supposedly had delivered the overcoat and suit. Bonny was charged, convicted, dismissed from the Sûreté, and sentenced to six months in prison.

When he came out broke and broken, he went back to Bordeaux, where he was born and where he found work as a shrimp fisherman; there was nothing else. Some days he and his family went hungry. Finally his energy, or perhaps anger, began to return. Leaving his family behind, he went back to Paris.

For the next few years he made a living of sorts as a freelance journalist. He became quite a good reporter. Inasmuch as detection and journalism demand much the same instincts, this is not so surprising.

Then came World War II. The German blitzkrieg rolled across France. Editors ran for the unoccupied zone, and newspapers shut down. Bonny's freelance market evaporated. In Paris he looked for work, but there was none. Then someone he met in a café sent him to see a man called Henri Lafont, who operated one of the new *bureaux d'achat* that had sprung up under the occupation. It was Lafont's business to buy up goods, mostly luxury goods, for resale to the Germans. The conquerors of France had all the money in the world and would pay three or four times the original price. Lafont could be found, Bonny was told, at 93, Rue Lauriston.

Bonny walked uphill from the Kléber metro station towards what was soon to be the most sinister address in France. He saw mostly what anyone can see today, for in Paris the storefronts may change, and the style and shape of the cars in the street, but not the angle of the sun falling on the pavement, and rarely the buildings.

A shabby street, narrow and dark in the otherwise chic sixteenth *arrondissement*. No trees. All buildings the same height more or less, four stories. These days there are cars parked solidly along both curbs and only one lane open for traffic in the middle. It would have looked different to Bonny, for almost no cars moved in Paris during the occupation, though Lafont had many and Bonny was soon to have one himself.

Today the building at 93, Rue Lauriston houses the Chambre de Commerce Franco-Arab. Its facade is plain, almost without decoration. A more banal-looking building could not be imagined, though the door — glass in a wrought-iron frame — is one and a half stories high. In Lafont's day I believe this door was sheet steel painted black so that no one could fire bullets in, or hear loud voices or screams.

Inside Bonny met Lafont, who struck him as charming, seductive, bright. Though barely able to read and write, Lafont struck most people that way. He was tall, powerfully built, with piercing black eyes, and he portrayed himself to Bonny as a successful businessman now engaged in sticking it to the hated occupiers of their country. He offered the ex-detective a job as the number-two man in his firm, and Bonny accepted.

Lafont's real name was Henri Chamberlain. He was born in Paris in 1902 and from early adolescence had been your average, all-around crook: burglary, car theft, forged checks, larceny, assault. He had been in jail when France fell, a convict marching with a labor battalion. He was "liberated" by a Stuka that came down strafing. So were three other men, two Germans and a Swiss, all three in prison as suspected spies. The four men made it to Paris to the Hotel Lutetia, where German Intelligence was installed. The three spies, reporting in, had brought along their new friend Henri Lafont, whom they introduced all around.

By the time Bonny met him, Lafont was running several black-market outlets, and was sharing profits with his German benefactors. Presently he began to throw sumptuous parties, to which all Paris came. Now he was bringing profits and intelligence both. He had many mistresses, whom he flaunted. In the years to follow, Mme Bonny refused to attend dinner parties at the Rue Lauriston. She was offended by the presence of the immoral women.

For a time Lafont installed the Bonnys in a suburban villa, but the detective didn't feel comfortable and moved back to his little apartment. Lafont forced on him, he later claimed, a red Jaguar, a rich man's car. It made Bonny uncomfortable, but he drove it. There were plenty of ration cards for gasoline, food, clothes. He was able to dress well again and to dress his wife and son well, though Paris as a whole was already short of textile goods. They ate well too, though Paris was short of food. The son became popular at school because an invitation back to the Bonny house after classes meant something to eat. To Bonny, though he would disavow it later, his new lifestyle proved that he had made his comeback. He was again someone who counted in Paris and the world.

About 350,000 cars had circulated in Paris in the year before the war — for a population of 2.3 million. Now there were 4,500. Most ran rarely or never. The city, which had consumed 60,000 cubic meters of gasoline per month, now had access to 650. There had been 3,500 buses operating in 1939; now there were 500. Paris had become a silent city, the loudest noise the tap-tap of people's wooden shoes on the sidewalks. Not only had leather disappeared from the shops but so, virtually, had clothing of any kind. Women restyled what they owned until it fell to pieces. They made new clothes out of curtains, drapes, bedspreads, while these things lasted. After that they could buy if they wished clothing made of hair. The barbers still worked and had found a market for what fell to the floor.

There came to be almost no coal or wood for heating and no soap that would give a lather. The food shortage got worse. Before the war Paris had received 68,000 tons of meat per year and 132,000 tons of fruits and vegetables. By the eve of the liberation this was down to 20,000 tons of meat, 61,000 tons of fruits and vegetables.

Bonny meanwhile lived as well as he wanted to, and Lafont lived sumptuously.

But Lafont decided his black-market businesses were not profitable enough. Why not put together a personal police unit to scout out hoarded or black-market goods that could be confiscated and resold?

Why not indeed? But where to get trusted men? Lafont's idea of trusted men was not like your idea or mine. He went into the prisons and culled out about two dozen dangerous convicts. Some he had known before. Some he knew by reputation. He gave them guns and badges. Overnight the crooks became the cops, and no one who caught their eye was safe. Hoarding was a crime; buying or selling on the black market was a crime; attempting to get oneself or one's capital out of France was a crime; listening to news broadcasts from London was a crime; being a Jew was a crime. From such "criminals" money and valuables could be extorted: pay up or go to jail. The house at 93, Rue Lauriston began to fill with paintings and tapestries, with gold and silver.

Sometimes members of the gang would come upon a house or apartment where no valuables were left. Residents would be dragged back to the Rue Lauriston, taken down into the basement, and tortured until they remembered where their missing goods could be found. Or they would be tortured into signing over title to lock boxes or bank accounts.

Jews were especially vulnerable. The police from the Rue Lauriston were at the door, and everyone inside trembled. Gang members would extort money and possessions from Jews on the threat of turning their children over to the Germans — and then turn the whole family over anyway. Wherever they went they sowed terror. They became known as the Gestapo of the Rue Lauriston, and after that, more simply, as the Bonny-Lafont gang.

From time to time certain of them got tired of even pretending to be policemen and went back to outright burglaries and armed robberies. Occasionally one or another was arrested by the regular police, charged with some heinous crime. Lafont would complain to the Germans, and his men would be released. They committed a number of murders. Sometimes they got into arguments and killed each other.

Bonny had come to work bringing with him two accountants, perhaps honestly imagining that his job was to straighten out Lafont's paperwork. Later he claimed to know almost nothing of what went on, claimed that no torturing ever took place in the basement to his knowledge.

Ordinary Parisians knew who he was. People took shots at him from ambush. He kept a bodyguard. But he was not comfortable with bodyguards either and decided he did not need one. He himself was armed — normal for the policeman he considered himself once again to be. He could defend his person without help.

Lafont took German nationality and began to wear an SS uniform. He gave the ex-detective a uniform too, but Bonny refused to wear it. Lafont began to use his network of informants to infiltrate Resistance cells. Bonny did nothing to stop him and took part in several raids. His defense in court was that he had to, because it was the law. During one raid he had the misfortune to arrest Geneviève de Gaulle, the general's niece. He arrested her personally. He didn't know her name at first, though he learned it soon enough. Informants had pointed her out as active in the Resistance, and he grabbed her. Later, when he had been condemned to death, his lawyer appealed to de Gaulle for clemency. The general did not accord it. Geneviève, who was sent to the concentration camp at Ravensbrück, survived the war.

And so it went, the good years, the years of being somebody again. It ended more abruptly than Bonny might have hoped. In the summer of 1944, with the American armies approaching Paris, he and Lafont and their families fled the Rue Lauriston in three cars. The Bonnys went in the red Jaguar; Lafont, his two children, and his mistress of the moment (a "superb" brunette, according to contemporaries) went in a Bentley; and Lafont's chauffeur drove a backup Citroën. They had arms, money, false passports, false identity cards, false papers for the cars. They had all the false tax stamps and rubber stamps needed to change their identities and the cars' identities as often as might prove necessary. They hid out at a farm in a village near Sens, about sixty miles southeast of Paris, waiting for the propitious moment to strike out for Spain and safety.

Bonny, the career policeman, should have known better. No one can pass unnoticed in a village. In a different big city it might have been possible. And to arrive in a caravan of expensive cars —

in a country where cars had become an oddity — was asking for it.

They hid the cars under hay in the barn and began to wait, but a squad of Resistance fighters descended upon the farm, having heard about the cars. They needed them, they told Lafont, who came to the door. They believed Lafont's false passport, his lies; they didn't want him, just the cars, which they made off with, leaving a receipt. Lafont was obliged to send to a confederate in Paris for more cars. The confederate, with the Allied armies even closer, went to the police instead. The real police.

Who rushed south to the village, surrounded the farm, and moved in so quickly that no shots were fired on either side.

In police custody in Paris, Bonny typed out his official interrogatory himself, just as he had typed out so many others for those he had himself arrested. It was as if he were still a policeman. He wanted everything to be correct.

Finally the trial began. It was not quite regular, though more nearly so than most other "trials" that took place during those times, when so much had to be done so quickly. Thus there were two magistrates and four jurors, instead of three and nine. The four jurors were all drawn from Resistance fighters. With altogether eleven defendants in the dock, it was not so much a trial as a recital of extortions, pillages, robberies, tortures, murders. Lafont, when interrogated by the court, was neither repentant nor afraid. He boasted that he had got what he wanted and had no regrets. "I lived like a king," he said.

Bonny in his turn had plenty of regrets. He wanted to explain it all away.

The verdict was never in doubt: death.

In jail Bonny became intensely religious, and the old Stavisky-Prince case tormented him. He was allowed no visitors, but his son bribed the jailers and after dark was let into Bonny's cell. They spent most of the night in there, and Bonny talked of the murder of Prince. Yes, the magistrate was indeed murdered, and it was Bonny himself who had set it up, on orders from "on high." He was a suspended detective at the time, awaiting his corruption hearing. When asked to do away with Prince so as to end the scandal and save the republic, he had had no choice. None at all. That was why his later investigation had looked so clumsy. How could he "get to the bottom of the Prince case" when he was involved himself? And of course the higher-ups had then abandoned him.

On the last morning of his life he told the same story to the police doctor, a man he had worked cases with, whose job it would be to pronounce him dead.

We have only his own word for it, a kind of deathbed confession. Perhaps it was true. Or perhaps he was hoping that so explosive a revelation would cause the authorities to keep him alive a bit longer. If this was his tactic, it failed.

The escort was heavily armed. Bonny and Lafont were driven to the place of execution. Their death warrants were read aloud. Lafont sucked voluptuously on the cigarette offered him, but refused the rum. "What are you here for, Pop?" he said to the chaplain at his side. "You want me to listen to your gibberish? Go ahead then. I'm leaving for God's place in a moment. You don't have something you want me to tell Him, by any chance?"

Bonny made no statement. He was wearing a jacket that was too small for him. Strapped to the post, he trembled, whether from fear or only from the dawn cold of two days after Christmas was impossible to tell.

Paris Three
LAFAYETTE, WE ARE HERE

Behind this wall at 35, Rue de Picpus there come together a number of strands of French history, and some of American history as well. It is a plain address on a plain street in the working-class twelfth *arrondissement*. It is not mentioned in guidebooks. There are no tourist buses pulled up outside. The first time I came here I wasn't sure it was the place, because from the sidewalk nothing shows. I had been round and round the block searching. I kept coming upon two great wooden doors in the wall with a smaller wooden door inset into one of them, and finally I opened the small door and peered inside. I saw a large gravel courtyard surrounded by buildings, including a church. The concierge's loge was off to the right, together with a sign: "Visits permitted only from two o'clock to four."

A woman of about 60 answered my knock. This was the right place, she said, but it was now five past four and closed.

I gave her a smile. I was late by only five minutes, I said, and actually I had been here on time, but I couldn't find it —

"*Je regrette, monsieur.*"

I don't know why I persisted, for I knew Parisian concierges. But I had come all the way from America, I told her. I was going home tomorrow. I was only five minutes late. This was my last chance to see something important to me.

"*Je regrette, monsieur.*"

It occurred to me to slip her 50 francs. But to succeed at bribing people takes a certain grace. "Perhaps if I give you something you could make an exception," I said. Instead of just doing it I had had to announce it first. Beautiful.

Her manner became haughty. She said "*Je regrette*" again and closed the door on me.

There was an iron door in the wall beside the church. It was locked. I knew what was behind it. I wanted to go through it, and couldn't.

I went into the church. The usual gloomy church, lit principally by candles. About a dozen nuns wearing the elaborate white habits of my youth knelt in pews in prayer, keeping a permanent vigil there. They worked around the clock in relays. That's what they did for a living. They belonged to the Order of the Sacred Heart and were semicloistered. I watched one or two new ones come in and others go out. I had forgotten there were nuns who still dressed in such habits, that prayer vigils still existed.

In the lateral chapels, immense white marble plaques bordered in black were fixed to the walls. On them were inscribed the names, ages, professions, and dates of each of the victims out in the garden. I walked over and peered up at the names, first in one chapel, then in the other. Some were familiar to me. The nuns on their knees paid no notice. There were about 1,500 names in all. For a moment 1,500 living people marched through my head. The impression it made was overpowering, and I resolved to make one more try at the garden.

A side door up by the altar rail might lead out into the garden. I went through it. The worst that could happen was that I would run into some nun; if so, I would bluff my way past her. I had gone through grade school with nuns like this. I was not afraid of nuns.

But I had come out into a corridor, not the garden, and I met not one nun but three. The first two gave me a startled look. The third said sharply, "*Monsieur, vous désirez quelque chose?*" And she pointed, exactly in the manner of my grade-school teachers, back in the direction I had come.

Thoroughly humiliated, I went back into the church, out the front door, and back to my hotel.

Today I knock again on the concierge's loge. Some months have passed. This time she is all smiles. I am acquainted with few important people in France, but one is the Count de Chambrun, a descendant of Lafayette, who has called her on my behalf. Normally, she tells me with a smile, visitors are not permitted at this hour. However, she's always happy to make an exception for a guest from America like me. I smile right back. Clearly she does not remember me. I remember her well enough. She hands me a heavy bunch of keys and points to the gate to the garden. I tip her 50 francs. It would seem churlish not to. The money disappears into her apron and she thanks me profusely.

The keys are as big as the keys to a jail, and I open the iron door and go through.

The garden is much bigger than I had thought: about 300 yards long, about 60 wide. It is bigger than some parks, an enclave of greenery entirely surrounded by buildings. There are long alleys of trees, mostly horse chestnuts and lindens, and flat sweeps of lawn. The cemetery is in the far right corner. Its gate is locked too — the French lock up everything. But one of my keys opens it, and I go in.

Lafayette's grave is easy enough to find, for over it flies an American flag. I don't know when the flag was first put up, but it has never come down. It flew all during the German occupation, which surprises me less than it evidently does some people. Probably, like most modern tourists, the Germans didn't know it was there, nor the tomb, nor even the garden. Lafayette's wife Adrienne lies beside him, I note, and George Washington de Lafayette behind them both. Just beyond these tombs under the trees, stones mark the place where are buried almost 1,500 headless corpses.

At the start of the Revolution this was a convent, as it is now, but the nuns were forced out, their sacred vessels, paintings, and stained glass confiscated, their chapel demolished and its stones sold to builders. A man named Riedain rented the property from the state, lived in one of the buildings, and in partnership with another man ran what was called a *maison de santé et de détention* — a euphemism for a kind of prison hospital. Actually what they ran was a profitable extortion. "Enemies of the nation" (a great many euphemisms were in vogue at this time) could claim to be sick, get themselves sent here, and, for as long as their money or their relatives' money held out, avoid the guillotine. Usually they did not stay long. As more and more goods and property got confiscated, as relatives got arrested too, they were dumped back into the mainstream, en route towards what the men in charge called the Sword-Blade of the Law — the populace, being less pious, called it the National Razor.

By the summer of 1794 the guillotine and the nauseating odor that went with it had been moved several times. Death by decapitation was incredibly messy. The blood pooled on the paving stones underneath. The executioner had a hose and at the end of each day's work would hose off the scaffold, the blade, washing more blood down among the stones. In the summer heat it decomposed rapidly, attracted flies, and gave off a stench. Whole neighborhoods first stank, then protested.

In June of 1794 the instrument was moved again, just in time for the start of the Revolution's busiest summer. Over 1,300 men, women, and children were executed in a month and a half at the new site, the Place du Trône, today's Place de la Nation, which is four or five blocks from where I stand. Thirty-eight heads were lopped off on the first day, including 26 belonging to members of the Toulouse parliament, 42 heads two days later, and 61 the day after that. The record seems to have been 68 on July 7, including the 80-year-old Abbé de Salignac Fénélon (some accounts say he was 69), who had founded a home for the small orphan boys who were the chimney sweeps of Paris. A detachment of weeping boys followed the tumbrel to the scaffold, where the priest asked that his hands be unbound so he could give them a final blessing. The entire mob went to its knees as he traced the cross in the air. Ten days later, singing hymns, a convent of Carmelite nuns, about whom Poulenc later wrote an opera, genuflected to their Mother Superior, climbed the steps one by one, and were decapitated. There were 16 of them in all. One was a novice. Two were 78 years old.

Next the heads of Lafayette's mother-in-law, her mother, and one of her daughters rolled into the basket, all for the crime of being aristocrats; and the head of André Chenier, 31, poet, about whom Giordano would write an opera 100 years later. Chenier's crime was that he had written articles in the *Journal de Paris* protesting the excesses of the Revolution.

Day by day the guillotine worked. It killed the rich and poor, the known and unknown, 1,109 of them men, including at least one 17-year-old boy; 197 of them women, including 51 nobles and 23 nuns, the rest being for the most part maids, hairdressers, and seamstresses from noble households.

The problem became what to do with the corpses, and one morning Riedain woke up and found that a hole had been broken through the wall at the bottom of his garden. Hordes of men were chopping down his fruit trees, digging vast ditches in his lawn, building a heavy door into the breach in his wall. Riedain rushed up and protested. The nation has need of your place, he was told. The ditches got deeper and deeper. He shouted, pleaded, got nowhere. He ran off to plead before the proper ministry. What about his prison hospital? He was doing important work for the Revolution. Again he got nowhere. The first ditch was twenty-five feet long, fifteen wide, twenty deep. The second was even bigger, thirty by twenty by twenty-four.

Night fell, and here came the cartloads of corpses into the garden. Men worked by the light of torches. The headless male, female, and adolescent bodies were first stripped, then dumped naked into the hole. The heads were shaken out of sacks. Sometimes one or another escaped and was booted in like a soccer ball. The bloody clothing, meanwhile, was being inventoried by scribes to be sold.

It rained a lot that summer and the garden turned to mud. The carts were heavy and some nights the men could barely push them up to the edge. Night after night the carts came through, and the corpses fell one upon the other in the ditches, where they were sometimes covered by a light dusting of lime. The ditches remained open, and through the neighborhood on every night breeze moved clouds of stench. After almost two months, neighborhood outrage reached such a pitch that the guillotine was moved back to what is now the Place de la Concorde in front of what is now the Crillon Hotel. But at night fresh corpses continued to arrive here. Finally the order was given: the immense ditches, containing now about half of all the victims of the Terror, were to be filled in. The depths were measured. In the first ditch the headless corpses lay eight feet thick, in the second only five.

Altogether more than 3,000 people were executed in Paris alone, among them many of the best men France had. More than 110,000 others, including all the rest of France's best, had fled abroad, where they stayed. Napoleon, 30 years old, walked into an empty capital and took over.

By 1802 some of the émigrés had trickled back to Paris, many wanting to visit the graves of guillotined loved ones. In most cases they were unable to find out where they were, for although the executions had taken place in public, the burial details had worked at night and in secret lest grief or rage provoke demonstrations. Officially, the mass graves at 35, Rue de Picpus did not exist. But the surviving Noailles sisters, Adrienne de Lafayette and Pauline de Montagu, learned of a lacemaker who had followed the cart containing the corpses of her father and brother.

The girl led them here.

The two women decided to buy the property. But they had no money anymore and so were obliged to sell subscriptions to other bereaved relatives, the ones they knew, the ones with blood as blue as their own. In time they invited the present order of nuns to establish a new convent here and to build a new church over the ruins of the old.

They also set aside a corner of the garden as a private cemetery for themselves — this cemetery in which I stand — with the result that I walk now past tomb after tomb of counts and marquesses and princes and dukes and their female equivalents. There can't be such a conglomeration of nobility anywhere else in the world. Hardly a commoner's tomb anywhere. It is very strange. The commoners are all back there under the trees, headless, buried twenty feet deep, indistinguishable from the aristocrats who died with them.

I am quite alone in this enormous garden, and I walk over to look at the wall where the breach was made for the carts. The carts were painted red so the blood would not show, or at least not show so much. The breach is still visible. After the Revolution it was filled in with stones that are not quite the same color. Also the lintel is still there — the great thick beam that the workmen embedded in the wall so that the doorway would not collapse on the horses and carts.

There are plaques by the breach and more plaques on the wall that surrounds the mass graves — to the sixteen Carmelites, to André Chenier, and to others. If you enjoy reading such things, this is the place for you. You will be busy a long time. Nor is there any similar place elsewhere. There were mass graves in other parts of Paris at the time, but as the city expanded the others were built on; this is the only one extant.

The 1,500 people piled together under my feet, plus that many again who lie today under buildings, were all beheaded by one man, Charles-Henri Sanson. Sanson, who was 50 years old in 1789, came from a family of executioners. The Sansons were themselves the executioners, or were related to the executioners, of eighteen cities in all, and Charles-Henri was the fourth generation in an unbroken line from father to son to serve as executioner of Paris. After him the post would go to his son, and then his grandson, six generations in all before the line petered out.

At the beginning executioners were not allowed to marry outside the profession. By law their houses were painted red. If they had daughters they were sometimes obliged to nail a sign to the front door to warn suitors away. The baker baked their bread apart, and in church their pew was set apart. Commissions brought to them were not handed over but tossed at their feet.

Their job was even messier at first than it later became. In addition to merely killing people, the early Sansons and their relatives and colleagues in other places also had to cut off hands, cut off ears — the left one first because it was thought to control sexual activity — and stretch people out on the wheel so as more easily to break their legs with iron bars. If the court's sentence called for it they had to peel a criminal like an orange with red-hot pincers or stretch him on the rack until all his limbs were dislocated. Sometimes the executioner used the retentum immediately, or almost immediately. The retentum was a cord so fine the mob couldn't see it. The executioner strangled the victim, then performed the heavy stuff on the corpse. Whatever happened, eventual death was certain. Vagrants and petty thieves were hanged. Homosexuals were burned. Bad women or bigamists were scourged. Serious felons were decapitated: swords for the nobility, axes for commoners. Executions were popular entertainment. To get the best places, spectators began to gather the night before; they lit fires, bought food from vendors, who abounded.

The first four Paris Sansons were all named Charles, the last two Henri. The sire of the dynasty was an army lieutenant stationed in Rouen who had the misfortune to fall in love with the Rouen executioner's daughter. He was, in more ways than one, invited into the family. At his first execution, when ordered to start clubbing the condemned man, he is said to have fainted. This was the origin of the legend that the Sansons were at heart kind, sensitive, gentle. There would be more publicity of this nature during the Revolution. Once inside the profession this first Charles found he could not get out. The top job in Rouen being already taken, he moved to Paris, where he made a name for himself.

His son, the second Charles, performed his first execution at 18. The prisoner was a woman who had tried to poison her husband. The windows all around were selling, it was said, for 50 louis d'or apiece. The boy's father ordered him to sword off her head. Butchery. He was trembling so much it took him five or six swings.

The third Charles inherited the post at 7, his father having willed it to him on his deathbed. His mother, née Marthe Dubut, had to hurry him over to the public prosecutor's office, where she pleaded for the appointment to be approved, and it was. From then on the child had to witness every execution to make it legal. He did not himself perform one until he was 18. At 35 and in bad health he resigned — one almost wants to say abdicated — in favor of his oldest son, the Charles-Henri of the Revolution, who was then only 15 — too young. Back to the public prosecutor went Marthe Dubut, dragging her grandson by the hand. The boy had been assisting his father on the scaffold from the age of 11, she testified. He was certainly experienced. Grandma claimed the job as the family's right, and again got her way.

This newest Sanson was supposedly the most softhearted of the lot, and the execution of a man who had murdered his mistress's husband is offered as proof. Charles-Henri, by then 16, could not watch. A mulatto assistant began bludgeoning the man while Charles-Henri looked away. The mistress, meanwhile, was being made to watch; she was later hanged.

Soon afterwards a man named Damiens stabbed Louis XV. Although the King was only nicked, Damiens was sentenced to horrendous torture. Knowing himself too tenderhearted to carry out the sentence, the boy executioner (so the story goes) went to his grandmother for help. Marthe Dubut must have been one tough lady. She summoned one of her other sons, who was executioner at Reims, and they bought strong horses. On the appointed day the boy and his uncle went to the conciergerie, where the prisoner had his arms dislocated by *estrapade* and his feet twisted in the boot. Onwards to the scaffold, where the uncle held the would-be renegade's hand in the brazier and an assistant began peeling off his skin with red-hot pincers. Other assistants poured boiling oil and boiling lead onto the wounds. The limbs were then attached to the four horses, which tried three times to pull the man apart. Finally his limbs had to be severed with axes. Every rooftop around was crowded with people.

This was the climate in October 1789 when Joseph Guillotin, 51, a medical doctor and delegate, made a speech in the Estates Général. A quick and humane method of capital punishment had to be found, he argued. All persons regardless of rank should be similarly executed. Torture must be abolished once and for all. There should be no confiscation of the condemned man's property — justice did not permit the nation to ruin his family as well. After execution his family should be allowed to claim his body if it wished.

Guillotin was from Saintes. He had once studied for the priesthood in Bordeaux. He had left to study medicine in Paris and was by now an extremely high priced doctor — consultations cost 36 livres, about double what others dared charge.

Guillotin began to research capital punishment. He found engravings by Dürer, by Cranach, that showed primitive guillotines. He found descriptions of such machines elsewhere, and he brought this information to Charles-Henri Sanson.

The executioner, we are told, had grown tall and strong. His features were classic, his manner pleasant. He took himself seriously, and he was a snob. He had tried to call himself the Chevalier de Longval, but this did not catch on. He had tried to dress himself in blue, the color reserved for the nobility, had gotten officially reprimanded, and so took to wearing green coats stylishly cut. His title was Bourreau — axman — which he found undignified, and he had petitioned the King to be called instead the Executor of Criminal Judgments. The King, now Louis XVI, had so decreed it. The people went on calling him Bourreau anyway — or else, cynically, Monsieur de Paris. He played the violin and the cello, how well we do not know, and was friends with Tobias Schmidt, a maker of harpsichords.

It was to Schmidt that he brought Dr. Guillotin's ideas. It was Schmidt, whose name has barely come down to us, who designed the guillotine, but it was the humane Dr. Guillotin whose name got attached to it. He came to be seen as one of the villains of the Revolution, and even of history. During his lifetime — he lived until 1814 — he often seemed an object of horror, or else an object of fun. People who passed him in the street would shake their head or give themselves karate chops to the back of the neck. He died a disillusioned man.

In March of 1792 Sanson and Schmidt submitted their designs to a government official at the Tuileries. The King came in and looked them over. He was an enthusiastic amateur locksmith, and it is said that he made suggestions for improving the design of the machine that would ten months later lop off his own head.

The first guillotine was built, and on April 15 Sanson tried it out on some live sheep. Two days later he decapitated three corpses — two men and one woman — in the courtyard of the hospital at Bicêtre, while a crowd of officials, including Dr. Guillotin, looked on. Eight days after that it was used on a thief named

Jacques Pelletier. It worked so perfectly that Tobias Schmidt the harpsichord maker got orders for thirty-four more. Someone is supposed to have said: I hope this doesn't make killing people too easy.

The Terror began the next year, and a guillotine mentality, guillotine fads, swept over the city, together with insane rumors. Did severed heads feel pain, was the guillotine humane or not? Learned men, and some not so learned, disputed this point. Experiments were conducted on heads. When pricked with a knife point, tongues were said to retract into the mouth; when turned to the sun, pupils were said to dilate. Charlotte Corday's cheeks were said to have blushed when one of Sanson's assistants slapped her face as he showed her head to the crowd. The general belief seemed to be that severed heads continued to feel pain until they had cooled.

Meanwhile, there were charms for bracelets in the form of guillotines, and toy guillotines for children. Small guillotines were sold to farmers for beheading chickens. At dinner parties similar guillotines beheaded tiny dolls; out flowed a red liqueur into which men dipped their fingers, women their handkerchiefs. Songs were written. Cartoons appeared, in one of which Sanson himself lay bound under the blade; according to the caption he had guillotined everyone else, so there was no one left to guillotine but himself.

Sanson had four assistants, then seven; two tumbrels, then nine. Some days he worked from dawn to dark. He complained of overwork, of burgeoning expenses. He kept asking the Committee of Public Safety for more money; eventually he got it, a bonus of 20,000 livres. Between March 1793 and July 1794, a period of 502 days, he, his brothers, his sons, and whatever other assistants were on the scaffold with him killed 2,362 people. Sensitive? Softhearted? Some were people Sanson knew and had had official contact with; others he came to know, for the ride to the place of execution was frequently long, sometimes two hours or more, and he would converse with them. In addition there were rain delays — Paris is a rainy place — and a rainy, bloody scaffold with that great snaggletooth hanging overhead was too dangerous to work on. While the rain lasted, executioner and condemned prisoners alike would huddle under the scaffold, and again Sanson would converse with them. Sometimes he would apologize for making them wait.

He executed everyone sent to him, no questions asked, nine men over 80, sixteen artists, twenty-five writers, the King, the Queen, the actress Marie Grandmaison and her 18-year-old serving girl, and, eventually, Danton, Robespierre, Public Prosecutor Fouquier-Tinville, and most of the others, the signers of the death warrants, the very men he had been taking his orders from.

Under the Revolution he became, in his own eyes at least, a figure of importance. As he saw it he was respected everywhere he went. He was certainly good at his job. The mass graves in this garden attest to that. He once killed twenty-one men in thirty-eight minutes. He made them get out of the carts and stand in rows facing away from the scaffold. One by one he ordered them to mount the steps. On top their legs were bound together with ropes. Their arms were already bound. They were strapped to the bascule. Their heads were tipped into the lunette. The two halves came together and locked. Down came the blade. Unstrap him. Undo the ropes. Into the basket with him. Next.

Such speed was possible because virtually none of the victims made a fuss. They were all too proud. The rich were especially haughty. They looked out over the cheering mob, their lips came together in what was close to absolute contempt, and they went to their deaths without so much as a grimace. Madame du Barry, once the mistress of Louis XV but now a raddled, middle-aged woman, did kick and scream. It took three men to hold her while her hair was cut and her arms bound. But she was the exception. It was the opinion of a number of witnesses that if everyone had behaved just like her the public would have sickened of the spectacle much more quickly than it did; the Terror would never have lasted so long.

As far as Sanson was concerned the Revolution produced only one tragedy. One day his son Gabriel, who had been assisting him on the scaffold from the age of 11 but who was by then a grown man, was parading around the perimeter showing someone's head to the mob. He fell off the edge and was killed instantly. There were railings around every scaffold after that, but Sanson, it was said, was never the same.

The guillotine devoured nearly everyone who came near it, with one glaring exception — Sanson himself — which seems, on the face of it, incredible. He was arrested twice. A Royalist press was found in a room in his house that he had rented out. He argued his way out of that one. Later on he and his two brothers were arrested and charged with being Royalist sympathizers — they had hanged, clubbed, and broken the King's enemies for years, had they not? What else could they be? A charge like this was sufficient to send scores of men to the scaffold, but the Sanson case posed a special problem: who do you get to execute the executioners? In the 1790s you could not just phone up some other town and fly in a substitute. Meanwhile, death warrants were piling up on somebody's desk. People were waiting to be executed, and there was no one to do it.

So again they let the Sansons go. Soon afterwards Charles-Henri became so busy and also so essential that he was never bothered again.

There were not even recriminations once the Terror finally ended. Outraged or grief-stricken relatives might have come forward. None did. There might have been cries for revenge, but if there were no one heard them. By the standards of the Nuremberg trials Sanson would certainly have been arrested and prosecuted as a war criminal. But this was not 1945. He was a government functionary. He had obeyed orders. He had done his job. He died in bed in 1806.

By then he had been succeeded by his son. Later came his grandson, sixth and last in the line, who got himself fired. He lost his job, and his descendants lost their jobs at the same time. Between 1840 and 1847 this last Sanson guillotined only eighteen people. He was supposed to be a tenderhearted executioner too, and this is offered as the reason he gave himself to gambling and fast women. He felt an intense revulsion for who he was and what he did that could be assuaged in no other way. But the result was unfortunate: he went heavily into debt and faced debtor's prison.

He pawned the guillotine for the sum he needed, 3,800 francs. He was hoping to be able to redeem it in time.

But someone took a shot at the King (for France had kings again now). The would-be assassin was caught, and the authorities went looking for the executioner. Then they went looking for the guillotine. At first they couldn't find either. Finally Sanson came back. He was 48 years old. The authorities redeemed the guillotine for him, the execution took place, and then they sacked him, and the family dynasty, after just under 200 years, was over.

A new one promptly started. Louis Deibler became Monsieur de Paris. In 1870 the number of executioners was reduced to one, whose jurisdiction encompassed the entire country. There was only one guillotine too, plus a spare, of course; he and it moved about the roads as needed. Monsieur de Paris had become Monsieur de France. Louis Deibler was succeeded by his nephew Anatole Deibler, who was succeeded by his nephew Henri Desfourneaux, and then by André Obrecht, another nephew of Anatole, who performed the last public execution in 1939 and who later was credited with having "perfected" the guillotine — he put ball bearings instead of grease in the grooves. The great blade still weighed seventy pounds — now it dropped more quickly. When it spoke, people listened. With it Obrecht executed 387 criminals to 1977. He was something of a natty dresser. That is, he became famous for wearing his hat while he worked. There was perhaps something subliminal there — his clients had nothing to wear hats on. He kept going until he was 78 years old, then retired in favor of his nephew by marriage, Marcel Chevalier, the present incumbent and perhaps the last in history, for France abolished the death penalty in 1981.

Every country has its "traditional" method of execution. The Spaniards garrote, the English hang, the Americans electrocute, and the French guillotine; and although the result is the same in all cases, it is the last-named that has so fascinated the world. The very thought of it, it is said, is enough to make a man feel a chill on the back of his neck. No method is "nice," nor are they always instantaneous. Men in electric chairs jerk and sometimes fry. Men hanged sometimes squirm, strangling, for some time. However, the sensibilities of onlookers are not assaulted. The mess is self-contained. Hanging, garroting, electrocution — these can seem almost euphemisms for killing. The guillotine, by contrast, is graphic, noisy, bloody — the real thing.

And so to a good many people, though not to the French,

who remained married to it for so long, it has seemed by far the most horrible method of judicial death. The condemned man, philosophically speaking, is more than executed. His arteries fountain after he is dead, and he goes into his coffin mutilated, his head under his arm, retribution having been carried out seemingly even on his corpse. He will remain both killed and mutilated until the end of time. This is a heavy notion, and everyone who ever pondered the guillotine as a method of execution (condemned men in their cells have tended to ponder it a lot) has had to come to grips with it.

Lafayette is not in either of the mass graves. I stand looking down on the great stone that covers his tomb. There is nothing dramatic written on it. Only the American flag that flies over it night and day, year after year, tells part of his story.

Lafayette in 1792 commanded one of France's three armies in the field in a war against Austria. The French officer corps was deserting in droves, and behind the armies was chaos. In Paris the mob had invaded the King's chambers, forced indignities upon him, and held him at pike point for several hours. Lafayette wanted to march on the capital to restore order, but to him this sounded like a military coup; it was against all the principles he lived by. His solution was to ask the other army commanders to march with him, but they would not do it.

So he rode to Paris alone, one man who stood for what was right for France, and burst into the National Assembly and demanded the return of strict constitutional government. Not only did no one listen, but there were cries for his arrest. He barely got out without being seized.

When he had ridden back to his post near the Belgian frontier, he called out the troops and, when they had assembled, asked for a renewal of their oath to the nation, the law, the King. The soldiers instead muttered oaths to Liberty, Equality, and the National Assembly.

Meanwhile the assembly ordered Lafayette's arrest. "Freedom will be in danger," proclaimed Robespierre, "as long as Lafayette is head of an army."

Knowing what arrest would mean, Lafayette gathered some

of his officers and rode into Belgium. He was hoping to get to the coast to take ship for America. "There we will find the liberty which no longer exists in France," he wrote his wife. It was August 1792.

But he was arrested by an Austrian patrol. He was hated and feared by the Austrian Emperor and by the Prussian King as well. He had brought on the French Revolution. He was an enemy of kings, one of the most dangerous men in Europe, a threat to all their thrones.

Turned over to the Prussians, he was thrown into a dungeon near Berlin, and the years began to pass. Later he was moved to other dungeons. He was kept under appalling conditions in tiny, dank cells that were sometimes belowground. Armed guards watched him around the clock. He was without medical attention or proper food. He was not allowed exercise and his clothes rotted on his back. There was hardly enough air to breathe. In summer he nearly suffocated. In winter there was no heat. He could neither send nor receive letters. He got no newspapers. Communication with the outside world having been entirely cut off, he had no notion what had happened to his family, which, under the circumstances, was just as well.

For behind him his goods and property had been confiscated. His wife and children were penniless, forced to live on money sent by President Washington or borrowed from Gouverneur Morris, the American minister to France. And then Adrienne de Lafayette too was arrested. The other Noailles women were in the same prison, all of them awaiting execution. The day came when the others were taken out and guillotined: her sister, her mother, her grandmother, who was over 80. Adrienne was left behind, probably because of vigorous protests by Morris. She was not released until January 1795, six months after Robespierre's fall and the end of the Terror.

Lafayette by then was at Olmutz in Austria; he had been in dungeons two and a half years, had seen no one except his jailers in eight months, and did not know if his wife was still alive. Suddenly his cell door opened and she walked in on him. Traveling on a false passport, she had made it to Vienna, where she had won from the Emperor permission to live with her husband in his cell.

To her he looked like a ghost. He was thin and weak and had lost much of his hair, and she nursed him month after month while her own health deteriorated.

By 1797 France was being governed by a directorate, and its armies in the field, led by a new young general named Napoleon Bonaparte, were victorious everywhere, so that the Austrians sued for peace. The directorate ordered Napoleon to make the release of Lafayette part of the peace treaty.

The treaty was signed, but Lafayette remained locked in his dungeon while the Austrians tried to extract assurances from him, imposing conditions for his release: that he would never again set foot in the Austrian Empire, or the German states, or France, but would sail at once for America. But even after an incarceration of more than five years Lafayette would agree to none of this, and six more months dragged on. Finally the Austrians released him anyway.

For two years after that he lived in exile, first near Hamburg, then in Holland, his return to France forbidden by the directorate, for he was now more a hero than ever, and the mob might decide to make him King.

The directorate was overthrown and replaced by a consulate, three men, one of them Napoleon, who called himself First Consul. Napoleon was afraid of Lafayette also. Permission to reenter the country continued to be denied.

Finally he rode into France on a false passport and settled down thirty-five miles southeast of Paris in a fifteenth-century feudal château that had belonged to his wife's family. There were dependencies and some hundreds of acres of farmland. The nearest village was Rozay en Brie about two miles away. The château had five towers and a moat but had been empty for years. The Lafayettes' first job was to make it habitable, though they had almost no money. Their second would be to make the farm pay. Some of their confiscated properties would come back over the years, but at first the château — it was called La Grange — was all they had.

Lafayette notified Napoleon that he had ended his exile on his own authority and that he intended to stay where he was.

The First Consul's reaction was an explosion of rage, but in

the end he did nothing, for he and his government were too new
for him to risk taking on a hero of Lafayette's stature.
The two men did meet. Lafayette asked for an audience and
was received with pretended cordiality. Later during a banquet
Napoleon drew him aside, and a rather strange conversation took
place.

"You must have found the French looking coldly upon liberty," Napoleon said.

"Yes, but they are in a condition to receive it."

"They are thoroughly disgusted with it," said Napoleon.
"Your Parisians. Your shopkeepers. They want no more
of it."

"I did not use those words lightly, General. I am well aware
of the crimes and follies which have profaned the name of liberty.
But the French are perhaps more than ever in a condition to receive it. It is for you to give it to them; it is from you that they
expect it."

Napoleon recognized that Lafayette's prison martyrdom had
made him the symbol of liberty the world over. He recognized
also that Lafayette stood ready to oppose him.

As for Lafayette, he saw the younger man's vaunting ambition, but also his intelligence. He intended to live out his retirement
as a country farmer, he told Napoleon, who nodded. The two
men parted. Lafayette went back to La Grange.

The château at La Grange still exists, of course, but is closed
to the public. It has belonged since 1955 to the aforementioned
Count de Chambrun, who has restored many of the rooms as
they were in Lafayette's time. Chambrun also discovered trunk-
loads of his ancestor's papers in some of the attics.

Chambrun rarely goes there. He says he doesn't have time.
Though now in his eighties, he is a bustling little man who still
goes to the office Saturdays and even Sundays. He says he takes
off only about three hours on Sunday afternoons. He is an international lawyer with a posh, largely American clientele. He was
partly educated in America, has been admitted to the New York
bar, and his firm occupies an entire floor of a building on the
Champs Elysées. His own office is twenty feet square and its
ceiling looks twenty feet high. The corridor leading to it is fifty

yards long. On his walls are signed photos of Roosevelt, Marshall, Eisenhower, and others. He is a man interested in impressing visitors. When I asked for permission to visit the château so that I might write about what it must have looked like to Lafayette, he refused; he said he would make arrangements for me to tour the grounds, if I wished.

We did tour the grounds one day. The approach is down a long alley of trees. The moat has a stone bottom. There is an oak tree in the garden said to be 1,000 years old. After gazing up at the tower in which Lafayette kept his office, we went away.

La Grange is really the province of Chambrun's wife, Josée Laval, daughter of Pierre Laval, the executed wartime premier. At the upper levels of French society, disparate historical strands are as entangled today as they were in Lafayette's time. Chambrun, who has written a number of books seeking to rehabilitate the reputation of his late father-in-law, has written also that he wishes to make La Grange into a small private museum. This may happen once the old couple has passed on, but so far it is a museum no outsider has seen.

Napoleon's rule became arbitrary. Because La Grange was three or four hours from Paris by carriage, Lafayette took an apartment on the Rue d'Anjou as well, and he began to make his opinions known. His public role was not over, he realized. He wrote hundreds of letters to powerful men both in France and abroad. He spoke out around dinner tables. As Napoleon's despotism increased, so did Lafayette's criticism. He was outspoken, and he was fearless. Napoleon's reaction was to try to shut him up with flattery, with offers of offices, appointments, an ambassadorship — and the riches that went with them. Lafayette, who frequently had more debts than he could pay, refused every time. Napoleon, having created the Legion of Honor, sent emissaries to ask Lafayette to accept the highest decoration. The hero answered that the idea was ridiculous and asked that his name be stricken.

Napoleon made himself First Consul for life, then submitted this decision to the people in a referendum. Approval was virtually unanimous, 3.5 million to 9,000. Lafayette not only voted no but wrote on the register: "I cannot vote for such an office until such time as public liberty shall have received sufficient guarantees. Then and then only will I give my support to Napoleon Bonaparte." He then sat down and wrote a letter to Napoleon describing his vote and affirming his opposition.

Lafayette's wife died. He was brokenhearted and would never marry again. He broke his thigh in an accident and walked with a limp for the rest of his life.

He moved in the highest circles. He attended a dinner party at Joseph Bonaparte's house and was seated next to Lord Cornwallis, his old adversary from Yorktown, to whom he spoke his mind. Afterwards Napoleon summoned him: "According to Cornwallis you have not yet seen the error of your ways."

"What error? Is it an error to love liberty?"

"I regret the manner in which you express your views on the actions of the government."

"I do my best to avoid talking politics, but whenever anyone asks me whether your regime is in accordance with my ideas of liberty, I say no. I wish to be a prudent man, General, but not a renegade."

Nothing happened except that George Washington de Lafayette was forced to resign from the army.

In 1805 Napoleon crowned himself Emperor. The armies he led went from victory to victory. "Everybody has learned his lesson," he said in 1812, "with one exception, and it's Lafayette. He has never given an inch. He is quiet now, but I tell you he is ready to start all over again."

It was 1814 before General Napoleon, as opposed to Emperor Napoleon, finally began to lose. The allied armies won a bloody battle in Champagne, then entered Paris. Lafayette watched them march in, then locked himself in his room and burst into tears. It was France he wept for, not Napoleon, who was exiled to Elba. Napoleonic despotism was over, or so the world believed. Louis XVIII, the guillotined King's brother, having agreed to a constitution that guaranteed all the personal liberties then considered possible, and with a healthy push from the English, was restored to the throne.

Suddenly Napoleon had escaped from Elba. Louis XVIII ran

for his life. Lafayette ran for a seat in the new Chamber of Representatives, for Napoleon, although he had reached Paris and reclaimed his throne, had found himself obliged to accept all the new liberties that the vanished King had conceded, this Chamber of Representatives among them. Now 57 years old, Lafayette was back in public office. As fearless and inflexible as ever, he was at last in a position to do Napoleon real harm.

His chance came within weeks of being seated: on a battlefield in Belgium called Waterloo, Napoleon's armies were crushed. The Emperor rushed back to Paris intending to raise new armies. But in the Chamber Lafayette jumped up and began to harangue his colleagues. He proposed that the Chamber, of which he was a vice president, declare itself in permanent session; any attempt by Napoleon to dissolve it would be considered treason. The ministers of police, war, interior, and foreign affairs should be summoned to the Chamber at once and be so advised. The independence of France was in danger. The country must be saved. Napoleon must go.

The hero of the American Revolution, the champion of liberty, was taking a fearful risk. Supposing in this test of wills and of strength that the winner was Napoleon. What would happen then? And already voices were being raised against Lafayette. What about honor? What about duty to the Emperor?

Lafayette made still another speech to the Chamber. "Have you forgotten what we've done for him?" he cried. "Have you forgotten that everywhere our children's and our brothers' bones are bearing witness to our fidelity — in the African desert, on the banks of the Guadalquivir, the Tagus and the Vistula, on those freezing fields in front of Moscow. During the last ten years and even longer, three million Frenchmen have died for a man who now wants to go on fighting the whole of Europe. We've done enough for him. Today our duty is to save our country."

He demanded that the Emperor be deposed, but no one would agree. They argued most of the night. By the next day Lafayette had won them over. A message went to Napoleon: he must abdicate. When he refused, Lafayette sent him another message. Either he abdicated or Lafayette personally would ask the Chamber to depose him.

Napoleon abdicated, and was exiled to St. Helena, a tiny island in the south Atlantic.

Obviously Lafayette hoped for a new and democratic France. It was a vain hope. Imposed by the conquerors from the outside, Louis XVIII was returned to the throne. The populace accepted him. The populace wanted peace at any price. Almost alone, Lafayette resisted. In the Chamber as in conversation, in his letters, in public speeches, he kept demanding democratic reforms, complete freedom of the press, complete freedom of religion, the victory of right over privilege, the restoration of the people, the end of arbitrary rule. He continued to reject all honors. There were those who called him naive, or even stupid. "He had only one idea his whole life long," Chateaubriand later complained.

The idea was liberty.

I was self-taught, Lafayette himself said. America was my only school.

In 1824 President Monroe invited him to America; he would send a warship to get him. Lafayette's vast fortune was long gone. Nonetheless, he refused the warship; he would come by ordinary packet. His visit lasted thirteen months. He found a real nation in place of the collection of towns he had left behind forty years before. It was prosperous, well governed, with good roads. The people went delirious over him. They called him General Lafayette or else simply "Our Marquis." In Boston in front of the new monument at Bunker Hill, 200,000 people acclaimed him. Afterwards there was a banquet for 4,000 people — "Where I announced," he wrote home, "that having now celebrated the liberation of the American hemisphere the toast for the next fifty years would be To the Liberation of Europe."

He toured every state. He visited Mount Vernon, where he asked to be left alone before Washington's tomb. He went on to Monticello, where Jefferson was waiting for him on the porch. Lafayette was 67, Jefferson 81. The two old men approached each other hesitantly, then rushed into each other's arms. Two other guests arrived — Monroe, who had just left the White House, and Madison, who had held office before him. The three ex-presidents and the symbol of liberty on two continents sat down to lunch. Afterwards the two others departed, leaving Jefferson and Lafayette alone. At each stop up to then Lafayette had spoken in English; now Jefferson wanted to speak in French, so they did.

Lafayette was the first foreigner ever to address both houses of Congress — but he wasn't a foreigner, he had American citizenship too. Congress, knowing he was broke, voted him $250,000 and land in Louisiana that he later sold; his financial worries were over for as long as he might live.

On the eve of his departure the new president, John Quincy Adams, presided over a dinner in his honor. It was September 6, 1825, his 68th birthday. "To February 22, the birthday of George Washington," said Adams, raising his glass, "and to September 6, the birthday of the Marquis de Lafayette."

Lafayette, when he rose to speak, said: "To July 4, the birthday of liberty."

The next day the president and all of Washington came down to the banks of the Potomac as he sailed away for the last time.

The King had ordered the Paris press to ignore Lafayette's triumphal tour of the United States. His speeches had been widely circulated nonetheless, and there were those in the King's circle who wanted him arrested when he debarked at Le Havre. But a vast crowd turned out to greet him, and he got a hero's welcome instead. Other receptions were planned in cities on the road back to Paris. The police closed some of them down, but elsewhere there were balls, illuminations, fireworks. More than ever Lafayette was the hero of the common people of France.

He began a crusade for free public education and in this was fifty years ahead of his time. He began to urge that France come to the aid of liberals and revolutionaries everywhere: in Greece, Poland, Italy, Portugal, Spain, Latin America. He wanted to export revolution. He himself aided all these movements as much as he could and received their leaders in his house. His speeches on behalf of democracy were printed and widely discussed, and they seemed fiery for their day. When his publisher was arrested for rebellion, Lafayette demanded that he be arrested himself, as they were his words that the publisher had printed. The charges against the publisher were dropped.

The King had died childless. The new King was Charles X, still another brother of the guillotined Louis XVI, who desired

only a return to the *ancien régime*. He toured the provinces to prove
his popularity — prior to dissolving the Chamber. Lafayette
toured right behind him to prove that the people wanted even
more democracy than they had. The King dissolved the Chamber
anyway and abolished freedom of the press. Lafayette rushed to
Paris, whose people rose up against the new decrees. The Chamber
met in urgent session. All turned to Lafayette, who was now 72
years old. He was asked to appoint a municipal commission to
run the city. He refused; it would be undemocratic, he said. The
deputies must do it themselves. But the National Guard came back
into existence — almost spontaneously, so it seemed — and Lafayette agreed to take command. "The confidence of the people
of Paris calls me once again to the command of its public force,"
he announced. "I have accepted the duties entrusted to me with
devotion and joy as I did in 1789. . . . I will not explain my position, my feelings are well known. . . . Liberty will triumph or
we will die together."

"My feelings are well known . . ." In another time of crisis
128 years later de Gaulle would decline to explain himself also,
saying only, "*Je vous ai compris.*"

The old hero began issuing proclamations that were placarded
on every wall. Once again he was in the thick of revolution.

The Chamber refused to deal with the King at all and began
looking for a replacement. There were only two available choices,
the Duc d'Orléans, who was descended from the younger branch
of the royal family, or Lafayette. The Duke was known as a liberal.
He was one of the few nobles who had supported the Revolution
in 1789, at which point he had been 16 years old. At 20 at the
height of the Terror he had fled to England. Afterwards he had
lived two years in America.

There was no question whom the people wanted: Lafayette.
They would take him any way they could get him. He could be
president of a new republic, even president for life. He could be
regent for the deposed King's grandson. He could be dictator, if
he chose. He could be the French Washington. And with his National Guard behind him he already held all power in his hands.
He could just do it. He need not wait for the consent of the people.

But there was no fraud or deceit in him. Simply to arrogate

power unto himself like any of the despots of the past was something he would not and could not do. Nor was there any machinery in place to elect him president. He did not believe the French people were ready for a republic anyway. France was not America. He did announce publicly that "the Royal family rules no more," and this ended any chance that Charles X would be accepted back, whatever concessions he might make; it ended also any possibility of a regency for the grandson. He announced that power came from the people, that before any decision was made the people should stipulate their conditions. In this way the crown would be given at the same moment that the stipulated guarantees were proclaimed.

The Chamber continued to debate. All waited for Lafayette to decide what he would do — would he take power or not? What government was France to have? A mob surrounded the building in which deliberations went on. Its temper was described as increasingly nervous.

Lafayette or the Duc d'Orléans?

Fearing a republic, refusing to seize power himself, Lafayette announced that he would back the Duc d'Orléans as King, news that the mob received with coldness.

Lafayette and the Duke were brought together. The conversation, according to Lafayette's memoirs, went like this. "The constitution of the United States is the most perfect there is," said Lafayette.

"I agree with you," said the Duke, and he began to speak of his years in America. "But do you think that France and public opinion are in a state to adopt it?"

"No. What the French people need today is a popular throne surrounded by republican, thoroughly republican institutions."

"I agree with you."

There was only one way to make the mob accept the Duke as King. Seizing a huge tricolor flag, Lafayette brought the Duke to the window for all to see, wrapped both of them in the flag, and embraced him. And the mob went wild.

Most of the stipulations Lafayette had demanded were enacted into law within a few months. The Duke took the name Louis-Philippe and called himself not King of France, but King of the

French. He said he reigned by consent of the people, not by divine right. He was the "citizen king" and for a time made no move without Lafayette at his side. As Stendahl was to write: "The admirable Lafayette is the anchor of our liberty."

They soon fell out, of course. The King began to move as close as he dared to the absolute power of his ancestors. Lafayette, wanting to distance himself from the King, resigned from the National Guard, stepped back from the government, and began to renew all his old demands for liberty: the voting privilege must be opened up to an ever-greater electorate; groups of citizens of whatever size must be allowed freedom of assembly; detention without charges must be abolished; press freedom must be enhanced and judicial reform carried out.

At 76, he caught cold and took to his bed. He wrote letters, he wrote a speech that he sent to Paris to be read for him. His cold did not get better. He grew weaker, and after nearly three months, with his family clustered around him, he died.

His passing was mourned by everyone, even the King, or so he claimed; and the funeral mass was attended by everyone in Paris who even pretended to importance. But troops with fixed bayonets lined the packed streets as his cortege wended through. The government had forbidden public demonstrations. There were so many soldiers that in places the cortege could barely be seen. But the crowds were quiet. There was no outburst. "Hide your faces, Parisians," wrote Armand Carrel, "the funeral of an honest man and a true lover of liberty is going by."

Burial in this cemetery in which I stand was, like de Gaulle's so many years later, private. Only family and close friends were permitted to enter.

When he had returned from America ten years previously Lafayette had brought back with him a trunk full of dirt. Ordinary dirt. It may have come from Virginia, whose troops he had led, or from Brandywine, where he had been wounded. When he died he wanted to be buried in American soil, he said to those who asked. And he was and is.

Commemorative ceremonies take place here most years on July 4. The ambassador comes, together with important French officials and whatever American dignitaries are in town. One such ceremony — one of the most significant ones — occurred July 4, 1917. The latest French offensive had recently been crushed in still another awful bloodletting, and after it the French army had mutinied. The German invaders were on the move, and the war seemed lost. But present in the cemetery that day were Gen. Pershing and his staff, having just landed with the first units of the American Expeditionary Force. Pershing made a speech: Lafayette had come to America to help when it mattered, and now when it mattered the Americans had come to help in their turn. The saviors of France were at hand. Pershing, or perhaps one of his aides, then said: "Lafayette, *nous voici.*"

Paris Too

We lived at 6, Rue Villaret de Joyeuse, just off the Avenue
de la Grande Armée. For the first time in our lives, unlike the
penniless writers and artists who had inhabited the Left Bank in
the twenties, my idols, we were not poor. For the first time in
years I had a salary, $190 a week. The paper paid a cost-of-living
allowance as well, plus half the rent; it paid for our car, including
garage, and for the kids' schooling, and for all of my travel, meaning that for not very much more P. could come with me. Sometimes if it was fairly close, all four of us would go. I filed stories
from Lisbon to Stalingrad, now Volgograd. I was sent to North
Africa for a war and to Ireland for a horse race. I worked in eighteen
different countries in all, if you count places like Monaco and
Andorra. We thought ourselves rich. We thought we might live
in Paris forever. The whole world seemed open to us. I was writing
books and articles on the side, and people were buying them,
which was new and a miracle, and during our first year in Paris
I doubled what the paper paid me and, as the law was then written,
paid no taxes. I earned over $30,000. A year or two afterwards I
got involved with a movie director my age and mentioned this
sum to him. He said he himself earned half a million a year, but
that I was doing very well, nothing to be ashamed of.

We began to buy antiques; we filled up our Paris rooms with

them. And paintings for our Paris walls — we met indigent young artists and went back to their dingy studios and sometimes bought their work, and in the flea market we bought the portrait of a cardinal dating from 1620. We went to museums. We bought art books and learned about people like Dürer and Watteau we had barely heard of. We learned about opera and bought complete recordings. We went to concerts. There were public dress rehearsals at the Théâtre des Champs Elysées on Saturday mornings — whoever heard of going to concerts at such an hour? But it was possible because the kids were in school — French schoolchildren had Thursdays off instead. We sat enthralled by music we were hearing for the first time. We would come out at noon dazzled by what we had heard, and by the brightness of the day. We would stand on the sidewalk with the afternoon, the whole weekend ahead of us.

Our apartment had five marble fireplaces, one in each room, and wedding-cake ceilings, and parquet floors. It came with a kind of barred jail cell of a wine cellar below street level, the racks already in place, in which we began to collect what are now fabulously expensive wines, cheap enough at the time; no one was much interested at the start of the sixties. The great wines in the shops were all from the '52 and '53 vintages: Bonnes Mares from the Comte de Vogue cost $3 a bottle, the Bordeaux first growth $6.

Also we had a maid's room up under the mansard in which lived our Spanish maid with, later, her husband. She was a bit younger than we were. Her name was, inevitably, Carmen. She was a fine cook, and our two little girls were crazy about her. She spoke poor French, and poor Spanish as well; her native tongue was the dialect of Galicia. She worked six days a week from before breakfast until the lunch dishes were done, and again from about 5:00 P.M. until after dinner, and we paid what she asked, $90 a month, plus room and board and a month off in summer — a fortune to her. She was saving up to go home, buy an apartment, and live like a rich woman, she said.

There were only seven apartments in our big corner building, one on each floor. The maids' rooms, up under the eaves, one for each apartment, were all occupied by Spaniards, and most nights they apparently had great and noisy times up there. There was a toilet and sink on the hall but no running water in the rooms, and no heat either, apart from electric heaters. In summer, trucks loaded with discarded furniture and Spaniards standing up would leave Paris, and a month later the trucks would come back bringing only the people. The husbands worked the factories around the city, and the wives not only cooked and cleaned but went out with the string bags to do the food shopping as well; the language on the lines at the shops each afternoon was Spanish, or a variation of Spanish, and many of the villages on the other side of the Pyrenees must have been virtually depopulated.

Most of the young artists whose paintings we bought were Spanish too. They lived in dilapidated and sometimes condemned buildings on the Left Bank, and I don't know anyone else who bought their paintings besides us. To keep eating they sang and played guitars in bars at night, receiving, usually, only tips. Night after night we went to these bars and listened to Spanish songs and rhythms that to us were strange, exciting, and new. Spain became prosperous and even democratic after Franco died, but at the time of which I write he was still in power, and year after year there was this great Spanish exodus not only to France but to Germany, Switzerland, and the Low Countries as well.

Later, as I understand it, the Spaniards in Paris were replaced by Portuguese and later still by Turks.

Those were the years also of France's struggle to extricate herself from the war in Algeria. There were seven of us working out of the paper's Paris bureau, covering mostly the political side. It was a big story, and often we would have three bylined pieces on the front page and others inside. It was as if Paris were the center of the world, not only France's world but New York's as well.

Assassinations and atrocities took place day after day in Algiers, Oran, and other cities of North Africa. The Paris papers — there was only minimal television in France as yet — were full of horror stories. When the violence spread to Paris it was in the form of plastic bombs that exploded regularly on one street or another; we used to get frantic letters from America suggesting that we come "home," or at least send the children "home." The headlines I was helping to furnish were a good deal more frightening than real life — more frightening, that is, to them than to us.

The army in Algeria rebelled, or at least its generals did, and one night the prime minister came on radio and television: paratroops from Algeria were in the air en route to Paris to overthrow the government, he said. Civil war was threatened. In the bureau we waited until dawn for something to happen, from time to time going out to look around. The alarm may have been true; perhaps the plane or planes turned back. One by one the rebel generals and also some colonels were arrested; one general received a death sentence, though it was never carried out.

Finally the treaty granting independence to Algeria was signed, but this brought only new problems. Hordes of French colonists poured back into France, refugees who had to be integrated into a country that blamed them for all the killing so far and did not want them under any circumstances.

It put the Paris populace in a sullen mood. A layer of hatred blanketed the city. Nothing, it seemed, could make anyone smile, and ordinary transactions in stores could become unpleasant before they ended. Despite its beauty, Paris is a gloomy place at the best of times — from October to May the sun rarely shines — and these were worse times than most. One day I measured with a light meter normal Paris daylight under normal northern European cloud cover; it showed six stops down from sunlight. Gloomy light plus gloomy news — no wonder everyone felt surly and snapped at everyone else.

The bureau was on the Rue Caumartin, near the Opéra. Most days when I was in Paris I would work all morning at home on my own stuff, then go to the bureau after lunch, boarding the metro at the Argentine station, which was on our corner. The trains came in on rubber wheels with a soft whoosh. After a time it became hard to remember the ferocious clangor of the New York subways. I would ride five stops and come up out of the ground beside the Jeu de Paume and walk to the bureau along the Rue Cambon. It was on the fourth floor of a narrow office building, a long, narrow room with desks. The bureau chief had a separate office in the front, as did the resident columnist in the back. The rest of us were out in the open. There was a second narrow room alongside. In it were the teleprinter machines and the three or four operators, who were Frenchmen. None of them spoke one word of English, though they could type it out accurately enough. They sent our stories to New York, and also stories that had originated in French Africa, French Indochina, and elsewhere, for Paris was the hub for all these places. The Belgian Congo — now Zaire — was in turmoil at this time. In Indochina — nobody thought of it as Vietnam yet — the monks were just beginning to set themselves ablaze. I watched the story of the first of these public immolations go through Paris; in New York the desk either shorted it or killed it outright, I forget which, on the grounds that it was not significant.

In the Paris bureau one's first job each day was to approach the bulletin board to read the "fronting." The paper had about forty bureaus throughout the world, and the fronting was sent out to all of them overnight. It informed us in journalistic shorthand how New York had played our stories that morning, whether they had been "fronted," "insided," "shorted," "held over," "not used" — whatever. You could see how your career was going from the fronting, and so could everyone in every other bureau around the world, and one day I watched one of the correspondents come into the room, walk up to the fronting, and then, after a moment, start to cry. Too many "not useds" and you were on your way back to New York, where there were no cost-of-living allowances, no perks, and no glamour. Everybody knew it, and it led to a certain tension, not only in our lives but also in our relationships with each other. I had thought before I got there that once in the bureau I would be awash in team spirit and good feeling — like being on a sports team. It wasn't so. For the most part, no one socialized with anyone else. I was the youngest and by far the least experienced of the paper's men in Paris, or anywhere else abroad for that matter, and when I would turn up in one of the bureaus in some other country, most often I would be greeted with a suspicion and hostility that never failed to disconcert me.

At my desk I would work through the afternoon, making my phone calls and travel arrangements, writing the day's piece, and carrying it in to the operator to transmit, sometimes watching over his shoulder to make sure he got it right; writing also, in that era before easy transatlantic phone calls, hundreds of letters to New York to the paper's editors, to magazine editors, to publishers, to my agent, to family and friends. Our lives were here, but nearly everyone we cared about and depended on was there. Being a foreign correspondent was a lonely business, and in time this would weigh on me.

Outside the bureau windows the gray light of Paris would fade into evening. The street lamps would come on. Sometimes going home I would share a taxi with one of the other correspondents. We would walk down to the taxi stand on the Boulevard Haussmann and make our way from the front of the line to the rear, asking each chauffeur if he would take us. Most would not. These men were waiting for a fare that would take them out towards the working-class districts in which they lived. Their direction was not our direction. After five or six rejections, some of which were delivered in tones as surly as possible, we would turn away towards the metro. In Paris at that hour finding a taxi was, to say the least, traumatic. Five or six rejections in five minutes is a lot. Sure they had come only from dumb cab drivers. Sure. You could tell yourself that. Some nights it helped a little.

There was an American writers' colony in Paris then too. The impoverished expatriates of the twenties would not have recognized it. Most of its members were famous and, as writers go, rich. They were not young. They were men who wrote only bestsellers. They seemed to me very impressed with themselves. They tended to frequent the same cafés as the Hemingway crowd thirty and forty years before: the Brasserie Lipp, the Coupole and such — cafés that by now were as renowned and expensive as themselves. They inhabited Paris as you would inhabit an expensive hotel. James Jones had bought an apartment on the Ile St. Louis. There may be more elegant, more expensive addresses in Paris, but not many. He lived with his wife and two children and gave dinner parties attended by celebrities. William Saroyan, Irwin Shaw, Mary McCarthy, and James Baldwin all lived or had lived in Paris. William Styron and Kurt Vonnegut were frequently in town.

Jones was at the center of this group, though he seemed to have an inferiority complex towards it due to having come out of the army rather than Harvard or Princeton; he had not even come out of New York. His ambition seemed to be to get accepted by the others as a literary equal. To my mind he was a more important writer than all the rest of them put together; I thought *From Here to Eternity*, which I had first read in a barracks in Ohio, the supreme literary work by an American in my lifetime, and once told him so, embarrassing both of us. One night at a dinner party I heard another guest ask him what he did for a living. "I'm a writer," said Jones, adding with what seemed to me false modesty, "trying to be, anyway."

The other guest clapped him on the shoulder. "I hope you make it," he said sympathetically. Although all writers spend most of their lives being anonymous, this kind of thing must have been hard for Jones.

He was a rough man who sometimes farted or belched in public. He used four-letter words in mixed company at a time when this simply was not done. He would call them out across dinner tables, shocking everybody. To be around him in someone's house made me very uncomfortable.

Saroyan made me uncomfortable too. He lived alone in what sounded like a fifth-floor walkup on I believe the Rue Taitbout, which is near the big department stores and not a chic address. Saroyan had once been richer than anybody but had gambled it all away. Not once, but many times. Now he seemed to be barely getting by. He once spoke of an assignment he had just got to write an essay for the side of a breakfast-food box. The idea amused him and the money was good. He did not believe in doctors. He said that when sick he knew only one cure, to stay home and drink gallons and gallons of water.

Other than that he did not say much. He would stand in a corner behind his walrus mustache, silently watching, and for the most part his mustache hid whatever his thoughts or feelings might be.

All these people were separated from us by age, success, and fame, and we were not confident enough to invite them to our house. There was one thing more. They seemed to belong to a closed circle, a writers' circle. They would admit celebrities more famous than themselves at least on a temporary basis, but seemed unlikely to make room for a young foreign correspondent and his wife. What I imagined to be their attitude surprised me. A writer was supposed to be looking outward, not inward, I had always thought; writers were supposed to observe others, not congregate together; study the outside world, not themselves. These men seemed to travel to each other's Alpine chalets or Mediterranean villas a lot. With the possible exception of Saroyan, all were rich enough to invite such visits, to accord each other such visits, and it seemed to prove how close they all were with one another. I envied this.

In Paris we had too few friends. The intrabureau rivalry seemed to preclude the possibility of new ones, and those we had left behind in New York and Nice were all too young and financially shaky to drop in on us here. These big writers seemed to me lucky in this respect. I wanted to be a big writer myself someday. None of them seemed to recognize this ambition, though I hoped they would, for then the possibility of achieving it might have seemed more real to me.

We missed having friends and blamed Paris. In fact we had reached the age when the intimate friendships of youth would have dissolved in any case; we did not yet realize that past a certain age one could never form such friendships again.

Our children were learning to read. They went to school until 6:00 P.M. There was no schoolyard, no facilities for play. If the weather was fine, which was rare, they were taken for a walk in the afternoon along the Avenue Foch, moving in a crocodile two by two under the trees. Or else for a few minutes during recess they were allowed to chase each other around the chairs. At not quite 6 years old, one of them was taking dictation, a regular subject, writing out sentences like "*René d'abord observe le calme absolu, il admire le joli décor du bord de la mer de la côte du Calvados.*" They spoke French to each other, English to us.

They were often sick. Whooping cough dragged on most of one winter; first them, then all four of us. On Sundays it seemed essential to get them out into the country. We would drive out each time in a different direction: to the Normandy beachheads;

to the clearing in the woods at Compiègne where the Armistice was signed in 1918 — and where Hitler came for a second signing in 1940; to the cathedral at Chartres, which somehow escaped every single war and revolution for 800 years and whose windows give new meaning to the word blue.

They and we learned French history on the spot where it happened. Sometimes they got it a bit wrong.

We drove to Rouen and showed them the Place du Vieux Marché, where Joan of Arc was burned at the stake by order of the English in 1431; from there we went to the cathedral, which was badly damaged by English bombs in 1944; and after that to Beauvais, which possesses only half a cathedral, a structure so bizarre that even a 6-year-old recognized at once that something was wrong with it. "Papa," she said, "did the English come through here too?"

The explanation for what we were looking at was less violent, more human. Begun in 1238, the Beauvais cathedral was designed to be the hugest in Christendom. Alas, the architects were less gifted than they pretended, and in 1284 the walls of the nave caved in. It took immense amounts of money and forty years' more work to save what was left: the apse, the choir, a transept of sorts. Extra pillars had to be planted and old ones reinforced. Double layers of flying buttresses were laid on. All these special supports are of course still visible today, and some look more than ordinarily peculiar.

During the centuries that followed, attempts were made to resume construction. Funds were begged. By 1550 there was enough to build a steeple. The architects were still thinking big. They built a tower with a cross on top that reached 500 feet above street level. The height of a fifty-story building. In a village.

Four years after the tower was pronounced finished, it collapsed.

That was the end of attempts to finish the cathedral at Beauvais, and what is left is this huge, flat-faced half-church, higher and flatter than any other and strange indeed to see.

We visited one by one the châteaux of the Loire. At Blois there hung a painting which purported to represent the murder of the Duc de Guise there in 1588. The two little girls loved gory stories of this kind. The painting fascinated them. It was winter, the group we had joined was a small one, and the guide began to play to them. *"Le Duc était là,"* he told them, pointing to the spot. *"Les assassins étaient là."* He declaimed his lines like an actor. He crouched, lunged, was impaled on blades, died. He was superb. The little girls' eyes got bigger and bigger.

Guise had been the most powerful lord in the kingdom. He was head of the Catholic League and head of a plot to depose Henri III in favor of himself — or so the King believed. Eight impoverished noblemen in the King's employ attacked him with daggers as he crossed the King's bedroom. The Duke was a huge man. They got his cloak wrapped around him so he could not draw his sword. Daggers kept plunging through clothing into his body. Still he dragged the pack of them across the room and felled five before he went down. He lay at the foot of the King's bed. The King came in and, it is said, slapped the dead man's face, saying: "God, how big he is. He looks even bigger dead than alive." The King, who would himself be assassinated eight months later, ran off joyfully to tell his mother, Catherine de'Medici, then attended mass in a nearby chapel.

We went outside and stared up at the famous octagonal spiral staircase, one of the glories of French Renaissance architecture, that dominates the front of the château. Richly decorated in carved stone, it forms a series of open balconies, and each time the King threw a ball or banquet, they would be crowded with lords and ladies watching the arrival of other lords and ladies. The little girls liked that idea too, but the murder was what they talked about on the way home, the part about the daggers and about the victim wrapped in his cloak. And after that, whatever the château or museum we took them into, they always asked if there was a picture of the murder of the Duc de Guise. Often there was, and after that they would look at other pictures too.

We took them several times to Chantilly, thirty miles north of Paris, to visit what to my mind is the most rewarding château in France, though it is not on the Loire, was never the home of kings, and as a tourist attraction the Michelin guide awards it only two stars out of a possible three, a rating I found then and still find incomprehensible.

The château rises out of what must once have been considered
a moat but which is almost a lake. Sometimes when the light is
right and there is no breeze to ruffle the water, there are suddenly
two châteaux, one floating above the other. The approach across
a stone bridge is very fine. Below swim many plump orange fish.
The children loved to hang over the balustrade to watch them.
Like most of the great châteaux of France, this one is not a
single building but an accretion of buildings, part Gothic, part
Renaissance. There are domes and turrets, a spire, many chimneys.
The result, odd as it may sound, is extraordinarily harmonious
and handsome. Apparently there were châteaux on this spot for
most of 2,000 years. The newest part was built between 1875 and
1881 by the Duc d'Aumale, who was a passionate art collector.
Like America's robber barons, the Duke, who was the fifth son
of King Louis-Philippe, seems to have looted other châteaux and
churches of whatever pleased him: *boiseries,* stained glass, ceilings,
painted panels, carvings, altars, statuary, and splendid furniture.
The supreme possession of the Duke then and the museum now
is the fifteenth-century illuminated manuscript known as the *Très
Riches Heures du duc de Berry.*

The château's paintings spill out through ten galleries and, in
the way they are disposed, resemble no other museum in the
world, for they are grouped not by period or nationality or style
or even painter, but are hung in the order in which the Duke
bought them, or most liked to look at them. One entire gallery
seems to contain only his personal favorites. In some others the
canvases extend from floor almost to ceiling. An academic curator
trying to impose discipline wouldn't have lasted a day in the
Duke's employ. He wanted it his way, and although he willed his
château and its art to the Institut de France, the parent body of
the Académie Française, it was with the proviso that no changes
could ever be made inside or outside, nor could any of the works
ever be loaned to any other museum.

Therefore the château's treasures, and they are significant, can
be seen only here: works by Raphael, Botticelli, Piero di Cosimo,
Filippino Lippi, Carracci, Guido Reni, Ribera, Philippe de Cham-
paigne, Nattier, Drouais, Watteau, Ingres, Poussin, Corot. There
is a collection of fifteenth-century miniatures, another of sixteenth-

century French portraits, and a third of nineteenth-century academic paintings by contemporaries of the Impressionists — it was the former rather than the latter, don't forget, who were the giants of their day. And, yes, there is also a painting of the murder of the Duc de Guise; this is a museum that was a hit with the children at once.

The château's gardens are a joy to stroll about in; there are huge trees, sculpted hedges, carved lawns, plus reflecting ponds, pools, and canals in multiple shapes. And on one side stretches what may be the most beautiful grass racetrack in the world, a perfect little jewel that is open for race meetings only a few days a year.

Chantilly is the capital of thoroughbred racing in France. This town of 10,000 was — and is — home to 3,000 or more racehorses, 1,000 exercise boys, about 180 trainers.

Horse racing came to France from England around 1830. English owners came, English trainers, punters, and grooms, and also English youths to muck out stables, many of whom, like the sailors who manned the wooden ships of the British navy, were press-ganged out of London bars and sold across the channel into virtual slavery. The first races were on the Champ de Mars, where the Eiffel Tower is now. At that time the forests surrounding Chantilly were famous for stag hunting. Since the sporting crowd already knew the town and felt comfortable there, this seemed to make it a perfect horse-training site. The English trainers set up forthwith, soon to be joined by English hotel keepers, publicans, and bookmakers, and finally, to save the souls of all these people, English parsons.

Naturally they built their houses in the English way, houses that are still there, many of them inhabited now by their descendants, Frenchmen with English names. And one of our pleasures was just to walk along the streets under the trees looking in at all the English manor houses and mansions, here in a small French town.

Sometimes we had to step aside to let horses go by. The sight of so many sleek colts that close up, their coats polished like furniture, is extraordinarily pleasing. There is a French-style horse, or so it is said, which differs from American or English ones, for there has been almost no new blood here for 150 years. French owners sometimes bred cousin to cousin — even first cousins at times. The inbreeding has produced a horse that is fine boned, high strung. Sometimes I would study a group of them and wonder if anyone could really see the difference. I certainly couldn't.

I had an editor who loved the sport, and so I had to write about it more than I cared to, particularly if an American horse came to Paris to race. I would drive out to Chantilly to watch the workouts in the forest at dawn. There were long, straight, two-mile-long alleys through the trees. I would stand with the trainers and wait for the horses to come galloping by. The sun was not even up yet. There was no sound and almost no light. Usually we heard the horses before we could see them, the heavy breathing, the thudding hoofs, and then suddenly they were upon us, "lads" on their backs, thundering past a few feet away.

I would talk to the trainers and jockeys, rarely to owners, and afterwards have lunch at one of the small restaurants in the town. To this day there are no comfortable hotels in Chantilly, no famous or swanky restaurants. It's a country town. But in autumn there was always game on the menu. I would go over my notes and then go back to the bureau and write my story, and it would appear in the paper in New York the next day.

I became interested in the lads — the English word, its meaning somewhat corrupted, had come over intact into French. They were undersized French kids 14 years old and up, perched atop sometimes priceless horse flesh. The ones I talked to loved horses, and riding was a joy, but normal childhood, I saw, was for them over. In some cases there was tragedy in the making.

These were boys who didn't go to school anymore or stay up late or eat junk food. They had signed contracts binding them to their trainers as apprentices until they were 21. They got room, board, and pocket money and dreamed about one day becoming rich jockeys, an idea that was most likely put into their heads by someone else, possibly a parent hoping to make a fortune from inside tips. They were accepted by the trainers because they seemed especially small for their age and because their parents, who were always checked out, were small as well.

They were up at 5:00 A.M. in summer, 6:00 A.M. in winter,

even though small boys love to sleep. They rode their three lots of horses each morning, which took about ninety minutes per mount, then mucked out stables, sifted oats, rubbed down coats the rest of the day. At night they lay in bed and worried about growing. Most were so young they imagined they could stay tiny just by wanting to.

They ate and drank almost nothing day after day: a single cup of coffee for breakfast, salads and small portions of grilled meats at lunch and dinner. Year by year they got older and, inevitably, bigger. They were hungry all the time. No more than two in ten, according to the statistics, ever got to be jockeys.

I went to do a story in Chamonix — we all went, and I hired a ski instructor for the little girls, a young woman who had once raced on the national ski team, who took them out onto the gentle hill behind the hotel. A French jet fighter, swooping low over the Vallée Blanche, had sliced through an aerial cableway, dropping the car onto the glacier and killing some of the passengers. It was over by the time I got there. I never saw it, but I got some good descriptions and wrote about it. The Vallée Blanche offered both the highest skiing in Europe, the start being at 12,700 feet, and the longest run down, about eleven miles. You couldn't even ski it in winter, for the snow so high up was not safe, and the people who got killed in the cable car were not skiers but sightseers. Spring was the time for the Vallée Blanche, and that spring I came back alone and engaged a guide to take me up there.

Chamonix is at 3,300 feet. It is full of smart hotels and smart shops. In the early morning, with our skis and poles over our shoulders, the guide and I crossed the bridge over the torrent that pours through the town and walked down the road towards the *téléférique* station. It was April and the buds were bursting over the road. There was a warm, sweet odor in the air, and in the fields the cows were munching ripe new grass.

The guide's name was Henri Théolière, he was 41, and in summer he guided climbers, he said. In the pockets of my parka I was carrying a camera and two oranges, for there would be nothing to eat on the way down. Henri had some fruit and candy bars, and in his knapsack he carried survival gear. This was in case I should crash and half kill myself. He had showed me some of this stuff before we started out. He had some clever collapsible splints that could be made to fit any bone I might break. He practically guaranteed that he would be able to get me down. It occurred to me that these professional guides were braver than one realized. They would go up there with just about anybody.

The ride to the top of the Aiguille du Midi took thirty minutes, including one change of car. The last part was straight up the sheer flank of the mountain. It was something like those outdoor elevators you see these days, except that it was not attached to any building. It dangled, it swayed. If the wind rose any further it might dash its brains, and mine, against the mountain.

When we came out of the station I saw that up here it was winter — it would always be winter — and to get to a level spot where we could put on our skis we clambered downhill for 200 yards along a knife-edged ridge of snow. On one side of the edge was Chamonix, straight down. On the other was a precipitous plunge into the Vallée Blanche. Poles had been driven into this ridge and a rope strung along them. Nothing more substantial could be built because at this altitude the snow kept shifting.

At last it was possible to clamp on skis. We were facing towards Italy, towards the high, blinding sun. The Mont Blanc, Europe's highest mountain, was on our right. Below us dropped the great bowl of the valley, ringed by the multitude of high, jagged peaks that are the needles of Chamonix. The view from where we stood was stunning.

The guide pushed off and I followed. There was no track. Each of us made his own track. The snow was firm in the sun and my skis ran smoothly. On top of the solid base was the barest film of powder that had fallen during the night, erasing the tracks of the day before. The expanse of snow was so huge, so white, so silent, that it was possible to feel that no man had ever been this way before, and I glided downwards, one gentle ess after another. There was no other sound than my skis, no other movement but Henri and me. I was almost overcome with the joy of it.

It was easy skiing, and if we stopped often it was to admire the mountains, and the air, and the breathtaking view. Or we would come to crevasses and stop to peer down into them. The icy walls were blue or green, and some were so deep we could not see the bottom. Sometimes we stopped to watch climbers, tiny specks of color and movement high up on some sheer wall. Mostly they didn't move, they just clung, while Henri entertained me with stories of the terrible accidents that tended to befall climbers — skiers too — up here.

The Mont Blanc was the first of the world's great mountains to be climbed. Two men from Chamonix, a doctor and a dealer in animal skins, did it in August 1786, battling not only the mountain but the popular supposition that no human being could survive at such altitudes. Nowadays 2,000 people attempt the climb every year, 300 make it, and two dozen or so become corpses — every year. Henri and his colleagues bring them down in bags. The Mont Blanc is a dangerous mountain. It is 15,771 feet high, and its summit, however exquisitely pure and beautiful today, is subject to violent, freakish weather.

Henri certainly knew a lot about tragedy. I did not like watching the tiny clinging figures, especially with Henri's symphony playing in my ear, so I pushed off and we continued down.

Under my light parka I wore a single sweater. I was sweating and overdressed. Henri kept me from getting lost, or from falling into crevasses, and he took me through only the best snow. He was a good companion. We skied onto the Mer de Glace, which is formed by four glaciers that join in a kind of corridor and pour imperceptibly, inexorably downhill. The Sea of Ice is an extremely noisy place — or at least it was that day. As we leaned on our poles breathing deeply, we could hear the snow and ice splitting and grumbling all around us.

We came out onto a kind of plain where someone had built an igloo, known as "the dining room." Some days, according to Henri, people carried up soft drinks and sold them. Today the igloo was empty, though around it sprawled several skiers resting in the sun. We took our skis off and rewaxed them, for the slope was getting gentler, the snow wetter. I ate the last of my oranges, and Henri his last candy bar, and we started down again. At the end we were poling ourselves along, and soon after that the snow ended. We shouldered our skis and hiked downhill over rock falls and steeply descending trails for forty-five minutes until we came to the main road, where taxis waited. I was famished and thirsty. Every muscle in my body ached, I wanted a bath and some cream for my sunburned face, and after that I wanted to write a piece about it for the paper. It had been a glorious experience, and I wanted to share it if I could. It was a day I thought I would remember all my life. And so far I have.

We had another baby, and afterwards I was told to go to the *mairie* to register her birth. There the clerk got down a ledger nearly a yard high with thick, parchmentlike pages, and he showed me where I was to inscribe the new baby's name, sex, and date of birth, and her parents' names. He watched me while I did it. This was the official birth registration, and it was in my handwriting, and everything else for the rest of her life would be only a copy. She could go there and look at that handwriting some day, if she chose, perhaps on a day long after her father was dead. The clerk closed the ledger and put it back on the shelf beside all the other ledgers from past years, decades, maybe even centuries; it would remain there who knew how long. I remember that I stood somewhat stunned, my head filled with half-formed ideas. Some had to do with the succession of the generations, the continuity of families, cities, nations. But mostly I was fixed on what seemed to be the rightness of it all — that the father should register the birth of his daughter, not the hospital, not the state. It was as if France knew something America had not yet learned.

The paper's columnist sent flowers to the hospital, but no one else did, and no one at all came to visit. A sense of aloneness came over me. We had no family in Paris, of course, no old friends, no one to help if we got in trouble, no one to share anything with, even a new baby. There is a vulnerability to being a foreign correspondent. I had been feeling this more and more strongly. The birth of the baby accentuated it. I kept going into more and more countries not my own, nosing about, sometimes not speaking the language, sometimes misunderstanding in an important way a language I thought I did speak, always wondering if I could get the story I had come for, and get it out, and then get myself out. If I got lost or sick or shot or arrested — I was young enough so that these seemed remote possibilities, but they did exist — there would be no one to help. The paper might help, of course. Might try to. But it had very little clout in Europe. The paper was not something I had great confidence in.

This had gone on year after year. It had perhaps gone on too long.

In Paris apartment buildings, the heat goes on and off by date, not temperature. Usually the heat starts November 15 and goes off April 15, and God help you if a cold snap occurs before or after. The baby was born April 13. The air temperature was forty degrees on the day we brought her home, and it was not much warmer inside our apartment.

When the weather did not warm up the next day, nor the next, I sought out our concierge and begged for heat. But the matter was out of her hands, Monsieur. I offered to pay for the heat myself, but this was not possible. Only a majority vote of the tenants could get the furnace put back on.

Seven families lived in the building, so I needed three votes to go with my own. Since every other tenant was as cold as we were, I expected no difficulty. But I had reckoned without the mood of bitterness and distrust that so pervaded Paris at the time.

The first tenant I polled said he was gone all day and a fire sufficed at night. He could hardly be expected to pay for the comfort of other tenants, could he?

The next tenant was going away for the weekend and naturally could not vote for heat on days she wouldn't even be home. A third tenant lived on the top floor and said the sun heated her apartment enough. "What sun?" I almost shouted. Everyone knew that in Paris the sun didn't come out until June.

I rang the fourth bell, desperate by now. I explained about the new baby. I pointed out that less than a dollar a day per apartment would pay for the oil to heat the building. At last this tenant wrote on the ballot: "No for me, yes for the baby."

That gave me one vote, and I got another from a family not obliged to pay for heat because of some peculiar arrangement with the landlord. The vote was three to three as I rang the last bell. A disheveled young man in a silk dressing gown appeared. He looked scared. Behind him through a half-open door I caught a glimpse of a bare leg, or so I imagined. An expression of relief came over his face to find it was only me. Hardly listening to my plea, he voted yes, and we had heat at last.

I decided this anecdote typified Paris. Americans would never have behaved in such a way, I believed, because Americans were nice. A strange sort of homesickness was setting in. And I was becoming bitter about Paris.

About a year later we got into a taxi on the Champs Elysées at midnight, and the driver tried to gouge us on the fare. I told him off, adding gratuitously: "You French are all alike."

To which he snarled in reply: "If you don't like it, go back where you came from."

Clearly it was time to leave, and presently we did. When I think of Paris now it is with affection. I lived there longer than in any city except the one in which I was born, and when I come into its streets it is like renewing an old love affair. I know where everything is. I feel alert and alive. I don't regret not having lived in Paris as a young man, because I did.

But this was not my mood at the time. Once back in America I wrote an article for the old *Saturday Evening Post* called "I Hate Paris in the Springtime." I got $1,500 for it, and I have never been able to remember it without shame. It mentioned the bad weather, the roaring inflation, the constant one-day strikes, and of course the balloting for or against heat. It mentioned a good deal else too, but not what was most important: that Paris — the French — had taught me everything I know about how to live.

"Every man has two countries," Benjamin Franklin said, "his own and France." Not every man, certainly. Some. One, anyway.